Arrested Development in India
The Historical Dimension

PART I

THE CONCEPT OF ARRESTED DEVELOPMENT

Arrested Development in India
The Historical Dimension

Edited by
CLIVE DEWEY

R

The Riverdale Company
Riverdale, Maryland
1988

First Published 1988
ISBN 0-913215-08-2
LC Card No. 85-62580

Published in the United States of America by
The Riverdale Company, Publishers
Suite 102, 5506 Kenilworth Avenue
Riverdale, Maryland 20737

By arrangement with
Manohar Publications
1 Ansari Road, Daryaganj
New Delhi - 110002

Text photoset by The Word and Printed in India at
P.L. Printers, C3/19 Rana Partap Bagh, Delhi 110009

PREFACE

Although there are more historians working on Indian economic history in British and German universities than there are in the rest of Europe put together, they have few opportunities to pool their findings or discuss their plans. Personal contacts tend to be restricted to cursory exchanges at general-purpose conferences of orientalists or spasmodic encounters in archives in India. The barriers to the transmission of published work are less formidable, but they still exist. It is impossible for any university library in Germany to stock the full range of English language periodicals in which research on Indian economic and social history is published; and no university library in the United Kingdom, with the possible exception of that of Oxford or Cambridge, tries to stock the full range of German periodicals in which German Indianists publish their work. Moreover, only a minority of the British scholars working on South Asia read German with sufficient fluency to make full use of their German colleagues' discoveries. As a result, the two sets of scholars lack the instinctive grasp of research in progress on the other side of the 'linguistic divide' which is essential in planning long-term projects. The breakthroughs which German historians have made in the study of Indian 'temple culture'—by applying traditional Indological skills—and the sophistication of British analyses of agrarian structures and commercial organisations are examples of historiographical revolutions which have proved difficult to transmit in their entirety.

The Workshop at Schloss Hochhausen at which the papers in this volume were originally delivered was an attempt to overcome these obstacles to international cooperation by bringing together the majority of the younger historians of South Asia in both countries. The theme of the Workshop—the 'arrested development' of the Indian economy—reflected the need to draw as much current research as possible into the common net. Sooner or later, every historian of South Asia has to address himself to the sources of growth and stagnation in the Indian economy; and a great deal of work has been done in related fields, such as peasant stratification, whose full implications for growth have yet to be spelt out. The fact that the great majority of the historians in the United Kingdom with a research interest in Indian economic history delivered papers at the Workshop suggests that the choice of arrested development achieved its immediate objective; it gave everyone a chance to show the relevance of the work they had in hand. But themes as complex and all-embracing as arrested development have their drawbacks. It is virtually impossible to do them justice with the limited manpower available. If there were as many economic historians working on South Asia as there are economists working on the United Kingdom, it would be possible to draw up the perfect blueprint for a model conference. Experts on every issue worth discussing could be invited to attend; their authoritative statements could be dovetailed into a logically-structured programme; and the subject of arrested development could be definitively disposed of, for years to come.

Sadly, there are only a dozen scholars in U.K. universities with a research interest in the economic history of South Asia, a huge and heterogeneous subcontinent. Inevitably, there are gaps in our collective knowledge; immense areas which are only superficially researched, or not researched at all. It is impossible to pluck ready-made experts on every subject out of some bottomless pool; there is no pool, only a slowly evaporating puddle. Moreover, the denizens of the puddle are understandably reluctant to abandon their existing research projects while they work up pieces commissioned by workshop 'managers' who have absolutely nothing to offer them in return, except the privilege of attending their workshop. With no leverage to exert—no riches, power or fame to confer—conference organisers are well-advised to temper their ambitions to the prevailing wind, and accept whatever contributions their colleagues are prepared to offer, provided they bear some relationship to a sufficiently broad theme—the alternative being a finely-focused *tête-à-tête*. It would be absurd, therefore, to expect this collection of papers—or any other collection of papers—to provide the definitive solution for a problem which has exercised Indian economic historians since the subject was invented, and will doubtless go on exercising them until the discipline dies of inanition. It is a little like fighting on the western front. There are no magic theories or methods which will guarantee a decisive breakthrough; India's history and development economics teach one the same lesson: grand offensives always get bogged down in the mud. The best one can hope for is to inch a little further forward along a limited sector of the line. If the Heidelberg Workshop took a few of the possible causes of India's backwardness a step further—if it re-examined some of the old scapegoats and added a fresh candidate or two to the list—that is as much as any merely mortal workshop can be expected to achieve.

* * * * *

The structure of the book reflects the organisation of the Workshop. The first section addresses the central concept of 'arrested development' from two diametrically opposed directions. Professor Rothermund's brief discussion paper was circulated several months before the Workshop took place, in the hope that a summary of some of the commoner assertions in the field would give the participants a clearer idea of the probable agenda by injecting a little empirical stuffing into a complicated abstraction. It is published here, with only a few verbal alterations, as a record of the contentions which paper-givers disputed when they came to sink their deeper—if narrower—shafts. Colin Simmons' magisterial examination of the recent climacteric in development economics and its implications for economic historians was written in reaction against many of the theoretical assumptions underlying Professor Rothermund's *aide-memoire*. It calls into question the utility of the whole notion of arrested development as a framework for the analysis of Indian economic history. Impartial judges may decide that everything depends on the definition employed. If the term is taken to mean something terribly culturally-specific—if references to arrested development imply acquiescence in all the theories put forward by 'liberal' development economists in the 1950s and 1960s—then its utility is very dubious indeed. But if arrested development means something much simpler and more flexible—if it involves no more than the belief that India was in some sense backward, and a rough check-list of potential causes—it may supply an 'organising idea' for workshops still to come. The fact is that historians habitually use the ideas they borrow from economics with far less rigour than any self-respecting economist would feel obliged to do, because they lack the data which make theoretical sophistication worth-while. As a result, their robust building-bricks survive the collapse of the economists' more elaborate sophistries. They gain in durability what they lack in precision.

The second section of the book—like the second session at Heidelberg—is devoted to the historiographical revolution which has overtaken conventional views of the eighteenth century. Where historians once saw only anarchy and impoverishment, revisionists see 'state formation' and the stimuli to economic growth which the emergence of new polities supposedly supplied. Dr. Stein's contribution to the Workshop was an exceptionally timely review of the work of three of the pioneers of this new interpretation. Readers who are daunted by the sheer size of Dr. Bayly's *magnum opus,* or Dr. Perlin's occasional forays into the portentous, or the inaccessibility of Dr. Washbrook's unpublished manuscripts, will welcome guidance across an unfamiliar and sometimes puzzling landscape; and Dr. Stein's article is the intellectual equivalent of a trusty native guide. The correlations which the Baylys draw between the structure of different kinds of pre-colonial state and the structure of the market will delight a different audience: connoisseurs of the revolution, who already know all there is to know about state formation before the coming of the British. The typology they construct may be, as yet, a collection of largely empty boxes; but demand is such a neglected factor in Indian economic history—and their approach is so original and stimulating—that an entire 'school' would be justified in spending years of research pumping a little hard data into their receptive categories.

The third section—on the colonial state—is normally an invitation to tot up the blessings and the curses of the raj by passing value judgements on the reasons policies were adopted rather than the effects they had. All the papers on British policy delivered at Heidelberg were intended to correct the resultant imbalance between the plethora of articles on policy formation and the paucity of articles on implementation. Before the emergence of comprehensive development programms, it could be argued that the defence budget—which absorbed somewhere between a quarter and a third of India's public expenditure in peacetime—was in some senses the most important 'economic policy' of them all; and my own case-study of the tract containing the largest recruiting-ground and the biggest cantonment in British India shows how military expenditure had sufficient multiplier effects to convert a profoundly backward area on the brink of a Malthusian abyss into one of the most prosperous regions in India.

Rather than unravelling the repercussions of a single policy, Chris Christensen examines the aggregate influence of the full range of British policies on a single zone, the north-west frontier. His dissection of the interplay between the Pathans' political culture, the natural resources of their tribal territory, and the techniques of tribal management which the British gradually evolved is a minor masterpiece of compression. Peter Robb's painstaking analysis of the impact of the Bengal Tenancy Act of 1885—the most important piece of tenancy legislation the British ever enacted—on the balance of power in rural Bihar makes a pathbreaking contribution to the on-going debate over 'land control' and land reform in British India. In its open-minded fidelity to an extremely valuable (but under-utilised) body of records, it sets new standards for research on Indian agrarian policy. The last study of the state—Tom Tomlinson's paper on the rupee ratio—represents a return to a historic battlefield, full of bimetallic ghosts; fortunately, he discusses the potential consequences of a rising and unstable rupee with a lucidity and a caution which is rarely found in contemporary financial commentators.

The largest section of the book treats the largest sector of the economy. The four papers on agricultural growth and agrarian structure range from Bates' exceptionally detailed reconstruction of the economy of one of the most fertile farming zones in India—the Narmada valley—to Islam's painstaking re-working of the agricultural statistics for the undivided Punjab. Although methodologically distinct, their work arrives at equally pessimistic conclusions. Bates emphasises the retardative effects of agrarian exploitation; Islam claims that Blyn's estimates (showing significant agricultural growth) should be revised downwards. Charlesworth and Stone—who occupy the middle-ground, methodologically speaking—are more optimistic. Charlesworth's examination of the impact of the depression suggests that the peasantry of Bombay escaped comparatively unscathed; while Stone's return visit to the canals of the United Provinces shows how irrigation engineers went on improving their efficiency long after they were built. The last two papers in the book—dealing with labour in the handicraft and factory sectors—continue this 'upbeat' note. Handloom weavers and jobbers in the Bombay cotton mills have been castigated for their economic inefficiency; Konrad Specker and Richard Newman gallop to their defence. Konrad Specker's summary of his doctoral thesis—which has just been published in German—confirms what many Indianists have long suspected: that the handloom weavers, far from collapsing in the face of factory competition, displayed a remarkable capacity for survival well into the twentieth century. Newman's comparative study of labour sub-contractors in China and Japan acts as a vital 'control' on their Indian counterparts, and argues that jobbers were a rational adaptation to the economic environment.

* * * * *

The British participants in the workshop have reason to be grateful to the institutions and individuals who made their visit to Heidelberg so profitable and so pleasant. Despite retrenchments on every side, the U.K. Economic and Social Research Council and their West German counterpart—the Deutsche Forschungsgemeinschaft—anticipated the 'Anglo-German initiative' which will shortly promote academic co-operation between the two countries, and awarded generous grants towards the cost of travel and subsistence. The choice of Schloss Hochhausen as a venue for the workshop was inspired. Count and Countess von Helmstatt showed us how high the standard of south German hospitality can be. The cuisine was proof, if proof is required, that British universities inhabit a culinary black hole in a gastronomic disaster area; while the house and grounds—a friendly amalgam of eighteenth century elegance and nineteenth century romance—imposed their own civility on our debates. But most of all, we are grateful to our German colleagues. Some very distinguished scholars working in related fields—

one thinks of Professor Fischer from Berlin or Professor von Albertini from Geneva—acted as commentators on British papers or took leading parts in the ensuing discussions; and they did both these things in the language of the workshop, which was English. The fluency and clarity of the German participants' presentations was the greatest possible reproach to our resolutely monoglot culture, and their willingness to engage in scholarly debate in the language of their guests was a much-appreciated courtesy. Lastly, there is Professor Rothermund. As head of the Sudasien Institut at Heidelberg, he has done his utmost to encourage visits to Germany by British historians; as joint-organiser of the workshop, the whole burden of the local arrangements fell on him; and it is to him that I should like to dedicate this book—without his knowledge or permission.

CLIVE DEWEY

Burton Overy
October 1986

CONTENTS

1

PROBLEMS OF INDIA'S ARRESTED ECONOMIC GROWTH UNDER BRITISH RULE

DIETMAR ROTHERMUND
University of Heidelberg

The sole purpose of this discussion paper is to provoke discussion by defining some of the basic issues which must be on the agenda wherever Indian economic historians meet together. Marxist, nationalist and revisionist contributions to debates on the lack of capital accumulation, retarded industrialisation, and peasant stratification—to cite only three examples—have stimulated a great deal of research. The publication of the Cambridge Economic History of India has provided an encyclopaedic survey of the field, but in the nature of things such collective efforts generally fail to establish a 'common line'. The present note cannot fill this gap: it merely attempts to list leading problems in a crude chronological order. Modern economic history, influenced by the timeless rigour of current economic theories, often loses sight of the crucial aspect of timing. Of course, historical sequence does not necessarily imply causality and 'economic history in a nutshell' invites detailed qualification at every point.

No need for capital accumulation in pre-colonial India

The lack of capital accumulation has been frequently discussed in the debates on India's economic history. Was the transition to capitalism just around the corner when the British conquest put an untimely end to its further development? This question is asked without due regard to the functions of capital as a factor of production. Capital only becomes important when the other factors of production—land and labour—are scarce; capital is then invested to enhance their productivity. In pre-colonial India land and labour were abundant and there was no need for capital investment. The accumulation of merchant capital and state capital which did take place helped the elite extract a larger surplus from artisans and peasants—a surplus which was devoted to consumption, more particularly the consumption of unproductive services (which included the maintenance of cultural specialists as well as many retainers and an enormous military establishment).

No linkage effects of foreign demand under the East India Company

The East India Company was a very advanced commercial organisation with many innovative features (combination of monopoly trade abroad and auction sales at home, leasing rather than building of ships, management of cost and timing, corporate intelligence, functional hierarchy, transferable personnel, and so on; but none of these features made an impact on the Indian economy, they only served to make the appropriation of surplus production of artisans and peasants more efficient. Production for export—even if it increased very rapidly as in Bengal in the 18th century—did not change the structure of production; it was accommodated within the prevailing 'cottage industry' mode. The influx of silver also made no difference to the mode of production; it merely facilitated appropriation.

The parasitical symbiosis of Britain and India

When the representatives of the East India Company discovered how easy it was to capture the levers of power in India through their organisational superiority, they established a connection which can be compared to that of a parasite with its host. The parasite uses the structure of the host for his own sustenance. It interferes with this structure only to strengthen its hold; it has no incentive to subvert it. In this way the British in India carefully adopted the heritage of their indigenous predecessors. The copiously recorded *obiter dicta* of British administrators which imply that they were reshaping everything in accordance with latest British ideas are misleading.

The impact of deflation in the first half of the 19th century

After the parasitical symbiosis was established much of the silver which had been pumped into India by the East India Company was extracted again. Furthermore, the conspicuous consumption of the earlier political elite was replaced by the more austere life-style of the British bureaucrats. A severe deflation kept prices down and limited the purchasing power of the Indian people, which delayed the expansion of the Indian market for British goods. As the industrial revolution progressed, however, British manufactures flooded the Indian market; and Indian artisans were only able to compete (for a time) because low crop prices made it possible for them to cut their (survival) costs. This was a more important impediment to the rise of a modern Indian industry than the British imports themselves. An Indian textile industry could only capture the domestic market after a rise in food prices reduced the weavers' flexibility.

Reflation, price movements and population growth in the late 19th century

From about 1876 the influx of depreciating silver reflated the Indian economy, pushed up crop prices and contributed to population growth. The terms of trade were in favour of agriculture, the peasantry could retain a larger surplus as revenue settlements and rent enhancement lagged behind, and more children could be better fed. Rising prices, a steady growth of population and a slight improvement in living standards encouraged demand for imported as well as indigenous industrial goods. But the expansion of modern industry in India was checked by a scarcity of capital investment. Land and trade both yielded higher returns than industry. After the free influx of silver was stopped in 1893 and a deflationary policy was adopted, a combination of factors—the increasing export of foodgrain, a reduction of storage and crop failures—led to a major crisis in the 1890s. Famines and epidemics checked population growth, which stagnated for the next two decades.

Relative prosperity and stability in the early 20th century

The years before the First World War were in many ways exceptional. Population growth stagnated while agriculture and industry expanded, producing a definite increase in per capita national income. India's export surplus grew and the currency reserves which built up in London made it possible to put the rupee on a gold exchange standard, as well as strengthening London as the financial centre of the world. The money supply remained relatively tight, however, and capital accumulation for industrial investment was still very limited. The British-Indian government secured sufficient income from customs and other taxes to let the real pitch of the land revenue drift downwards with inflation, maintaining the profitability of land as an investment. The railways—which had been in the red during the 19th century—also yielded a profit, as expenditure on construction fell and the utilisation of the network increased.

The impact of the First World War

The war affected the Indian economy in many ways. The partial interruption of trade routes provided a kind of protection for India's industries which rose to the occasion by fully utilising installed capacity rather than expanding their plant, as investment goods could not be imported during the war. The British-Indian government realized the usefulness of Indian industrialisation—but once the war was over these brave plans were soon shelved. The war also had negative effects, particularly the unprecedented inflation. Rising silver prices (which increased the intrinsic value of rupee coins) pushed up the exchange rate; at the same time more silver had to be imported to keep up with the expanding money supply. Then a bad harvest in 1918 drove foodgrain prices through the roof. This inflation, however, did the peasantry no good. Crop prices remained high during the next decade, but the terms of trade for agriculture actually declined. The peasants' purchasing power fell and the hopes of the industrialists who imported investment goods in the immediate postwar years were disappointed. For a predominantly agrarian country like India it was especially unfortunate that the terms of trade for agriculture which had improved from the 1870s to the war now declined—with a brief respite in the late 1920s—until they reached a very low level in the years of the Great Depression.

The structural effects of the Great Depression

The Great Depression was caused and perpetuated by a worldwide contraction of credit. This contraction was perhaps even more severe in India than in the industrial countries of the West. As far as the general mode of agrarian production was concerned India had not progressed much beyond the level of subsistence agriculture, but due to the prevalence of rent and revenue payments in cash even the smallest peasant was compelled to sell a good deal of his produce and was also involved in credit relationships. At least half of the peasantry was more or less permanently indebted. Rent, revenue and debt service could not be easily adjusted to the low level of agrarian prices. Moneylenders now tend to foreclose mortgages and to buy up land rather than to extend credit. They also profited from the sale of distress gold which they extracted from their debtors. The quest for land kept land prices at a stable high level in spite of the severe reduction of agrarian prices. Only a limited amount of capital which was withdrawn from moneylending in the years of the depression was invested in small scale industrial activities. Oil presses and rise mills were examples of such investment, but the amounts invested in this way were negligible. The sugar industry was the only major success story: aided by a protective tariff this industry grew rapidly and achieved almost complete import substitution within a very short time. The cotton textile industry also benefited from protective tariffs and made some headway through import substitution. But new investment in this industry was limited, and production was stepped up by operating existing plant more intensively.

In general, import substitution was impeded by the high exchange rate of the rupee which was maintained by the British in the teeth of Indian opposition. The outflow of distress gold made it easy to stick to this rate which acted as an import bonus. Of course, this also made imported investment goods available at attractive prices. But nobody buys investment goods just because they are cheap, if he is not assured of a market for his products. The prospects for this were very bleak in India. The purchasing power of the rural masses declined during the depression and the small urban population (which benefited from an increase in real income due to low food prices) did not constitute a market large enough for profitable import substitution. Protective tariffs without imperial preferences, a quick devaluation and a public works programme financed by loans raised by the government at the low interest rate prevailing after 1932 would have greatly stimulated economic growth in India, but only an independent government would have been able to adopt such a policy.

Inflation and deformation in the Second World War

Unlike the First World War, the second one gave hardly any growth impulses to the Indian economy but subjected it to an even greater amount of inflation. The currency in circulation increased about three times from the pre-war to the post-war years and prices trebled in keeping with this development. The government bought up an increasing proportion of India's industrial output which could not be expanded very much because investment goods could not be imported. Increasing demand and limited capacity pushed up prices. The interruption of imports and the purchasing power of those who shared war time profits also contributed to a rise in prices. Finally the government arranged for gold imports so as to counteract this trend. The earlier outflow of distress gold was to some extent neutralised, but those who bought this gold now were hardly the same people who had to part with it earlier. The sequence of depression and war made the poor poorer and the rich richer, perpetuating a long-term trend in India's economic development.

At the same time the Government of India changed under the impact of the war from a *laissez-faire* law-and-order administration to a large scale interventionist machine. Manmade famines led to procurement and rationing, while stores purchases for the war had brought the government into close contact with Indian industry. The Five Year Plans of independent India could hardly have been conceived without this legacy of the war economy and its interventionist administration. At the end of the war India was left with an economy troubled by structural deformation. An investment goods industry was still conspicuous by its absence. The machinery installed in the existing factories was outdated and worn out because of the war effort. War time profits had accrued to a very small class of capitalists who had not been able to play a productive and innovative role under the prevailing circumstances. The whole trend of the time had encouraged the financial wizard and speculator rather than the constructive industrial entrepreneur, and in the countryside traders and rich peasants had consolidated their hold on the land and on the service of the rural poor whose ranks had increased in numbers.

The only apparent benefit which India enjoyed at the end of the war was the balance accumulated in the Bank of England which represented the result of India's enforced saving. The Government of India procured everything on credit during the war, turning India from a debtor into a creditor of Great Britain. This made the attainment of independence much easier, as there was no financial risk in granting independence to a creditor. But the defects of the economic structure could not be so easily mended with the help of these accumulated balances. A good deal of this money was frittered away by importing consumer goods for those who had reaped war profits.

Conclusion: India's arrested growth under British rule

This brief survey of India's economic history has shown that economic growth was arrested under British rule in various ways at different periods of time. In most instances it would be wrong to assume that this growth was arrested intentionally *by* British rule. British rule could often be blamed only for not implementing measures which could have removed obstacles to economic growth. In the parasitical symbiosis even progressive elements of British rule such as a modern civil service and a highly developed legal system turned into impediments to economic growth. The disciplined civil service was used to run the old agrarian state more efficiently and thus to perpetuate its structure. The legal system based on the freedom of contract, the protection of credit, the facilitating of commercial transactions when implanted into this agrarian setting only served to enhance the control of the rich over the poor. Older relationships of patron and client were replaced by new patterns of debt service which in the rural environment often meant actual servitude.

Even the opening up of India in terms of the expansion of infrastructure, the only major line of British investment in India, did not contribute to a balanced economic growth. A national market did develop in this way, but it grew up under the tutelage of the world market. For a brief period in the early 20th century India's association with the world market seemed to show a positive trend, but then the sequence of war, post-war stagnation, depression and once more war, affected India negatively, and not having an independent government India could not adopt an economic policy of its own. India's economic policy was not even determined by the viceroy in New Delhi but was guided in all important matters by the British government in London. Now it so happened that London lost its pre-eminent position as the financial centre of the world in the First World War and imperial control became more self-conscious and painstaking and less grandiose than before. Also India's managed currency was more amenable to manipulation in the imperial interest than in the period of the open mints (which were only kept open as long as this was in line with imperial interest). Fears about a defaulting India whose debts would have to be paid by the British government were no idle dreams but a real menace in this period of London's reduced financial staying power.

The paradox of the postwar period was that imperial control tightened and preferences and safeguards were imposed while India lost much of its earlier economic importance for Great Britain and *vice versa*. Impediments to economic growth were created by this paradoxical relationship. When India attained independence capital accumulation for productive investment was still very limited. Of course, some factors which had prevented capital accumulation in pre-colonial India were operative even then. Labour was more abundant than ever but land was comparatively scarce and fetched a price quite out of proportion to its actual productive utilisation. Capital investment in irrigation, for instance, which would have greatly enhanced the productivity of the soil was nevertheless rather limited.

Institutional rural credit which should have been sponsored on a large scale to encourage such investment did not make much progress under British rule although the legal and organisational framework was provided by the state (Registrar of co-operative societies, etc.). The field was left to the traditional moneylender who did not finance investment. In fact, his interest rates were usually so high that they discouraged investment. The British inherited the institution of taccavi loans—which the revenue authorities disbursed with a view to increasing the revenue-paying capacity of the peasantry—but bureaucratic procedures made such loans difficult to obtain. Moreover, in the 19th century when land revenue was a mainstay of British-Indian finance the revenue authorities concentrated on the collection of revenue and were not eager to lend money, while in the 20th century, when land revenue became less important for the budget, there was less incentive to give loans enhancing the future revenue-paying capacity of the peasantry. The private banking system in India which developed along British lines was not geared to investment in agriculture or industry, but only provided short-term credit for commercial transactions. The managing agencies to some extent played the role of investment banks within the limited sphere of their operations which were restricted to export-oriented plantations and industries in Eastern India. Actually they invested very little and derived much profit from their astute operations.

Just as the impact of the British-Indian state that of British private capital was very marginal as far as India's economic development was concerned. India received only a small share of British overseas investment (about ten per cent) and one can hardly speak of any positive interaction of the British and the Indian economy. It is, therefore, no accident that in the recent economic history of Britain, edited by Floud and McCloskey, there is hardly any mention of India in the first volume and only some passing references to the marginal 'gains from the empire' in the second. This may perhaps be true and the 'parasitical symbiosis' mentioned above should not be taken to mean that the British economy as a whole drew its sustenance or even derived major benefits from India. The term has been used only to indicate the limited function of British rule in India. In fact, once this kind of parasitical symbiosis was established the maintenance of British rule became an end in itself.

2

'ARRESTED DEVELOPMENT' IN INDIA—WORTHWHILE EPITHET, HOSTAGE TO FORTUNE OR PLAIN UTOPIANISM?

COLIN SIMMONS
University of Salford

Do the very titles of scholarly gatherings matter? Are they of any real significance in themselves, or are they convenient umbrella terms which are sufficiently provocative to attract the relevant academics, sufficiently 'important' to warrant public subsidy and sufficiently plausible to persuade some reluctant publisher to accept the collected papers? Even if they are only 'empty boxes' which are never properly filled, the particular choice of wording is often intriguing and, like the tucked-away sub-title of many a grandiosely phrased monograph, reveals more about the organisers' ambitions than appears at first sight. In the present case 'arrested development' cannot fail to arouse curiosity, alert critical instincts and raise—I suspect—a few eyebrows. For the phrase not only begs the question of whether, and in what sense, 'development' was arrested—it also assumes that the phrase has a categorical and unambiguous ring.

Now, although we are fortunate in having Professor Rothermund's introductory *Note* which attempts to provide some perspective for further discussions, it gives very little guidance on the meaning of the central term. Indeed, no definition is offered at all, and it displays no awareness that economists distinguish between economic growth and economic development, so that the terms cannot be considered as either interchangeable or synonymous. Similarly, the five earmarked sessions on the conference programme do not offer us any real clue as to a possible ordering framework: they could just as comfortably fit into any symposium on modern Indian economic history. Since neither 'arrested development' nor 'arrested economic growth' are self-evident terms, the purpose of this paper is to argue that economic hisorians should be conscious of their very different implications. In view of the debate that is presently raging over the question of how to perceive and measure development, this is an issue of real substance and not one of semantic carping.

Taking 'Arrested Development' for granted

> 'The cause of Indian poverty is not the rate of population growth but the fact that India is a case of arrested economic development'. K.M. Munshi, *The Ruin That Britian Wrought* (Bombay, 1946).

The proposition that a national economy has experienced a condition of 'arrested' growth and development during a particular phase, cycle, long-run period or even, *pace* Simon Kuznets,[1] an entire epoch in its modern history is reasonably widespread and altogether unexceptional. Contemporary politicians, a whole host of media pundits, and academic authors have deployed the term to evoke—and perhaps provoke—a sense of dissatisfaction with a given economic performance. Their plaints are generally accompanied by an attempt to saddle a specific target—an individual, a group, an institution, or even an entire socio-economic system—with responsibility for an undesirable state of affairs. Who or what is considered culpable seems, in large measure, to be dependent upon the prevailing orthodoxy of the ruling establishment. Thus, over the last decade or so, intransigent trade unions, backward-looking corporate managers, and avaricious oil sheikhdoms have all been castigated for arresting—if not bringing to a standstill—Western economic progress, whereas the Group of 77, who ostensibly represent the great majority of Third World governments at UNCTADs and other rhetoric-inducing colloquia, condemn the current international monetary system (for imposing crippling debt-service burdens), the nefarious practices of the multi-national corporations (such as transfer princing), and the maintenance of neo-colonial international trading relationships (which 'under-value' commodity exports and 'over-value' manufactured and infrastructural imports).

Now although the proponents of these ideas may well believe that they are valid explanations, it is surely not unduly cynical to suggest that they also serve an enormously important political function. They can be used to provide propaganda to unite one's allies and discredit one's opponents; they can also distract attention from more fundamental issues. Few serious students of political economy would wish to gainsay the considerable advantages conferred by such postures, nor deny attributing these sort of motives to influential publicists;[2] however, if we wish to probe rather deeper and investigate more fully the substance of the basic charge of arrested growth and development, then we need a clearer and more precise knowledge of the meaning and nature of the phenomenon itself.

The allegation that colonial rule 'arrested' the development of the subcontinent fulfilled all three functions in the work of the early Indian nationalists. In this sense Dietmar Rothermund's paper on arrested growth under the Raj[3] can be regarded as one of the most up to date airings of a very extended line of writing. But this long tradition has paid relatively little attention to the meaning of the key phrase, despite its lengthy lineage.[4] Until the late 1960s and early 1970s, it was perfectly feasible to engage in learned discourse on the subject of economic growth and development without bothering overmuch about strict definitions, because economists specialising in Third World problems were quietly confident that they knew what constituted growth and what constituted development, while economic historians were perfectly happy bobbing along in their wake.[5] Thus if we set aside the divide between Marxian and Liberal-Orthodox paradigms, their respective approaches as to what constituted development and underdevelopment have always been very different of course[6]—it would not be an exaggeration to say that the dominant mode of thought in Western academic circles had a very firm and categorical view of both economic development and growth.

Over the last decade, and especially over the last five years, this virtual unanimity has completely collapsed under the weight of an avalanche of new writing (see the Bibliographical Appendix). Growth and especially development are no longer uncontentious terms: great controversies ebb and flow around them. The great majority of economic historians, including those researching Third World problems, have yet to incorporate these fresh insights and reservations into their framework of thought—Indianists generally have always been far less receptive to theoretical 'advances' than their colleagues interested in Southern Africa and Latin America.[7]

Professor Rothermund's piece is a good example of a genre which takes growth and development as read and makes no attempt to distinguish the one from the other. Professor Rothermund also chooses to discuss arrest within a quasi-chronological framework on the grounds that modern economic history, influenced by the timeless rigour of current economic theories, often loses sight of the crucial aspect of timing—although several branches of neo-classical economic theory are far from timeless (and not particularly rigorous). Indeed the modern theory of economic growth is consciously highly dynamic and now includes sophisticated modelling for expectations,[8] and if we widen the ambit of economics to embrace the now thriving work of Marxist scholars,[9] Professor Rothermund's position is patently erroneous. Although we may all harbour grave reservations about the deployment of national income accounting techniques to data-scarce Third World societies,[10] we cannot escape the fact that growth and development are surely *processes* that operate through time.

The closest Professor Rothermund comes to providing his readers with a clue to his own understanding of the nature of arrested growth and development lies in his somewhat curious notion of 'parasitical symbiosis'. Unfortunately, a parasite cannot have a symbiotic relationship with anything or anybody since it is defined (O.E.D.) as being an animal or plant living in or on another and *drawing nutriment directly from it,* whereas symbiosis is an association of two different organisms living attached to each other *to their mutual advantage* (my emphasis). Moreover, it is surely flying in the face of the evidence to argue that the 'host' economy was unchanged by imperial rule. The commercialisation of some primary activities, the new structure of the balance of payments, the creation of a sizeable proletariat and the demograhic 'revolution' are changes too fundamental to be ignored, whether they constituted 'transition', 'dislocation', 'disruption, or 'destruction'.

Before anyone can prove that the Indian economy suffered from 'arrested' growth and development under British rule, we need to scrutinise four separate but inter-related sets of assumptions:

1. there is general agreement concerning the meaning and measurement of economic growth and economic development;
2. we can appeal to the 'actual record' for confirmation or denial;
3. we can characterise the fundamental direction of the economy prior to alleged arrest and in the subsequent (post-1947) period;
4. we are able to identify the major cause of arrest and can specify the counter-factual alternatives.

1. Defining 'Arrested Economic Development'

From the emergence of modern Development Economics and the somewhat wider field of Development Studies in the aftermath of World War II, to the end of the second so-called 'Development Decade' in the early 1970s, there was widespread agreement about the meaning and measurement of economic growth and economic development. Both Western-based academics and, with a relatively short time-lag, the governments of many of the 'emerging', de-colonising Third World states arrived at this consensus. It would be an exaggeration to suggest that all interested scholars subscribed to this general view—and even more of an exaggeration to claim that all Third World regimes were eagerly receptive to the sort of policy implications which flowed from the analysis. Countries influenced by the spectacular twentieth century material advances of the U.S.S.R. remained outside the orbit and, after the publication of Paul Baran's seminal study, a small group of radical intellectuals began the task of updating the ideas of Marx, Rosa Luxemburg and Lenin.[11] There was also disquiet within the Liberal-Orthodox tradition. Progress in Welfare Economics cast doubt on the equating of growth in per capita income with an increase in welfare;[12] and reservations about the technical feasibility of measuring growth in less developed countries[13] by standard national income accounting methods started to come to the surface. Investigations into how to improve the processing of a largely flimsy data base exposed the magnitude of transactions within the non-monetised sector, and the potential of alternative indices (such as steel production, school enrolment or telephones) was explored.[14] These criticisms, however, were either swept aside (i.e. politely listened to and then ignored) or marginalised in the heady atmosphere of 'hope' generated by the ever-increasing flow of funds towards development studies.[15]

	Economic Growth	*Economic Development*
Meaning	A sustained rise in per capita income and output	Structural change drawn up on the basis of the three-sector classificationary model devised by Irving Fisher, Colin Clark and Simon Kuznets
Indicating Technique	National income accounting	A declining share of both net domestic product and labour resources devoted to the primary sector; a corresponding rise in the secondary sector, especially industrial manufacturing; the tertiary sector remaining roughly neutral during the initial phases and then rising fairly rapidly
Prognosis	Bounded optimism depending upon the ability of host countries to attract capital inflows, and packages including technical assistance	Qualified optimism depending upon the achieved rate of growth and the consolidation of a liberal international trading framework and a degree of domestic economic planning which would supplement—but not supplant—the normal price mechanism

The real challenge to this smug consensus came in the most direct and brutal of ways: the Third World failed to live up to the economists' expectations. One of the earliest cracks in the entire edifice of the 'modernisation' theory was the recognition that growth and development were really quite separate animals. The detailed empirical study of Liberia by Clower and his associates in the mid-1960s—entitled *Growth Without Development*[16]—concluded that the "rapid growth in production . . . had little developmental impact".[17] Of course Liberia was shrugged off as a special case because of its small size, its relative 'obscurity', and its special relationship with American multinationals, notably the Firestone Corporation. The authors, also, were not very well known in the field at the time. But further criticisms gradually emerged, and the stocktaking exercise which the Establishment conducted at the end of the 1960s (the Report of the Lester Pearson Commission),[18] heralded the onset of a major onslaught. Historically impressive—and indeed unprecedented—per capita income growth in a number of 'representative' Thirld World countries was not having the predicted ameliorative effects: the 'gap' between poor and rich countries was widening not narrowing; absolute poverty was increasing, not diminishing; income distribution was becoming more highly skewed; unemployment was deepening and widening; cumulative foreign trade deficits were causing acute strain on the balance of payments; the 'industrialisation first' strategy was draining resources from agriculture and many former food exporters were struggling to feed their own people; the ever-expanding cities were in crisis; populations were burgeoning; the environment was being laid waste; governments were reneging on their own policies (land reform was the classic example); etc., etc. As the Western economies lurched from unparalleled prosperity to deep recession, resources began to be diverted to problems 'closer to home' and all talk of 'development decades' ceased.[19]

The unity, if not the homogeneity, of the Third World's economic problems—one of the ingrained assumptions of this first generation of development experts—was also exposed as a dangerous myth. No amount of rhetorical proclamations could disguise the impossibility of arriving at a single 'Southern' position on any issue of substance—as the series of embarrassingly inconclusive summits designed to forge a 'New International Economic Order' proved.[20] The rise in the price of oil, and the industrial and export-led successes of the four 'Asian Tigers' (Taiwan, South Korea, Hong Kong and Singapore) divided the L.D.C.s among themselves—a fact that even the World Bank was belatedly compelled to concede in its successive *World Development Reports.*[21] But the two Brandt Commission studies were perhaps the most visible symbol of the disintegration of the consensus. Their content matters less than their reception. Although their emphasis on the common interests of 'North' and 'South' was phrased in such a way as to appeal to the self-preservation instincts of even hard-line conservatives, not one of their many recommendations has been accepted by any major country.[22]

Two inter-connected responses to this catalogue of unpalatable events may be discerned. The intellectual hegemony of the Liberal-Orthodox School of development studies has crumbled in the face of frontal assaults aimed at their most cherished ideas. Nothing is sacred, not even dualism, Lewis' two-sector growth model, Harrod-Domar's incremental capital-output ratio, the zero marginal productivity of farming labour, vicious-circle conundrums, low-level equilibrium traps, Rostovian 'take-offs', growth poles, green revolutions, the theory of demographic transition, migration processes, import-substituting industrialisation strategies, benefit-cost analysis, fiscal federalism, planning initiatives within a mixed economy framework or the balanced 'versus' the unbalanced growth dichotomy. In the case of Development Economics, this broadside came from the neo-Marxists (in uneasy alliance with the post-Sraffa Classicists) and the resurgent neo-Classicals. The nucleus of the neo-Classical alternative is reasonably straightforward, and may be conveniently—if crudely—summarised as 'getting the prices right',[23] i.e., it is a plea for the untrammelled operation of free market forces, especially with respect to international trading.[24] Although the Marginalist Revolution dates back to the 1870s, it has been widely held that neo-Classical doctrine had little to say about the problems facing the underdeveloped world until relatively recently. For many years the notions of Peter Bauer and his colleagues Bert Yamey and Harry Johnson were considered to be fringe irritants at best and antediluvian curiosities at worst. As a result, however, of a combination of interlocking forces—the demise of Keynesian ideas and the rise of Supply-Side economics, the ascendancy of the new Right in Western governments, the disappointing performance of planning regimes in the Third World, and the I.M.F.'s insistence on financial orthodoxy as a condition for alleviating debt burdens—there has been a conscious attempt to develop a mainstream economic perspective.[25]

The neo-Marxists are more difficult to pin down, because there are so many ideological disagreements within the canon.[26] After Baran (and in no particular order) we may identify the following approaches: 'the development of under-development' (associated with the early writings of André Gunder Frank[27]), the 'core-periphery' analysis (Samir Amin); the theory—or rather theories—of 'unequal exchange' (A. Emmanuel); 'World Systems' theory (Immanuel Wallerstein, Terence K. Ranger and, more generally, the F. Braudel Centre, New York); the 'Dependency' School (at first dominated by Latin American authors such as T. Dos Santos, F. Cardoso, Oswaldo Sunkel and Celso Furtado, but now extended to West Africa and the Caribbean); the multinational corporations as agents of a new form of imperialism (Hugo Radice and many others); the 'modes of production' controversy (John Taylor, Hamza Alavi and others); and finally a number of sturdily 'independent' scholars who share one important common outlook—a great sense of dissatisfaction with virtually everything written by other Marxists.[28] This confusion would, of course, be further compounded if we were able to take proper cognisance of theoretical developments in Marxist economic theory (including the confrontation with the neo-Ricardians), the more applied writings on the economies of the newer parts of the Communist world (China and Cuba in particular), and the implications stemming from work in Marxist philosophy (especially from the Althusserians) and political theory.

Mainstream developmentalists reacted to the crisis in their 'discipline' by taking up a bewildering succession of new causes: income distribution; unemployment; the 'special' case of women; human capital formation (primary schooling in particular); structural imbalances (the so-called 'hypertrophy' problem of the informal service sector); exchange entitlements (A.K. Sen's 'discovery' of the 'real' causes of famines); conservation; the connections between health, nutrition and fertility; the physical quality of life; and—in Michael Todaro's influential text-book—low self-esteem and limited freedom.[29]

The suspicion that these notions were nothing more than a kind of intellectual fashion parade encouraged a number of orthodox economists to undertake a purposeful enquiry into the history of the Tradition to discover what had gone wrong and whether there were any basic principles which could be salvaged.[30] Several influential academics have questioned the validity of any sort of development economics. Dudley Seers—one of the founding fathers of the discipline, a key figure in the establishment of the Sussex-based Institute of Development Studies, an advisor to many Third World governments and a man directly involved in the creation of the Ministry of Overseas Development—has actually declared his subject 'dead'.[31] As far as he and his disciples are concerned, the way forward is to apply the tools of Development Economics to the states on the periphery of Europe (Iberia, Yugoslavia and Greece): they are no longer of any use to their original destination.[32] Seers' nihilism, however, is less popular than proposals for a return to mainstream economics, i.e., a judicious combination of neo-Classical and neo-Keynesian outlooks.[33] By concentrating upon the 'special' features of Third World economies, the discipline supposedly lost its real moorings: the notion that economic theory, born out of Western experience, was somehow 'inapplicable' in non-Western settings has begun to be jettisoned.[34] Sir Arthur Lewis' presidential address to the American Economic Association in December 1983 is a clear signal, emanating from a voice of great authority and experience, of a real desire to 'return to the fold'.[35] Most development economists, however, have yet to declare their colours. So much intellectual capital has been sunk into the Tradition that novel viewpoints are unlikely to be accepted overnight.

What then are we to conclude from all this? A schematic picture of what is left of the notion of economic development ('growth' has been lost somewhere en route)[36] might look something like this:

1. The *positive* statement that economic development is a tangible and historically-specific phenomenon—something that has already taken place in the West and Japan[37]—although the search for a concise internally consistent theory capable of explaining why it happened in particular regions and not others has met with little success. The

possibility of its extension to other parts of the globe is shrouded in controversy, but it is now widely acknowledged that simple replication/duplication is well-nigh impossible.[38]

2. The *quasi-Eurocentric* statement that such a development path is the norm.
3. The *normative* statement that economic development should be the goal of all societies, especially those suffering from abject poverty.
4. The *prescriptive* statement that development can be engineered *if only* governments or private citizens take the necessary action.
5. The *idealistic* statement that development cures all (or virtually all) economic, social, political and strategic problems.
6. The *qualitative* statement that it can be widely recognised, even by non-professionals!
7. The *quantitative* statement that development is, at least in principle, amenable to precise measurement.

Econimic historians exploring the labyrinth of modern Development Economics have to choose the meanings and indicators which are relevant to their particular task. They can no longer afford to mix up positive with normative statements; be fuzzy about the line that separates explanation from policy prescription (even retrospectively); ignore the difference between a process that 'happened without being consciously willed by anyone',[39] and a conscious development drive; or fashion indicators without due regard to their contexts. Few economic historians and fewer specialists working on the imperial Indian economy have attempted to grasp these sort of nettles—let alone adopt a consistent view of them. This lacuna weakens our perception of the entire course of modern economic change: witness our facile use of words like 'arrested' with any semblance of conviction. The task of rectifying this situation is daunting, but the potential returns are high. A detailed study of the Indian case could supply a novel typology of economic development/underdevelopment. Instead of borrowing concepts from the extant body of theory, Indian economic historians could conceivably enrich it.[40]

Resorting to 'the Record'

Whichever theories and indicators are employed, there is no

escaping the intractability of the data on imperial India or the limitations of all-India generalisation. Many of the aggregative and averaging procedures that lie close to the very core of modern research methodology (both Orthodox and Marxist) are inapplicable as a result. Neither the nation state nor traditional class structure are self-evidently appropriate units of analysis in South Asia.[41] The huge land mass (the size of Europe less eastern Russia) is fragmented by vastly different geomorphological, topographical and metereological conditions; political divisions (584 Princely States ranging from 'giants' such as Hyderabad to tiny village fiefdoms); varied administrative practices (e.g. the three main types of Land Revenue regime); and the different dates at which particular territories came under British rule. The problems of generalising about India over space and through time are neatly highlighted by the scepticism that has been recently expressed concerning national indices of agricultural output and labour productivity.[42] As one specialist (Clive Dewey) has put it: All-India averages combine opposing trends—catastrophic deterioration in Bihar with rapid expansions in the Punjab—to give an impression of general stagnation; the averages of super-provinces blend the performance of heterogeneous farming types.[43] He goes on to argue that the future lies with detailed studies of the agricultural statistics of quite small areas.[44] Now just how small these areas should be is, of course, a matter of individual judgement; but there can be little disagreement that what Myrdal (in another, albeit related, context) has called 'false aggregation' applies here.[45] The credibility of presenting the processes of industrialisation and de-industrialisation as all-India phenomena is likewise strained. M.D. Morris and A.K. Sen have asked why modern indigenous entrepreneurship flowered in Bombay, but not in Calcutta, during the heyday of the Raj;[46] while A.K. Bagchi has argued that regional stratification can be an aspect of the general processes of the uneven development under colonisation.[47]

Just as there are intense horizontal differences, there are also significant vertical divisions. The 400-million-strong population (1947) was not only differentiated along class lines, but also with respect to religion, race, caste and language. In study after study anthropologists and sociologists have brought out the highly hierarchical nature of Indian society.

Since there are no satisfactory general answers to issues such as changes in the relative standard of living of different castes—*Harijans*, say, as opposed to *Brahmins*—the painstaking local-level works of scholars such as Cohn and Kessinger (who focus upon closely delineated villages) or Timberg and Bayly (who have put the microscope on particular merchant communities) are invaluable.[48] But we cannot tell, as yet, how 'representative' and 'typical' these particular case studies are, and there is still no agreement on how best to study the nature of class formations or even how to characterise the dominant mode of production.[49]

The data base itself is probably superior to that of other Third World countries, and an enormous amount of information is available on particular activities. There is a fine run of international and inter-regional trade returns, a vast body of material on the railways, and a detailed series of decennial censuses of population. But many of the most basic quantitative sources are riddled with incalculable margins of error. The agricultural statistics are the classic example of just how shaky much of the ground really is. Over the last decade a mounting body of research (conducted by Dewey, Islam, Heston and others) has pinpointed their basic deficiencies: surely no amount of ingenious re-working is ever going to compensate for their imperfections? There are also some gaping voids. The papers of the great majority of the modern India's most ubiquitous form of modern business organisation—the Managing Agency—have disappeared without trace.[50] As a result, we cannot work out, with any pretensions to accuracy, the long run trend of real per capita output, the relation between farm output and population growth, the fate of 'native arts and crafts', the savings-investment and capital-output ratios, or aggregate series of employment, money and real wages.[51]

One of the main factors responsible for the uneven quality of the data is the peculiarly heterogeneous character of the economy itself. A confusing amalgam of capitalism, custom and state involvement produced a hybrid economic structure—one in which entirely different methods of production, distribution and exchange co-existed side-by-side. At the most obvious points of interface—the factories in the large cities, and the mines and plantations in the up-country areas—highly developed forces of production mingled with a whole variety of pre-capitalist relations; thus captains of industry resorted to all manner of institutional devices to secure a ready supply of raw labour and to maintain control over their employees.[52]

At the other end of the economic order—India's half a million or so villages—a 'significant' number of transactions were non-monetised, and a 'substantial' part of total rural output (including services) was not marketed.[53] In fact, over much of what might be termed the 'traditional economy', factor and product markets in the sense much-loved by neo-Classical theorists, simply did not exist. A great many rural dwellers did sell some of their output and many of them responded to price changes in the approved 'rational' manner. Tens of thousands also left their villages to enter expanding labour markets. But we are still a long way short of being able to determine the proximate degree of their participation in modern (i.e. capitalist) market transactions. The inescapable conclusion is that *even if* we accept the simplest (and now almost discredited) indicators of economic growth (per capita income and output change) or economic development (the predicted structural shift), *and* swallow our reservations about national income accounts, *we still cannot meaningfully appeal to the 'record' for confirmation or denial of the charge of arrest.*

Take population: at the most basic level a knowledge of aggregate population size is necessary to derive time series estimates of per capita income and output. Prior to the pioneering all-India census undertaken in 1868-72, we are in the realm of conjecture and educated guesswork. Leela and Pravin Visaria admit, in their recent overview of the pre-census period, 1750-1870, that the data base is very weak[54]—and it speaks volumes that the various attempts to estimate the total population circa 1800 have produced wildly variant figures ranging from 100 millions to almost twice that number.[55] The census reports themselves tell us far too little about births, deaths (especially famines), marriage rates, life-expectancy, migration, density, urbanisation and age structure.[56] In consequence, the great twentieth century demographic watershed—imperfectly captured by the 1921 Census—is difficult to explain, which makes it difficult to assess the trend rate of change of per capita income over the inter-war period.

Commencing with Dadabhai Naoroji's pioneering calculations for 1867-68,[57] there have been many attempts to construct an index of average real per capita incomes for both particular years (point estimates) as well as for changes over time (series estimates).[58] The argument about the material condition of the population played an important part in the polemical battle between Nationalists and Apologists[59]—a debate which re-surfaced in the 1960s with the publication of Morris' provocative 're-interpretation' article.[60] But despite the labours of the heirs of Professor V.K.R.V. Rao, we are not in sight of convincing estimates covering the whole period.[61] Only for the last five decades of imperial rule do we have a reasonably tolerable set of figures, those provided by Siva Sivasubramoniam.[62] Before the middle of the last century we are on such dangerously uncertain ground that only Morris has been prepared to venture any sort of opinion at all, and his 'tentative' findings are based on 'hunch'.[63] For the period 1850-1900 Moni Mukherjee has stated that 'our knowledge . . . is nearly non-existent, and although the position is somewhat better in respect of the more recent decades, we cannot say with certainly that today (1969) our level of per capita income is higher than in 1900 or in 1850s'.[64] No amount of tinkering with accounting conventions—the choice of base year for the derivation of a price deflator; the choice of production series (especially with regard to the weighty agricultural sector); the allowance made for different geographical coverage; the value placed on the output of the tertiary and handicraft sectors; and the choice of estimates of non-monetised production and transactions—can overcome the deficiencies of the data.

Even if it were possible to construct a reliable index of per capita income,[65] it would still say nothing about distribution; and here again we must admit to yet another awesome gap in our knowledge. Despite the work of Dharma Kumar and J. Krishnamurthy,[66] we are not in a position to test any of the general hypotheses regarding regional income shares[67] or its social distribution. Only Angus Maddison has been brave (or reckless) enough to venture any firm views on social distribution,[68] and his estimates for the *single* year of 1938 need not be taken too seriously.[69] Surrogates such as the availability of food or access to education[70] raise as many problems and have produced few worthwhile results.[71]

To investigate the pattern of structural change—our second indicator after national income—we need to know the total net domestic product of the three major sectoral groupings. Discounting the crude backward extrapolation exercise conducted by Heston (from 1899-1900 to 1868-69),[72] nothing is available prior to the turn of the twentieth century. From 1900-01 to 1946-47 we do have Sivasubramoniam's estimates—his exploration of the rise of the secondary sector is especially valuable,[73] but his series is still highly tentative and for crucial categories such as the small-scale handicrafts is no better than informed speculation. Further down the line, the share of resources consumed and released by the three sectors over any period of time to 1947 is still *terra incognita*. Thanks to the decennial census, most work has been centred upon the occupational structure (labour resources). But J. Krishnamurthy's various studies only cover the twentieth century because the primary evidence before 1901 is so defective, and there are many problems that cannot be overcome—not least the question of (self) employment by artisans—at any point in time.[74] Thus one of the most important issues of modern India's economic history—the charge of de-industrialisation and the fate of the 'handicraft' workers[75]—can only be discussed in rather vague or regionally specific terms.[76] It may be that more unconventional (and certainly more interesting) approaches[77] and an altogether wider range of source material will produce results worth having; but at present we are not in a position to test any of the 'first order' indicators of economic growth and economic development against the record.

The Economy before and after 'Arrest'

The character of the economy before and after the alleged arrest is seldom discussed. Even in a long academic career, it is difficult to master three distinct epochs; and the specialists in each of these three periods live in worlds of their own. They ask different sorts of questions; they struggle with vastly different source materials; they belong to different disciplines (the development economist is usually a social scientist; the students of the British and pre-British periods tend to be historians without much training in economic history); and they rarely enter into dialogue with each other.[78] This means that one of the key standards of the proponents of arrest[79]—that growth and development was taking place during the pre-Plassey period—is rarely made with any conviction.[80] Many of the Nationalist writers believed in the existence of the Golden Age: thus for Romesh Dutt, pre-British India 'was a great manufacturing as well as a great agricultural country'.[81] Subsequently, a number of scholars looked for the kind of economic growth and development that occurred in the West, or the obstacles which supposedly prevented an 'industrial revolution'.[82] Latterly, a few historians have consciously avoided examining the indigenous economy in terms of Eurocentric-type pigeon holes,[83] and may yet supply fresh insights into the growth and development processes. The main conclusion to be drawn from both approaches is that few specialists would not feel that the Nationalist School has been vindicated; indeed the new generation of writers would be distinctly uncomfortable about even thinking in such terms.[84]

Since 1947 there has been both economic growth and economic development in India, judged by the more obvious criteria. Average real income per capita has risen (albeit 'disappointingly' slowly and with considerable fluctuation), and there has been a relative shift of resources away from the primary sector towards both manufacturing and (less welcome) tertiary activities.[85] But not even the most sanguine observer would take much comfort from these results, because the setbacks have been so grave.[86] Bumper wheat crops co-exist with severe malnutrition, and nuclear power stations with bullock-carts. And how should we construe the great population increase? As a drag on absolute gains or an enhancement of the ultimate resource? After almost four decades of formal political independence the question of whether India has 'developed' remains tantalisingly elusive.

Causative and Counter-Factuals

The Nationalist School and their latter-day equivalents have no doubt about the identity of the culprits responsible for India's arrested growth and development and suppress evidence running counter to their preconceived ideas. But over the last twenty years or so, an increasing number of 'Orthodox' scholars have begun to challenge the much wider—but obviously closely related—issue of the intensity of the imperial economic impact, and neo-Marxists are no longer content to simply blame the Raj for causing arrest without exploring the precise ways in which the forces unleashed by capitalism and imperialism 'distorted' the economy. Unfortunately, the current 'state of the art' does not permit us to separate the effects of British rule from the on-going economic life of Indian society. It is possible to list the laws the British enacted, but what impact did they have? Equally important, the non-official community obviously made a significant impression. But how is it to be evaluated? The fact that the imperial impact varied over space and time complicates the issue. If, for example, we focus upon foreign trade policy, we need to consider the specific mechanics of mercantilism, free trade, and discriminating protection.[87] The British economy was itself in transition, and it is difficult to disentangle the effects of this from the forces at work in the world economy—into which it was so profoundly integrated.

The extensive theoretical literature on imperialism treats the functioning of the colonial state in the most superficial way, and gives little guidance to students trying to work out its power to arrest. The early Marxist theories of imperialism do not have very much to say about the actual processes of economic change under foreign rule; rather they purport to explain the reasons that lay behind the metropolitan quest for empire.[88] The widely quoted work of historians of imperialism (such as Robinson and Gallagher, David Fieldhouse and D.C.M. Platt) does focus upon 'imperialism on the ground', but contains no 'theories' (in the sense of testable hypotheses) about the course of economic activity in the periphery.[89] The neo-Marxists have made relevant and important contributions towards developing a theory of imperialism but there is wide and deep disagreement over basic issues,[90] and the link between this work and the study of particular economies has often been tenuous. The Classical economists, the neo-Keynesians and the present generation of 'new' economic historians[91] have developed some useful methodology—the refinement of a special type of cost-benefit analysis applied to trade relations is an example—but there is no equally useful general theory which could be applied to India.

The notion of some hypothetical alternative is implicit in the charge of 'arrested' development. Three sorts of counterfactual propositions may be identified. The Raj could have pursued an entirely different set of economic policies; a possibility which is hardly worth spending much time considering, because there are such an infinite number of 'could' and 'should' variations. Then one can speculate about what might have transpired had India escaped colonialism altogether. Would she have forged a new, dynamic economy on Japanese lines, or would her fate have been similar to that of China? Everything depends on our assumptions concerning emergent state formations. Lastly, there is the intriguing possibility that India would have been subjected to colonial rule by a different power or at different dates. Again, without specifying a great many economic and non-economic variables it is difficult to say anything very meaningful about either postulate. Indeed, because of the inherent problems of discussing these sort of grand scenarios, those few 'new' economic historians interested in imperial history prefer to confine their purview to a rather narrow set of issues such as the effect of a tariff or the 'social savings' conferred by the coming of a railway system. Such tasks, though more obviously manageable, are a long way from the big question of 'arrested' development.

The methodological problems posed by comparisons between Indian and other—principally Third World—economies are equally daunting, since the 'quality' of colonial rule differs so much.[92] Even if we could agree upon a set of criteria to evaluate economic performance on a comparative basis[93]—and even if we were in possession of a run of reliable data to fill in the appropriate equations—such an exercise is more likely to open a Pandora's box of contention than to illuminate the course of long-run change.

Conclusion

The main conclusion to be drawn from our discussion is that neither arrested economic growth nor arrested economic development are worthwhile epithets. Our ideas about the meaning and measurement of both growth and development have changed too radically over the last decade or so, and the notion of arrest is too utopian a concept. It implies that if only the Raj and done something else (which, invariably, is never properly specified) then there would never have been any retardation: this is quite unrealistic in view of the very nature and needs of the actual colonial state. A rejection of the term and all it stands for is not a position of nihilism—on the contrary it serves the purpose of clearing out a useless item of baggage that we have been carrying around for too long.

BIBLIOGRAPHICAL APPENDIX
NEW THINKING ON GROWTH, DEVELOPMENT AND UNDERDEVELOPMENT

This list is illustrative rather than exhaustive and refers to those works which discuss the meaning or measurement of economic growth and economic development and underdevelopment. Where feasible and for the sake of brevity, survey-type literature (e.g. A. Brewer, 1980) has been used as a surrogate for fuller citation referencing.

1985

J. Galtung, 'Development Theory: Notes for an Alternative Approach' mimeo, International Institute for Environment and Society, Preprint 185-11, Berlin.

E. de Kadt, 'Of Markets, Might and Mullahs: A Case for Equity, Pluralism and Tolerance in Development', *World Development*, 13(4).

F. Stewart, 'The Fragile Foundations of the Neo-Classical Approach to Development', *Journal of Development Studies*, 21(2).

M. Todaro, *Economic Development in the Third World*, London, 3rd Edition.

J. Toye, 'Dirigism and Development Economics', *Cambridge Journal of Economics*, 9.

1984

K. Basu, *The Less Developed Economy: A Critique of Contemporary Theory*, Oxford.

M. Bronfenbrenner, 'Review Essay of Hirschman's Esseys in Trespassing', *Economic Development and Cultural Change*, 32(3).

Capital and Class special issue on the New International Division of Labour, 22, Spring, esp. the papers by R. Jenkins, A. Lipietz and W. Andreff.

R.H. Chilcote, *Theories of Development and Underdevelopment*, Westview.

B. Hettne, 'Development Theory and the European Crisis', unpublished paper presented to the 4th General Conference of the European Association of Development Institutes, Madrid, September 1984.

Journal of Development Economics, Symposium on 'Technological Change and Industrial Development', 16(1-2), September-October.

Journal of Development Studies Special Issue on 'Third World Industrialisation in the 1980s: Open Economies in a Closing World', 21(1).

D. Lehmann, 'The Rise of the Jet-Set Proletariat', *Times Higher Education Supplement*, 27 April.

W.A. Lewis, 'The State of Development Theory', *American Economic Review*, 74(1).

G.M. Meier, *Emerging from Poverty*, Oxford.

G.M. Meier, *Leading Issues in Economic Development*, Oxford, 4th Edition.

G.M. Meier and D. Seers (eds.), *Pioneers in Development*, Oxford.

W. Nafziger, *The Economics of Developing Countries*, California.

S.N.H. Naqvi, 'Development Economics in New Cloths', Pakistan, *Development Review*, XXIII (2, 3).

S. Roy, *Pricing, Planning and Politics: A Study of Economic Distortions in India*,

I.E.A. Occasional Paper 69, London.

N. Smith, *Uneven Development*, Oxford.

C. Suriyakumaran, *The Wealth of Poor Nations*, London.

Symposium on Reassessing Development Experience in *World Development*, 12, esp. the papers by Adelman, Singer, Scitovsky and Fishlow.

P. Worsley, *The Three Worlds: Culture and World Development*, London.

1983

C.A. Barone, 'Dependency and Marxist Theory', *Review of Radical Political Economy*, 15(1).

J. Bhagwati, 'Development Economics: What have we Learned?', Discussion Paper No. 36, International Economic Research Center, Columbia University, October.

H.J. Bruton, 'The Search for a Development Economics', Research Memorandum Series RM-87, Center for Development Economics, Williams College, Mass., November.

R.H. Chilcote and D.L. Johnson (eds.), *Theories of Development: Modes of Production or Dependency?*, Beverley Hills.

K. Choi, *Theories of Comparative Economic Growth*, Iowa.

K. Cole, 'Economic Theory and Development Studies', *Journal Ekonomi Malaysia*, 7, June.

J.E. Elliott, 'J.A. Schumpeter at 100 and the Theory of Economic Development at 72', *Working Papers in Economics*, No. F.H.06119, University of S. California, March (unpublished).

C. Furtado, *Accumulation and Development*, Oxford.

P. Hall, *Growth and Development: An Economic Analysis*, Oxford.

D. Lal, *The Poverty of Development Economics*, I.E.A., Hobart Paper 16, London.

P. Leeson, 'Development Economics and its Companions', *Manchester University Discussion Papers in Development Studies*, No. 8304 (unpublished).

P. Limqueco and B. Macfarlane (eds.), *Neo-Marxist Theories of Development*, London.

F. Perroux, *A New Concept of Development: Basic Tenets*, London.

A.K. Sen, 'Development: Which Way Now?', *Economic Journal*, 93, December.

R.M. Sundrum, *Development Economics: A Framework for Analysis and Policy*, London.

A.P. Thirwell, *Growth and Development: With Special Reference to Developing Economies*, 3rd Edition, London.

J. Toye, 'Commentary: The Disparaging of Development Economics', *Journal of Development Studies*, 20 (1).

G. White, R. Murray and C. White, *Revolutionary Socialist Development in the Third World*, Brighton.

The World Bank, *IDA in Retrospect: The First Two Decades of the International Development Association*, Oxford.

World Development, Special Issue, 'Economic Development and the Development of Economics', 11(10), edited by G. Rosen, esp. the essays by Chenery, Streeten, Solow, Weiskopf and S. Roy.

1982

H. Alavi and T. Shanin (eds.), *Introduction to the Sociology of "Developing" Societies*, London.

H. Alavi *et al.*, *Capitalism and Colonial Production*, London.
A.K. Bagchi, *The Political Economic of Underdevelopment*, Cambridge.
P.T. Bauer, *Equality, the Third World and Economic Delusion*, London.
M. Bienefeld and M. Godfrey, *The Struggle for Development*, London.
A.M.M. Hoogvelt, *The Third World in Global Development*, London.
K.P. Jameson, 'A Critical examination of "The Patterns of Development", *Journal of Development Studies*, 18(4).
I.M.D. Little, *Economic Development: Theory, Policy and International Relations*, London.
I. Livingstone (ed.), *Approaches to Development Studies: Essays in Honour of A. Mackintosh*, London, esp. Part 1.
F.I. Nixson, 'Beyond Economic Development', *Manchester University Discussion Papers in Development Studies*, No. 8203.
P.W. Preston, *Theories of Development*, London.

1981

H.W. Arndt, 'Economic Development: A Semantic History', *Economic Development and Cultural Change*, 29(3).
L. Currie, *The Role of Economic Advisors in Developing Countries*, London.
P. Fourie, 'The Illusive Concept of Development', *Development Studies on Southern Africa*, 4(1).
M. Gersovitz (ed.), *The Theory and Experience of Economic Development: Essays in Honor of Sir W.A. Lewis*, London.
D. Goodman and M. Redclift, *From Peasant to Proletariat*, London.
A.O. Hirschman, *Essays in Trespassing: Economics to Politics and Beyond*, Cambridge.
R.J. Holton, 'Marxist Theories of Social Changes', *Theory and Society*, 10(6).
I. Livingstone, 'The Development of Development Economics', *O.D.I. Review*, 2.
H.G. Mannur, 'Development Economics and Economic Development—Old Theories and New Prospectives', *Indian Journal of Economics*, LXII (2-4), July.
B. Munslow, 'A Critique of Theories of Socialist Transition on the Periphery', unpublished paper presented to the Development Studies Association Annual Conference, Oxford, September.
P. Streeten, *Development Perspectives*, London.
P. Streeten *et al.*, *First Things First: Meeting Basic Human Needs in the Developing Countries*, London.
P. Streeten and R. Jolly (eds.), *Recent Issues in World Development: A Collection of Survey Articles*, Oxford.
M.P. Torado, *Economic Development in the Third World*, 2nd Edition, London.

1980

I. Abdulla, 'What Development?', *International Development Review*, 22(2-3).
V.V. Bhatt, *Development Perspectives: Problems, Strategy and Policies*, Oxford.
A. Brewer, *Marxist Theories of Imperialism*, London, 1980.
K.P. Clements, *From Right to Left in Development Theory*, Singapore.
J. de Bandt, P. Mardi, and D. Seers, *European Studies in Development: New Trends in European Development Studies*, London.
J. Friedman, T. Wheelwright and J. Connell, *Development Strategies in the Eighties*, Sydney.

F. Fröbel, J. Heinrichs and O. Kreya, *The New International Division of Labour*, Cambridge.

I.D.S. Bulletin, 'Teaching Development at Graduate Level in Britian', 11(3), esp. essays by J. Toye, C. Leys, R. Apthorpe and D. Seers.

J. Love, 'Prebisch and the Doctrine of Unequal Exchange', *Latin American Research Review*, 15(3).

N. Mouzelis, 'Prospects for a Theory of Third World Formations', *Journal of Peasant Studies*, 7(30).

I. Sachs, *Studies in the Political Economy of Development*, Oxford.

D. Seers and C. Vaitos (eds.), *Integration and Unequal Development*, London.

W. Warren, *Imperialism: Pioneer of Capitalism*, London.

1979

F.H. Cardoso and E. Falleto, *Dependency and Development in Latin America*, Berkeley.

H.B. Chenery, *Structural Change and Development Policy*, Oxford.

R.A. Flammang, 'Economic Growth and Economic Development: Counterparts or Competitors?', *Economic Development and Cultural Change*, 28(1).

J.K. Galbraith, *The Nature of Mass Poverty*, Cambridge, Mass.

K.Q. Hill (ed.), *Towards a New Strategy for Development: A Rothko Chapel Colloquium*, New York, esp. essays by Hirschman, D. Seers, P. Streeten, B.S. Minhas and G. Ohlin.

D. Lehmann (ed.), *Development Theory: Four Critical Studies*, London, esp. essays by D. Seers, W. Nafziger and H. Bernstein.

D.A. Nugent, J.B. Yotopoulis, 'What has Orthodox Development Economics Learnt from Recent Experience?', *World Development*, 7(6).

Proceedings of the I.S.S. 25th Anniversary Conference, *Development of Societies: The Next Thirty-Five Years*, The Hague.

C.H. Rao and D.C. Joshi (eds.), *Reflections on Economic Development and Social Change: Essays in Honour of Prof. V.K.R.V. Rao*, Bombay, esp. the chapter by H. Singer.

D. Rimmer, 'Some Origins of Development Economics', *I.D.S. Bulletin*, 10(4).

J. Robinson, *Aspects of Development and Underdevelopment*, Cambridge.

I. Roxborough, *Theories of Underdevelopment*, London.

D. Seers, 'The Birth, Life and Death of Development Economics', *Development and Change*, 10(4).

D. Seers, 'The Meaning of Development', *International Development Review*, 11(4).

D. Seers, 'Back to the Ivory Tower? The Professionalisation of Development Studies and their Extension to Europe', *I.D.S. Bulletin*, 9(2).

J. Taylor, *From Modernisation to Modes of Production*, London.

I. Wallerstein, *The Capitalist World Economy*, Cambridge.

C. Wilbur (ed.), *The Political Economy of Development and Underdevelopment*, New York, esp. the essays by K. Griffin and P. Henriot.

1978

L. Currie, 'The Objectives of Development', *World Development*, 6(1).

P. Deane, *The Evolution of Economics Ideas*, Cambridge.

A Foster-Carter, 'The Modes of Production Controversy', *New Left Review*, 107.

B. Higgins, 'Development Economics in the US: A Comment', *Journal of Development Studies*, 15,(2).

G. Williams, 'Imperialism and Development: A Critique', *World Development*, 6(7 and 8), July and August.

1977

R. Brenner, 'The Origins of Capitalist Development: A Critique of Neo-Smithian Marxism', *New Left Review*, 104.

F. Cardosa, 'The Originality of Copy: CEPAL and Development', *CEPAL Review*, 4.

C.P. Kindleberger and B. Herrick, *Economic Development*, 3rd Edition, New York.

E. Laclau, *Politics and Ideology in Marxist Theory*, London.

C. Leys, 'Underdevelopment and Dependency: Critical Notes', *Journal of Contemporary Asia*, 7(1) 1977.

D. Morawetz, *Twenty-Five Years of Economic Development: 1950 to 1975*, Washington.

M. Nash (ed.), *Economic Development and Cultural Change: Essays in Honour of B.F. Hoselitz*, Chicago, esp. the essays by G. Ranis, G.V. Papanek, S. Kuznets and T. Schultz.

J. Nyilas (ed.), *Theory and Practice of Development in the Third World*, Budapest.

A. Phillips, 'The Concept of "Development"', *Review of African Political Economy*, 8, January-April.

Pugwash Symposium, 'The Role of Self-Reliance in Alternative Strategies for Development', *World Development*, 5(3).

C.G. Reynolds, *Image and Reality in Economic Development*, New Haven.

P.S. Sang, *Growth and Development: A Physical Output and Employment Strategy*, Oxford.

O. Sunkel, 'The Development of Development Thinking', *IDS Bulletin*, 8(3).

1976

S. Lall, 'Conflicts and Concepts: Welfare Economics and Developing Countries', *Wrold Development*, 4(3).

A. Foster-Carter, 'From Rostow to Gunder Frank: Conflicting Paradigms in the Analysis of Underdevelopment', *World Development*, 4(3).

I. Livingstone, 'After Divorce: The Ramarriage of Economic Theory and Development Economics?', *Eastern Africa Economic Review*, 8(1).

J.W. Mellor, *The New Economies of Growth: A Strategy for India and the Developing World*, Cornell.

W. Nafziger, 'A Critique of Development Economics in the US', *Journal of Development Studies*, 13(1).

T. Szentes, *The Political Economy of Underdevelopment*, 2nd Edition, Budapest.

M. Wolfe, 'Approaches to Development: Who is Approaching What?', *CEPAL Review*.

1975

American Economic Review, 'A Re-assessment of Development Economics', 65(2), esp. essays by I. Adelman and S.A. Resnick.

H. Brookfield, *Interdependent Development*, London.

H. Chenery and M. Syrquin, *Patterns of Development 1950-70*, London.

G. Kay, *Development and Underdevelopment: A Marxist Analysis*, London.

W.A. Lewis, 'The Diffusion of Development', in T. Wilson and A.S. Skinner (eds.), *The Market and the State*, Oxford.

I. Oxaal *et al.* (eds.), *Beyond the Sociology of Development*, London.

H.W. Singer (ed.), *The Strategy of International Development: Essays in the Economics of Backwardness*, New York.

1974

H. Chenery *et al.*, *Redistribution with Growth*, Oxford.

A. Foster-Carter, 'New-Marxist Approaches to Development and Underdevelopment', in E. de Kadt and G. Williams (eds.), *Sociology and Development*, London.

L. Lefeber, 'On the Paradigm for Economic Development', *World Development*, 2(1).

J. Taylor, 'Neo-Marxism and Underdevelopment', *Journal of Contemporary Asia*, 4(1).

NOTES

All references to *op.cit. followed by a date* can be found in full in the Bibliographical Appendix.

1. Professor Kuznets has long argued that the last two centuries form a distinctive epoch or era in world economic history with the institutionalisation of rapid economic change being its essential characteristic: for him it is an epoch of 'modern economic growth' which he defines in very broad terms, see his *Modern Economic Growth: Rate, Structure, Spread* (New Haven, 1966) Part I; *Economic Growth of Nations: Total Output and Production Structures* (Cambridge, Mass., 1971) Ch. 1; and the succinct Nobel Lecture, 'Modern Economic Growth: Findings and Reflection's,' *American Economic Review*, 63 (1973). Although he admits to the 'highly uneven' spread of growth and its 'limited outreach' I find this general argument unsatisfactory on account of its basically Western vision. For some contrasting views and some alternative temporal suggestions cf. J.D. Gould, *Economic Growth in History* (London, 1972) Ch. 1; W.W. Rostow, *The World Economy : History and Prospect* (London, 1978) Part 2; A. Maddison, *Phases of Capitalist Development* (Oxford, 1982); and L.G. Reynolds, 'The Spread of Economic Growth to the Third World', *Journal of Economic Literature*, XXI (1983).

2. In the last few years a number of attempts have been made to apply some of the principles of economic theory—especially the concept of maximisation—to political and electoral analysis, cf. A. Peacock, *The Economic Analysis of Government* (Oxford, 1979); D.K. Whynes and R. Bowles, *The Economic Theory of the State* (Oxford, 1981); and J.E. Alt and A.K. Chrystal, *Political Economics* (Brighton, 1983)

3. D. Rothermund, 'Problems of India's Arrested Economic Growth under British Rule' *supra*.

4. There is now a solid body of work on the history of economic thought as applied to India and this substantially improves the chance of unravelling particular threads of thought, cf. H. Furber, 'The Theme of Imperialism and Colonialism in Modern Historical Writing on India' in C.H. Philips (ed.) *British Historians and India* (London, 1963); E. Stokes, *The English Utilitarians and India* (London, 1959); P.J. Marshall (ed.), *Problems of Empire: Britain and India (1757-1813)* (London, 1968); K.N. Chaudhuri (ed.), *The*

Economic Development of India under the East India Company 1814-1858 (Cambridge, 1971); W.J. Barber, *British Economic Thought and India 1600-1858: A Study of the History of Development Economics* (Oxford, 1975); S. Ambirajan, *Classical Political Economy and British Policy in India* (Cambridge, 1978); B. Chandra, *The Rise and Growth of Economic Nationalism in India* (New Delhi, 1966); B.N. Ganguli, *Indian Economic Thought: Nineteenth Century Perspectives* (New Delhi, 1978); N.V. Sovani, 'Indian Economics and Indian Economists', *Indian Economic Journal* 21 (1), (1974); and B. Datta, *Indian Economic Thought: Twentieth Century Perspectives 1900-50* (New Delhi, 1978). For the general imperial context—in which India figures prominently of course, see D. Winch, *Classical Political Economy and the Colonies* (London, 1965); R.N. Ghosh, *Classical Macroeconomics and the case for Colonies* (Calcutta, 1967); B. Porter, *Critics of Empire* (London, 1968); B. Semmel, *The Rise of Free Trade Imperialism* (Cambridge, 1970); and J. Cunningham Wood, *British Economists and the Empire 1860-1914* (London, 1983).

5. Cf. D. Cannadine, 'The Past and Present in the English Industrial Revolution 1880-1980', *Past and Present,* 103 (May 1984) esp. 149-159.

6. The differences between 'bourgeois' and Radical approaches were well brought out by T. Szentes, *The Political Economy of Underdevelopment,* 1st ed. (Budapest, 1971) Part 1. Other attempts to perform the same sort of task by A. Foster-Carter, 1976, *op. cit.*, K.P. Clements, 1980, *op. cit.*, and L. Lefeber, 1974, *op. cit.*, have, in my view, been far less successful—partly because they have been written almost in aspic and have been rapidly overtaken by the serious splits that have opened up within the two main-line traditions.

7. For some discussion of these issues see my 'De-industrialisation, Industrialisation and the Indian Economy, c. 1850-1947', *Modern Asian Studies,* 19 (2), 1985. It is also interesting to note in this context that John Latham, who writes in a basically neo-Classical vein, obviously mis-titled the first of his ambitious two volume work on the modern economic history of the Third World, *The International Economy and the Underdeveloped World* (London, 1978): by the time the second volume appeared, underdeveloped had given way to *Thı Depression and the Developing World, 1914-1939* (London, 1981)!

8. For an outline of neo-Classical growth theory see J. Meade, *A Neo-Classical Theory of Economic Growth* (Oxford, 1963), and D. Simpson, *The Theory of Economic Growth* (London, 1983). For an interesting re-interpretation of the older Classical approach see W. Eltis, *The Classical Theory of Economic Growth* (London, 1984).

9. Most of the major English-language publishing houses—however staid and conservative their reputation—now have an extensive list of Marxian economics titles.

10. For an excellent discussion of the many pitfalls see D.J. Casley and D.A. Lury, *Data Collection in Developing Countries* (Oxford, 1982). As far as historical data are concerned some of the more obvious intractabilities are discussed by S. Kuznets *loc. cit.*, L.G. Reynolds, 1983, *op. cit.*, and, more narrowly, P. Bairoch, 'International Industrialization Levels from 1750 to

1980', *Journal of European Economic History* 11(2), 1983, esp. 311-333.

11. P. Baran, *The Political Economy of Growth* (New York, 1957).

12. For an excellent discussion of the dangers of this tendency see J.D. Gould, *op. cit.*, 5-11, and E.J. Mishan, 'GNP—Measurement or Mirage?', *National Westminster Bank Quarterly Review*, November 1984.

13. Whether the first letter of this acronym stood for 'late' or 'less', its euphemistic tone was entirely deliberate.

14. The standard early references are M. Gilbert *et al.*, *Comparative National Products and Price Levels* (Paris, 1958); W. Beckerman, *International Comparisons of Real Incomes* (Paris, 1966); and W. Beckerman and R. Bacon 'International Comparisons of Income Levels: A Suggested New Measure', *Economic Journal*, LXXVI, September 1966.

15. For an informal discussion of development thinking and practice during this period see G.M. Meier, *Emerging from Poverty: The Economics that Really Matters* (Oxford, 1984) Chs. 1-4, and G.M. Meier and D. Seers (eds.), *Pioneers in Development* (Oxford, 1984), esp. the Introduction.

16. R. Clower, G. Dalton, M. Harvitz and A.A. Walters, *Growth Without Development: An Economic Survey of Liberia* (Evanston, 1966).

17. Ibid., vi.

18. *Partners in Development: Report of the Commission on International Development* (London, 1969). This Report was of course the precursor to the two Brandt Commission Reports which appeared in 1980 and 1983.

19. One sign of the supposedly new air of 'realism' pervading the corridors of Western Liberal establishments was the relegation of 'good causes' to a single years' duration: thus 1982 was declared a 'Habitat' year (under the inspiration of that tireless idealist Barbara Ward) in order or bring attention—and perhaps action—to the plight of the millions of shanty dwellers living in Third World slums.

20. Two useful sources of reference for these summits (plus the more technical meetings convened in order to hammer out commodity-wise agreements) are the Editorials of the *Third World Quarterly*, vol: 1, 1979 onwards, and the journal *Development Dialogue*, vol. 1, 1981, onwards.

21. *World Development Report(s)*, 1979 onwards, especially the Appendixes.

22. There is now a large critical literatre on the Reports, especially the first (1980) *North-South: A Programme for Survival* (London); see the special number of the *I.D.S. Bulletin* devoted to 'Britain on Brandt' 12 (2), 1981, and the article by C.H. Kirkpatrick and F. Nixson, 'The North-South Debate' in *The Three Banks Review*, 313, September 1981.

23. The phrase has recently been coined by Deepak Lal and clearly represents the view of the new Radical Right ginger-group—the London-based Institute for Economic Affairs. See Lal: Hobart Paper, *op. cit.*, 1983.

24. Although I have showed the underlying unity of the neo-Classical school nevertheless it is necessary to distinguish between two different streams within it. The first stresses the need for *governments* to consciously correct market failure by a rigorous programme of intervention if necessary: the possibility of 'distortions' requires an ever-alert and vigilant monitoring

authority: Professor R.W. Schultz and the Chicago school are the best-known proponents of this view. The second argues that in an imperfect (in the competitive sense) world there is a case for a degree of state intervention ('encouragement' rather than 'control') as far as the 'internal' economy of the Third World is concerned, but denies that anything positive can come from tinkering with 'external'-orientated activities—the exchange rate should be entirely left to 'pure' market forces, and no tariffs or quotas are permitted. The major adherents to this approach are writers such as Ian Little, Bela Belassa and Deepak Lal.

25. A.W.A. Lewis, *op. cit.*, 1984, D. Lall, *op. cit.*, 1983, A.K. Sen, *op. cit.*, 1983, P. Bauer, *op. cit.*, 1982, A. Hirschman, *op. cit.*, 1981 and I. Livingstone, *op. cit.*, 1981. At a more general level we should also note Mrs. Thatcher's recent ennoblement of Peter Bauer and the great flurry of attention given over to a consideration of the work of the new neo-Classicists of *The Times*, 22 August and 9 September 1983.

26. Cf. A. Brewer *op. cit.*, 1980, P. Limqueco and B. McFarlane (eds.), *op. cit.*, 1983 and P. Worsley, *The Three Worlds*, *op. cit.*, 1984, for an outline of the difference within the 'School'.

27. It is well-known that this writer qualified certain aspects of his position in the late 1970s and we must be careful to distinguish between a Mark I and a Mark II Frank.

28. I have the following people in mind, the late Bill Warren, Geoffrey Kay, Nicos Mouzelis, Gavin Kitchen, Peter Worsley and Colin Leys. Adding to the confusion the last named author (Leys) has recently confessed to having undergone a substantive change of mind, and has now all but disclaimed important conceptual sections of his pioneering study on East Africa, *Underdevelopment in Kenya* (London, 1977).

29. M. Todaro, *op. cit.*, 1981, 72-76; and *op. cit.*, 1985, 88-91. Here Todaro has drawn heavily upon Denis Goulet's influential work *The Cruel Choice: A New Conception on the Theory of Development* (New York, 1971).

30. All of the following works contain discussion of at least some aspects of the recent history of Development Economics: Lewis, Meier, and Seers, all published in 1984; A.K. Sen, Leeson, *op. cit.*, 1983; Little, Nixson, *op. cit.*, 1982; Arndt, Hirschman, Livingstone, Streeten, Fourie, *op. cit.*, 1981; Warren, Toye (in the *I.D.S. Bulletin*), *op. cit.*, 1980; Streeten (in K.Q. Hill, ed.), Seers (in *Development and Change*), Rimmer, Flamming, *op. cit.*, 1979; Deane, *op. cit.*, 1978; Phillips, Sunkel, Morawetz, *op. cit.*, 1977; Foster-Carter, Livingstone, *op. cit.*, 1976; Adelman, Resnick (both in the *A.E.R.*) *op. cit.*, 1975; Foster-Carter and Lefeber, *op. cit.*, 1974. For an interesting article which takes a rather longer—and more idiosyncratic—view, see P. Selwyn, 'Johnson's Hebrides: Thoughts on a Dying Social Order', *Development and Change* 10, (3) 1979.

31. D. Seers, 'The Birth, Life and Death . . .', *op. cit.*, 1979.

32. Cf. D. Seers and C. Vaitors (eds.), *op. cit.*, 1980; J. de Bandt, P. Mardi and D. Seers (eds.), *op. cit.*, 1980; and D. Seers, 'Back to the Ivory Tower? The Professionalisation of Development Studies and their Extension to Europe' *I.D.S. Bulletin*, 9(2), 1977. Some writers have recently taken this

shift to heart and indeed have gone a step further—see M. Minogue, 'Development and Underdevelopment in Britain and Ireland', *I.D.S. Bulletin*,8 (4), 1977.

33. They see A. Hirschman, 'The Rise and Decline of Development Economics' in his *Essay in Trespassing, op. cit.*, 1981.
34. Dudley Seers and Gunnar Myrdal were in the vanguard of the original attempt to distance Development Economics from its parent. The former has not only done an about-turn on this basic issue as noted above—but has also tried to reconcile neo-Classical and neo-Marxist views, see his 'The Congruence of Marxism and other neo-Classical Doctrines' in K.Q. Hill (ed.), *op. cit.*, 1979. In my view the reasoning behind this latter position is not at all convincing.
35 W.A. Lewis, A.E.R., *op. cit.*, 1984.
36. This is a simplification of course. Thus the solid and painstaking work on purchasing power parities conducted by Irving Kravis and his team of researchers has begun to make an impact and cause controversy. For the most recent discussion of P.P.P. see L.H. Officer, *Purchasing Power Parity and Exchange Rates: Theory, Evidence and Relevance* (Michigan, 1983); the articles by Kravis, 'Comparative Studies of National Incomes and Prices' and Robin Morris, 'Comparing the Incomes of Nations', both in the *Journal of Economic Literature,* 22 (1), 1984; and the respective studies by M. Keren and J. Weinblatt, S. Swamy and Paul Samuelson on 'International Real Income Measures', all in the *Economic Journal,* 94, June 1984.
37. According to the *World Bank Development Report, Passim*, 15.6% of the World's population live in 17 advanced industrial market economies, and a further 8.2% live in 6 East European Communist countries.
38. Rostow's work on stages is evidently enjoying something of a renaissance, see M.M. Postan, 'Walt Rostow: A Personal Appreciation' in C.P. Kindleberger and G. di Tella (eds.), *Economics in the Long View: Essays in Honour of W.W. Rostow,* vol.1, (London, 1982), B. Supple, 'Revisiting Rostow', *Economic History Review,* 37 (1), 1984, and his own article, 'The World Economy since 1945: A Stylized Historical Analysis', *Economic History Review*, 37 (2), 1985.
39. H.W. Arndt, *op. cit.*, 1981.
40. Hamza Alavi and his colleagues have tried to perform the same sort of task for one branch of neo-Marxism by putting forward the notion of a distinct 'colonial' mode of production on the basis of the subcontinental experience under imperial rule, see his essay in *Capitalism and Colonial Production, op. cit.*, 1982. A further attempt along these exploratory lines has been made by Frank Perlin in the context of the pre-British period, see his 'Proto-Industrialization and Pre-Colonial South Asia', *Past and Present*, No. 98, 1983.
41. Until the appearance of more up to date volumes and a more convincing exposition of the methodology, Immanuel Wallerstein's 'new' unit of analysis—nothing less than the entire capitalist world economy—it is difficult to judge the usefulness of modern world systems theory, see his *The Modern World System*, 2 vols., (New York, 1974-80).

42. Originally sparked off, of course, by the reactions to George Blyn's seminal study which came out in 1966, the debate continues to smoulder to this day.

43. C. Dewey, '*Patwari* and *Chawkidar*: Subordinate Officials and the Reliability of India: Agricultural Statistics' in A.G. Hopkins and C. Dewey (eds.), *The Imperial Impact: Studies in the Economic History of Africa and India* (London, 1978).

44. *Ibid.*

45. In his study of post-Independent India, *Asian Drama* (London, 1968) vol. I, Part I.

46. M.D. Morris, 'The Growth of Large-Scale Industry to 1947' in D. Kumar and M Desai (eds.), *The Cambridge Economic History of India, op. cit.*, and A.K. Sen, 'The Commodity Pattern of British Enterprise in Early Indian Industrialisation, 1854-1914', in the *Proceedings of the Second International Conference of Economic History* (Paris, 1965).

47. A.K. Bagchi, 'Reflections on Patterns of Regional Growth in India during the Period of British Rule', *Bengal Past and Present*, XCV, 1, 180, 1976. A similar viewpoint—but in a slightly different context has been expressed by R.S. Chandavarkar, 'Industrialisation in India before 1947: Conventional Approaches and Alternative Perspectives', paper presented to the Cambridge Economic History of India Conference, 11-13th April, 1984, and now published in *Modern Asia Studies*, 19 (2), 1985.

48. For specific reference to the work of these authors see N. Charlesworth *British Rule and the Indian Economy, 1800-1914* (London, 1982) and C. Bayly's extensive bibliography in his *Rulers, Townsmen and Bazaars North Indian Society in the Age of British Expansion* (Cambridge, 1983).

49. The mode of production literature is now vast. For two useful survey articles see D. McEachern, 'The Mode of Production in India', *Journal of Contemporary Asia*, 6 (4), 1976, and J. Harriss, 'The Mode of Production Controversy: Themes and Problems of the Debate' in I. Livingstone (ed.) *op. cit.*, 1982. The debate now takes in 'colonial', 'feudal', 'semi-feudal', 'pre-capitalist'. 'Asiatic' and other modes.

50. Thus to take one specific example amongst many, Sri Prem Preshad, erstwhile Managing Director of Bird-Heilgers has owned to destroying the bulk of the records of the agency and all its constituent parts.

51. See W.J. Macpherson, 'Economic Development in India under the British Crown, 1858-1947' in A.J. Youngson (ed.), *Economic Development in the Long-Run* (London, 1972). Although this survey is now somewhat dated the basic position on data remains almost the same today as it was at the time of writing.

52. For details of these entrepreneurial devices as they were used in one particular industry see my 'Recruiting and Organising an Industrial Labour Force in Colonial India: The Case of the Coal Mining Industry c. 1880-1939', *Indian Economic and Social History Review*, 13(4), 1976. Many other studies of the growth of the labour force makes the same sort of points—though with different degrees of emphasis.

53. Refer to W.J. Macpherson's evidence, 'Economic Development in India

. . .', *op. cit.*, 133.

54. In the *Cambridge Economic History of India, op. cit.*, 2, 486.

55. Cf. I. Habib, 'Population' in the *Cambridge Economic History of India*, vol.1, T. Raychaudhuri and I. Habib (eds.), 1981; M.D. Morris, 'The Population of All-India, 1800-1951', *Indian Economic and Social History Review*, XI (2-3), 1973; and, of course, K. Davis, *The Population of India and Pakistan* (Princeton, 1951).

56. This point is clearly made by Ira Klein, 'Death in India', *Journal of Asian Studies*, 32(4), 1973.

57. In his *Poverty and Un-British Rule in India* (London, 1871).

58. See M.M. Mukherjee, *National Income of India: Trends and Structure* (Calcutta, 1969), Appendix II for details up to the point of publication.

59. The debate was sparked off by W. Digby's book *'Prosperous' British India*, (London, 1901).

60. M.D. Morris claimed that there was 'substantial' growth in per capita incomes over the nineteenth century in his 'Towads a Re-interpretation of 19th Century Indian Economic History', *Journal of Economic History*, 23(4), 1963.

61. M.M. Mukherjee *op. cit.*, A. Maddison, *Class Structure and Economic Growth: India and Pakistan since the Moghuls* (London, 1971); S. Sivasubramoniam, 'National Income of India, 1900-01 to 1946-47', unpublished Ph.D. dissertation, Delhi School of Economics, 1965; A. Heston, 'National Income' in the *Cambridge Economic History of India*, vol. 2, *op. cit*.

62. S. Sivasubramoniam *loc. cit.* We should also note that Heston's recent essay *ibid.* (which formed the basis of his joint article with Robert Summers, 'Comparative Economic Growth: 1870 to 1970', *American Economic Review*, 70 (2), 1980) rests on a number of highly dubious—and disturbing—assumptions. For critiques see A.K. Bagchi's pithy remarks in his review of the *Cambridge Economic History of India*, vol. 2, in the *American Historical Review*, April 1984; A. Maddison's note, 'What did Heston Do?', and Irfan Habib's 'Studying a Colonial Economy—Without Perceiving Colonialism', papers presented to the Cambridge Conference on Indian Economy History, April 1984; and Pramit Chaudhuri's review (also of the C.E.H.I.) which appeared in the *Economic Journal*, March 1984, 193. After Sivasubramoniam, Moni Mukherjee's study comes closest to providing us with a workable set of figures.

63. M.D. Morris, 'Towards a Re-interpretation . . .', *op. cit.*, 1963.

64. M. Mukherjee, *op. cit.*, 37.

65. Though much maligned, national income per head is undoubtedly an index of great convenience in that it reduces a whole host of variables to one composite number (or series), and therefore provides an opportunity to simplify, quantify and effect comparisons over time, space, and international frontiers.

66. D. Kumar and J. Krishnamurthy, 'Regional and International Economic Disparities since the Industrial Revolution: the Indian Evidence' in P. Bairoch and M. Levy-Leboyer (eds.), *Disparities in Economic Development*

Since the Industrial Revolution (London, 1981), 361.

67. The method chosen by Kumar and Krishnamurthy to measure regional distribution is that of using variations in the shares of the labour force in agriculture in the major provinces. Whilst the major finding of Kumar and Krishnamurthy—they argue that regional inequality rose only marginally—is broadly consistent with a number of other recent studies (cf. J. Hurd, 'Railways and the expansion of Markets it India 1861-1921', and M.B. McAlpin, 'The Effects of Expansions of Markets on Rural Income Distribution in Nineteenth Century India', both in *Explorations in Economic History* 12, 1975) it conflicts with other evidence (see Heston and Summers, *op. cit.*, 97) as well as common sense!

68. A. Maddison, *Class Structure, op. cit.*, 67-70.

69. *Ibid.*, 68.

70. Following the publication of M.D. Morris', *Measuring the Condition of the World's Poor: The Physical Quality of Life Index* (New York, 1979) there now exists a large critical literature on the P.Q.L.I. measure itself—most of it in the journal *World Development*.

71. See Kumar and Krishnamurthy, *op. cit.*, 363.

72. A. Heston, 'National Income', *op. cit.*, 1983, Table 4.3A, 397. Strictly speaking these calculations only possess curiosity value. Presenting numbers like this in tabular from *can* give a misleading impression: the caveats are tremendous.

73. S. Sivasubramoniam, *op. cit.*, and his article 'Income from the Secondary Sector in India, 1900-47', *Indian Economic and Social History Review*, 14 (4), 1977.

74. For the most recent see his survey of 'The Occupational Structure' in the *Cambridge Economic History of India*, vol. 2, Chapter VI.

75. There is now a large volume of writing addressed to this subject. For a discussion of the bibliography see my 'De-industrialisation, Industrialisation and the Indian Economy c.1850-1947', *op. cit.*, 1985, esp. footnotes 19 to 20.

76. That is Gangetic Bihar.

77. Such as those of M. Desai, A.K. Bagchi. P. Twomey, K. Specker, G. Pandey and R. Chattopadhyay, see note 75 above.

78. One doesn't have to wade through the entire text of the *Cambridge Economic History of India*, to be struck by the differences of approach between—and indeed within—the respective parts of the two volumes.

79. A second i.e., that of arrest in terms of some hypothetical or potential standard is briefly discussed below.

80. If I understand Professor Rothermund's remarks under 'No need for capital accumulation in precolonial India ' (in his 'Problem of India's Arrested Economic Growth . . .' *op. cit.*, 2) he appears to be arguing that economic development was *not* proceeding prior to the mid-eighteenth century and that the transition to capitalism was not 'just around the corner'. I find it logically inconsistent to talk about arrest in one breath

and yet admit to no ongoing development in the preceding period in the next.

81. R.C. Dutt, *The Economic History of India*, vol. 1, *Under Early British Rule: 1757-1837* (1st Indian edition, New Delhi, 1976) XXV. One of the modern generation of Nationalist writers, R.S. Sharma, in his 'Cottage Industries: 1857-1947' in V.B. Singh (ed.), *Economic History on India* (Bombay, 1965), has gone so far as to say that 'before the advent of the Europeans, specially during the 17th and 18th centuries, India was the industrial workshop of the world'.

82. Cf. Tapan Raychaudhuri's essay 'A Re-interpretation of 19th Century India Economic History' in M.D. Morris *et al.* (eds.), *Indian Economy in the 19th Century* (Delhi, 1969), and I. Habib, 'Potentialities of Capitalistic Development in the Economy of Mughal India', *Journal of Economic History*, 29 (1), 1968. Both these authorities have contributed much new writing since then—not least their contributions to the *Cambridge Economic History of India*, especially vol. 1, *op. cit.* I suspect that neither Professor Habib nor Professor Raychaudhuri would be entirely comfortable with my reading of their work and my putting them in this category: but the two early essays quoted here certainly convey this impression.

83. For a short review of this new approach see Burton Stein's paper 'Arrested Development, But Where and When?', in this volume.

84. I have the work of Frank Perlin and Chris Bayly in mind here.

85. See V.K.R.V. Rao, *India's National Income 1950-1980: An Analysis of Economic Growth and Change* (New Delhi, 1983).

86. For some discussion of the 'mixed' record cf. P. Bardhan, *The Political Economy of Development in India* (Oxford, 1984); P. Chaudhuri (ed.), *Aspects of Indian Economic Development: A Book of Readings* (London, 1981); P.S. Jha, *India: A Political Economy of Stagnation* (Bombay, 1980); and V.N. Balasubramanyan, *The Economy of India* (London, 1984).

87. Though it could be argued that all of these might well have had the effect of 'arresting' India's development, they need to be considered separately.

88. See E. Stokes, 'Late Nineteenth Century Colonial Expansion and the Attack on the Theory of Economic Imperialism: A Case of Mistaken Identity?', *Historical Journal*, 12, 1969, and N. Etherington, 'Reconsidering Theories of Imperialism', *History and Theory*, 21 (1), 1982.

89. Historians are generally not themselves in the business of formulating tightly-constructed theories of Empire.

90. See A. Brewer, *op. cit.*, for details of "internal" disagreements.

91. For an outline of the Classical and neo-Keynesian arguments see M.B. Brown, *The Economics of Imperialism* (London, 1974). For a sample selection of cliometeric work see M. Edelstein, 'Foreign Investment and Empire 1860-1914' in R. Floud and D. McCloskey (eds.), *The Economic History of Britain since 1700: vol. 2, 1860 to the 1970s* (Cambridge, 1981) 86-97; S. Lebergott, 'The Returns to U.S. Imperialism 1890-1929', *Journal of Economic History*, XL (2), 1980; L.E. Davis and R.A. Huttenback, 'The Political Economy of British Imperialism: Measures of Benefit and Support', *Journal of Economic History*, XLII (1), 1982; and the interesting 'inter-

nal' controversy between Davis and Huttenback and D.O. Flynn and D. St. Clair, 'The Social Returns to Empires', *Journal of Economic History*, XLIII (4), 1983.

92. For an interesting discussion of this issue see L.J. Reynolds, 'The Spread of Economic Growth to the Third World', *op. cit.*, 1983.

93. Such as that suggested by H.B. Chenery and M. Syrquin, in their *Patterns of Development 1950-70* (Oxford, 1975).

PART II

THE EIGHTEENTH CENTURY

3

ARRESTED DEVELOPMENT': BUT WHEN AND WHERE?

BURTON STEIN
School of Oriental and African Studies, London

One of the legitimate complaints about the *Cambridge Economic History of India*[1] was the failure of its editors and its several participants to formulate a developmental sequence for the economic history of the Indian subcontinent, one that explicitly denied the implicit stages of something which was supposed to be 'the traditional economy' and something supposed to be 'the modern economy'. The division of the two volumes of the *Cambridge Economic History* around the middle of the eighteenth century, if anything, seemed to confirm the traditional-modern dichotomy, and in the absence of any coherent argument to the contrary, that old, counter-productive bifurcation of the history not only has been permitted to stand, but received validation insofar as such a work confers it.

As a contributor to the first Cambridge volume, I bear the same responsibility as others—including the editors—for the missed opportunity to, if nothing else, deny any place for a view that equates economic development and growth, or 'modernization', with westernization in the form of colonial dominance. This view, it might have been thought, had been widely discredited theoretically and empirically along with most of the other baggage of modernization analysis; surely, that discrediting was well enough advanced by the end of the 1970s when the Cambridge volumes were ready for the press. Or, so it would seem.

Actually, however, there was a lively enough spirit of the

modernizationists among those who convened to consider the matter of 'arrested development' in Heidelberg during the summer of 1984; if it was a ghost, it was a hardy one, and it appeared to inhabit the house that Professor Rothermund built in his framing paper for the conference and this volume setting out the 'problems' of 'arrested development' in South Asia. I say 'appeared' because in the opening of his paper his remarks about the lack of capital accumulation during pre-colonial times were so brief and general that I may have misunderstood him, but I think not. He said:

> Capital only becomes important when the other factors of production—land and labour—are scarce; capital is then invested to enhance their productivity. In pre-colonial India land and labour were abundant and there was no need for capital investment.

The specific importance that he attached to capital—to its significance for production—is fully justified, and if his general position were not merely asserted, but demonstrated, it would have explained a great deal about the pre-colonial economic order; that is, it would have permitted us to speak of this pre-colonial mode of production as pre-capitalist. Though he concedes the existence of 'merchant capital' and 'state capital', neither are seen to be implicated in production, but only in the extraction of artisanal and peasant production for elite consumption. This has the familiar ring of the Asiatic mode of production, or Polanyi substantivism, about it. Familiar it may be, but is it correct?

A new historiographical view which has begun to emerge on pre-colonial India suggests that Rothermund is wrong. This new view alters our understanding of the broad course of economic development as well as any consideration of 'arrested development', for it asserts that there was impressive commercial and paleotechnical industrial production present from at least the early eighteenth century, and that these productive forms required and utilized both merchant and 'state' of capital. It further asserts that these capital-dependent forms of production were destroyed in the later nineteenth century and with that destruction, British colonial rule extinguished endegenous change or growth in the economy of much of India. This description may not make the recently writings of

C.A. Bayly, David Washbrook, and Frank Perlin[2] seem original at all. Is this not, after all, a restatement of the positions of R.C. Dutt and Dadabhai Naoroji and other critics of British rule in India?

Several of the central propositions of the 'new' view do in fact restate propositions found in the formulations of nationalist historians; among them are: recognition of the high degree of commodity production in eighteenth century India, especially by artisans; the pervasive linking by financial institutions of petty commodity production with urban, regional, and international markets in many parts of the subcontinent; and the role of the pre-colonial state in stimulating production and trade through various means (e.g. court and military expenditures). With earlier writers, the 'revisionists' speak of the destruction of these economic relationships and their potential by the specific policies of the colonial state or, less directly, by the logic of the processes set in train by British colonial control.

But, in certain other crucial respects, the emergent revisionist view is different. Little is said about the looting (or 'drain') of existing wealth by early British officials or the destructive costs of imposing British peace and order. The very idea that there might have been a national economy in pre-colonial times seems to be denied and with that the notion that the imposition of British rule prevented a pre-colonial, 'national' economy from developing into a modern industrial economy. The new view also rejects the justifactory premise of imperialist historiography that the eighteenth century was a time of chaos from which India was rescued by British rule. A further difference with their predecessors is the wider range of evidence considered; analysis is no longer dependent on the demi-official, administrative histories of the late nineteenth century, but involves new sources not available or not consulted at that time and later. Lastly, there is a shift in focus from one that is exclusively north Indian—the domain of the great Mughal state—to the western and southern peripheries of that seventeenth century state, though Bayly's work has opened even the Mughal heartland to an examination of the same general forces that are found at the peripheries. Why certain of the conditions which seem to inspire the alternative view being examined here were first observed at the edges of the Mughal state has less to do with objective historical conditions than it does with historiographical conceptions which have persisted about the Mughals and the presumed relationship between an imperial polity and its economic substructure.

It might therefore be said that evaluations of the Indian economy over the last two centuries—and presumed 'arrested development'—have returned to an earlier historical view, one produced by politically committed nationalist scholars who were documenting a degradation of the Indian economy as a result of colonial rule. I say 'return' because the fashion of our scholarship, especially economic history, was overtaken by modernization theory which was wholly preoccupied with explaining why industrialization in particular and economic modernization in general failed to occur in South Asia. Beginning with Marx and Weber, modernization theorists, influenced by functionalist sociology, explained these failures in terms of the absence of specific pre-conditions. Modernization theory in its time seemed to reconcile the contradictions between the dominant schools of economic-historical study of South Asia—nationalist and imperialist—when in fact what modernizationists did was to take over the imperialist view. Economic history of the modernization persuasion has not been politically neutral as its practitioners have claimed; it has been politically loaded in favour of hegemonic capitalism. The new view is thus a return to a consideration of the role of the explicitly political in economic-historical interpretation.

Of the three writers that constitute the core of the new view—Bayly, Washbrook, and Perlin—the work of the first is the most finished and, possibly, limited in its scope. Bayly rejects what he calls the 'Black Century' conception of the eighteenth century,[3] and he provides a strong counter-argument for the economic and political vigour of the period. Imperial decline was attended by important economic changes during the eighteenth century. These include the rooting of formerly peripatetic imperial officers and minor service officials in small towns and the establishment there of a 'gentry' class comprising local magnates—not previously part of the Mughal regime—as well as erstwhile officials; the increasing homogenization of a merchant class in the numerous, small urban centres of the Gangetic plain; the development of solidarity relations between increasingly powerful, local, rural magnates and the bazaarmen of these towns; and the evolution of a new culture among merchants in particular, one emphasizing religious piety as a gauge of creditworthiness. The political-economy context in which these new formations of the Gangetic area emerged was based upon three interlinked and flexible relationships. First were relations of agrarian dependency and patronage in which the rural elite of village level society was assimilated to towns under the dominance of a service-gentry; this added to the already high degree of social differentiation among rural social groups, some 40 per cent of whom were not engaged in cultivation. Secondly, the rural economy became a provisioning hinterland for elite consumption in towns. Finally, there was a recycling of state resources, derived from taxation, to meet the demand of the elite for luxuries, which established a nexus between revenue collection and trade. The cash of merchants and bankers was a vital channel for transferring land revenue, often realized in kind, into the hands of the state; merchants and bankers also provided advances to state officials, often secured by the right to collect land and other revenues; finally, proceeds from revenue transactions were converted into commodities by merchants at the peripheries of a state for transport and sale at the centre thereby yielding a cash revenue to pass to the state and a profit for the merchant to be redeployed in subsequent transactions.[4]

That warfare of the eighteenth century was destructive is granted by Bayly. The invasions from the north-west by Nadir Shah in 1739 and by Zeman Shah in 1797-99 and the wars attending the formation of the Sikh, Maratha, and Jat states disrupted economic relations. Bayly holds, however, that these disruptions have been exaggerated. Much of the loot seized in these wars was sold in India, and markets quickly recovered, or bazaarmen moved to other places in an orderly way. Moreover, the era of state-building resulted in the proliferation of royal courts and new markets to serve the elites of the 'compact despotisms' based on Turkish ordinance and European infantry. A prime example of this sort of transformation was the state of Haidar Ali Khan in Mysore.[5]

Bayly's conclusions are that economic decline was limited during the eighteenth century, losses in one area being recouped elsewhere and richer farming tracts gaining additional cultivators, artisans, and merchants. The 'commercialization of royal power' begun under the Mughals spread to meet the needs of military organization and the state capitalism upon which these economies were based. Older commodities, such as cotton and indigo lost some of their dominance, but others, such as opium, became more lucrative, and all evidence points to the robustness of the coastal trading around the subcontinent. There was a significant redeployment of Indian merchant capital calculated to achieve greater control of labour through control over revenue collection, and there was a progressive unification of a commercial class drawn from the great merchants of old imperial cities and the humble bazaarmen of the countryside. Both met in the *qasbah* quarters and the small, permanent markets (*ganj*) attached to them. The entire infrastructure required for the trade and ultimately the dominion of Europeans was created in this allegedly 'Black Century'.[6]

Frank Perlin's work is less finished than that of Bayly and is, accordingly, more ambitious. In several important papers based on the records of seventeenth and eighteenth century Maharashtra he has sought to define the character of the 'old regimes' of India. He sees the central process in these old regimes as the complex interaction between two kinds of forces: centralizing state-building and local, household-dominated forces. Prior studies of this period and its processes he sees as flawed by the division of scholars between those holding 'taxation-centric' conceptions of states implying a political superstructure bearing down upon a passive social base and those holding an equally distorting vision of old regime societies viewed from the bottom up where the centralizing element is denied. In a recent formulation of his position on the late pre-colonial period, he outlines the 'administrative order' and the economic sub-structure revealed by the rise of Shivaji's regime in the seventeenth century and its subsequent transformations in Maharashtra.[7]

Perlin discovers the 'infrastructural underbelly of what we call the state' in the administrative forms employed by the 'great households' of seventeenth century Maharashtra. The Bhonsles, for example, first amassed a miscellany of patrimonial and prebendal rights over land which they then succeeded in converting into a directly-managed domain, or *khalsa,* in the manner they had learned from the sultanate regimes of the Deccan. This learning from others, Perlin says, was general in India, and he speaks of a 'library of categories and techniques', including ideas like *khalsa*, which was widely known in the Deccan and used by the great Maratha households for their interior administrations and subsequent state-building. Paper records and accounts were another element of this: the clerk and accountant, *kulkarni* and *deshpandi*, served great households and enhanced the administrative mechanisms at their disposal. Measurement and monetary systems added to this, and, along with clerks and accountants, spread freely around the Deccan thereby permitting the adoption in many places of cash revenue systems based on land surveys and records. In the process, older rights and entitlements were transformed. Heritable, patrimonial rights and properties became interchangeable with resumable, prebendal entitlements through money sales. Ideologically, there was tension between the centralizing state forces and older usages of local peasantries which resulted in the convening of assemblies (*gòta*) to protect the latter from the former. Terms like *watan* and *saranjam* respectively refer to patrimonial and prebendal rights and properties; they also refer to two, opposed, yet interacting, notions of rights. Larger and more powerful households operated in the worlds of both forms—the royal court and the peasant village—the two being linked by the economic power of great households founded upon landholding, control of labour, capital investments in agricultural improvements, and trade and banking. Such 'right accumulating households' of the seventeenth and eighteenth centuries were also strategically placed to benefit from the spectacular development of trade and production for foreign markets at the same time as they were creating new state forms and new areas of agrarian settlement.

David Washbrook has yet to publish his several papers on the late pre-colonial economy of South India, but many of his arguments are expansions of the insights of his monograph, *The Emergence of Provincial Politics: The Madras Presidency, 1870-1920.*[8] His papers deal with the economic and social restructuring of merchant capital in the Coromandel area between 1750 and 1850. The major change that he traces is the retreat of merchant capital from its post-Vijayanagara role of sustaining states by providing the money skills necessary for fiscal institutions of the time to that of petty local usury within defensive local caste and kinship bodies by the later nineteenth century. During the eighteenth century, he finds

Indian agents of European officials, or *'dubashes'*, taking contracts for revenue farms, and money-lenders, *'sowcars'*, providing a major part of the capital which the East India Company and private European traders needed for the conduct of their businesses. Funds were moved from one European trade centre (factory) to others and from fort to factory by means of Indian bankers' bills until about 1800. Indian merchants at this time were involved in the widest range of commodity transactions, selling everything from cloth to copper and rice to rubies, as Washbrook put it. The social composition of Coromandel merchants encompassed more than those from castes who specialized in trade, for included were Brahmans and members of dominant landed groups such as Tamil Vellalas and Telugu Balijas and Muslim grandees from the court of the Nizam of Hyderabad.

By 1830, this system pivoting upon Indian merchants had changed. The cloth trade had become a Company monopoly and trade in such valuable commodities as opium, indigo, tobacco and spirits was either subject to Company monopoly or was given advantageously over to the management of European agency houses, thus excluding major Indian merchant participation. The most important change, though, involved the revenue system. By 1830, tax farmers everywhere in the growing territories of the Madras Presidency had been replaced by European civil administrators and Indians were removed from the nexus of revenue collection, currency operations and remittance financing. The most serious implications of these changes by the end of the first third of the nineteenth century was that Indian finance was excluded from all but the most local and riskful levels of the agrarian system. At the same time, Anglo-Indian law froze certain previously flexible forms of rights, by, for example, limiting the sales of *mirasi* and *inam* rights in which Indian financiers had long invested.

The withdrawal of Indian merchant capital under these assaults and the curtailment of investment of state capital (i.e., revenue collections) in agricultural production, as had been practised in pre-colonial times, had the most destructive impact upon the Coromandel economy. Areas of high agriculture there had always faced labour deficits owing to the abundance of land in the interior, as Rothermund observed. Productive capital derived from revenue collections had long served to fix labour in the best agrarian regions through investments in improved cultivation. With the reduction in the scope of Indian merchant capital during the first half of the nineteenth century, the institutional system for the maintenance of these regions weakened. This resulted from the reduction of older incentives to Indian bankers to invest in agrarian production from which they shared benefits as tax farmers; it also resulted from the Company's changes in the financial operations of wealthy, land-owning temples and their extensive *inam* and *mirasi* rights which placed at hazard the portfolio interests of Indian merchants and bankers who had perviously purchased these rights. Because the Company could not or would not compete in the existing system of agrarian and trade relationships, it forcibly seized control of that system. By doing so, Washbrook argues, the British destroyed an eighteenth century system which reproduced the Coromandel economy through the participation of merchants in the fiscal operations of the state and were its agents for the redistribution of state resources through investments in trade and in agricultural production.

Despite differences of emphasis, our three revisionist authors emphatically deny the assumption of eighteenth century chaos which has been a fixture in the historiography of India for so long and survives intact in modernization theories about the economic history of subcontinent. All three writers describe flexible interrelations among political, social, and economic institutions and practices of the late, pre-colonial epoch; and all of them recognize the degradation of long-standing relations that resulted from the impact of colonial policies of the first half of the nineteenth century. With respect to the economy, in particular, their findings clearly contradict Professor Rothermund's remarks on 'capital accumulation' in pre-colonial India.

Bayly and Washbrook comment directly upon Rothermund's position. Bayly spoke of money-lenders, along with landlords, as owners of capital factors of production such as stock, tools, seed, fertilizer, and the application of these to cultivation, especially for the production of cash crops like cotton. Revenue farmers—whether merchants or 'service-gentry'—regularly invested part of their collections in production, while rural magnates bought sugar presses, planted fruit orchards, and provided the initial developmental costs of specialist farmers and ordinary farmers in newly colonized areas of the Gangetic plain. The advances (*taccavi*) of merchants supported the specialized production of agricultural raw materials, notably cotton. Washbrook goes further; he makes productive investment by those involved in the fiscal processes of eighteenth century states the cornerstone of his reconstruction of the late pre-colonial rural economy of south-eastern India. There, during the early eighteenth century, the Brahman and Vellala rural elite dominated two major capital-accumulating and investing institutions of the pre-colonial period: temples and co-parcenary (*mirasi*) villages. When to these two strategic institutions, the elite added the resources they enjoyed as revenue farmers, a major 'circuit' of community production and reproduction was closed. And like their counterparts in the Gangetic region, as Bayly describes them, South Indian rural magnates regularly provided productivity loans to cultivators.

Perlin, for his part, postulates an even greater degree of linkage between the productive base of Maharashtra and the most advanced political and economic sectors of Indian society during the seventeenth and eighteenth centuries. He posits a long-standing relationship, marked by tension and contradiction, between local, patrimonial forms and rights (*watan*) and state officials, markets, and fiscal institutions. Here, the same men and prominent families were parts of both sectors, and the extensive use of money enabled rights to be transferred from the one to the other. Hence, trade, revenue collection, and agricultural and artisanal productivity were pervasively entangled. Family records are adduced by him to demonstrate the widely ramified involvement of merchant and landed families in state functions. At the same time, these households deepened their local positions of wealth and power through purchases of *watan* rights to village headmanships and other local offices.

In short, each of the writers deals not only with the mobilization of capital and its employment in production, but each also sets out, at least in outline, how trade, revenue and production were structured to reproduce the complex economic systems of the late pre-colonial age. Given Professor Rothermund's reasoning about capital in relation to other factors of production in pre-colonial South Asia, none of this should have happened, nor, therefore, should it have been possible to suggest something like 'arrested development' by the middle of the nineteenth century. Yet, there it was. Still, the processes that linked trade ('merchant capital') and revenue ('state capital') with productive investment have not been fully worked out in any of the regions of the subcontinent covered by the Bayly, Washbrook, or Perlin. It may be of value to examine some of the evidence on productive investment in the Ceded Districts of the Madras Presidency around 1800 as a means of more completely disconfirming Rothermund's supposition.

My biographical research on Thomas Munro[9] has required a detailed analysis of the economic structure and history of the Ceded Districts of Madras where he worked out what has since been called 'the Munro System' of *ryotwar* revenue administration between 1800 and 1807. Because this high and dry plateau tract had such bleak economic prospects, the Ceded Districts in Munro's time can be used to test one of Professor Rothermund's key assertions—that capital investment in agriculture did not occur and was not necessary owing to the superabundance of land and labour. It is a limiting case with considerable explanatory potential.

On the face of it, Rothermund's general observation that there was a great plenitude of land and labour in pre-colonial times, that these productive factors were virtually free resources, seems unexceptionable. Yet, there is no question that in pre-colonial South India, his assertions and assumptions about the land-man ratio and the consequences of this for productive capital utilization must be fundamentally qualified, if not wholly denied.

There were the riverine basins of the Kaveri, Palar, Kistna and Godavari where land was not abundant, but scarce, and rights to a portion of it, or to a share of its irrigated production, was a valuable property, and saleable. This is certainly true in the Kaveri and Palar regions during the eighteenth century following Washbrook's arguments, and, according to the recently published research of N. Karashima, it was found as early as the thirteenth century in South India.[10] This is what *mirasi* tenure in the Coromandel lowlands meant during the eighteenth century, when that Hindustani term replaced older terms, such as the much older Tamil word, *kāṇiyatci*. Elsewhere, variants of this proprietorial right to the output of scarce/wet lands had almost the same meaning: *janma* tenure in the monsoonally-watered fields of the Malabar coast of

Kanara.[11] Even in such places as Cuddapah in the Ceded Districts *vīsabaḍi* tenure had the same meaning. It seems, however, that this sort of property was not bought and sold as were *mirasi* rights in other places, perhaps reflecting the limited penetration of commercial forms in what were to become the Ceded Districts in comparison with the lowlands on either of the coasts of the peninsula. Nevertheless, this form of tenure over valuable irrigated lands involved a substantial portion of Cuddapah, indicating that even in the inhospitably dry Deccan, there were zones in which land improved by capital works such as irrigation tanks and channels was very valuable. In such places, where neither land nor labour were abundant in any meaningful economic sense, it says something about the risks to human survival in these dry ecotypic regimes that agricultural labourers of the deltaic eastern and monsoonal western littorals were prepared to suffer the humiliating degradations of untouchability in return for a reliable supply of food.

In the uplands of the peninsula, including the Ceded Districts, where the great majority of the agriculturists were wholly dependent on rainfall and where the potential for irrigation was very limited, land was indeed abundant. Under Munro's administration, only half of the cultivable land of the Ceded Districts was actually under crops at any time and of this, almost half was under *inam* tenures paying an average seven per cent of the regular revenue.[12] In general, land possessed so little value partly because there was insufficient labour available for its cultivation and it was costly to bring into production. Preparing the black clay soils in many parts of Bellary, Cuddapah, and Anantapur in the Ceded Districts reportedly cost as much per acre as several years' revenue demand and involved very substantial capital inputs in the form of large bullock teams for ploughing the heavy clays, high costs of fertilization and weeding, as well as deferred production of up to three years before achieving a crop of cotton, indigo, or grain. The limiting factor of production here was capital in the form of draught animals, ploughs and other implements, fertilizers (meaning pasturing animals), in the form, too, of sufficient resources for several years of subsistence before the first crops were realized, and, I would add, in the form of the specialized knowledge required for the production of dry grains and other crops.

In the Ceded Districts of around 1800 the population density was a mere 75 per square mile, the proportion of irrigation was a slight three per cent, and the majority of cultivators moved incessantly about the region seeking the best terms they could find for their meagre capital resources and the labour of family members. Yet here, in a region that became notorious for its susceptibility to drought and famine during the later nineteenth century, Munro discovered considerable commodity production. Much of this was petty and for local consumption, but other commodities found their way to ports on both coasts of the peninsula and to other towns. Among these commodities were raw cotton, as well as finished textiles and yarn. Cotton was cropped or intercropped with jowar and other millets in an eight year rotation. About 70 per cent of cotton was consumed locally, near the point of cultivation, spun and woven by full-time weavers and by part-time agriculturists by whom it was either consumed within the family, bartered, or sold locally. Another 10 per cent of cotton production was shipped by bullock to other places in the Ceded Districts, for example the fine cottons of Cuddapah in the east were shipped to Adoni in the centre, or to Bellary in the west where there were places in which specialized weaving was carried out. Some of the output from these weaving centres was exported to Mysore (much of the Ceded Districts having been ruled from Mysore during the late eighteenth century), to the Nizam's territories in Hyderabad or the Nawab of Arcot's capital at Walajapet. The rest was consumed in the Ceded Districts.

The trade system of the tract included a network centered in Hindupur in the south-central part of the Ceded Districts. That town was established in the late eighteenth century by a military commander serving Haidar Ali Khan, the ruler of Mysore. Though this officer bore the title of 'Bahadur' before his name, Jungamkote Krishnappa was probably a Lingayat from the town of Jungamkote, near Kolar, in Mysore.[13] He is said to have established the trade centre (*'pettah'*) of Hindupur in the late 1780s and attracted merchants to the place by waiving all customs duties for a period of three years and by offering other facilities for profitable trade—warehouses, bazaar sites under the supervision of merchants, protected roads—all financed from land revenue collections, that is, from 'state capital'. It is possible that the founder of Hindupur was following the example of a fifteenth century chief, one Chikkaraya Timme Gauda who had established the town of Jungamkote in his Kolar chiefdom to which he invited Lingayat merchants from northern Karnataka who were facing religious persecution. Alternatively, the Bahadur may simply have been following the orders of Haider Ali intent on increasing commercial production as his son, Tipu Sultan, was to be later.

Hindupur attracted trade from a large region extending from the crest of the western ghats, around Nagar, in Kanara, a major gateway onto the peninsular upland from the western coast; trade goods also came from the southern Maratha country, and from Hyderabad. Products of the tract later called 'the Ceded Districts' were added to those from these other places to compose large pack trains bound for Walajapet, 300 miles from Nagar. From the Arcot capital, commodities were bulk-broken for sale in the Nawab's territory as well as for shipment to the Company's territories in the Chingleput '*jaghire*', near Madras. Lionel Place's reports from there[14] refer to trade centres connected with Walajapet and managed by local magnates who combined landed dominance with fiscal offices; Place also reported a lively sale of *mirasi* rights and *inam* privileges, pointing to a high degree of commercialization of patrimonial rights.

Some agricultural products entered the commerce of the Ceded Districts of the late eighteenth century through sharecropping. Arrangements of this sort focus attention upon the application of merchant capital to commodity production. Sugar cultivation, for example, involved capital investments by merchants of the western parts of the Ceded Districts and of Mysore, called *vartaka*. The latter provided cane cuttings to cultivators, and undertook, also, to supply additional draught animals, fertilizer, sod, and fuel for reducing the syrup to jaggery, as required by the cultivators with whom the product was shared. In return, the *vartakas* took 60 per cent of the crop for trading. Cultivators entering into this share arrangement were often among the most substantial of the region. They commanded stock, tools, and labour; in some cases such substantial cultivators might engage a labourer to carry out the cultivation on their behalf in return for a 20 per cent share of the yield, the balance being divided between the wealthier farmer and the merchant investor. Another element of sugar production in the Ceded Districts was that about 5 per cent (one share in twenty) was paid to village servants (*āyagāndalu*) on whose village lands the share-crop contract occurred as a payment called *'barra ballati'*, from the Marathi *bārābalutā*.

There are two things that might strike us about sugar production in the Ceded Districts. One is that merchant capital was apparently necessary even though the cultivators who entered into share contracts may have been substantial ones. Partly, this can be explained by the relatively backward state of commodity markets in the Ceded Districts at the time and the need for merchants, therefore, to invest in commodity production in order to assure a supply of the commodity for trade; there was also a simultaneous need for cultivators, given the backward state of markets there, to secure a certain outlet for the crops they produced and even to use, or have available, additional productive factors provided by merchants. A second striking feature revealed by the share system of sugar production was the surcharge upon that production for the benefit of the village community; that charge can have been no small part of the profits of such arrangements. Here we see a defensive form of commodity production, one in which the principal agents sought to reduce risks of losses by sharing in an enterprise that neither merchant nor rich cultivator was prepared to undertake alone.

The emergent historiography on the transition from the late pre-colonial period to the time that the British imperial regime took its mature form—i.e., from 1700 to 1870—has the most important implications for larger questions about economic change in the subcontinent. As the various strands of this emerging economic historiography are tested against older interpretations, against each other, and against additional empirical analyses, conventional ideas about distorted and 'arrested' economic processes will have to be modified. Principally, of course, it will be necessary to see the first century of British colonial rule in a quite different way, as the late Eric Stokes argued.[15] He was the first to reject both the imperialist and the nationalist distortions of Indian economic history and to insist on the significant economic continuities of the late pre-colonial period. This obviously places the imperial intervention into the Indian economy during the later nineteenth century in a different light. Another set of benchmarks must be considered and a reassessment of the broad tendencies of the complex Indian economy must be undertaken before distorted and 'arrested' forms—if this is what they are to be labelled—can be properly identified.

Evidence from the transition period of the late pre-colonial era makes Professor Rothermund's specific proposition about capital in pre-colonial India untenable, however tempting it has long proven to define the base agrarian structure in his terms. My research on the eighteenth century Ceded Districts, as well as my research and that of others on much earlier times, points to a condition very different from that supposed by Rothermund, and it is important to bear in mind how much of an economic backwater the Ceded Districts were then and continued for long to be. Judging from the work of other scholars mentioned here, the productive uses of state and mercantile capital were very considerable everywhere in eighteenth century India, and possibly much before; capital was as vital in maintaining the pre-colonial economy of India as it was for the colonial regimes in the several parts of the subcontinent covered by the studies touched upon in this note.

NOTES

1. Cambridge University Press, 1982 and 1983.
2. C.A. Bayly, *Rulers, Townsmen and Bazaars: North Indian Society in the Age of British Expansion, 1770-1870* (Cambridge, 1983). D.A. Washbrook, 'Some Notes on Market Relations and the Development of the Economy of South India, c. 1750-1850', presented to the Leiden workshop on Comparative Colonial History, 1981; 'Commerce and Credit in South India: the Transition to Colonialism, 1770-1830', presented to the South Asia Regional Center, University of Pennsylvania, 1984; and his published paper: 'Law, State and Agrarian Society in Colonial India', *Modern Asian Studies,* 15 (1981). F. Perlin, 'The Pre-Colonial State in History and Epistemology: A Reconstruction of Social Formation in the Western Deccan from the Fifteenth to the early Nineteenth Century', in H.J.M. Claessen and P. Skalnik, eds., *The Study of the State* (The Hague, 1981); 'Of White Whale and Countrymen . . .', *The Journal of Peasant Studies,* 5 (1978); 'Proto-industrialization and Pre-colonial South Asia', *Past and Present, 98 (1983);* Growth of Money Economy and some Questions of Transition in late Pre-colonial India'. *The Journal of Peasant Studies,* 11 (1984).
3. Bayly, *op. cit.*, 460.
4. *Ibid.*, 64.
5. *Ibid.*, 459-60.
6. *Ibid.*, 463.

7. F. Perlin, 'State Formation Reconsidered', *Modern Asian Studies*, 19 (1985), 415-81. This issue is devoted to papers from a conference at Selwyn College, Cambridge, on the *Cambridge Economic History of India* volumes, held in 1984.

8. Cambridge University Press, 1976.

9. Much of this discussion of the Ceded Districts is drawn from the collection of Thomas Munro's papers now lodged in the India Office Library and Records, London, European Manuscripts, *Munro Collection*, F/151. Munro (1761-1827) served in the Madras army of the East India Company from 1780 to 1792 when he began a career as civil administrator rising to the governorship of Madras in 1819. For recent and balanced assessments of his career see: Nilmani Mukherjee, *The Ryotwar System in Madras, 1792-1827* (Calcutta, 1962) and T.H. Beaglehole, *Thomas Munro and the Development of Administrative Policy in Madras, 1792-1818* (Cambridge, 1966).

10. *South Indian History and Society; Studies from Inscriptions, AD 850-1800* (Delhi, 1984).

11. H.H. Wilson, *A Glossary of Revenue and Judicial Terms* (Calcutta, 1940), 231-32.

12. This is my calculation based upon statistics gathered by Munro for submission to the Madras Board of Revenue in 1806, *Munro Collection*, F/151/file 106.

13. India Office Library and Records, *Mackenzie Collection*, 'General', vol. II, 201 and B.L. Rice, *Mysore, A Gazetteer Compiled for Government* (London, 1897), 2, 108 ff.

14. Place's papers on the Chingleput jaghire are found at the India Office Library and Records in several volumes of the 'Board's Collections' [the Board of Control].

15. 'The First Century of British Colonial Control of India; Social Revolution or Social Stagnation?' *Past and Present*, 58(1973).

4

EIGHTEENTH-CENTURY STATE FORMS AND THE ECONOMY

CHRISTOPHER AND SUSAN BAYLY
St. Catharine's College and Clare Hall, Cambridge

The apparently limitless proliferation of powers and principalities in eighteenth-century India is one of the main reasons why its political history has appeared to be anarchic. It is therefore understandable that a younger generation of historians concerned with Indian social formations and the nature of the market in the immediate pre-colonial era might shy away from consideration of the state, or at best assume the existence of a universal if decayed Mughal model of the agrarian system. Yet even if the notion of political chaos and economic decline is rejected as too facile for a whole century and the whole subcontinent, the historical record provides constant examples of states directly involved in the process of production, trade and exchange with both negative and positive results. One priority therefore is to develop a basic typology of pre-colonial state forms as they related to economic activity and to each other. This paper suggests some initial lines of approach to this problem and how such a typology might be used to reinterpret the political conflicts of eighteenth-century India and their sometimes degenerative economic consequences without retreating to the stereotypes of chaos and anarchy.

Rather than adopting the usual method of describing states in terms of revenue-collecting machinery and government the paper begins by looking at changing patterns of consumption and management in seventeenth- and eighteenth-century

India. Consumption provides a key which links the ideology of royal court centres and elite groups with the actual workings of the economy. The notion of 'management' of men and resources has similar advantages. It distances us from the teleological and ethnocentric assumptions which go with the idea of development. It also points to the need for a sociology of knowledge in analysing the nature of the pre-colonial political, commercial and religious elites.

The diffusion of new styles of consumption throughout India in the seventeenth, eighteenth and nineteenth centuries seems to be the crucial link between the changing political and moral order and the changing economy. Most important was what might be called the Muslim *ashraf* style. This term is better than Mughal because the form of consumption it embodied spread far beyond the actual bounds of Mughal rule; in the south it followed the pattern of the Deccani Sultanates and had roots independent of the Mughals in Bengal also. It was spread as much by gentry who established small-town centres embellished with tombs, groves and public baths as by the supposedly centralised kingdoms. Finally, *ashraf*, a specifically Islamic notion of right conduct and outward observance is peculiarly appropriate as it is quite different from Hindu conceptions of 'inner rightness'—purity and restraint—embodied in the equivalent term *bhallalog* or *bhadralog* (lit. 'good people'). Just as Muslim gentlemen were distinguished in part by their outward observation of prayer, ablution and *haj*, so they adhered to an appropriate style of life and consumption. Contempt for nakedness and 'barbaric' garments such as the *sari* was matched by a connoisseurship in fruits, meats and milk products.

The Muslim expansion into eastern, central and southern India meant therefore the expansion of a style of consumption and its appropriate specialists and markets. Muslims introduced high quality wheat, fruit gardens and meat markets (albeit limited) to their core areas in the south such as Kurnool, Ginjee, Arcot, Vellore and Tinnevelly where rice, pulses and vegetable gruel had been the dominant foods before. Tailors, embroiderers and shoemakers were planted and settled in response to their more elaborate and involuted forms of dress. Tomb shrines and secular royal buildings and public baths greatly extended the architectural range of the earlier Hindu states. Even in the kingdom of Vijayanagar there is a striking distinction of categories between Hindu templ art and the Islamised secular buildings which are dottec amongst them in the ruins of Hampi [Fritz *et al.*, 1985].

When we turn to markets and trade it becomes clear tha many of the origins of entrepreneurial endeavour in immedi ate pre-colonial India were related to these rapidly diffusin patterns of consumption. Hide traders in central and south India were very prominent in inter-regional trade. The famou *bidri* iron-ware of the Deccan established itself as iron drinkin and eating vessels became appropriate to a Muslim or Islamis ing gentry in the south; much of the buoyancy in land value and land sales around the small-town centres was related t mutations in rights over valuable grove and garden lands o which melons, guavas, jack-fruit, roses, mangoes and othe tokens of gentility were produced.

The dynamic consequences of new patterns of consumptio were not, of course, limited to Muslims. At the most super ficial level, new military techniques involving firelock guns cannon and massed heavy cavalry were necessarily adopted b Hindu kingdoms, spreading employment for Muslims an Portuguese ('Topaze') artisans. Politically too, the domestica tion of the Maratha kingdoms within Mughal state forms afte the 1730s led to a slow acceleration of Muslim styles of con sumption amongst them and the rather late urbanisation c ritual centres such as Pune and Satara.

It seems likely that there were expansive propensities als within Hindu society proper. The 'confusion of orders' tha occurred with the social mobility of Hindu and Sikh peasan leaderships during the eighteenth century (predominantl drawn from the Jat and Kunbi castes) promoted the 'spirit c imitation' which Bouglé [Pocock, 1971, p. 153] assumed di not exist in Indian society. Massive programmes of templ building amongst the Wodiyar rulers of Mysore, the Nayaka and Poligar inheritors of the Vijayanagar sovereignty als helped populate their new sacred centres with artisans, artist and stone traders. But the new style representing bodil wealth and spiritual 'success' may have spread beyond th courts also. The key image here is the deity Krishna. Krishn devotionalism was the most vital religious movement in six teenth- and seventeenth-century India, finding especi favour amongst the middle and high castes in Bengal and th eastern Gangetic India, but also influencing the religious lif of Mysore and the Kauvery Delta. (cf. Breckenridge, 1980) Levelling, anti-ritualist, even austere in their first phase, the rituals and worship of Krishna were often sumptuous, sensuous and luxurious in their later stages. Krishna is often shown (in the emerging Tanjore glass-painting style, for instance) as a gaudy, epicene manbaby, delighting in consuming the fine things of the natural world—milk, butter, sweets and women's love.

The sumptuousness of Krishna worship and of the veneration of the high God Vishnu with which he was most closely associated had an obvious effect on temple specialists who appear to have encouraged the increasing use of sweets, sugar and milk in offerings. But the style of 'enjoyment' (*lila*) may also have had implications for the life-style of the Hindu middle castes, especially merchants and urban artisans for whom sweets and milk products, silks and garlands became more common items of consumption. All three of these products—sugarcane, milk and flowers—required capital, protection, specialist cultivation or production and delicate systems of marketing. They all figure prominently in extant lists of trade goods into pre-colonial towns and they all yielded healthy profits to producers and merchants. Their implications for political power are apparent more indirectly. The establishment of flower gardens was an essential symbol of both Hindu and Muslim royalty; as for sugar, travellers noted the cultivation of cane—the strongest proof of firm government, as cultivation and maturation took so many months. Finally, alongside this the rapid expansion of pilgrimage especially to sites connected with the Krishna legend or to the great Vishnu temples (Tirupati in Andhra, above all) represent a kind of ritual service industry concentrating personnel and trade at nodal points of economic growth.

The second determinant of pre-colonial social change could be called *management*: the diffusion of the skills of accounting, prediction and the combination of resources through the subcontinent. It went wider than entrepreneurship or enterprise since it meant that the ruler, the merchant, even the priest, assumed knowledge of calculations in each other's world [Perlin, 1985]. Yet it was not strictly development as economists and nationalists have sometimes assumed. Certainly, there were notions abroad that the ruler and merchant should combine to defeat want. There is, for instance, a fine miniature of the Emperor Jahangir shooting down the demon Famine with a bow and arrow [V and A, 1982, p. 40], and exhortations to ministers and governors in Hindu and Muslim states for the protection and feeding of the people were common. But inventories like the Mughal revenue manuals and the gazetteers in the Peishwa's *daftar* were not plans for growth so much as guides to good management.

There were several aspects to the growth of management in this broader sense. Most important was the expansion of political accountability which involved the incorporation of local chieftains, powers, tribes, and other bodies into the scheme of ranking of the Indo-Muslim state and to a lesser extent into categories of office associated with the Hindu state of Vijayanagara and its successors. As Muslim rule expanded into the Deccan and the far south these local potentates were beaten into the form of *zamindars* and *mansabdars* of the 'Mughal Empire' as earlier Hindu rulers of Rajasthan and other northern territories [Ziegler, 1978] had been incorporated in the fifteenth and sixteenth centuries. Even if the power of the state of Arcot, or Hyderabad, remained nominal the creation of a *mansabdar* (imperial military officer) out of a *poligar* (local Hindu chief) implied a concept of accountability, of salary and of representation at court. A nominal tribute was entered in the books.

The formal political rationalisation of the subcontinent in terms of a counting of resources and money tribute greatly extended the opportunities for literate specialists and 'accounters'. Throughout north India the term *mutsaddi* seems to have been used for this class of men of business [Devra, 1979]; on a grander scale the term *amil* was conflated with the term *mostajir* which implied revenue farmer [Barnett, 1980], indicating that Persian methods of estate management were coming to be seen more and more as a kind of investment and a potentially marketable commodity.

Though rights, shares and honours with distinctly religious connotations became bound up with this general growth of accountability and exchange, what was happening was not really the creation of a secular domain for business such as has been posited for early modern Europe. Management still served the sacred order in the prevailing ideology. But it is interesting to see that a distinct class of 'management' brahmins had emerged out of the priestly order by the eighteenth century. The concept of *apadharma* (the temporary cessation of caste religious duty) had always allowed the brahmin to take to government or trade in the 'Age of Destruction', of course. But the term *lokika* brahmin as distinguished from *pandit* or *pujari* used in the eighteenth century south to imply a 'worldly' or 'business' brahmin suggests a perception of the separation of functions which is quite striking.

These clues will need to be followed up in the context of the education of specialists in the late pre-colonial period. At a superficial level (the level of missionary observers) Indian systems for the diffusion of knowledge remained entirely traditional and dominated by religion. Yet there is some evidence that within the general bounds set by classical learning both the Hindu and Muslim traditions of scholarship were becoming more flexible and more appropriate to the expanding domain of management and accounting during the period 1600-1800. In the Delhi schools of the Waliullah tradition which provided judges and registrars for north India, law and philosophy were accorded considerable importance, but the content of legal discussion was often quite practical matters of property rights, relations with Hindus and so on. The *fatawa* or pronouncement by doctors of the law became a flexible way of dealing with problems of inheritance, marriage, sharing and transactions which faced people in their everyday lives [Rizvi, 1982]. Similarly, the rationalisation of the teaching syllabus, the Dars-i-Nizamiya, associated with the great north Indian teaching schools, Firangi Mahal, was designed to create a rounded Muslim scholar who could operate in the world of worship and the world of business with equal facility [Robinson, 1984; cf. Cole, 1984]. Something similar in the drawing together of strands of esoteric knowledge into a comprehensible system for daily use appears to have been taking place among Hindus, particularly at the teaching centres of Benares and Gaya. It was in the sixteenth century that groups of Brahmins particularly from central and southern India came to Benares to form teaching institutions as regular and regulated to be called a 'college' by early British observers. Medicine, astronomy, astrology and Hindu sciences of grammar, logic and natural forms were taught. These developments and the rapid pace of recension of Hindu legal texts and commentaries suggest a response to a political and public domain where ordered knowledge was becoming increasingly significant [Buchanan, 1838, ii, 729ff; cf. Phillips, 1717].

Such a background helps to explain the greater visibility in the seventeenth and eighteenth centuries of tightly-knit bodies of specialists in learning, accounting and management. Though the writer caste—the Kayasthas—were known in earlier texts as a category it was apparently in this period that Kayasthas became a significant political force at Muslim courts, and in many cases acquired land rights. Similar groups of skilled literary people elsewhere rose to greater heights. The Muslim Nevayat lineages of the Konkan coast spread inland into the Deccani kingdom, abandoned their heritage as ship-borne merchants and soldiers, and became a tightly-knit group of Islamic administrative specialists who ruled the early kingdom of Arcot and acquired considerable power in Mysore. Chitpavan Brahmins, pre-eminently a class of accounters and managers, rather than priests, seized power in the Maratha states from the middle of the eighteenth century. As with the lokika brahmins of Mysore the Chitpavan administrators and their clients had formed by the end of the eighteenth century a definite 'curial' interest with its own voice and aims and leader in Nana Farnavis [Wink, 1986]. This style of *mutsaddi raj* (rule by men of business) was not really a bureaucracy in the Weberian sense of secular, rational administration because the administrators were simultaneously enhancing and complicating their religious role. Farnavis and his party were *gurus* as well as administrators for the Maratha warrior nobility. A late eighteenth-century visitor to a Maratha revenue court in Gujarat noted how the court of justice presided over by a Chitpavan Brahmin had become a quasi-temple where villagers did *puja* (prayer) as well as registering rights. This sanctity departed from the place 'on becoming the abode of an Englishmen' [Forbes, 1813, ii, 347].

The greater influence of merchant corporations in several parts of India in the late seventeenth and early eighteenth centuries should be seen as part of this powerful administrative culture. It lays behind the complaints of the older Muslim literati that 'grocers' and 'men of low origins' were rising to power and that the public offices sanctioned by Muslim law were being parcelled out and sold off like melons. Important as were the internal lines of trust and credit between merchant people, much of the corporateness of the merchant *mahajan* or *sabha* (councils) [Bayly, 1983] came about through participation in a wider administrative culture. In this context it is interesting that the famous form of double entry accounts which was almost standard throughout Indian cities by the eighteenth century is attributed to the intervention of Mughal finance ministers, particularly Todar Mull.

The key feature of eighteenth-century Indian elite culture was in fact the close interpenetration between the worlds of the revenue administrator, the court priesthood, the merchant and the military mercenary captain. This facilitated a rapid circulation of resources from warfare, through agrarian patronage to religion and kingly display.

Resources

So far this paper has been deliberately oblique in approaching the question of state and economy. That is to say it has argued that the diffusion of various culturally reproduced patterns of consumption and a general style of management were prior to the creation or mobilisation of resources in the Indian economy, in that they provided a rationale for the exploitation of the internal economy. One aspect of these prior changes was the accommodation of the political order of Muslim India to its Hindu predecessors which had profound economic consequences. Before one asks why new roads, bazaars, trade routes and agricultural populations were coming into being, one must ask why these things should be so. Otherwise on the standard methodology of economic history changes in human societies becomes a simple measurement made against the surface patterns of western European history.

New resources were, of course, available in seventeenth- and eighteenth-century India to be consumed and managed [Habib, 1965]. But these resources themselves were generated by the cultural as well as the material requirements of indigenous elites.

The creation of a more homogeneous agricultural society consuming and producing a wider range of products was itself the consequence of the settlement of previously mobile and semi-nomadic people by bodies of lords and gentry who sought to reproduce a high Muslim life-style or patterns of Hindu worship supported by a complete and stratified Hindu order. This process can be studied in the long-term around Delhi where Sheikh gentry slowly captured bodies of Gujar, Bhatti and Jat nomads and introduced them to intensive wheat agriculture, to cities, and often to Islam [e.g. Rizvi, 1980, p. 45]. This process was impelled by a Muslim notion of what constituted a civilised life. Agricultural settlements were often based around shrines of members of Sufi religious orders and were pinned down by the creation of mosques and other locations of communal worship. The consumption by the gentries of fruits, melons, tobacco and sugar modified local patterns of agriculture which in turn raised the value of land and created the potential for the circulation of land rights. Such settlements appear to have been a key feature of endogenous economic change in north India. *Poligar* warrior settlement in the dry parts of south India had a similar consequence. The minor, but cumulatively significant, technological changes (the introduction of Persian wheel irrigation and iron-shod ploughs) mentioned by Habib grew out of this expansion and elaboration of elite Muslim and lordly Hindu life-styles throughout the countryside [Habib, 1982].

At a wider level attempts to order and integrate new territories into the Mughal Empire, or into later regional principalities, created new economic resources. The expansion of Bengal muslin production and Gujarat silk production was the consequence of political integration. The centre had to become the great consumer of such goods in order to secure the payment of these provinces' land revenues and to obtain the allegiance of their elites and craftsmen [C. Bayly, 1986]. It is true that unintended economic changes could direct the attention of kings to new, wealthy tributaries. But the process was self-reinforcing: culture and polity reproduced the economy as often as economic changes moulded indigenous politics.

Even the exogenous changes associated with the inflow of bullion from Portuguese, Dutch and English sources operated within a political and cultural context. The emperors and their eighteenth-century successors needed the bullion inflow in order to oil the wheels of military politics, paying cash salaries and disbursing funds to attach to themselves the most important notables. In the mid-eighteenth century the Nawab of Arcot went heavily in debt to European moneylenders of Madras. These loans were used to found charitable bequests and religious institutions to secure the allegiance of his Tamil subjects; they paid for the cavalry he badly needed; but they were also accumulated specifically to built up amongst the Company servants a body of political support devoted to his cause.

Competitions and Dynamism

Dynamism within what might be called the supply side in modern economics (management) and within the demand side (consumption) both derived from competition within pre-colonial society. Both Weber and Bouglé [Bouglé in Pocock, 1971], within their respective spheres, argued that it was the absense of competition on western European lines which kept India in its rigid mould and prevented capital formation and investment. This was because they both (rightly) failed to see the emergence of class or status competition on western lines. In India, however, there existed different forms of competition which served to promote the better accumulation and management of resources. First there was the process of change in religion and life-style which saw 'sectarian' competition in the building up ot holy places, saints' shrines, patterns of pilgrimage and devotional worship. The competition between established temple centres and new *bhakti* cults with their own heavily endowed institutions promoted growth, trade nd new styles of consumption.

At another level tension and competition within the Muslim state system and the (segmentary) Hindu polities on which it was superimposed provided another type of buoyancy [Stein, 1985]. Several authors have recently noted the accumulation of patrimonial rights (village zamindari, hereditary *inam* or *watan*) under the surface of the temporary, prebendal rights of the Islamic kingdoms (*jaghir, saranjam,* temporary *inam*) in the course of the late seventeenth century and the eighteenth century. Now in a recent doctoral dissertation at Leiden, Andre Wink has provided a simple, powerful argument which helps link tension, 'gentrification' and economic change. He develops the notion of 'rebellion' (*fitna, fitva*) as a basic characteristic of Indian politics [Wink, 1986]. Though condemned by theorists in both the Muslim and Hindu traditions, 'rebellion' in this sense is a crucial technique of building empires by alliance on the internal frontier of Indian empires.

The king operates deeply inside the territory of his enemy the 'counter-king' (here the Mughal and the Peshwa) to built up alliances by the concession of rights to local magnates. Once rights have been given by the counter-sovereign or rebel, the sovereign must validate and even extend them. Thus conflict within the Mughal universal realm leads inevitably to its gentrification by the creation of more and more patrimonial rights. In order to be sure of their local power these newly gentrified magnates must initiate what Wink (in an attempt to avoid development) calls *mise en valeur*: the settlement of non-occupancy tenants, tradesmen and artisans. This, it might be argued, has a particularly expansionist consequence as much of the land thus given in rights was on the frontier of cultivation, barren or underpopulated.

So we can begin to resolve the problem at the heart of immediate pre-colonial social and economic history. This is the question of how the conflict the British saw as anarchy is compatible with the dynamic local changes which they and more recent writers perceived in the economy. Rebellion (*fitna*) led to the creation of rights which led in turn to management, new patterns of consumption and reconcentration of agricultural resources.

Eighteenth-Century State Forms

Having observed some of the general forces lying behind economic change in pre-colonial India, it is important to go back to the question of diversity. The political and ecological contexts within which these changes worked themselves out varied greatly from one part of the subcontinent to another, even between one village and the next. Gentrification took on a different form in north India where village level *zamindari* rights had long existed and in the Deccan where it was the headship and perquisites of village management *(patilki)* which was the right which the gentry sought to accumulate [Stokes, 1978; cf. Perlin, 1985]. It is essential also to avoid the grip of the model of the Mughal-type centralised, cash-revenue state which has so long dominated the literature because it appealed both to the British and Indian historians of pre-colonial India. Indian state forms were patently more diversified than this model will allow and consequently the outcome of the economic changes which these different forms encouraged were more varied. At present the only incipient change in the pre-colonial economy seems to be that set forth by Habib in his influential essay: that a cash-paying free peasantry might have transformed themselves into a labour-using yeomanry through the extension of 'self-cultivating' types of land rights (*khudkasht*) [Habib, 1969; cf. Satish Chandra, 1976].

On the other flank of this Scylla of the Mughal model, itself increasingly suspect, lies the Charybdis of mind-breaking diversity which other historians find so infuriating about Indian studies. All we seem to be able to offer is the notion that it was all different region by region, district by district or even village by village. What is needed perhaps is a very simple typology of state-agriculture forms which are not simply regional variations dressed up as models.

It must first be admitted that the basic units of agrarian relations were enormously diffuse at the village level. In all parts of the subcontinent cash revenue paying villages were interspersed with villages paying in kind; villages where a free peasantry existed were found side by side with villages or village groups where deep agrarian bondage was the norm and the elites were involved quite directly in the finance and direction of agricultural operations. In the same way one finds villages with an ethic of egalitarian peasant brotherhood side by side with those with a most involute system of caste ranking dominated by brahmins.

Yet ecology and the operation of the state and the elites operating over long periods of time ensured that in different sub-regions one or another of these basic units predominated and so certain types of agrarian system emerged. Their variety was great but it may be possible to develop a few crude ideal types if we simply take two basic variables: the weight of state revenue demand whether in cash or kind and the degree of social stratification. The first variable bears on the power and intrusiveness of the state; the second on the question of distribution and the role of caste. Out of these variables we can generate four types of state-agrarian forms.

A. Low stratification and low state demand

This type was associated with pioneer peasant brotherhoods. Caste categories were open, reflecting the need to attract new cultivators and agrarian servants in an area of relatively low

C. High stratification and high state demand

In this type the state, through a semi-prebendal bureaucratic elite similar to the Javanese *priyayi*, intervened more deeply in the processes of production, distributing seed and controlling water. The state sought to retain complete control of the grain market and payments were in kind. The state used the grain monopolised to provide a buffer for bad years, to sell back to the cultivator at notional money rates when his own stock had been exhausted. It also used the grain heap to provide for ritual specialists, temples and pilgrims in massive system of redistribution. Grain was exported to provide essential cash income, but in view of seasonal variations there was a tendency to build up large artisan industries in order to provide a second source of export earnings and for internal redistribution. In this type deep social stratification was apparent with large numbers of tied cultivators for use on state and religious works. Large scale redistribution tended to reproduce systems of caste ranking in relation to temples or other religious institutions. Economic development was expressed in terms of greater and greater agricultural intensification and the build-up of artisan industries in temple-town complexes. Merchants would be large-scale, state-patronised monopolists who exported through thriving port centres like Javanese *shahbandars* or through well developed inland entrepots The weaknesses in such a system derived from defective water and labour control and inadequate cash earnings to support military protection.

The best example of such a type appears to be Maratha Tanjore before 1770. Under Raja Shahji at the beginning of the eighteenth century Tanjore is supposed to have produced the enormous amount of 32 *lakhs* of cullums of paddy per annum (c. 400,000 tons) from 5,735 villages [Madras Board of Revenue, 1801-2]. Allowing for exaggeration and the nominal nature of assessment, this nevertheless must have accounted for a not insignificant part of the subcontinent's total grain production, a fact borne out by the extensive scale of its rice exports: to the dry south, to Kerala, and to south-east Asia. This production was carried out by teams of bonded husbandmen (*parakudis*) who could be drafted or sold, but owned their ploughs, unlike Keralan slaves. Their efforts were supported by large bodies of water-management specialists. The state appears to have provided the cultivators with seed at nominal prices, to have assessed a proportion of the crop and made a division in kind at harvest which reflected the state of the season. The state share of the grain was sold by sponsored merchants to external markets or redistributed on a massive scale to religious and cultural institutions which in turn parcelled it out to ritual dependants, etc.

Raja Serfoji claimed at the beginning of the nineteenth century that his forefathers before 1760 had supported nearly 1,000 large temples and charitable feeding houses. These *chatrams* received consignments of state rice which allowed them to feed upward of 40,000 specialists and pilgrims per annum, including 'Jogues, Jungums, ateets and byragies [varieties of religious mendicants]', teachers of Vedas, doctors and orphans. The connection of much of this ritual activity with the great pilgrimage to Rameshwaram illustrates the whole theme of this paper. Rameshwaram, legendary stopping point of the hero Ram, was a Vaishnavite pilgrimage centre which seems to have risen in importance in the sixteenth and seventeenth centuries. The new patterns of consumption emerging in the region spurred on the state's effort at management and made possible new accumulations of resources, but the state's role and form differed dramatically from that obtaining in the other types discussed here. So too, the nature of caste was made more involute and hierarchical by the intervention of the state. Whereas in other systems temple festivals relied on corporate or unorganised manpower in the great car pulling rituals (*brahm-utsavams*), here it was the state which drafted in labour for festivals. Nor was the intervention of the state directed wholly to the support of Hindu institutions. The role of Muslim Maralkayyar (seaborne) merchants in trade out of the port cities, especially Nagapattinam and Nagore, encouraged the rajas to give large benefactions to the great Sufi shrine of Nagore with its contacts throughout south-east Asia [S. Bayly, 1986]. Catholic Christian mercantile activity was reflected in the growth of the Virgin cult at Velanganni. The need for a wider base for export earnings was fulfilled with huge cloth transhipments through these ports to the Dutch Indies, Europe and West Africa.

Features approximating to this type were also found outside

investment for seventeenth and eighteenth century north India was a particular target for the Sikh war-bands. Again, though economic change and the expansion of agriculture was advanced in the Maratha homelands, the breakdown of the Mughal revenue pump starved them of the silver with which to maintain their system and purchase precious items from outside. Thus Peshwa Balaji Baji Rao advocated Maratha expansion both to the north and the south. Elaborating the symbolism of the holy rivers Ganga and Cauvery he remarked that the 'sterility' of the lands around Pune could only be remedied if the Marathas united the 'streams of gold' flowing along these rivers under their own control; bullion would water the dry lands of the Deccan' [Sen, 1958, pp. 59-60]. And while it is true that the Marathas ultimately reproduced a dynamic revenue and agricultural system even in the land which they plundered and put under their danegeld (*chauth*) the evidence suggests considerable short and medium term disruption of agriculture and the destruction of urban centres.

Type B (low stratification and high demand) similarl sought an expansion of dominion in order to maximise cas revenue and payments for its prebendary elites who woul otherwise cut into the state's own restricted demesne (*khalsa* and create gentry rights. Wherever it expanded therefore thi type sought to turn payments in kind into cash payments disrupting in the process the delicate systems of redistributio and water control which characterised C and D. Internall unbalanced the centralised cash revenue system tended t pressure the peasantry into revolt thus precipitating labou shortages; this was noted some years ago by Irfan Habib. Th remedy was further expansion, or possibly as D.H.A. Kolff ha suggested a much more general resort to slave labour than h been thought characteristic of the Mughal state. Certainly, th seizure of cultivators and other specialists was a prime obje of the later campaigns of Hyder and Tipu in Coorg, th Carnatic and Kerala.

In this context the incursions of the sub-Mughal forms of t Arcot Nawabi and the Mysore of the sultans into the kingdo of Tanjore after 1760 provide an interesting case study of ho the meeting of two radically different pre-colonial stat agrarian forms led to involution and collapse. Two process occurred in Tanjore. First the absence of a cash revenue led t invaders and their captive kings to farm out the right to ta the produce of villages on a system called *tunkhwal*. Intermediaries called *phatakhdars* began to consolidate themselves in the countryside in return for cash-payments as the court desperately sought silver rupees to pay its tribute obligations. At the same time merchant moneylenders (called *sahukars*) penetrated into the villages, lending money to peasants who could otherwise not pay their newly-monetized revenue obligations [Madras, Board of Revenue, 1801-2]. Secondly, the decline of the state's role in agriculture led to a degeneration of watercourses, a rapid collapse of production, and the decay of the many thriving coastal towns which had existed in the previous era of redistribution and payment in kind.

An important by-product of the collisions between the various pre-colonial state forms was the emergence of fissures within Indian social organisations which in some cases pointed forward to the more developed 'communalism' of colonial rule. Thus the conflict between monopolising monarchs on the west coast (Malabar, Cochin, type D) and their *shahbandar* merchant communities lay behind a flare up of the Islamic militancy associated with the later Mappilla outbreaks. In north India the conflicts between Muslim gentry coming in from outside and Hindu peasant-gentry represented by the Sikhs and Jats underlay land-wars in which communal tensions were clearly present [Muzaffar Alam]. Even in Tanjore and the south historical changes in forms of caste conflict represent particular sets of historical events which are partly related to the impact of the state. It may be true as Appadurai argues that the famous conflicts between Right and Left hand castes in Tamil Nadu and Karnataka represent a paradigm of social tension through time. But the meaning of these disputes varied considerably from those of Vijayanagar. In Madras they were confounded with battles between Company's agents. In Tanjore after 1770 they seem to be related to the degeneration of the state purchasing system and the rise of the *phatakhdars* within the disintegrating kingdom.

Conclusion

This paper has addressed itself to the question of the relationship between the state, caste and the agrarian order in eighteenth-century India as an essential background to the changes

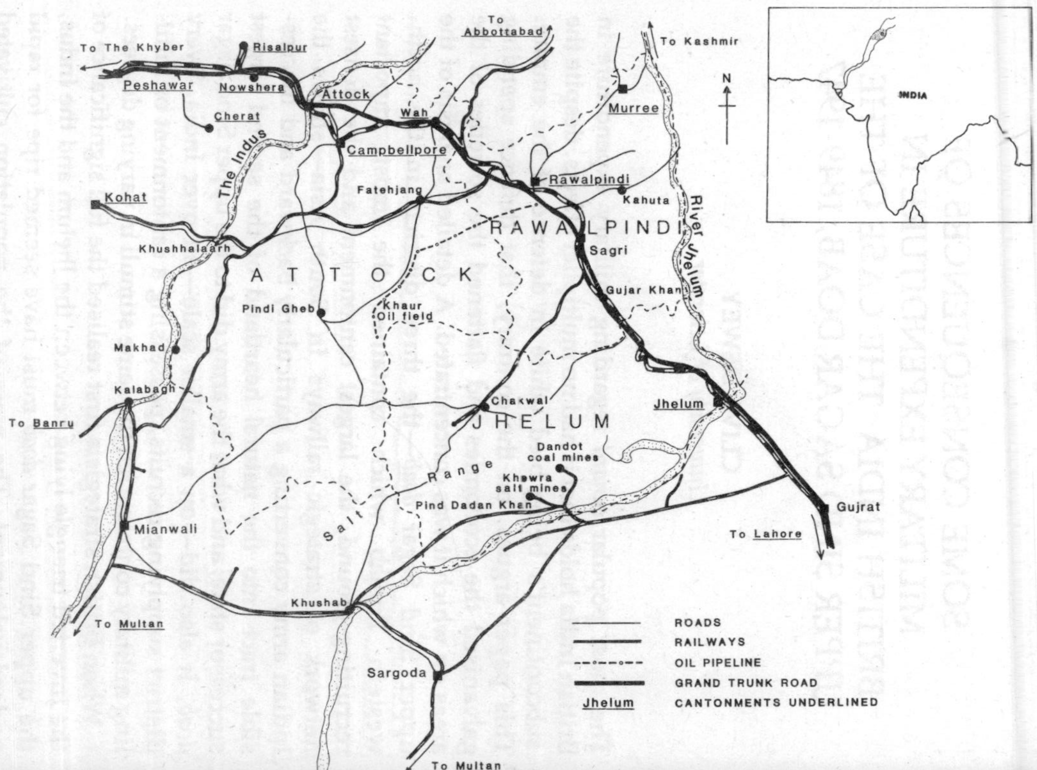
INDIA
N
To Kashmir
River Jhelum
Murree
To Abbottabad
Kahuta
Rawalpindi
RAWALPINDI
Sagri
Gujar Khan
Jhelum
JHELUM
Dandot coal mines
Khewra salt mines
Pind Dadan Khan
Salt Range
Gujrat
To Lahore
Chakwal
Khaur Oil field
ATTOCK
Wah
Attock
Campbellpore
Fatehjang
Pindi Gheb
Risalpur
Nowshera
To The Khyber
Peshawar
Cherat
The Indus
Kohat
Khushhalaarh
Makhad
Kalabagh
To Banru
Mianwali
To Multan
Khushab
Sargoda
To Multan
ROADS
RAILWAYS
OIL PIPELINE
GRAND TRUNK ROAD
Jhelum
CANTONMENTS UNDERLINED

by its comparative aridity and broken terrain. The monsoon rains were unreliable, the watertable was too low for profitable well-irrigation, and the surface of the land was cut up for canals or tanks. At its worst, the tract degenerated into an endless expanse of tangled ravines and steep ridges, which hill torrents carved out of bare rock. The same conformations that precluded high farming inhibited communications. There was exactly one metalled road in the entire *doab* and all the unmettaled tracks were impassable by wheeled vehicles, so pack animals and human porters were the only means of carriage. The absence of an agricultural surplus and the high cost of transport put paid to commerce; and the low level of commercial activity put paid to urbanisation. The 'towns' of the *doab* were jumped-up villages which managed, for the moment, to annex a few low level government offices or the transactions of some fertile oasis.

The only dynamic element in this otherwise stagnant situation was the population. Between 1855 and 1881 the population of the three *doab* districts rose by almost one-half: twice the growth-rate of the rest of the Punjab. Given the impossibility of increasing agricultural output indefinitely, a Malthusian catastrophe appeared inevitable. In the event, the crisis was averted. Although the population went up by 140 per cent, the income of the peasantry went up faster still. An immense influx of pay and pensions derived from military service swamped agriculture as the great determinant of consumption and investment. The profits of cultivation and carriage soared, as military expenditure generated new markets. A century of military town-building culminated in the designation of the largest cantonment-city as the provisional capital of Pakistan. The *doab* acquired one of the best networks of railways and roads in India, because of the strategic importance of communications. There was even a 'show' of industrialisation, heavily concentrated in the building trades and extractive industries. As a result, the inhabitants of the *doab* were better-fed, beter-clothed, better-housed and better-educated at independence than they had been at annexation. They were also comparatively free. All the peasants' natural masters—landlords, moneylenders, traders, officials, kulaks—were weakened when their erstwhile dependants obtained access to resources provided by the army.[1]

contradictory. It appears among the letters and articles written by Indian army officers whenever the Military Department wanted to put pressure on the Finance Department to raise the army's pay scales; and it appears, also, in some surveys which the Board of Economic Inquiry conducted during the Second World War. All the officers, writing at a time when the real value of the soldiers' pay was at its nadir, stress the low size of remittances; while the surveys almost certainly inflate them because wartime earnings were so high and in some theatres of war there was nothing to spend money on. Probably the best one can do is to posit a period of low remittances between the Afghan war and the First World War, when soldiers still had to provide their own rations and the purchasing power of their pay scales in terms of food was falling; a period of comparatively high remittances between the wars, when soldiers had free rations and benefited from deflation in the 1930s; and two periods—the world wars—of bumper remittances.[7]

The proportion of the remittances which was invested supposedly varied according to the land-hunger, professional eminence and tribal values of the recipients. Large families with tiny holdings and a single sepoy in their ranks were unable to match the investment rates of less fecund families with big holdings and several native officers. High-ranking tribes, also, were unlikely to match the agricultural improvements made by middle-ranking cultivators; just as middle-ranking cultivators were unlikely to spend as much as their ritual superiors on ceremonies or litigation.[8] But even if the exact percentages are elusive and variable, the main consequences of the great influx of pay and pensions are fairly clear.

Consumption

The most important item in almost any peasant family's budget is food, and the most immediate effect of the influx of pay and pensions was a growth in the demand for foodstuffs. In 1884/85—the only year for which figures are available—the North-Western Railway carried four times as much grain into Rawalpindi as it carried out. The city and cantonment must have consumed more food than the district could supply at a very early date, and distinct food deficit zones soon emerged in the countryside as recruits withdrew their labour from cultivation and access to off-farm income cut the tenuous links between subsistence agriculture and population growth. The population of Murree—one of the tehsils which got most out of the army—went up three times over between 1881 and 1961; and less than halfway through this miniature explosion, population densities (on a comparatively unproductive cultivated area) reached twice the levels obtaining in the far more fertile plains. A survey of two bloated villages in 1941-42 revealed that they were buying in between three-quarters and seven-eighths of their food, and the deputy commissioner warned his superiors that 'the land will not support the (people). Any decrease in recruiting would be disastrous.'[9]

This growth in the number of consumers—coupled with rising cash incomes—had an entirely predictable effect on prices. In the 1860s the price of wheat, far and away the most important crop, was lower in the Sind Sagar *doab* than in almost any other region of the Punjab. Fifty years later, grain prices in Rawalpindi were higher than in any other district—and the margin widened whenever the peasantry's income from the army went up: in 1917-20, when soldiers' families were spending the profits of the First World War; in the 1930s, when deflation increased the purchasing power of the sepoys' fixed pay and pensions; and again during the Second World War, when huge pay increases swept a high proportion of the able-bodied *doabis* into the army. The prices of other foodstuffs were just as buoyant as the price of grain, because military service gave recruits a taste for a more varied diet. The standard ration for Muslim troops included far more meat, vegetables, milk, eggs and sugar than peasants normally ate at home; and soldiers who were used to eating well in cantonments were loath to go back to the more monotonous meals of their youth. The great beneficiaries of this sustained increase in the demand for widening range of agricultural products were the tracts and families which managed to produce a surplus, especially if they were protected from outside competition by poor communications. Deficit tracts and deficit families lost out whenever food prices went up; but they still reacted in exactly the same way—by intensifying their cultivation, to minimise the amount of food they bought in.[10]

The demand for artefacts, especially textiles and hardware, went up with the demand for foodstuffs. Soldiers who lived in cantonments were exposed to a range of factory-made goods

The collapse of crop prices after 1928 forced families to realise their liquid assets, despite the opposition of the wives; and the *doab's* net imports of bullion turned into a massive outflow. The goldsmiths who made small fortunes selling the ornaments made even larger ones buying them back at distress prices, melting them down, and selling the bullion for export. But the 1920s boom and the windfall profits of the depression were the Indian summer of the *sunars* in the upper Sind Sagar *doab*. The soldiers' relatively fixed incomes enabled them to hold onto their jewellery, and by the time crop prices recovered, fashions had changed. When Darling asked a registrar of cooperative societies to describe the differences brought about by mass enlistment during the Second World War, he replied:

> You will not see a single woman here with a nose ring . . . Their ears, too, used to be pierced in half a dozen places, so many ornaments did they wear; in Gujranwala the older women have a dozen holes. Now women tend to have one gold ear-ring in each ear; this is because it is more beautiful.[15]

Sometimes the increased demand for luxury foodstuffs and luxury manufactures went together. Just as rice and wheat required different sets of implements and utensils from the point at which the seed was put into the ground to the point at which the grain was put into the mouth, the introduction of a new beverage involved the introduction of a new technology. Milk-based drinks could be prepared and drunk using traditional clay or metal vessels; but tea-drinkers needed equipment designed for tea alone. Soldiers who caught 'the tea habit' in camps or cantonments popularised tea drinking in the recruiting-grounds after the First World War, and their families became great consumers of tea-sets as well as tea leaves. A soldier with a wife and two children told Darling that they drank tea

> twice a day with milk and *gur* and each ate a *paraunta* (a griddle-cake of unleavened bread fried in *ghee*) with it. He put the cost at twelve annas a day . . . (A) headmaster thought the habit a bad one—'it makes men weak'—but one rustic said, 'I cannot even walk until I have drunk tea', and others said that when they did not drink it, they got headaches and constipation . . . Whatever its effects . . . the habit . . . is spreading southwards

from the more martial to the less martial areas.[16]

Hence the crockery in the Chakwal bazaars: the cups, saucers, jugs and pots piled high on the traders' stalls.

The service sector seems to have done as well out of the growth in military incomes as the cultivators with a surplus to sell and the craftsmen whose wares stayed in fashion. Lawyers benefited from a boom in litigation and priests welcomed the onset of the Islamic revival; two tendencies which were financed, in part, by pay and pensions. The majority of the 15,000-odd civil cases which got into the courts in a normal year in the 1920s consisted of suits for the repayment of petty debts, brought by Hindu moneylenders against Muslim cultivators. They were a by-product of the peasants' insecurity and lack of reserves, and they were comparatively inexpensive. A court of first instance rubber-stamped the plaintiffs' claims—the defendant might not put in an appearance and the moneylender might never execute his decree. It was a way of obtaining legal recognition of a debt and putting pressure on a debtor to pay up; that was all. The army did nothing to encourage this sort of suit; on the contrary, by giving the peasantry the cash to repay their debts and stand up to the moneylenders in court, it may even have kept the level of litigation down.

Over against the petty debt cases there were others: much more costly suits which would never have been initiated or would never have been pressed so far if it had not been for the endemic factionalism—the 'passionate and revengeful spirit'—which divided all the leading families and the great majority of the villages into hostile camps. Technically, such suits were generally disputes between neighbours over titles to land. In reality, the land was only a means of getting a feud into court, and the ostensible parties were only representatives of their factions. The real objective was to do the opposing faction down, by setting up a public trial of strength. Thousands of rupees had to be raised to pay skilful pleaders to pursue suits up to the High Court; platoons of witnesses had to be carefully rehearsed until they corroborated one another's perjuries; clerks had to be bribed to falsify official records, and *munsifs* had to be squared to ensure that they delivered appropriate judgments. The 'party' which could do all these things most effectively—which could use the British courts to expropriate its opponents—struck fear into the hearts of its leering at the women who walked down to river or the well with pitchers on their heads. 'An imprudent word, a sharp reply, a curse, a blow, and maybe a riot and murder will ensue.' Then the clients gathered round their patrons; the quarrel spread to the neighbouring villages; and everyone, from the headmen down to the lowliest scavengers, was sucked into the dispute. As the Attock gazetteer put it, 'false witness whenever needed (was) an implied condition of tenancies.' Sometimes the waves of intrigue originated with the lower orders: a fracas among menials in some hamlet in the hills could convulse the *maliks* of an overgrown village in the plains. But however the latest round of factional violence originated, it always ended the same way: with a rash of expensive court cases, civil and criminal.[21]

Court cases were one kind of 'extravagance' financed by pay and pensions; Islamicisation was another. There were all the signs of an Islamic revival in the Sind Sagar *doab* a generation before communal sentiment led to the creation of Pakistan. When the allies went to war with Turkey, Muslim soldiers serving in the Indian Expeditionary Force in Mesopotamia naturally wondered whether the only consequence of their courage and privation would be the annexation of the holy places by unbelievers; and the Punjabi Mussalmen who came home in 1919 felt the tug of the *khilafat* movement, which protested against the dismemberment of the Ottoman empire among assorted *kafirs*. Ayub Khan's father, a retired risaldar-major, had 'a vague but strong sense of Muslim nationalism', sent his son to the local *maulvis* to learn the Koran off by heart, and told a visiting *alim* that his only desire was

> to die under the flag of Islam. But where is that flag? There is no Muslim country today which is free. They are all dominated by colonial powers.[22]

In one of the most heavily-recruited villages in Jhelum, the veterans who fought in the First World War added a fifth mosque to the four they already possessed; and what the 'most martial' villages did in spades, the rest of the *doab* did in *parvo*.

The rash of mosque-building was inseparable from an up-grading in the quality (and cost) of the *ulema*. Mosques needed priests to serve them, and superior mosques warranted a superior class of clergy. The traditional *mullah* in the *doab* was a village menial who inherited his clients from his father, read the contract at their weddings, laid out their bodies when they died, took his fees in *chapatis* and grain, and did a little weaving on the side. He was too poorly educated to expound the *Koran*, and his counsel was neither sought nor taken. From the *khilafat* movement onwards, the *panchayats* in charge of mosques began putting up the money to import *maulvis* trained in the great Muslim seminaries in Delhi and the United Provinces. They wanted men capable of applying the *shariat* to local disputes and the issues of the day. Particularly pious soldiers were prepared to lay out large sums of money giving their sons a Muslim education, in the hope that they would join the ranks of the religious scholars; and enlightened landlords employed the more reputable members of the *ulema* to settle disputes among their tenants which they were perfectly capable of settling themselves. But the most learned *maulvi* still counted for nothing, in the western Punjab, alongside the most ignorant *pir*. The *pirs*, holy men who inherited their *baraka* (or religious charisma) from their still holier ancestors, were the religious aristocracy of the *doab*. Every Muslim was supposed to be the *murid* of a particular *pir*, and every disciple owed his religious counsellor unquestioned obedience.

Some of the *pirs* did *piri-muridi:* they went on regular tours round their followers, handing out charms against infertility and ill-health in return for alms. Darling met a young *pir* who had just returned from a six week trip round the western Punjab with twenty sheep and goats, six cows and Rs. 600 in cash, 'the price of the forty or fifty charms given daily'. Other 'saints—generally the custodians of the richest shrines—disdained the easy pickings of *piri-muridi* becuase they could make more money staying in one place and waiting for their disciples to make pilgrimages to them. In either event—whether they were peripatetic or sedentary—their incomes from offerings went up, as their followings expanded and their *murids'* pay and pensions rose. The networks of religious clientage were closing round the martial castes. With the progress of the Islamic revival, it became harder and harder for a *doabi* to do without a *pir*; and at a time of general prosperity, it became harder and harder to keep offerings down to customary levels.[23]

Islamicisation also increased the cost of pilgrimages, ceremonies and *purdah*. Outside the ranks of the *ulema*, it is difficult to think of anyone in the upper Sind Sagar *doab* who made the pilgrimage to Mecca prior to annexation; and it is always possible that there was not one lay *haji* in the whole of the three districts. By the 1930s hundreds of *doabis* were performing the ultimate act of worship each year at a cost ranging between Rs. 200 and Rs. 630 for deck passengers; and many of them must have been soldiers or members of soldiers' families spending savings accumulated during lifetimes of service. Moreover, the *haj* was only the long-distance tip of a local iceberg. The improvement of communications encouraged pilgrims to visit shrines all over the western Punjab. The grave of Shah Chiragh drew thousands of worshippers into Rawalpindi city on four successive Thursdays; more than 20,000 pilgrims visited the shrine of Barri Latif Shah at the foot of the Margalla range, about nine miles north-east of Rawalpindi; and the biggest *mela* in the *doab* the three-day fair at Khanga Sydam Shah in Jhelum, was attended by crowds in excess of 50,000 people. Outside the *doab*, one of the most famous shrines of all—at Sakhi Sarwar in Dera Ghazi Khan—drew members of the martial castes 300 miles down the Indus.[24] It is more difficult to obtain evidence of expenditure on some of the major Muslim ceremonies, such as the formal hair-cutting of boys; but it seems almost certain that the cost of marriages rose. Bride-prices and dowries were lower in the Sind Sagar *doab* than in Hindu or Sikh recruiting-grounds, because Islam blurred caste distinctions and made the pursuit of brides and grooms of equal or higher ritual status so much less frenetic. The practice of cousin-marriage, which was virtually universal in the case of first marriages, also encouraged the exchange of brides. But bride-prices and dowries did go up when young bachelors and anxious fathers came home from the wars with gratuities burning holes in their pockets; and once the boom of the 1920s accustomed cultivators to higher standards of hospitality, it was difficult to resist the popular demand for more appetising food or more amusing entertainment at weddings. Guests, in return, were expected to give more expensive gifts.[25]

The collapse of crop prices after 1929 should have brought expenditure on ceremonies tumbling, and in areas which were wholly dependent on cultivation economies were made. But the purchasing-power of soldiers and pensioners on comparatively fixed incomes actually went up; and the cooperative movement's earnest attempts to persuade martial castes to reduce the cost of ceremonies ran into stiff resistance, mainly from the wives. *Tamashas* were the high spots of their secluded lives, and they were not prepared to give them up. Darling once attended a meeting at which a Muslim deputy registrar tried to persuade the Jodhras of Pindigheb to cut their expenditure on funerals from Rs. 500 to Rs. 50, only to run into opposition from a local *nawab*:

> 'I am old, and your father is old and we are *buzurg* (venerable). Is no more to be spent on us when we die than the cost of an *ekka* pony?' (i.e. a pony only fit to draw a crude two-wheeled trap). The (registrar) replied 'This proposal has nothing to do with *ekka* ponies, nor has the honour due to *buzurg* when they are dead; it is no matter to them what is spent. But (giving) a large feast (means) we must go to the *bania* and put our thumb mark to a bond. And what advantage have we?' The nawab was on the point of giving way when a message was brought him from his *zenana* that he should not yield, for on no account would they agree. And so in Pindigheb nothing has been done.[26]

Purdah probably absorbed a higher proportion of the soldiers' pay and pensions than all the other aspects of Islamicisation put together. The more strictly a family confined its women, the higher its *izzat*. There was no more conspicuous sign of a family's elite standing, and no more effective way of gaining status. Military service supposedly made soldiers much more conscious of their 'honour', and whenever military incomes rose, some of the gains were bound to be dissipated on the servants and labourers who were needed to do the jobs that the women of the household once did outside the house, from weeding the crops to marketing the produce.[27] An old captain born in the same year as the mutiny told Darling how the women had enjoyed much greater freedom to move around the countryside in his youth. 'But all this', he said,

> is stopped, and they mind their houses and children; and it is much better so . . . The children are better cared for, the house is better run, and needlework is done instead of cutting grass. There is modesty, too. Before they could be seen by anyone of their own tribe, but now only by those of their own village. When they go farther, they wear the *burqa* unknown in the old

days . . . Before we did not know the world, but we went forth serving in the army and we saw other countries. Now we have civilisation; (we do) what the *Koran* orders.[28]

Investment

Once families attained their 'targeted' consumption, they looked round for investments which would maintain their standard of living in the future; and the volume of surplus savings slopping round the *doab* was large enough to produce fierce competition for the limited number of viable investment opportunities open to the peasantry. Land was far and away the most attractive outlet for the soldiers' savings. Prices were so high that rents represented a pathetic return on the capital invested; no tenant could afford to pay an 'economic' rent. The profits of 'capitalist' farming—of employing labourers to raise crops for sale—were even lower. But land was safe. Despite occasional hiccups, it never really lost its value; and in the long term the gains from capital appreciation were immense. Prices fell during the depression and again after the Second World War, but in each case they fell from record levels, and the losses were soon recouped. Peasants who bought land in Rawalpindi in 1900 could have sold it for five times as much in 1940, or ten times as much in 1945; and the general level of prices in 1940, given the depression, was not so much higher than it had been 40 years earlier. Moreover, land enhanced the self-sufficiency of the family; one of the greatest peasant 'goods'. Families which outgrew their ancestral holdings acquired additional fields because they wanted to feed every member of the household from the produce of the family's labour on the family farm.

The most obvious way to acquire additional land was to redeem outstanding mortgages with possession, which is one reason why the repayment of old debts looms so large in all the surveys of soldiers' savings. The next step was to become mortgagees themselves. Between 1900 and 1940 competition from peasant moneylenders drove professional creditors—Hindus belonging to the commercial castes—out of the rural mortgage market. As long as they got the use of additional land, 'agriculturist moneylenders' were prepared to lend larger sums on easier terms than *sahukars*, because they were comparatively indifferent to the financial returns on their investment. The factors which dictated the *sahukars'* willingness to invest in land—rent levels and the profits of farming—were irrelevant to a set of mortgagees who were only interested in self-cultivation. Outside the belts of suburban market-gardening and the handful of high-farming zones, neither rents nor profits were high enough to attract most *sahukars*; they had better things to do with their hard-worked capital. As a result, agriculturist moneylenders held five-sevenths of the mortgages with possession in Jhelum in 1940; and the amount peasants borrowed from *sahukars* fell by 75 per cent in the course of a single settlement. For the first time in recorded history, the Muslim peasants of the western Punjab were meeting their own borrowing requirements.

The pattern of purchases underwent a similar transformation. Families in receipt of pay and pensions were prepared to pay such high prices for small plots in their natal villages that non-agriculturists were driven out of the land market. In the nineteenth-century the accumulation of Muslim land in Hindu hands worried British paternalists. They had nothing to worry about in the twentieth-century *doab*. Between 1900 and 1940 net sales by peasants to non-peasants came to less than one per cent of the cultivated area of Jhelum, and in the most heavily-recruited tracts the tide of alienations was completely reversed. 'Every village', a settlement officer reported,

> had its own price depending on the presence . . . or absence . . . of a number of landhungry pensioners . . . who knew of no other form of investment.[29]

Such descriptions conjure up visions of land-grabbing native officers engrossing entire villages and reducing their neighbours to the level of landless labourers. But before some theory of 'de-peasantisation' rears its inherently implausible head, there are three inconvenient sets of facts to be disposed of. In the first place, the areas under mortgage was small and diminishing. Peasants were redeeming mortgages faster than they were taking them out, and aggregate indebtedness was falling in real terms. At the outbreak of the Second World War less than 6 per cent of Rawalpindi and less than 7 per cent of Jhelum were subject to mortgages with possession: the lowest proportions in the Punjab. The shift in unsecured debt was in the same direction. Three years after partition, a survey of

19,000 households showed that the average debt per indebted family was lower in Jhelum than in any other district of the Pakistani Punjab: Rs. 271, compared with Rs. 575 in Muzaffagarh, a district further down the *doab* which had no tradition of enlistment.[30]

The position as regards sales is even clearer. A special inquiry into all the purchases of land by larger owners between 1922 and 1927 concluded that there was 'no sign whatever of larger owners swallowing up the smaller men', and settlement officers repeatedly stated that many—perhaps most—purchases were made by comparatively poor families: families which sent their surplus sons into the army because they had too little land to employ or feed them. There are even indications that sharecroppers and landless low-caste menials broke into the land market for the first time after the normal restrictions on recruitment were relaxed in their favour during the world wars. The corollary of these gains was the loss of land by larger owners belonging to the old locally-dominant tribes. In Attock it was 'usual to find the property of the larger landowner who is a drunkard or a gambler bought up by numerous small *zemindars* or even tenants', and a survey of big owners in the most heavily-indebted tehsil in Jhelum showed that thay were just as likely to sell or mortgage their land as smaller men. 'Men who owned over 100 acres', a settlement officer wrote, 'have sold practically everything to pay off their debts. Frequently purchasers have been tenants . . . who have . . . been in service.'[31] The data on *doab*-wide alienations confirms this local evidence; there was a steady drift of land, by way of sales and usufructuary mortgages, from high-ranking landlord tribes such as the Gakhars and the Janjuas to middle-ranking cultivator tribes like the Gujars and the Jats.[32]

It is true that the net gains by lower-ranking tribes were not particularly large; they only affected a minute proportion of the total cultivated area. But the slow rate of alienation is one of the greatest knock-down arguments against de-peasantisation. Despite a five-fold increase in prices, it took 40 years for one-sixth of Jhelum to change hands; and sales were least extensive in the circles with most military service. Pay and pensions did nothing to *force* reluctant peasants to part with their land; on the contrary, military incomes *prevented* sales by bridging the gap between a family's needs and the profits of its farm. As settlement officers were wont to point out, the combination of low (and falling) sales with high (and rising) prices 'might naturally be expected in a really prosperous district', because there were always 'far more people willing to buy land than . . . owners willing to sell'.[33] It was only in two sorts of tract that peasants seem to have parted with their land without putting up much of a struggle to retain it: in the areas where farming was most and least profitable. In the high-farming zones—the areas with the most fertile soils, assured supplies of water and good access to markets—the whole economy was so completely commercialised that land was bought and sold 'like any other commodity'. At the other end of the spectrum—in the most barren, arid and inaccessible areas—peasants were prepared to abandon their dwarf holdings for work which gave them a higher return on their labour.[34]

The final and perhaps the most conclusive evidence of the survival of a viable middle peasantry is the persistence of an egalitarian pattern of landownership, right up to the end of the British period. Altogether, three surveys of landownership were conducted between 1924 and 1939; two by the Board of Economic Inquiry, one by the Land Revenue Committee. All three arrived at virtually identical conclusions. In the Punjab as a whole larger owners paid two-thirds of the land revenue in 1938; in Rawalpindi and Jhelum only one-quarter of the revenue was paid by owners paying over Rs. 20 a year. The following year, small men with less than 15 acres owned three-quarters of Rawalpindi and two-thirds of Jhelum; in the Punjab as a whole they only owned one-third of the cultivated area. The limited areas cultivated by tenants and the derisory number of agricultural labourers reflect this fundamentally egalitarian pattern of landownership. In 1931, tenants at will cultivated only one-quarter of Rawalpindi and two-fifths of Jhelum: the lowest and one of the lowest proportions in the Punjab. In the same year, if the census classification of occupation is to be believed, there was only one agricultural labourer ('principal occupation') in 50 male adults in Rawalpindi, and only one agricultural labourer in 130 male adults in Jhelum.[35]

Next to land, housing was probably the most popular investment. Soldiers who had lived in 'lines' came home with new standards of comfort, and their families put up brick and stucco houses with pillared verandahs, low-walled courtyards, well-lit rooms and proper chimneys, in place of the traditional 'dungeon–like hovels: part of the great rebuilding of the rural Punjab which makes it difficult to find really old houses in many villages.[36] In one of the Salt Range settlements Darling visited during the depression, a third of the houses had been rebuilt since the First World War. They were

> all built of stone, and in some cases of stone so well dressed, evenly laid, and firmly mortared that it would be difficult to find better masonry work anywhere: all done, too, by local masons. Moreover, in marked contrast to the schools provided by the District Board, some of the houses were beautifully proportioned, and their smooth-plastered doorways pleasantly decorated with floral designs, as in Austria. There could be no doubt that the village had a sense of beauty and the craftsmen of the neighbourhood, whether mason or carpenter, a sense of finish. The deodar beams of the new raftered ceilings were well planed and accurately laid; and the cement floors, actually made by the women, left me wondering that in a remote village of the Salt Range one should find better floors than in an ordinary Punjab bungalow, and so spotless, even in the dark inner rooms, that it seemed a crime to tread on them booted.[37]

There were definite limits to the investment of pay anc pensions in cultivation, as distinct from the purchase of land as long as labour was comparatively cheap and crop price were comparatively low. There was no point in spending larg sums of money on labour-saving or output-maximising inno vations when the labour saved or the output gained failed t repay the necessary expenditure. The main contribution of th army was, therefore, to change the parameters within whic cultivators worked, by driving up wage-rates and inflating th price of foodstuffs. But pay and pensions did prime the pum of agricultural improvement by supplying cheap capital for th few 'lumpy' investments which were profitable. Milita families could afford to be 'best-practice' farmers; they had th money to spend on masonry wells and superior bullocks. The could also afford to experiment. Darling found native office who had served in France and Palestine putting into practi lessons they had learnt from Norman peasants and Jewi kibbutzin. Tractors made a particularly deep impression them: 'Let us have those machines here', an ex-prisoner- war said. The same men, or the same kind of men, acted links between the Department of Agriculture's demonstration workers and the rest of the villagers when the department first distributed improved grains or recommended improved practices. Outside the belts of market-gardening, ex-soldiers tended to be the first to sow improved wheat or raise a plot of vegetables or keep chickens.[38]

Peasant Enterprise: The Response to the Military Market

One can never be certain which came first: the enterprise or the army. The shrewder families undoubtedly saw how complementary cultivation and enlistment could be, and treated them as two halves of the same unitary business. They sent a son or two into the army to raise the cash which was necessary to develop the family holding, and they kept a son or two behind to work the farm and feed the soldiers' dependants. This neat division of functions had advantages all round, until the presiding patriarch lost his grip and the extended family dissolved among mutual recriminations.

The peasants who stayed at home to make what they could out of the burgeoning cantonments were almost as dependent on military expenditure as the recruits who went away. Settlement officers got into the habit of describing the economies of tehsils as revolving round the cantonments in their midst. The whole life of Rawalpindi tehsil supposedly centred on the army's creation, the biggest city between Lahore and Teheran:

> The great arsenal, the railway workshops, the commissariat supply stores and the city factories all draw their labour from the villages around Rawalpindi. The roads and railways (serving the army) demand constant labour. Eggs, milk, wood and above all, fodder, find a ready and profitable sale. The camping grounds are nearly always full of troops and the villages far from Rawalpindi can sell their fodder nearer home—fodder comes in very long distances from all over the tehsil. *Telis* spend (their) whole time in grass-cutting for officers in the cantonments and military grass farms . . . employ thousands cutting and storing grass. The increase in the number of carts since settlement is very high. The principal carting traffic is with Kashmir, but all round the cantonment, and in the season on the Murree road, the Rawalpindi carts ply for hire. The whole of the Kashmir road with its seething mass of cart and horse traffic is one huge markt for fodder, grain and miscellaneous supplies . . . All along the . . . road in the Murree tehsil . . . a multitude

> of small shops, *akka* stands, camping grounds and sometimes bazaars (have sprung) up. There are several villages in which the income from shop sites greatly exceeds the land revenue—there is one village in which the income exceeds the present land value a hundred times.[39]

A small hill station dominated by a large military sanatorium had just as great an impact on tribes like the Dhunds, who 'lived on the cantonment and civil station':

> Murree is the only market. All roads lead to Murree and *zemindars* carry their produce in for sale. The foodgrains produced in the hills are little sold, as few households produce more than they can eat, and the maize and rice grown in the hills are not much in demand . . . in the purely artificial and foreign bazaar. (But the station absorbs huge quantities of) fodder, potatoes and other vegetables, wood, sheep, goats and cattle, milk, eggs, fowls and all the hill fruits, walnuts, pears, peaches (and grapes . . . The *zemindars* also) keep carts, hire out bullocks, sell . . . wood, which is generally stolen, (and) do some day labour, but not a great deal . . . Keeping ponies for hire is a very profitable (side-line) in some of the worst villages. Others have more disreputable sources of income in connection with cantonments.[40]

When the cantonments really took off at the time of the second Afghan war there was plenty of scope for the intensification of agriculture over much of the *doab*, at least in the level plains. Despite mounting population pressure, pockets of low farming survived into the twentieth century. In four villages north of Rawalpindi, an Edwardian settlement officer discovered

> weeds and grass (springing) up . . . with a rankness unknown elsewhere . . . No hard weeding is ever done and the grasses choke the thinner crops. Weeding with the plough is done to all the important crops (but) in the wheat fields the ploughs are seen struggling among thriving weeds (and) everywhere the appearance of the fields is most slovenly. Little real ploughing is done: it is thought enough to merely break up the land for the seed. No irrigation beds are made, but the water is turned into the fields to run all over them with the result that some parts of the field get too much water and some parts too little, while manure is not seldom washed right out of the soil. Probably

> with half the water-supply and organied management the yields would be better . . . but the people are satisfied.[41]

Some forms of intensification—the continuous encroachment of the arable on the pasture and the waste, for instance—would have gone ahead in any case, as a result of population growth. But it is noticeable that the great expansion of the cultivated area in the tehsil with the largest cantonment occurred in a period in which the urban population was increasing by leaps and bounds, while the rural population was almost static. Between 1881 and 1901 the rural population of Rawalpindi tehsil rose by less than 10 per cent, while the population of the city went up by 66 per cent, from 53,000 to 88,000—and the growth of the city is really understated by taking 1881 as a baseline. Between the wars the cultivated area actually contracted a little, although the population went on growing, thanks to the expansion of alternative employment opportunities and the collapse of crop prices. The obvious implication is that the construction of the cantonments pushed cultivation to its somewhat elastic limits rather faster than population growth alone would have done.[42]

Other kinds of intensification were clearly aimed at the cantonment market. Fodder, for example, would never have been produced in such large quantities for the villages alone. The cavalry regiments, the officers' mounts, and the pack and draught animals belonging to the supply corps all had an insatiable appetite for hay, straw and pulses. Hay-making helped smooth out the labour-intensive peaks of the agricultural calendar in the hills; drought-resistant 'inferior foodgrains' such as *bajra* and *jowar* became a profitable alternative to less secure crops like maize, because they produced so much straw; and cultivators gradually discovered that the high fodder content of *moth* and *mash* made it worth their while to slot fertility-restoring pulses into otherwise exhausting rotations.[43]

There was one drawback to growing fodder. It was an easy thing to produce; it could be grown on poor soils with an unreliable water supply and very little labour. But the returns per acre were not particularly high; it was no solution for the problems of the large family on a tiny holding. Vegetables, fruit and tobacco were such a solution, at least in the areas suited to their production. The returns per acre in the market-gardening zones within easy reach of the cantonments were fabulous. The Pothwar plain which lay around Rawalpindi was one such area. As the city grew, *malliars* (members of gardening castes) working in conjunction with local *khatris* (members of the richest Sikh commercial caste) developed well-irrigation to an unprecedented pitch. Wells were sunk as if they were to last for ever, with cylinders of carefully-cut and mortared stones, masonry channels running through the fields, and proper sluices. Manure was applied with such intensity as to revolutionise the conservancy arrangements of the towns. Night-soil, instead of being a nuisance, became a highly-prized commodity sold in a fiercely competitive market; and all round the city regular applications turned patches of excessively sandy soils into the richest loams. But the most striking feature of *malliar*-farming was neither the input of water nor the input of manure; it was the input of labour. The market-gardeners lavished skill and effort on the ordinary operations of husbandry. They gave their crops more ploughings, more waterings, more weedings; they practised seed selection and experimented with new varieties; and as the military market grew, other castes in other areas emulated their best-practice farming.[44] The potato growers of Murree were a case in point. As the most lucrative crop in the tehsil, potatoes received

> more attention than any other crop. The land always lies fallow for the previous harvest and is carefully scraped and levelled before the crop is sown. Manure is nearly always . . . used. All the work is done by hand. The seed-trenches are made and the ridges built up by hand and the plants are carefully weeded. The English variety needs more cultivation, but bulks larger and ripens earlier. The price of potatoes changes with the season and great profit awaits the *zemindar* who can get his early potatoes to market before his neighbours. . . . Labour is generally employed to help with the sowing and weeding and this is paid for in cash. Except where the fields are close to the village site, they have to be watched day and night to keep pigs out.[45]

Pastoral farming was also promoted by the demand for draught animals and dairy produce generated by the cantonments. The growth of carting and the spread of well-irrigation drove up the price of bullocks, while the urban milk market made milch cattle more profitable. But the quality of the *doab*'s famous breed of Jatli cattle declined as the area of grazing contracted, and the milk yields of the hill cows was particularly low. By the turn of the century the shortfall in the milk supply was made good in suburban dairies, which stall-fed selected cows.[46] The same inexorable contraction of the pasture undermined the reputation of the *doab*'s horses. Fewer and fewer *zemindars* were prepared to raise animals which were costly to feed, required a great deal of looking after, and had to be kept for a long time before they could be sold. The army, conscious of its increasing dependence on imported Australian 'walers', did its best to encourage breeding. An army remount department was set up to centralise purchases; specifications were standardised; prices were stabilised; and horse fairs were organised at which large prizes were given away. The veterinary department even offered the services of government stallions free. But the real impact of the army's improvement programme was felt outside the *doab*, in the lower Jhelum canal colony, where tens of thousands of acres were distributed among peasant colonists on condition that they kept a branded mare and bred from it.[47]

Pack animals were a different matter. Given the unsuitability of cavalry in the hills and the sheer inaccessibility of so much tribal territory, frontier expeditions tended to be fought by long columns of infantry supported by even longer columns of baggage-laden mules. Mule-breeding, like horse-breeding, was actively promoted by the army; and unlike horse-breeding, it actually took off. It was so profitable that small groups of *khatri* traders who already used mules to carry their wares around the hills monopolised the contracts for carriage whenever expeditions set out. The secret of their monopoly was scarcity: donkeys and camels, rather than mules, were the traditional carriers of the *doab*—and they were still the main carriers over wide areas when the British left. Donkeys were democratic beasts. They were bred by small cultivators because they could be relied on to forage for themselves, needed very little attention, and could be sold young. Small traders also liked them, because they were cheap and sure-footed. Camels were aristocrats in comparison. The strings of pack camels which carried grain into the local fort-towns or station-*mandis* in the sandier tracts belonged to big *maliks*. When the army formed a camel corps stationed at Rawalpindi, one would have expected these *maliks* to be drawn into the business of supplying camels to the army; but most of the martial camels seem to have been bought in the really arid zones further down the *doab*, where breeders produced riding camels. It was indirect demand, the trade engendered by the army, rather than direct purchases that drove up the camel population.[48]

Carting was another outlet for peasant enterprise. The build-up of wheeled traffic in the parts of the *doab* which were passable was astonishingly rapid, once the army supplied the necessary roads and bridges. Between 1890 and 1909 the number of carts increased from just over 1,000 to more than 8,000, and a new phenomenon—the small cultivator turned carter-cum-petty trader—was born. There was no question of a small elite of rich peasants or rich traders monopolising the ownership of carts; carrying was a small man's game. It was one of the favourite ways in which peasants with holdings too small to absorb all their family labour worked up some off-farm income; the hill tribes, in particular, went in for carting as a by-employment in the slack season between sowing and harvest. During the summer months hillmen hawked their fruit and vegetables about the bungalows and bazaars of Murree; then, in the autumn, when the European population of the hill stations went back to the plains, they loaded up their carts and took their produce down to Rawalpindi. Direct marketing—direct from cultivator to consumer—was commonplace, and so was part-time trading among the peasantry. Every cart-owner was a prospective speculator in his neighbours' crops; and peasant carriers were just as adept at playing the markets as any *khatri*. Information as to prices was freely available in remote villages; carrier-traders were acutely sensitive to price; and a good deal of shopping-around took place, as they moved from one market to another in search of the best margin. In time, they even came to constitute a market of their own. The mass of bullocks and carriers constantly in transit along the great arterial roads of the *doab*—the Grand Trunk Road and the Kashmir Road are the best examples—consumed enough fodder and foodstuffs to stimulate the economies of all the villages in corridors hundreds of miles long.[49]

The same tribes that plied carts also sold their labour. The hillmen who moved down from their Himalayan villages to the low-lying cantonments at the beginning of the cold weather were just as likely to work as coolies. The public works in the plains—the strategic railways, the military roads, the fortifications—soaked up rural underemployment for miles around. In Jhelum there were the extractive industries: collieries, cement works, quarries and salt-mines. All depended on military patronage to a greater or lesser extent. Some villages 'sent almost all their able-bodied men to the Survey Department each winter' and a sizeable minority ventured even further afield. By the 1920s there were migrants from the upper Sind Sagar *doab* in every country in which the Indian army ever fought, from East Africa to China; and Gujar Khan virtually monopolised the stokeholds of the British steamers sailing out of Bombay. As one deputy commissioner put it, 'the Pothwari dialect can be heard on the lower decks of every P&O boat'. Once the army eased the villager out of his village setting and familiarised him with the notion of travelling long distances in search of 'service', there was no knowing where he would end up.[50]

Urbanisation: The Emergence of Cantonment Towns

It is always difficult to disentangle the contribution which military expenditure makes to the development of a town from all the other sources of urban growth: trade, industry, administration, religion. Fortunately, the only city in the Sind Sagar *doab*—Rawalpindi—was so completely a creation of the Indian army that the role of military expenditure is beyond question: the defence budget dictated the pattern of its growth. At annexation it was nothing special: just another Sikh fort with a bazaar at its gates commanding an important crossroads in the middle of a fertile plain. The army soon changed all that. Once British strategists realised that Rawalpindi was the perfect base for expeditions all along the north-west frontier—far enough along the Grand Trunk Road to be within easy reach of the full range of passes, and far enough in the rear not to be over-run by the first invader—the construction of the biggest cantonment in India was only a matter of time; and the cantonment turned the village of the Rawals into the third largest city in the Punjab, second only to Lahore and Amritsar.[51]

TABLE 1: CANTONMENTS IN THE GREATER PUNJAB: POPULATION 1881-1961

(in thousands: the figures in brackets are the total population of the cities or towns *including* their cantonments)

Cities and Towns	*1881*		*1921*		*1961*	
Dominated by Cantonments:						
Rawalpindi	16	(53)	46	(101)	143	(340)
Ambala	41	(67)	48	(76)	105	(181)
Ferozepur	19	(40)	25	(59)	46	(98)
Nowshera (Peshawar)	5	(13)	17	(28)	22	(44)
Abbottabad (Hazara)	2	(4)	8	(14)	15	(31)
Risalpur (Peshawar)*		N/A	8		11	
Bannu	4	(9)	6	(22)	8	(32)
Campbellpur (Attock)	0	(4)	6	(10)	4	(19)
Affected by Cantonments:						
Lahore	18	(149)	25	(282)	68	(1296)
Peshawar	21	(80)	25	(104)	47	(269)
Jullundur	9	(52)	12	(71)	42	(265)
Delhi	3	(170)	7	(240)	36	(2359)
Sialkot	12	(46)	15	(71)	20	(164)
Multan	10	(69)	12	(85)	18	(358)
Kohat	5	(18)	9	(28)	14	(50)
Jhelum	4	(21)	4	(18)	11	(53)
Mardan	2	(3)	3	(11)	5	(78)
Dera Ismail Khan	3	(22)	5	(39)	2	(46)
Cantonments in the Hills						
Dagshai, Kasauli, Jutagh, Sabathu (Simla)*	10		7		11	
	1	(2)	1	(3)	7	(13)
Bakloh, Balun (Gurdaspur)*	2		4			N/A
Dharmsala (Kangra)	1	(5)	2	(5)		N/A
Cherat (Peshawar)*	0		0		2	
Murree (Rawalpindi)	1	(2)	1	(3)	1	(4)
Post-Independence Cantonments						
Sargodha (Shahpur)					46	(124)
Wah (Attock)					37	(41)
Kharian (Gujrat)					12	(19)

*Pure cantonments: no towns attached.

Definitions:

'Dominated by Cantonments': Half or almost half of the total population of the city or town lived in the cantonment in 1921.

'Affected by Cantonments': Either a quarter of the total population of the city or town lived in the cantonment in 1921, *or* the cantonment contained at least 5,000 people.

Omissions: Very small cantonments (e.g. Attock Fort); cantonments which were too small relative to their 'host' cities to exercise much influence on them (e.g. Amritsar); and cantonments which were abandoned before the First World War (e.g. Dera Gazi Khan).

Sources: Punjab Census Report, 1921, Part II Table IV; NWFP Census Report, 1921, Table IV; West Pakistan Census Report 1961, Vol. 3, Tables 6 and 6A; India Census Report 1961, Vol. I, Part II-A(1), Table A-IV.

What happened to Rawalpindi was repeated, on a smaller scale, all over the Punjab. The nine largest cities all had cantonments, and two of them were as dependent on military expenditure as Rawalpindi. In the upper Sind Sagar *doab* the cantonment town was virtually the dominant urban type. Take away Jhelum, Campbellpur, Murree, Attock and Rawalpindi and there was precious little left. The old fort towns were generally in decay, with their military *raison d'être* gone. If they could capture a tehsil headquarters, like Tallagang and Pindigheb, the old strongholds of the Awans and the Janjuas, the influx of officials breathed a little life into them; and if they could carve out a share of some growing trade, as Pind Dadan Khan annexed the salt trade and Gujar Khan became a noted wheat market, they rode high for a time. But the general effect of the construction of the railway network was to decentralise trade. In the areas which were fertile enough to generate a substantial agricultural surplus, relatively obscure railway stations served as collecting-points for major commodity markets in distant cities such as Amritsar or Bombay; while a mosaic of rural *mandis*, really only overgrown villages situated in 'central places', mopped up the soldiers' remittances and the entrepreneurs' profits by distributing imported foodstuffs throughout the deficit zones and manufactures throughout the upper *doab*.

The railway stations and the rural *mandis* were free from octroi and market changes; that was one of their advantages over the towns. But their greatest asset was their proximity to producers and consumers alike. In a region in which the cost of transport by pack animals doubled the price of grain every few miles, the pressure to get crops into a railway wagon at the closest possible point was very strong. At the same time, the immobility of the average customer forced traders to bring imported goods to the peasants' doors. As a result, the commercial class was sucked down into the remotest villages; and the tiny scale on which their peasant-clients bought and sold set limits to the scale on which the vast majority of the *bania*-castes could operate. This 'dispersal of the traders' distorted the normal hierarchy of markets. The base of the pyramid was distended by a multiplicity of village-level transactions, and there was no export-crop boom to overcome this centrifugal tendency. There was only a perpetual haemorrhage from below, which left the cantonment-town to set the pace of urban growth.[52]

The Aldershot of the East

At first sight, the new cantonment town looks suspiciously like the old fort town writ large. They both, after all, performed much the same military functions. But cities like Rawalpindi were more than mere reversions to some atavistic Indian type; they were distinctively modern. They were alien artefacts, designed to meet the needs of an alien elite; and the larger the proportion of expatriates in their population, the more exotic the result. Europeans in Rawalpindi had numbers on their side, as well as political dominance. In 1921, with 5,700 Britons, Rawalpindi had the largest European community in the Punjab: in fact it had one of the largest European communities in the subcontinent, and the entire city was built to meet their requirements. In Rawalpindi, Anglo-Indians started out from scratch. In other cities—Lahore or Delhi, say—the cantonments were afterthoughts added onto Moghal city-centres; in Rawalpindi the cantonments *were* the city, and the great urban axis—the four mile stretch of the Grand Trunk Road converted into the inevitable mall—ran straight through them. There were no old buildings to dominate the townscape: no Red Fort, no Golden Temple. The fort built by the Thepuria governors was swept away soon after annexation; the *gurudwara* was rebuilt. Visitors supposed that they were entering a completely modern city, and in every important regard they were right. The building-styles and the town planning were consistently late-Victorian. Not even the new towns in the canal colonies could match the purity of Rawalpindi's 'public works functional' style, because only a small proportion of their buildings were designed by official architects; and no city in the Punjab had such automatic recourse to the 'Anglo-Saracenic' when it put up public edifices in need of *appliqué* decoration. There was no real

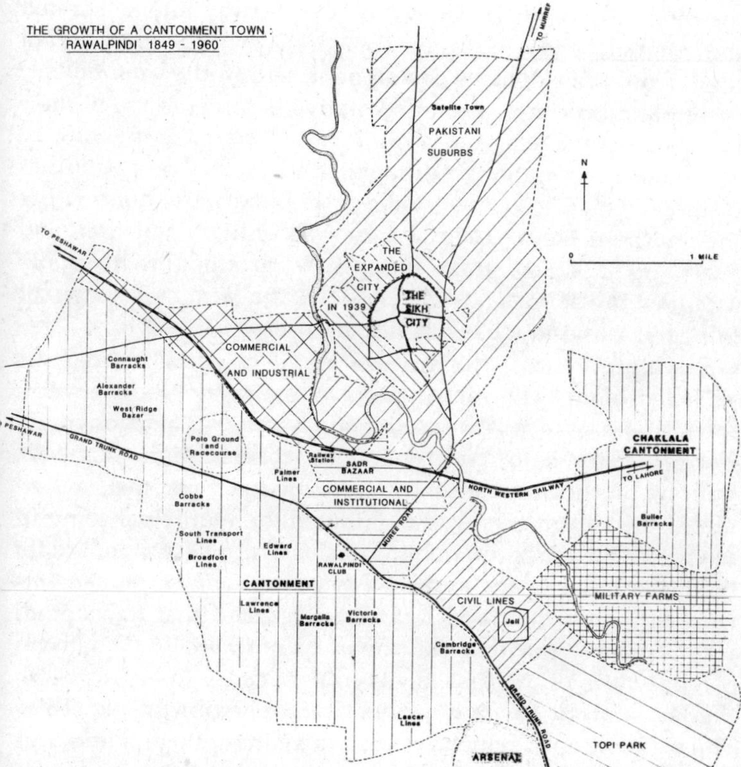
THE GROWTH OF A CANTONMENT TOWN:
RAWALPINDI 1849 - 1960
TO MURREE
Satellite Town
PAKISTANI
SUBURBS
N
0
1 MILE
TO PESHAWAR
THE
EXPANDED
CITY
IN 1939
THE
SIKH
CITY
COMMERCIAL
AND INDUSTRIAL
Connaught
Barracks
Alexander
Barracks
West Ridge
Bazar
PESHAWAR
GRAND TRUNK ROAD
Polo Ground
and
Racecourse
Railway
Station
SADR
BAZAAR
COMMERCIAL AND
INSTITUTIONAL
NORTH WESTERN RAILWAY
CHAKLALA
CANTONMENT
TO LAHORE
Palmer
Lines
Cobbe
Barracks
South Transport
Lines
Broadfoot
Lines
Edward
Lines
MUREE ROAD
RAWALPINDI
CLUB
Buller
Barracks
CANTONMENT
MILITARY FARMS
CIVIL LINES
Jail
Lawrence
Lines
Margalla
Barracks
Victoria
Barracks
Cambridge
Barracks
GRAND TRUNK ROAD
Lascar
Lines
ARSENAL
TOPI PARK
TO LAHORE

vernacular tradition, not even in the dependent native quarter. The layout of the city was cast in the same late nineteenth-century mould as its architecture. The basic principle of segregating different races and different classes was applied to Rawalpindi with a mathematical precision and lucidity. The river, reinforced by the railway line, separated the comparatively (but only comparatively) crowded Indian town from the extensive cantonment; within the cantonment, systematic 'zoning' separated native regiments from their European compeers; and within those two categories, every rank had its scrupulously differentiated place. Every building, from the gigantic arsenal to the rows of barracks dominating the southern half of the town, had its military function; and every open space, from the parade grounds to the polo ground, proclaimed its purpose in the army's scheme of things: it was a city that was singularly easy to 'read'.[53]

Rawalpindi was modern in other respects besides its physical plant. The municipality was a model local government in a province where self-government was a synonym for incompetence and corruption. In collaboration with the military authorities who had jurisdiction over the cantonment, the contractors who dominated the municipal committee provided a range of public utilities which set a standard for the other cities of the Punjab. The conservancy arrangements were efficient: the district gazetteer boasted that Rawalpindi was 'probably the cleanest (town) in northern India'. It was certainly one of the first towns in the Punjab to be lit by gas; the Rawalpindi gas-works came into operation in the 1860s. The water supply, which arrived via a nine-mile pipeline, was copious and unpolluted; the mission hospitals saved lives instead of squandering them; the schools got their 4,000-odd pupils through examinations; and the 60-acre public park (subsequently the 'Ayub National Park') was a *tour de force* of herbaceous borders. The inhabitants, also, were qualitatively different. The Indians, not just the expatriates, were distinctively modern—more literate, more mobile, and better housed. Rawalpindi had a significantly higher literacy rate than any other city in the north-western Punjab, and in 1921 the surrounding district was the most literate in the province, bar the wholly exceptional Simla. Clearly, the army's schooling rubbed off. The civilian education department could set up village schools until its budget allocations were exhausted, but it could never do what the army regularly did: give peasants in the principal recruiting-grounds the strongest possible incentive to become literate and numerate, by making promotion conditional on passing educational tests. Again the population of Rawalpindi, even after discounting the soldiers, was significantly more mobile than the inhabitants of any other city in the Punjab. Between the wars about two-thirds of Rawalpindi's residents consisted of immigrants, compared with one-fifth of Amritsar's; and five-sixths of the immigrants of 1921 came from outside the district: they were long-distance, not local, migrants. In many ways, Rawalpindi had the cosmopolitan population of a capital city long before it became the temporary capital of Pakistan. All it lacked was the high culture and the slums. If there was no university, there were few tenements either. A building survey of the three biggest cities in the Punjab in 1921 showed that there were only 305 buildings in Rawalpindi with more than five occupants per inhabited room (the standard measure of overcrowding), compared with 5,700 in Lahore.[54]

The Cantonment in the Sky

Every hill station in India benefited from military patronage, whether it had a cantonment or not. From the Himalayas to the Nilgiris, army officers spent short leaves or long retirements in the hills, and officers' wives endured cruel separations from their husbands in the plains. But most hill stations had other strings to their bows. As resorts, their clientele was co-extensive with expatriate society. Socialites hurled themselves into the summer season; dedicated *shikaris* fished passable imitations of Scottish trout streams or stalked poor substitutes for Scottish deer; while 'lovers of the picturesque' (as Murray's *Handbook* termed them) drank in the glorious scenery. In tea and coffee-growing tracts, the Darjeelings and the Ootacamunds were overrun by lonely planters bent on ruining their livers; in *zamindari* areas westernised landlords went to the hills to mingle with the ruling race. As workplaces, also, the hill stations developed a surprising variety of functions. Small armies of government servants invaded the summer capitals; missionaries working on the premise that high altitudes brought them closer to God turned towns like Ranchi into major religious centres; doctors and nurses treated convalescents, especially consumptives, in rough approximations to alpine sanitoria; and boarding schools taught underprivileged adolescents how to play compulsory games right through the hot weather, without exceeding the socially-permissible death rate.

Murree either failed to attract this range of patrons, or only attracted them in martial guise. The social life was humdrum compared to Simla, which monopolised visiting celebrities; the *shikar* was commonplace; and even if the distant views of the Himalayas were sublime, the immediate setting 'lacked interest'. There were no plantations within a hundred miles, and very few westernised landlords. The Government of the Punjab transferred its summer capital to Simla in 1875; religious institutions were restricted to the usual complement of churches; only a handful of civilian patients were treated in the local hospitals; and no one who was anyone sent their children to school in Murree. Yet the town survived, and went on multiplying its resident population ten times over each spring. The club gave the game away. The club at Murree was an 'annexe' of the club at Rawalpindi. In effect, the whole town was an extension of Rawalpindi; it was the Indian army at rest and play. The military road to Kashmir made Murree the most accessible of all the Punjab hill stations, and the largest concentration of British troops outside the British Isles was just 38 miles away. In the 1880s the journey from Rawalpindi by 'government hill cart' took less than five hours; travellers who were prepared to pay a little more for the 'express' (Rs. 16 instead of Rs. 10) could get there even faster (the express put on three horses to gallop up 'steep ascents', scattering strings of carts before it); and once the Punjab Motor Company started its regular taxi service in 1907—an astonishingly early date—there was nothing to stop 6,000-odd expatriates popping up to the hills for the day.

Murree's dependence on military expenditure was written into its fabric. Every road leading to it was a strategic road, built or improved by the army; every approach to the town passed through camps and cantonments; the biggest buildings were the barracks; the great sanitorium was reserved for soldiers and the only school marked on Bartholomew's map—the Lawrence School—concentrated on educating the sons of British 'other ranks'. The one large-scale industry, Dyers' brewery, sold the great bulk of its output to the troops; the

European shopping centre was full of shopkeepers from Rawalpindi who followed their customers to the hills; the native lines pullulated with regimental camp-followers; and the houses clinging to the sides of the 'Ridge' were generally let to officers. Murree also passed the crucial social test of an overwhelming military presence. In Rawalpindi district as a whole the ration of European males to European females in the 16-29 age group was seven to one. In Murree it was better, but not much better. It must have been a paradise for women and a standing incentive to 'irregular connections'.[55]

The 'Urban Village'

However rapidly they grew, there was no possibility of the cantonment towns urbanising the entire *doab*. There were too few of them; the gaps between the garrisons were too great. If the peasantry as a whole was to be sucked within the orbit of the city, towns had to develop on new sites in response to the general heightening of demand and the gradual erosion of the cultivator's self-sufficiency. There are signs that this is exactly what was happening, but the evidence is inconclusive, because the new towns in embryo were too small to be caught in the administrator's net. The basic census definition of a town demanded a population of at least 5,000—and in the whole of Rawalpindi district between the wars there was only one settlement which satisfied that requirement: the Aldershot of the East. Put another way, out of the 1,172 settlements in the district in 1931, 1,170 were classified as villages. Categories which are as exclusive or as inclusive as these conceal all the crucial distinctions. In the present instance, they conceal the existence of overgrown villages in the 2,000-5,000 band—there may have been as many as thirty of them—which were developing into embryonic towns at 'central places' all over the *doab*.[56]

These 'urban villages' were a transitional form. They still contained substantial numbers of cultivators and agriculture generated a substantial share of their income. But they fulfilled many of the functions and possessed some of the characteristics of towns. They were commercial centres with extensive hinterlands; they contained unusual concentrations of handicrafts; and they supplied a wide range of services to dozens of smaller settlements. Moreover, the inhabitants of an urban village, like the population of Rawalpindi, differed from their rustic neighbours in distinctly urban ways. They were more heterogeneous and more mobile, as well as better-educated and better-housed. The urban villages even looked different. They stood out from the general run of hamlets because their *abadis*—an *abadi* being the cluster of houses in the middle of each village—covered much wider areas and contained a higher ratio of *pucca* to *kachcha* buildings. But the 'urban' *abadi* was never big enough to burst through the 5,000 barrier and qualify as a town. To do that, it would have had to be *twenty* times the size of the normal hamlet.

The best-researched urban village—best-researched because the Board of Economic Inquiry happened to survey it during the Second World War—was a geographer's dream. Sagri fits all the elementary theories of location. It stood at the junction of three ecological zones—the hills, the ravine-gashed plateau and the fertile plain. The most important line of communication in the *doab*—the North-Western Railway, running parallel to the Grand Trunk Road—passed within sight of the *abadi* exactly halfway between the two most important markets in the district, 18 miles from Rawalpindi and 18 miles from Gujar Khan. As a commercial centre, it supposedly ranked immediately below these two towns. Large quantities of pulses and eggs were exported; but there was no export of foodgrains, because Sagri's hinterland was deficit tract with a moderately high propensity to enlist. It was the imports that mattered. They included—in the words of the Board's report—'everything from luxuries to vital necessaries of life'.

> Groceries (come) from Rawalpindi, tobacco from Mardan (112 miles away), hardware, hand fans, strings, leather and colts from Gujar Khan. Wheat, maize and *taramira* seeds are brought in from Lahore (163 miles), Sargodha (the capital of the nearest canal colony), and various places in the United Provinces (up to 600 miles). Cloth and hosiery are imported from Amritsar (almost 200 miles) and Gujar Khan; rice, tea and sugar from Sialkot, Gujranwala and Nazirabad (all between 110 and 120 miles away); and timber from Jhelum.[57]

There was no way that the population of Sagri could hav consumed the volume of goods pouring into the village, an more than they could have supported the *121* shops throug which they were distributed. There were 24 grocers, mainly selling foodstuffs; 10 haberdashers, mainly selling cloth; 6 'chemists' selling indigenous medicines; 6 butchers; 6 shoe shops; 6 jewellers; 5 tobacconists; 4 greengrocers; and so on, and so forth. All told, there was one shop for every six adults.[58]

Sagri's artisans were just as dependent on outside patronage as the local shopkeepers. There were 26 weavers, 20 carpenters, 15 families of potters, 14 shoemakers and 10 tailors; all following their traditional trades. There were also 15 carriers plying camels and donkeys between the *abadi* and the railway station; two crop-processing industries—flour-milling and oil extraction—brought into existence by the internal combustion engine; and a host of more specialised crafts, ranging from cloth-printing to cycle-repairing. The service sector, considering Sagri's size, was probably the most blatantly over-extended of all. The four schools drew their 900 pupils from a catchment area containing at least 20 villages; the population of Sagri must have gone up by one-third during school hours. The usual assortment of mosques and temples drew worshippers, especially non-Muslims, from a cluster of adjacent villages; the six *hakims* and the government dispensary treated patients within a few hours' walk; and the moneylenders did most of their business beyond Sagri's boundaries, as long as there was any business to be done. The net result of this expansion of the three 'urban' sectors of the village economy was a drastic reduction in Sagri's dependence on agriculture. Only 15 per cent of the population were wholly dependent on agriculture; half the population took no part in cultivation at all; and there were no signs that this drift from the land was ever likely to be redressed. There was no possibility of expanding the cultivated area—'even the courtyards . . . (were) sown'—and there were no gains in productivity to be made. Wells were unprofitable; the higher-yielding varieties distributed by the Department of Agriculture were unsuited to local conditions; and improved implements were unknown.[59]

Sagri's caste composition was as complicated as that of a small town. In origin it was a perfectly straightforward village, founded and owned by a single caste of Muslim Rajputs. On the eve of partition, when the Hindus and Sikhs who made up 28 per cent of the population fled to India, 35 of the 47 castes found in Rawalpindi district were represented in Sagri. The locally-dominant Muslim Rajputs were still the most numerous caste and still owned the great bulk of the land; but an astonishing influx of artisan and commercial castes had reduced them to a small minority (27 per cent) of the population. The most numerous artisan castes were the carpenters, weavers and potters; the most numerous commercial castes were the Muslim Sheikhs and the Sikh Sahnis. In total they easily outnumbered the Rajputs. But one of the most interesting aspects of Sagri's demographic history is the number of castes (18: just over half the total) which were only represented by a single family (11 instances) or three families at the most. It was this tail of thinly-represented specialists which made it possible for the urban village to provide an urban range of skills and services.[60]

Many members of the artisan and service castes were comparatively recent immigrants, in the approved small town way; and many of their children must have left the village. The artisans exported skills to major growth points like Rawalpindi, while the traders pumped their offspring into the professions via higher education. Half the Rajputs—the caste whose landholdings tied them to the village—were in receipt of income from military service; and service families were significantly more literate, as well as significantly more mobile, than pure cultivators. The commercial castes—more especially the Sikhs—were even keener on collecting qualifications; they set up two of the three private schools and pioneered female education. As a result of their efforts, there were 43 matriculates and 11 graduates in the village. More surprising still, there were two female graduates: a phenomenon virtually unknown in the rural fastness of the western Punjab in 1944.[61]

The same classes that raised Sagri's educational standards raised the standard of its housing also:

> The half of the inhabited site occupied by the commercial community (consists of) houses made of kiln-baked bricks (and well-paved) lanes with . . . good drainage. They have engaged a regular sweeper who is responsible for (the) sanitation of that part of the village. The other half, which is dominated by *zemindars* and menials, comprises houses of mud (with dirty uneven lanes and no) regular drainage system.[62]

The division of the *abadi* into two sections reflected the dualism of Sagri's economy. A traditional sector operating on customary lines was overlaid by a modern sector operating on market principles. There was a group of artisans attached to the families of cultivators in the time-honoured way. As hereditary *kamins*, they rendered customary services or supplied customary goods in return for a share of the harvest, paid in kind. At the same time, other members of the same castes were selling *ad hoc* services and goods to clients from surrounding villages, who invariably paid them in cash. One suspects that the division between the two sectors was more analytic than real; that *kamins* who found they could do better in the 'free market' went in for moonlighting or deserted their *jajmans* altogether. The breakdown of the traditional relationships between the cultivators and the shopkeeper–moneylenders was much more complete. There was no question of cultivators in Sagri keeping running accounts with shopkeepers–moneylenders, borrowing goods—even foodstuffs—during the slack season, and letting their creditors remove their crops from the threshing floor at harvest. Because of the influx of remittances, the Rajputs preferred to pay cash for everything they bought, and sold their crops at rates determined by supply and demand in distant markets. At most, they let debts pile up for a few weeks until the next remittance arrived. As sellers, there was no question of their indebtedness compelling them to part with their produce at depressed prices. The burden of debt was light, and wartime inflation made it lighter still. Moreover, 55 per cent of their unsecured debt was owed to relatives or friends. 'The moneylending class whether *zemindar* or non-*zemindar* (had) ceased to operate because of the Golden Laws passed by the Unionist Government' (which made it virtually impossible to recover debts from peasant defaulters).[63] The outcome of the cultivators' newfound solvency was something much closer to a perfect market for agricultural produce than one would expect to find in the normal hamlet:

> (Neither the seller nor the buyer) exercise any influence in fixing the price. The *mandi* of Gujar Khan is the only deciding factor. . . . Whether the grower sells his . . . produce to his family shopkeeper or to anyone else, cash is always paid on the spot. No instance was noticed where a grower sold to his

creditor at a rate lower than the prevailing village rates of the day.[64]

Clearly, the 'market' for labour and goods in Sagri was capable of operating with all the impersonality of a great city—and in that sense the quality of the inhabitants' relationships was distinctively urban.

The Improvement of Communications

To some extent the cantonment towns were a function of the improvement of communications. The Sikh army, outside Lahore, tended to be decentralised and peripatetic. A large number of small garrisons occupied strongpoints scattered all over the alien provinces Ranjit Singh incorporated in his empire, and much larger bodies of troops made regular sweeps through the countryside, collecting 'revenue' and living off the land. It was only when a major campaign was actually being fought that big troop concentrations took place outside the capital, and as long as Ranjit Singh was there to keep the regiments in hand, the concentrations were dispersed immediately the campaign was over. The British, on the other hand, kept the bulk of the Indian army in a small number of very large cantonments; and they only let regiments out of cantonments to go on active service or perform manoeuvres. Small parties would show the flag in recruiting-grounds or disturbed areas, and cavalry regiments went on long marches to the annual 'camp of exercise' at Rawalpindi; but their real homes were the cantonments, and there was always a feeling of being let out of school. This kind of 'sedentary assemblage' was encouraged by the construction of military roads and railways. They enormously enhanced the mobility with which troops could be concentrated at trouble spots, provided regiments were stationed at the nodal points in the network of communications; and, at the same time, they facilitated the transport of supplies to the nodal points at which troops were normally stationed. In war or in peace, the development of a limited number of lines of communication which were immensely superior to anything that lay between them played into the hands of strategically-sited cantonments like Rawalpindi. In 1849 the entire *doab* (with the possible exception of the Grand Trunk Road) was impassable by wheeled vehicles, and the prohibitive cost of transport by pack animals or human porterage restricted trade to short distances or luxury items. The fort town and the village craft were a logical response to this situation. There were still plenty of villages which could only be reached on foot in 1947, but the *doab* as a whole had one of the best communications networks in India. Over the century between annexation and independence, strategic railways and road built to meet the army's needs brought the agriculture of the most inaccessible tracts into contact with the world economy, dictated the fate of towns, and even encouraged a 'show' of industrialisation.

Steamboats on the Indus

A *doab*, by definition, lies between two rivers; and if the upper reaches of the Indus or the Jhelum had been as navigable as the middle reaches of the Ganges, a second Benares might have sprung up on their banks. Unfortunately, both rivers constituted obstacles to trade rather than trade routes. They nterrupted the flow of goods from east to west, without doing very much to help transport goods from north to south, because their channels were a boatman's nightmare. The ideal iver—from the bargee's point of view—is deep, slow-moving, and stable. In such rivers, boats with a draught deep enough to carry really substantial cargoes can be propelled long customary courses with a minimum of effort and risk. Neither the Indus nor the Jhelum remotely resembled the deal. In the dry season they shrank into tiny streams; in the wet season the current easily reached six or seven knots; their hannels were constantly shifting across flat flood plains; and ew obstacles to navigation, such as unsuspected shoals, were onstantly appearing. It took five weeks to get downstream to Karachi, and about four times as long to get back; trade was often suspended for months at a time, because the rivers were unning too high or too low; and boats were always running ground or sinking. Very few boatmen ventured beyond Makhad, at the extreme south-western tip of the upper *doab*; none braved the rapids above Jhelum, about halfway along the *oab*'s eastern border; and neither river had any navigable ibutaries, which meant that there were just two feasible outes, with 50 to 100 miles of upland between them. Water ansport might be cheap, but it was inaccessible and unreliable, and even if it had been readily available, it would still have been too slow for the army.[65]

Every outbreak of hostilities on the north-west frontier impressed the need for improved communications on British strategists, and every major campaign led to enhanced expenditure on the rivers which were closest to the major passes. The first Afghan war, the Sikh wars and the Umbeyla campaign all resulted in attempts to develop regular steamer services on the Indus and the Jhelum. The first government steamship appeared on the Indus in 1837, in anticipation of the war with Afghanistan; between 1862 and 1872 the 'Marine Department' of the Government of the Punjab spent Rs. 2.2 millions on its 'flotilla'; and the railway authorities only abandoned their steamboats in 1878, when 'through communication' between Lahore and Karachi was finally established. None of these attempts to increase the river trade had much effect. Even the most advanced paddleboat was economically inferior to the traditional country boats. Steamships cost too much to buy, maintain, and run. A paddleboat cost 200 times as much as the average country craft; it had to be repaired in government dockyards employing expatriate engineers; it had to be crewed by Scots officers; and there was no convenient source of cheap fuel. Above all, steamboats were caught in a technological trap. Engines powerful enough to breast the current were so heavy that the hulls lay too low in the water. Unless the cargo was kept to a minimum, the boats regularly ran aground on shoals. If they were equipped with ligher engines, they were unable to make headway upstream. So the steamboats died a natural death, and the army put its faith in railways and roads.[66]

Strategic Railways

The great bulk of the hundreds of miles of railway line running across the Sind Sagar *doab* in 1947 consisted of strategic lines which would never have been built, or would have been built much later, if the commercial criteria normally applied to railway extension had been applied to them. All told, 40 per cent of the North-Western Railway's track, some 1,500 miles, almost the entire network west of Jhelum, consisted of 'military frontier railways' whose low earnings pushed the entire network into the red, except for three years before the First World War (when wheat exports were at their height) and the

First World War itself (when military traffic choked the lines). Even arterial routes which were not technically classified as 'strategic' were often built for strategic reasons. The generosity of the original contracts with the guaranteed dividend companies reflected the government's desire to increase the mobility of the Indian army; and the routes chosen for the first railway lines reflected the desire to link up as many cantonments as possible. The first railway to enter the Punjab linked one cantonment (Meerut) to another (Lahore) by way of three more (Ambala, Jullundur, Amritsar); and the extension of that line to the frontier (in 1878-82) gave another seven cantonments main line stations. Four of them, Rawalpindi, Jhelum, Campbellpur and Attock, were in the upper Sind Sagar *doab*.

By the First World War, there were railway lines all over Rawalpindi, Attock and Jhelum. One line ran down the east bank of the Indus, another ran down the west bank of the Jhelum, while a third joined the two riverine lines halfway down the *doab*. At first none of them paid. 'The stations', a settlement officer reported, 'are numerous (but) desolate, (and) many of them do no goods traffic at all.' But the railways of the *doab* had a knack of generating traffic, in the same way that railways in the wild west called into existence the business which justified their construction. Rawalpindi alone would have justified the main line to Peshawar. In 1884/85, just two years after the railhead reached the cantonment in Peshawar, freight worth Rs. 2 million passed through the station at 'Pindi', compared with Rs. 3.3 million at the commercial capital of the Punjab, Amritsar. The mineral lines to the salt mines at Khewra and the collieries at Dandot also paid from the start, and the much longer country lines began picking up freight as the surplus agricultural tracts began exporting food to the deficit recruiting–grounds. But the railways, like the steamboats, had their technological limitations. They created narrow corridors along which communications were very good, but they left the bulk of the *doab* as impassable as ever. What was needed was a form of transportation which could reach out into every village in the three districts, and the internal combustion engine supplied it. The role of military expenditure in this 'final solution' for the problems of the *doab* was less obvious than the subsidies held out to the steamboats and the railways, but it was no less pervasive.[67]

Road Transport

The greatest road-builders in India were militay engineers, and the Sind Sagar *doab* was one of their favourite playgrounds. Predictably enough, the first road to be made passable for wheeled traffic was the Grand Trunk Road; but a whole network of military roads soon converged on Rawalpindi. Some were purely local. They connected the outlying defence works to the cantonments, and gave the Pothwar plain one of the densest and best-maintained road systems in the subcontinent. Other were arterial. The most picturesque road in the *doab*—the Kashmir road via Murree—was metalled and bridged as far as the frontier; two highly strategic roads ran across the Indus into Kohat and Bannu; and two more ran down the sides of the *doab*, towards the south. Similar, if smaller, networks converged on the other cantonments; and three enormously expensive bridges—at Attock, Khushalgar and Kalabagh—replaced the old ferries and bridges of boats across the Indus. Like the railways, these strategic roads had their limitations from the civilian user's point of view. The army had no interest in feeder roads, which left village tracks as impassable as ever; and towns with no military significance, such as Pindigheb, got nothing. It was up to the district boards to plug the gaps in the military net; and until the First World War it was as much as they could do to maintain the strategic roads which the army relinquished, once it got its railways. Then, in the 1920s, the provincial government began taking roads seriously; and the Unionist Party, which was heavily dependent on the martial lobby, skewed expenditure in favour of the great recruiting-grounds. By the 1930s the Punjab was spending more on roads (per capita) than any other province, and the settlement officer of Jhelum thought that the result was a 'very marked improvement' in communications.[68]

The most obvious consequence of military road-building was the immediate increase in the number of carts in the *doab*. In 1849 there were virtually none; by the 1880s there were more than a thousand, concentrated around Rawalpindi and Murree. The cart population peaked at about 8,500 in 1909, because the army was launching a frontier expedition; the norm between the wars hovered somewhere between four and five thousand. The growth of carting, paradoxically enough, was accompanied by an increase in the pack animals which wheeled vehicles were supposed to supersede. The number of donkeys and mules doubeld between 1885 and 1914, reaching its apogee in 1935. Even camels hit a new high in 1935. What was happening was quite simple. In the tehsils containing cantonments, which had fairly dense networks of passable roads, carts achieved an easy dominance. If one assumes that the average cart carried ten times as much as the average pack animal, the ratio of carts to donkeys/mules to camels in Rawalpindi tehsil in 1900 was 100:54:8. In Attock it was 100:54:11. But in the tehsils which contained no passable roads—especially the hill tehsils, which were cut up by ravines—pack animals retained a virtual monopoly; and as the volume of trade increased, so did the number of donkeys, mules and camels.[69]

The dip in the number of carts and pack animals after 1935 reflects both the depression—there was a certain delayed reaction—and competition from lorries and buses. It is difficult to trace the growth of motor transport in the *doab*, because the Government of the Punjab, which collected data on the whereabouts of every chicken in the province, never knew how many lorries or buses there were on its roads. But the number of lorries and buses in India went up more than seven times during the seven years between 1923/24 and 1930/31; and the increase in the upper Sind Sagar *doab* may well have been higher still. There were very few villages in Jhelum more than five miles from a regular lorry service, and the North-Western Railway, whose earnings fell by a third after 1926, was clearly terrified of road competition. At partition there must have been thousands of vehicles in the upper Sind Sagar *doab*, and during the post-independence transportation boom four times as many vehicles were registered in Rawalpindi as in any other district of the Punjab, bar Lahore.

It could be argued that the army supplied several of the crucial inputs which made the rapid introduction of motor transport possible, in addition to the original network of military roads. Enterprise, skills, capital and plant flowed out of the armed services into the hauliers' firms; and these flows account for the prominence of *doabis* in the transport industry in Pakistan today, just as they account for the prominence of Sikhs in the transport industry in northern India. The army gave its recruits a taste for machinery, and the means to indulge it. When the Board of Economic Inquiry asked a small sample of soldiers in Rawalpindi what kind of job they wanted after they were demobilised, *half* of them said they wanted to become drivers or mechanics; and detailed case studies of two heavily-recruited villages in the Sind Sagar *doab* showed that demobilised soldiers spent their savings and gratuities on driving lessons and army surplus lorries from the First World War onwards, albeit in a somewhat haphazard way. The Second World War enormously increased the number of soldiers who wanted to become hauliers, and also improved their chances of success. Punjabi Mussalmen were traditionally over-represented in the cavalry regiments which swopped horses for tanks, and a rough calculation suggests that about 12-13,000 trained as tank crews. At least 20,000 served in the motor transport section of the supply corps; and there must have been more again who learnt how to drive and maintain motor vehicles in the artillery, engineers and sappers. By 1946 there were army-trained drivers and mechanics in most of the villages of the Sind Sagar *doab*, and many of them had gratuities burning holes in their pockets. Sales of army surplus equipment—everything from ten-ton trucks to sets of spanners—coincided with their demobilisation; and if they failed to buy their way into the business of their dreams, it was no one's fault but their own.[70]

Industrialisation

It would be absurd to suggest that military expenditure precipitated an industrial revolution in the upper Sind Sagar *doab*. Given the centralisation of so much purchasing in the quartermaster-general's department and the tendency of purchasing officers to give contracts to established suppliers in the great industrial centres, bootmakers in Cawnpore and cotton magnates in Bombay did better out of military orders than any Punjab industrialist. But the fact remains that almost all the modern industry in the Sind Sagar *doab* in 1947 owed something to the army, and a few factories and mines were wholly dependent on military purchases or strategic railways. If there was any base at all from which further industrialisation could grow, it was due to defence expenditure.

Transport was clearly the greatest single beneficiary of the military's largesse. The army not only provided most of the infrastructure in the form of strategic railways and roads; it also generated a large part of the demand for haulage. Although the movement of troops and stores in peacetime can only have occupied a fraction of the North-Western Railway's capacity, military movements choked the system during both world wars; and a single frontier expedition could easily monopolise all the carts and pack animals for miles around, under legislation authorising their conscription. The railways—if one discounts the army itself—were the largest employers in the *doab*; and the railway workshops in Rawalpindi, with about 3,500 employees, were the largest 'factory'. They may well have constituted the second-largest factory in the province; only the railway workshops in Lahore seem to have been bigger. Judged by any of the conventional criteria—number of employees, complexity of product, range of skills, use of machinery—the railway workshops were ultra-modern factories in the 1880s; and they were still far in advance of anything else in the *doab* in the 1930s. They were schools of skill for managers and artisans; a pool of specialist labour on which other enterprises drew. They were also growing. It is often assumed that the multiplier effects of railway building were a one-shot thing: that India missed out on the multiplier effects of construction, because the railway network was built before the subcontinent got protection. But the rate of railway extension was almost as fast in the 1920s as it was forty years earlier, when the main line was being pushed through to Peshawar; and the great bulk of the expenditure was spent in India.

There were no comparable concentrations of ownership or employment where road transport was concerned. But even in the days of carts there were carriers like the 'Express Cast Company' who operated on a big enough scale to warrant the floatation of joint stock companies. The internal combustion engine ushered in an ever wider range of concerns. At one extreme there was the self-employed mechanic with his bag of tools and the owner-driver with his clapped-out truck; at the other extreme there were firms like the Pindi Automobile Company with a garage and showroom worthy of its nominal capital of half a million rupees, and hauliers with small fleets of buses and lorries running regular services all over the north-west. The 1920s were the golden age of the garage in Rawalpindi, and a large part of the garages' custom came from officers who owned cars and NCOs who rode motorcycles. The army maintained its own vehicles in its own workshops. The great ordnance works, which dominated the approach to the city from the south east, started out as a simple arsenal, a place where guns and ammunition were stored. Repair facilities and the manufacture of munitions were soon added to its original functions; and long before the First World War, the arsenal became the second-largest factory in the *doab*. By 1947, the mechanisation of the army had gone so far that specialist workshops were scattered all over the cantonment. The engineers, the sappers, the signals, the gunners, all had their vehicle parks and separate 'factories'.[71]

All the army-induced construction—the expansion of the cantonment towns, the new standard of housing in the villages, the completion of the railway network and the upgrading of the roads—produced a boom in the building trades. The leading contractors built up immense fortunes, and their employees became the best-paid craftsmen in the Punjab. The great philanthropists of the *doab*—the men who beautified Rawalpindi with temples and gardens, and left bequests for libraries and caravanserais—were almost all contractors; and one suspects that their influence on municipal committees, given their investments in urban real estate, was out of all proportion to their numbers. The *Wages Surveys* suggest that their workforce shared their affluence. With the possible exception of the notoriously prosperous canal colonies, carpenters and masons seem to have been paid higher wages in Rawalpindi than in any other region of the province. The local suppliers of building materials—who were protected by the high cost of transport—also benefited from the construction boom. Quarries strung out along the Grand Trunk Road supplied stone for public buildings and *kankar* for roads; the great cement works at Wah grew into one of the largest and most modern factories in India; the lumberyards at Jhelum, the biggest in northern India, felled the forests of Kashmir keeping the treeless plains in timber; and the brick-kilns which sprang up round every building site were a useful bolt-hole for redundant potters, when metal vessels replaced clay ones.[72]

Other extractive industries besides cement and quarrying were stimulated by military demand. The Jhelum coalfield was first explored and exploited as a source of fuel for the Indus flotilla, only to be abandoned because of the low calorific value of the coal and the difficulties of working narrow seams running through unstable shale or soft clay. The North-Western Railway reopened the mines and took out 81,000 tons of coal in 1899, but the same obstacles applied. Dandot never produced more than two per cent of India's output of coal, and the railway sold the mines after reductions in freight rates exposed them to competition with higher quality coal from Bengal. There were 1,700 men employed as colliers in the 1920s, but the industry never really recovered from the loss of the local market for steam coal.[73] The Khaur oilfield was more successful. An ex-PWD engineer, attracted by surface seepages, sank the first oilwells in the *doab* in 1870. Unfortunately, the outturn was minute and the Rawalpindi gasworks absorbed it all. As mineral oil became a major strategic resource, the pace of exploration quickened. At least a dozen companies sent out prospectors or made trial borings. The real breakthrough came in 1914, when the Attock Oil Company sank the 'Discovery' well at Khaur. By 1922 it had a refinery on the outskirts of Rawalpindi with a 40-mile pipeline leading to the oilfield. The proportion of the refinery's production which was sold to the army is not immediately apparent; but the military could easily have used the entire output, and during the world wars they almost certainly did.[74]

Lastly, there were the salt mines at Khewra: the great source of salt all over northern India, as a result of the government salt monopoly. The monopoly protected Khewra, but there was always the risk that the Salt Department would transfer its patronage to the open-cast mines in Kohat, where the cost of extraction was lower. Capital investment, mainly in tramways and drainage, combined with scientific working cut the cost of working salt at Khewra by four-fifths; but without the branch line linking the mines to the North-Western Railway the fate of the 1,000 salt miners would always have been in doubt, and without the strategic railway network there would have been no main line, much less a branch to Khewra.[75]

Manufacturing industries dependent on military demand were curiosities rather than a coherent industrial sector. The army's inexhaustible demand for boots and harness, coupled with the inexhaustible supply of hides and skins from the province's 24 million livestock, should have led to the modernisation of the local leather industry; but the impoverished and illiterate scavengers who monopolised tanning in the *doab* lacked the capital and the skill to produce high quality leather, and the local shoemakers and saddlers worked on too small a scale to establish new brand names in competition with the army's traditional suppliers in Cawnpore. A group of Khojas (Muslim traders who 'put out' raw materials to indebted artisans) got as far as floating a joint stock company to run a modern tannery; but the partners' inexperience soon brought 'The Punjab Tannery' to its knees.[76] Other ventures lasted marginally longer. The best-known industrialist in the *doab*, Rai Bahadur Buta Singh, set up the largest foundry and the largest tent-factory in the Punjab; and one Hardit Singh, another iron-founder, 'eked out a precarious living by ministering to various army needs'. The first large-scale bakery in the province seems to have grown up in response to the army's appetite for standardised food, at least for British troops; the Murree brewery, which had a branch in Rawalpindi, slaked their insatiable thirst; three ice factories cooled their tepid drinks; a tiny soap works—one of only two in he province—washed the sweat from their occidental bodies; and a couple of jobbing printers ran up their visiting cards, menus and invitations. But all the capital invested in these enterprises hardly equalled the value of the largest mill in the Punjab: the New Egerton Woollen Mill in Gurdaspur, which was heavily dependent on army contracts.[77]

The fate of the handicrafts of the *doab* is not yet clear. It seems probable that the overall picture was one of growth and adaptation, rather than collapse before an inrush of mill-made goods. The upper Sind Sagar *doab* was singularly devoid of famous industrial centres in 1849, just as it was singularly devoid of towns. In the central Punjab, every town had its speciality: arms and armour at Lahore, iron founding at Batala, and so on and so forth. But not one manufacture from the upper *doab* features in any of the five surveys of Punjab handicrafts written between the mutiny and the end of the First World War. Only the snuff-makers of Hazro figure in the reference books, and the snuff-makers seem to have done well enough out of the purchasing power of their soldier-customers. The official price and wage statistics—never the most reliable guides—imply that the standard village craftsmen (carpenters, masons and blacksmiths) made real gains in income. Between 1873 and 1905 (the years for which comparable series of index numbers are available), there were only nine years in which wages fell behind the price of wheat, and five out of the nine were famine years. Again, between 1909 and 1943—the dates of the first and last wages surveys—the pay of skilled men quadrupled, while the price of wheat only went up three times. There was even a certain specialisation of function, as cantonments undermined the hereditary bonds between craftsmen and cultivators. Smiths in some of the villages round Rawalpindi broke out of their traditional *jajmani* relationship with cultivator–patrons and concentrated on producing stirrups for the cavalry; doubtless other *kamins* followed their example.[78]

It is possible that the textile industry was the other side of the coin; that the bones of handloom weavers were bleaching all over the *doab*. But it seems unlikely. Weaving in old-established textile centres like Ludhiana was saved from extinction by the sepoy's demand for decorative turban cloths. Even if their wives dressed in imported chintz, the soldiery still 'gloried' in their brightly coloured and elaborately embroidered turbans. At the cheap end of the market, military families were major consumers of *khadar* and blankets; products protected from factory competition by their durability and the weavers' low overheads. There may even have been a revival of spinning (by soldiers' wives) during the hard times of the thirties; Darling claimed that there was such a revival in other recruiting grounds.[79] But all the evidence is too fragmentary to be conclusive, and it may be best to suspend judgment.

There are other, clearer cut, instances of decay. Boat-building has claims to being the one indigenous industry which 'strategic' expenditure positively drove into decline. The railway lines running parallel to the Indus stole the cargoes which the country-boats carried, while the railway bridges running across the river deprived the ferrymen of their livelihood. By 1893 there were fewer than 40 boats left at the two great *mallah* colonies at Makhad and Attock, and only one bridge of boats. But the decline of boat-building must have been swamped by the growth of cart-building. Even if one boat equalled ten carts, the 8,000 carts of 1909 represented a larger industry than the boatyards in their prime.[80]

The Social Consequences of Military Expenditure

> In the Jhelum District there is no class whose condition is not superior to that of the poorest classes in European countries.
> *Jhelum District Gazetteer* (1904)

> The daily food consumption [of] eleven families selected . . . from the different classes of the village . . . was recorded for three months. It was found that there was no marked difference . . . in [the] number of meals . . . or [the] kind of food consumed . . . There were many cases where families among the menials took more sumptuous meals than those taken by some of the more well-to-do landowners . . . The remarkable fact is that even the menials own land in [this] village.
> Ghulam Yasn, *Economic Survey of Sagri: A Village in the Rawalpindi District, Punjab-Pakistan, 1950* (Lahore, 1950)

> *Jang te Mahugai wich sare iko jache ho ghe nein. Sare roti khan lag ghe nein.* (The war and the high prices brought about equality. All were enabled to get their bread).
> Popular sayings, Ludhiana District, circa 1945: Ram Swarup Nakra, *Punjab Villages During the War* (Lahore, 1946)

The Emancipation of the Peasant

The impact of the army on the villages of the upper Sind Sagar *doab* was very similar to the impact of the market on some of the most heavily-commercialised parts of the Punjab: it dissolved traditional forms of dependency, without putting new forms of dependency—or at least equally personal forms of dependency—in their place. All the peasants' usual oppressors—landlords, moneylenders, traders, officials, kulaks—were weakened by the options it created. In the most backward tracts, the tracts which were unaffected by the army or the market, tenants were still 'serfs' at independence. They could do nothing new without asking their landlord's leave, and they had no right to anything beyond a bare subsistence. They were entitled to protection from rival predators and relief in time of famine; but that was all. In every important respect, they were *adscripti glebae*. Owner–cultivators in heavily–indebted villages were almost as badly off. Money-lender–traders 'harried the peasants at will', charging them usurious interest, forcing them to sell their crops at low prices, attaching their cattle and expropriating their land. At the same time, every petty jack-in-office—from the *patwaris* to the police—took as much 'squeeze' as they could extract from their inert and unresisting subjects; and in particular villages small oligarchies of rich peasants used their control over scarce resources—land, credit, leverage over the bureaucracy—to abstract whatever surplus their poorer neighbours managed to retain.

The position in the intensively-recruited tracts and the zones commercialised by the cantonments was very different. Like the rest of the *doab*, they had the advantage of a favourable start. The traditional lords of the land—locally-dominant tribes like the Gakhars and Janjuas—were weak at annexation because they lost control of the subordinate cultivators when the Sikhs misls overran the *doab* and by-passed the old revenue-intercepting intermediaries. Sikh *kardars* preferred managing villages directly; they could raise more money that way, and there was less risk of resistance. Then the incoming British refused to restore the *status quo*. As a result, less than a quarter of the *doab* was cultivated by tenants-at-will; and almost half the occupancy tenants and all the 'inferior proprietors' paid cash rents fixed at low rates which were rapidly eroded by inflation and gave landlords far fewer pretexts to interfere than kind rents would have done. The larger landowners' political disunity and incompetence as managers helped the tenants make the most of their strong legal position. Every landowning family was riven by feuds, which meant that every dissident tenant had potential allies among his social superiors; and every estate administration was infinitely corruptible. But it was the opportunities held out by the army that made the crucial difference. The old *sahu* tribes' hegemony was doomed once they failed to monopolise the military bonanza. Traditionally subordinate castes were at least as willing to enlist, and made far more effective entrepreneurs. As the officer corps was reserved for Europeans, many landlords' sons considered military service beneath them, because they would have been compelled to compete—for relatively petty prizes—on equal terms with their tenants. As entrepreneurs, also, they were handicapped by their archaic value systems, which equated particular kinds of profit with pollution and insisted on the maintenance of traditional forms of conspicuous consumption. Intensive cultivation and direct marketing—much less day-labour—were simply not done; lavish funerals, hard-fought lawsuits and 'four-walled' *purdah* were *de rigeur*. So the 'leading families' drifted into indebtedness, when multiple inheritance led to the subdivision of their ancestral estates; while their erstwhile tenants drifted into the army and cantonments, maximising their off-farm incomes.

The land market was the ultimate index of the different tribes' economic well-being. In the constant struggle to acquire and retain land, it was the middle-ranking cultivator castes who were most responsive to the army and the market, and it was the cultivators who proved the gainers. In the most heavily-recruited tehsils it was the soldiers who bought land; in Rawalpindi and Murree it was the men who made money out of the cantonments—contractors, carters, labourers; and in the high-farming zones, it was the high-farmers. Symbolic acts—such as forms of greeting or patterns of betrothal—reflected parallel changes in the tribes' social standing. At annexation, cultivator-tribes like Gujars and Jats universally accorded Gakhars and Janjuas the courtesy title of *raja*. Then mass enlistment ironed out tribal distinctions and owner cultivators began refusing to give their daughters to Gakhar husbands, because Gakhars refused to give their daughters in return. The 'democratic institutions, and 'widening franchise' of the 1920s brought the new levelling spirit into the open. 'Exhortations to combine to defeat a Gakhar or a Janjua candidate (became) the most effective election cry of a non-*raja* candidate.'[81]

The same tracts that resisted landlord dominance never gave the moneylending *sahukars* a chance to develop the 'commanding position' they occupied elsewhere. Only the feeble-minded became debt-slaves when it was so easy to go out and earn the money to repay one's debts. The fact that the price of land rose faster than the cost of living meant that owner cultivators could meet their needs by pledging or selling smaller fractions of their holdings; and even if they lost all their land, it was far from a disaster, 'because an able-bodied man (could) always keep his family' without it. He could also hope to re-enter the ranks of the proprietors by sending his sons into the army or going off to the cantonments; one settlement officer wrote of labourers repaying the mortgages they took out to buy land with the proceeds of three or four years work as coolies. The rise of the agriculturist moneylender and the debt relief legislation of the 1930s were the final nails the professional moneylenders' coffin. Whether he made his money out of service or enterprise, the agriculturist moneylender was generally prepared to advance mortgages on much more favourable terms than members of the commercial castes, if the mortgagor gave him the right to cultivate the land. At the same time, the Unionist Party's 'Golden Acts' made it virtually impossible to recover debts in any other way; and the *sahukars* had no wish to become farmers, because the profits were so low.[82]

The moneylender-trader's monopoly of trade—insofar as it ever existed—was destroyed by similar forces. The improvement of communications and the growth of demand intensified competition for the cultivators' crops and encouraged the growth of peasant marketing. Swarms of peripatetic traders—many of them lorry-owners—besieged cultivators in the high farming zones, offering prices only marginally lower than those obtaining in the local markets; while thousands of peasants took to carting crops to the towns, shopping round in search of the best deals. Traders could still make high profits out of violent post-harvest price increases; but commercialisation had a stabilising effect on prices, levelling out localised gluts and famines; and the normal post-harvest increases were built into the traders' expectations when they decided how high a price they could offer in order to obtain a crop.[83]

The *zulm* (tyranny) of the officials was also curbed by the soldiers' preferential access to the administration. If they had business to transact at a government office and some *babu* gave them trouble, they could appeal over his head with a good chance of getting redress, because British officials were terrified of unrest in the most important recruiting ground. District officers on tour made a point of talking to the soldiers, and deputy commissioners were always willing to receive native officers with distinguished records of service. When Darling went round the *doab* as commissioner of Rawalpindi, cavalcades of pensioners met him at the border of each *zail* and escorted him to martial villages, where squads of ex-soldiers were drawn up in full uniform, 'medals clanking on their chests', to present their collective petitions to the *sirkar*. The soldiery exerted just as much leverage over the Unionist ministers who were continuously in office during the closing decades of British rule. Unionist politicians knew that veterans constituted a majority of the electorate under a franchise skewed in their favour, and in the recruiting-grounds the leaders of the party were the leaders of the martial lobby. The provincial government's agrarian legislation and public expenditure, which consistently favoured the martial castes, were proof positive of the state's responsiveness to the interests of its peasant mercenaries.[84]

It seems unlikely that a distinct class of rich peasants (the now notorious 'village controllers') ever acquired enough power to 'rule' the most heavily-recruited or the most highly-commercialised settlements. The tendency of the Sikh *kardars* to develop a *ryotwari* system—dispensing with ever-lower sets of intermediaries until they dealt directly with individual cultivators—pulverised traditional village elites; and British attempts to impose a *mahalwari* system, reviving 'village republics' which never existed, fell foul of the *lambardars'* weakness. There was no class of *kulaks* from whom powerful headmen could be recruited, because the ownership of resources inside the villages was too egalitarian and access to resources outside the villages was too open. As a result, headmen who could exercise effective authority over their co-proprietors were an endangered species in the upper Sind Sagar *doab*; and the *biraderi*—the brotherhood of proprietors—had almost as much difficulty exerting their authority over the village artisans and menials. Client craftsmen and labourers could command such high wages in the cantonments or on the public works that they opted out of the *jajmani* system; and if they returned to the village, they were liable to return as co-proprietors.[85] According to the settlement officer of Gujar Khan,

> every menial whose work has a stable value outside his own village endeavours to save enough to buy a little land and to improve his social position. Fraudulent enlistment is very common, and there are many soldiers, and even native officers, who are accounted menials in their own villages. To such men as these landlessness is a constant disgrace and a constant danger, and they strain every nerve to acquire a little holding of their own, that they may be accounted *zemindars*.[86]

The one section of society which enjoyed *less* freedom as a result of military expenditure—the women who went into *purdah*—may well have been volunteers. It is difficult to see how half the population could have been confined without their consent, and seclusion had some fairly obvious attractions. A woman's segregation from unrelated men entitled her to a much higher degree of protection from the men to whom she was related. In Muslim districts to the south—districts which produced no recruits—women were as liberated, in one sense, as the most ardent feminist could desire. They could come back to their ostensible husbands after an absence of a few years, present them with a couple of strange children, and say 'God has increased your honour'. But they could also be bought and sold; they were expected to redeem bad debts by extending their favours to money-lenders; 'no girl was safe' from the local landlords; and they were constantly abandoned in ill-health and old age.

In a society so violent and so poor, the isolated woman was chronically insecure; and the 'free women' who were bereft of masculine protectors would almost certainly have leapt at the chance of entering a prosperous *zenana*. In the upper *doab*, women who fulfilled their prescribed roles—as chaste daughters, faithful wives and loving mothers—could expect the male members of their families to lay down their lives, if necessary, in their defence. *Purdah* was the outward and visible sign of this implicit contract—of the determination of both sexes to maintain stable family structures; and in the circumstances of the day, stabler families could be represented as a kind of progress. There were also more immediate gains. Women who went into *purdah* as a result of increases in their family incomes automatically acquired higher social status, did less work, and could concentrate on controlling the household. There are even suggestions that marriages became more companionable. One of Darling's informants told him that there was less wife-beating since men joined the army and saw the world. 'Now only childless wives are beaten', he said. Other witnesses claimed that the tyranny of the mother-in-law was coming to an end. Young wives 'took their mothers-in-law by the ears', while their soldier-husbands looked on.[87]

The net results of this general subversion of authority were not all good. Except for limited purposes, such as recruitment, the state lacked collaborators who could exercise much leverage over the mass of the population, which weakened its ability to attain almost any public objective. 'What can one do with such people?' a *tehsildar* is reported to have asked; and many policemen must have felt the same way. Rawalpindi tehsil was not only one of the most prosperous in the province; it was also one of the most criminal areas in the northern Punjab, and the villages which harboured the most hardened *dacoits* or nurtured the most bloodthirsty vendettas were often the richest.[88]

Arguably, the upper *doab* was a society which was losing the capacity to govern itself. Alternatively, it was always 'turbulent'—and the turbulence was becoming more apparent, as military discipline opened the peasantry's eyes to the possibility of order. If either of these contentions is correct, it may explain—in part—the popularity of the Islamic revival and the acceptance of military rule. A peasantry living through a period of rapid socio-economic change in a tract pullulating with faction and crime was anxious for the reimposition of some moral order. The *ulema* and the generals held out two kinds of order—one religious, the other military; the only kinds of order with which the villagers were familiar, above the level of the family; and the only kinds of order which were compatible with the patriarchal authority pervading the average villager's day-to-day life. When theocracy and militarism were combined in the same polity—when the priesthood went into alliance with the officer corps—it must have seemed as if 'there was no alternative' to the Zia regime.

The Mobilisation of the Notables

The 'general crisis of the aristocracy' which laid the old dominant tribes low was part of a reshuffling of the leading families of the *doab* according to their ability to meet the army's requirements. One of the reasons there was so much crime was that the British wanted their collaborators to do other things than catching criminals. They wanted them, above all, to supply recruits and fulfil army contracts. Families which could do these two things were promoted into the ranks of the officially-recognised notables; families which failed to perform their allotted tasks fell out of the *durbar* lists, and lost income and standing in the process.

The most spectacular of the casualties were the families that formerly stood at the pinnacle of the social system; the chiefs of the Gakhar tribe. 'No tribe', Sir Lepel Griffin rumbled, 'is more frequently mentioned in Indian history'. The Gakhars entered the *doab* in Mahmud of Ghazni's train; they murdered the emperor Shahab-ud-din Ghori after he suppressed their rebellion; they fought against Sher Shah and delivered up prince Samram to Humayun. The last independent Gakhar chief, Sultan Mukarab Khan (1739-65), was probably more powerful than any of his predecessors. But the Bhangi *misl*, marching out of Lahore, defeated his forces outside the walls of Gujrat; the other Gakhar chiefs murdered him; and the incoming Sikhs reduced them all to abject poverty, by confiscating the Gakhars' *jagirs* and imprisoning their leaders. Edwardes released the head of the tribe from a Sikh dungeon, and he 'did good service' during two crucial tests—the second Sikh war and the mutiny.

These were the last occasions on which the Gakhar elite really exerted itself. They were disappointed by the first regular settlement (1857-64) and sulked. They wanted to be the effective rulers of the *doab* again, and all the British gave them was the right to collect a nominal quit rent from their old estates—plus a few pensions, a few hundred acres of crown land, and the ancient Gakhar capital at Pharwala. As the Pharwala chiefs stopped helping the army and concentrated on their internal feuds, the British ran out of patience. Griffin thought the Gakhars were entitled to respect by virtue of their glamorous history, present misfortunes and undoubted courage; his successors looked at their descendants through more jaundiced eyes. A District Gazetteer published in 1907 publicly arraigned the Pharwala family as absolutely the most indolent' in the district, and when they did 'absolutely nothing' to assist recruitment during the First World War, the fact was publicly recorded in the district *War History*. Settlement officers who reported that the family was sunk in poverty were determined that the government should do nothing to alleviate the chiefs' distress. Gakhars as individuals made welcome recruits—they were the most heavily-enlisted tribe during the First World War—but their nominal leaders were *personae non gratae*.[89]

Chiefs belonging to less illustrious tribes stepped onto the escalator going up, just as the Gakhars were going down. The heads of the Dhanial tribe were a case in point. They took the winning side in 1848 because they were still resisting Sikh encroachments, and they sided with the British in 1857 when their arch-rivals, the Dhunds, sacked Murree. Thereafter they built up one of the most impressive military connections in the province. The family of the chief produced dozens of native officers; and the tribe, in consequence, produced thousands of recruits. They fought in every campaign in which the Indian army was engaged, and during the First World War there was a positive stampede to the colours. 'Every eligible male member of (the chief's) family, who was not already in service, enrolled himself in the army'. The chief's brother, son-in-law, and two cousins were all killed on active service; and their subsequent rewards were proportionately great. *Jagirs*, land grants, honorary magistracies, poured down on the leading Dhanials; and by the turn of the century the chief's position—given British support—was so strong that his word was law among adjacent tribes, not just his own.[90]

The survivors of the Sikh regime, notwithstanding the small number of Sikhs in the *doab*, also made effective military collaborators. The descendants of the soldier-priests who surrounded the gurus and managed to preserve their pre-eminence during the turbulence of the *misls* and the consolidation of Ranjit Singh's empire must have found the totally predictable British child's play in comparison. Some dynasties, such as the family of Baba Sir Khem Singh Bedi (died 1904), traded on their spirituality. The Bedis—once chaplains to the Sikh forces—became the spiritual leaders of all the Sikhs west of the Ravi and used their influence to produce large number of recruits in every crisis. In 1857 Khem Singh raised troops of his own; in 1878 he persuaded 1,500 of his followers to join the regiments marching against Afghanistan; and in 1914-18 his sons accompanied recruiting officers on tours of the Sikh colonies in the western Punjab, besides contributing Rs. 150,000 to the war loan. British patronage, plus the offerings of their followers, made the Babas one of the richest families (if not *the* richest) in the *doab*. Sir Khem was the recipient of a huge income in cash from *jagirs*, and he invested it in the development of a 14,000 acre estate—mainly crown land leased to him by the government—in tracts which were suited to canal irrigation. The subdivision of his estate among six sons was a setback; but each of them was richer than their father had been until he was more than halfway through his career, and they simply began the process of accumulation again.[91] The soldier-priests of Kountrilla went the other way. Unlike the Bedis, the Bakshis of Kountrilla specialised in military service and revenue-collection. They helped the last gurus resist Moghal persecution, fought in the Durrani invaders' armies, transferred their services to the Atariwala *sardars* in the days of the *misls* and commanded a couple of regiments when the Sikh army rebelled in 1848. Half the family joined the rebels; the other half joined Edwardes at Multan—and the Anglophiles never looked back. They rode down to Delhi, poured into the Sikh regiments, piled up commissions, diversified into the civil departments and came out of the First World War paying Rs. 16,500 in land revenue.[92]

Lastly, there were the contractors: the civilian purveyors of goods and transport, who grew up with the cantonments and dominated the new cities. The first generation, judging by the advertisements in the Rawalpindi Directory, were Parsis who entered the Punjab in Lord Gough's baggage-train and set up shop in Rawalpindi as soon as Dalhousie designated it a cantonment. They were soon eclipsed by the Khatri Sikhs who supplied Ranjit Singh's armies. Sardar Hardit Singh, a Khatri, made his family's fortunes during the decades on either side of the second Afghan war: the golden age of Rawalpindi's expansion. He ploughed the profits into building bungalows in the cantonment, which he let to British officers. He even owned the premises rented by the Rawalpindi Club. He made 'killings' supplying food and carriage, speculating in the grain trade, and lending money to local chiefs; and when his estate was finally taken under the court of wards because of quarrels between his children, the annual income amounted to Rs. 150,000: several times the pay and allowances of the generals who were his tenants. Rai Bahadur Buta Singh belonged to the next generation. His contracting turned him into an industrialist, with the largest foundry and the only tent factory in the Punjab. When the First World War broke out he sank Rs. 450,000 in the war loan, sent his son to Mesopotamia to see to the Expeditionary Force's tents, and set up a network of recruiting offices which enlisted thousands of men. When the district war history came to list the local notables who had made significant contributions to the war effort, contractors constituted a clear majority and Buta Singh's name led all the rest. They were the new burghers: the essential links between the commissariat and the peasantry, and the dominant force in the politics of the city they helped build.[93]

Conclusion

If the rejuvenation of upper Sind Sagar *doab* shows how great the power of military patronage could be, the north-western Punjab was only the beginning. There were other recruiting-grounds and other cantonments all over India; they must have experienced similar stimuli. Moreover, different approaches to the analysis of defence spending are bound to disclose fresh multiplier effects. The highest returns to future research are unlikely to come from additional case studies of areas like the Sind Sagar *doab*. A detailed dissection of a heavily-recruited village over a long period of time, identifying the changes in its economic activities and social structure which were due to enlistment; a history of Cawnpore relating the development of a great industrial complex to military orders; an appraisal of the massive purchases of military stores during the two world wars—purchases which altered the Government of India's attitude to industrialisation and wiped out its foreign debt; these are just three of the projects which must be undertaken before we arrive at a complete check-list of the *potential* effects of military expenditure.

One thing, however, is certain. Whatever the effects of military expenditure may have been, the army would have acted as a more effective force for modernisation if India had been forced to meet the full cost of its own defence, instead of benefiting from the economies of scale which the empire conferred on its members. A cursory examination of the growth of defence spending over the past fifty years strongly suggests that the cut-price security offered by the raj was a great deal cheaper than the arms-races of potentially hostile successor states. Defence expenditure in South Asia is now 170 times higher than it was in the 1930s, and the armed forces are approximately ten times bigger. However large the allowances one makes for inflation, or for economic expansion, or for the population explosion, the successor states still devote a higher proportion of the subcontinents' resources to defence than the imperialists ever managed to extract. The 'most-militarist' state, Pakistan, spends six per cent of its GDP on defence—two and a half times the level of the 1930s; and India shows every sign of catching up. Put another way, it takes four times the old proportion of males of military age to provide an inferior standard of security; and males of military age are the

	Armed Forces	Armed Forces including Para-Military	Percentage of Males of Military Age	Defence Expenditure ($m)	Percentage of Public Expenditure	Percentage of Gross Domestic Product
U.K. 1934	218,000	352,000	5.1	151	14/62*	2.8
India 1934	180,000	252,000	0.4	45	26	2.4
South Asia 1983	1,878,000	2,390,000		7,693		3.7
India	1,120,000	1,380,000	1.5	5,556	16	3.5
Pakistan	478,000	587,000	2.8	1,801	30	5.8
Bangladesh	91,000	171,000	1.4	161	19	1.5
Burma	179,000	252,000	5.6	175	24	3.1

*62 including the national debt (mainly incurred for defence)

Note: Males of military age are males between 20 and 40. Ceylon was garrisoned from India prior to Independence, and the 1934 figures for India's armed forces probably include the Singhalese garrison, but the 1934 figure for India's defence expenditure is unlikely to include the garrison's cost. The figure for India's defence expenditure in 1934 is, in fact, an average of the years 1931-40 at current prices, converted into dollars at 1984 rates. All the figures for defence expenditure omit a great deal of indirect expenditure (e.g. on communications, urban amenities and grants to veterans) which would never have been undertaken had it not been for the army's needs. The armies of native states have been counted as para-military in the Indian figures for 1934: a fair reflection of their quality. The 60,000 British troops in India have been lumped in with the Indian army proper. The estimates of GDP on which the last column is based need not be taken seriously, but the orders of magnitude suggested are in accordance with other evidence. The figures for defence expenditure and GDP are for 1981/2 (the last year for which comparable data were available), instead of 1982/3.

Sources: International Institute for Strategic Studies, *The Military Balance 1983-84* (London 1983); K.N. Reddy, *The Growth of Public Expenditure in India* (New Delhi 1972); *India Office List* (HMSO 1934); *Annual Abstract of Statistics* (HMSO 1934); B.R. Mitchell and P. Deane, *Abstract of British Historical Statistics* (Cambridge 1962); *The European Year Book 1983* (London 1983); K.N. Reddy, 'Indian Defence Expenditure, 1872-1967,' *Indian Ecomomic and Social History Review*, 7 (1970), 467-68, understates the growth of defence expenditure by omitting Pakistan, Bangladesh and Burma and taking 1967 as a terminus.

most productive section of the workforce. When some of the poorest countries in the world lavish more resources on defence than they allocate to their development drives, historians—as well as economists—are bound to ask whether the oppressive effects of military expenditure outweigh the multiplier effects. The upper Sind Sagar *doab* was one of the luckiest beneficiaries of the Indian army's largesse; but military expenditure in the *doab* sucked resources out of the rest of India, via taxation. Did this 'internal drain' exceed, in size, the more notorious external drain to England? And did it represent better value for money, or worse? Only further research will decide.

NOTES

I am grateful to the U.K. Economic and Social Research Council and the Research Board of the University of Leicester for grants towards the cost of the research on which this paper is based. The sections on 'Pay and Pensions' and 'The Social Consequences of Emancipation' are very largely summaries of more complex arguments worked out at greater length in three unpublished seminar and conference papers: 'Social Mobility and Social Stratification among the Punjab Peasantry: Some Hypotheses', 'The Army as Safety-Net: Military Service and Peasant Stratification in the British Punjab', and 'The Rise of the Martial Castes: Changes in the Composition of the Indian Army, 1878-1914'.

Abbreviations

AR	Assessment Report
DG	District Gazetteer
PBEIP	Punjab Board of Economic Inquiry Publication
PR(R)	Proceedings of the Government of the Punjab in the Revenue Department (Revenue Branch)
SR	Settlement Report

Copies of all the reports, gazetteers and proceedings cited can be found in the India Office Library and Records. Proceedings numbers in PR(R) references are italicised; the Roman numbers which follow refer to pages.

1. The 'before-and-after' descriptions of the *doab* are based on the district gazetteers (DGs), settlement reports (SRs), and assessment reports (ARs) of the three districts concerned. For a complete list with locations, see the entries under Rawalpindi, Attock and Jhelum in my 'Handlist of the Settlement Literature of the Greater Punjab' (forthcoming).
2. The relationship between a caste's traditional values and economic opportunities (on the one hand) and its propensity to enlist or cultivate (on the other) is explored in 'The Rise of the Martial Castes'. The key

sources are the passages in which settlement officers explained the distribution of income from service, or discussed the characteristics of the leading tribes. The assessment reports which A.J.W. Kitchin drew up during the 1902-07 settlement of Rawalpindi and the district gazetteer he subsequently compiled contain classic examples of the genre. See his *Gujar Khan AR*, Proceedings of the Government of the Punjab in the Revenue Department, Revenue Branch [PR(R)], October 1905, nos. *1-13*, 32-6; *Murree and Kahuta AR*, PR(R) November 1906, nos. *22-25*, 6-7, 15-20, 32-33, 39-40; *Rawalpindi AR* (Lahore, 1905), 16-18, 27-33; *Rawalpindi DG 1907*, 114ff, 163-64.

3. The reasons for the growth of Punjabi Mussalmen recruiting are analysed in my 'Rise of the Martial Castes'. The figures cited come from a miscellany of official sources. The annual *Caste Return of the Indian Army* (title varies) gives the size of the Punjabi Mussalmen contingent in the army from 1875 to 1942 (the first and last year for which the India Office Records have copies of the return). Data on peacetime soldiers and pensioners can be found in J.M. Wakeley, *Handbooks for the Indian Army: Punjabi Mussalmen* (Calcutta 1915; 2nd edn., Delhi, 1936); Roshan Lal Anand, *Soldiers' Savings and How They Use Them*, Punjab Board of Economic Inquiry Publication (PBEIP) No. 68 (Lahore, 1940), 5; Prem Nath Thapar, *Final Report of the Third Revised Settlement of the Jhelum District in the Punjab 1937-1941* (Lahore, 1948), 6; J. W. Johnston, *The History of the Great War: Rawalpindi District* (Lahore, n.d. but c. 1920), 2-4. The wartime peaks are treated in M.S. Leigh, *The Punjab and the War* (Lahore. 1922); *India's Contribution to the Great War* (Calcutta, 1923); Sri Nanda Prasad, *Expansion of the Armed Forces and Defence Organisation 1939-45* (Delhi, 1956), especially appendices 13-14; Johnson, *Rawalpindi War History;* M.S.D. Butler, *Record of the War Services in the Attock District 1914-19* (n.p. 1921).

4. The military participation ratios are taken or calculated from Wakeley's *Punjabi Musalmen;* Leigh's *Punjab and the War;* Johnson's *Rawalpindi War History;* and L. Middleton and S.M. Jacob, *Census of India 1921*, XV, *Punjab and Delhi* (two parts, Lahore, 1923), Part II, Tables VII and XIII. The rough estimates of the *doabis'* aggregate income from pay and pensions are based on data in the *Caste Returns;* Anand's *Soldiers' Savings;* Prasad's *Expansion of the Armed Forces;* and Ram Swarup Nakra, *Punjab Villages during the War*, PBEIP No. 91 (Lahore, 1946), chapter II. Details of military reward grants in the canal colonies are given in F.B. Wace, *Punjab Colony Manual* (rev. edn., Lahore, 1934), 103-5; annual *Reports on the Administration of the Punjab Colonies* 1901/2 to 1939/40; and Leigh, *The Punjab and the War*. The price of land in the 'British period' peaked in 1945/6: see *Agricultural Statistics of the Punjab, Pakistan, 1901-02 to 1946-47*, PBEIP No. 97 (Lahore, 1950), Table 49. Breakdowns of India's defence expenditure are available in *Budget Estimates of Expenditure on Defence Services, 1924/5-43/4* and *1946/7-48/9;* 'actuals' can be obtained from the *Statistical Abstract for British India* (title varies), *1911/21-36/41, 1946/7*.

5. *Jhelum DG 1883-4*, 118; *Jhelum DG 1904*, 252-6; R.G. Thomson, *Report of the Second Regular Settlement of the Land Revenue of the Jhelum District in the Rawalpindi Division of the Punjab* (Lahore, 1883), 75-9; W.S. Talbot, *Final Report of the Revision of the Settlement of the Jhelum District in the Punjab* (Lahore, 1901), 9; Prem Nath Thapar, *Jhelum SR*, 6, 13, 17, 23, 29; W.S.

Talbot, *Pind Dadan Khan AR*, PR(R) Oct. 1898, nos. 1-6, 34, 37; Prem Nath Thapar, *Pind Dadan Khan AR* (Lahore, 1941), 15-16; W.S. Talbot, *Chakwal and Tallagang AR*, PR(R) Dec. 1899, nos. 27-31, 30; Prem Nath Thapar, *Chakwal AR* (Lahore, 1941), 12; E. G. Wace, *Jhelum (District) AR*, PR(R) Feb 1882, no. 3 and Appendix, 8-9; W.S. Talbot, *Jhelum AR* PR(R) April 1900, nos. 12-16, 24-5; Prem Nath Thapar, *Jhelum AR* (Lahore, 1941), 11; M. L. Darling, Travel Diaries, 12 March 1932 and 20 April 1937, typescript, Centre for South Asian Studies, Cambridge.

6. Anand, *Soldiers' Savings*, 16-17.
7. Col. J.H. Green's complaints can be found amongst the Government of India's Proceedings in the Military Department, Nov. 1889, nos. 714-15; Lt. W.W. Norman published his critique in a prize essay, 'The Organisation and Employment in War of Native Cavalry', *Journal of the United Service Institution of India*, XIX (1890), 294. The survey was, of course, Nakra's *Punjab Villages*, chapter III.
8. Anand, *Soldiers' Savings*, chapter IV; Nakra, *Punjab Villages*, 8-9.
9. *Report on the Internal Trade of the Punjab, 1884/5*, Statement II; *Rawalpindi DG 1907*, 118ff, 163-4; D.G.J. Ibbetson, *Report on the Census of the Punjab, 1881*, (3 vols, Lahore, 1883), III, 494; Aslam Abdullah Khan, *Census of Pakistan, 1961*, vol. 3, *West Pakistan* (Karachi, n.d.), II-60; *Domestic Budgets (1941-42) of Thirty Families in the Murree Suburban Zone (Rawalpindi District)*, PBEIP No. 87 (Lahore, 1940), 8-11; W.G. Bradford, deputy commissioner, Rawalpindi, to commissioner, Rawalpindi, 5 June 1933 (a forecast report on a resettlement which never took place), PR(R) Dec. 1936, nos. 20-27 (actually bound in January 1937). Cf. Thapar, *Jhelum SR*, 6; Thapar, *Chakwal AR*, 12; C.B. Barry, *Pindigheb AR* (Lahore, 1926), 31-3.
10. *Report on the Revenue Administration of the Punjab* 1862/3-1870/1 (statement varies); *Report on the Season and Crops of the Punjab 1906/7-1946/7*, Statement VI; *Report on the Season and Crops of the North-West Frontier Province*, 1906/7-1944/5, Statement V; C.B. Barry, *Rates of Food Consumption by Zamindars in the Tallagang Tehsil of the Attock District*, PBEIP No. 6 (Lahore, 1925), ii-iii; M.L. Darling, *At Freedom's Door* (London, 1949), 61.
11. Thapar, *Chakwal AR*, 8-9; M. L. Darling, *Rusticus Loquitur* (London, 1930), 313; Darling, *Wisdom and Waste in the Punjab Village* (London, 1934), 63, 184, 289; Darling, *At Freedom's Door*, 61: *Domestic Budgets . . . of Thirty Families*, 6; Alma Latifi, *The Industrial Punjab* (Lahore, 1911), 4, 44, 52-3; Talbot, *Chakwal and Tallagang AR*, 32 J.H. Quereshi compares the expenditure of military and civilian colonists immediately after independence in his *Economic Survey of Eight Typical Villages in the Thal*, PBEIP No. 11? (Lahore, 1963), 141ff.
12. *Report on the Internal Trade of the Punjab 1884/5*, Statement II; Talbot, *Chakwal and Tallagang AR*, 32.
13. Darling, *Wisdom and Waste*, 63.
14. April Darling, Travel Diary, 82, typescript in the Darling Collection, Centre for South Asian Studies, Cambridge.
15. Darling, *Punjab Peasant*, 55-8; E. D. Maclagan, *Monograph on the Gold and Silver Work of the Punjab, 1889-89* (Lahore, 1890), 15; *Note on Sales of Gol*

and Ornaments in 120 Punjab Villages, PBEIP Pamphlet No.1 (Lahore, 1936), 26; the quotation is from Darling, *At Freedom's Door*, 60-1.

16. *Ibid.*, 61.

17. *Rawalpindi DG (Part B) 1935; Attock DG (Part B) 1933* and *Jhelum DG (Part B) 1934*, all Statements 34-35; *Rawalpindi DG 1907*, 88-9; Kitchin, *Rawalpindi AR*, 16-18, 21; Kitchin, *Fatehjang and Pindigheb AR*, PR(R) November 1906, nos. 26-29, 20; M.S.D. Butler, *Attock AR*, (PR(R) April 1904, nos. 1-12, 27; C.B. Barry, *Attock AR* (Lahore, 1925), 18; Barry, *Pindigheb AR*, 15; Barry, *Tallagang AR* (Lahore, 1925), 9ff; Barry, *Fatehjang AR* (Lahore, 1926), 20; Wace, *Jhelum (District) AR*, 10-12; Darling, Travel Diaries, page 10 of volume for 1931 and 13 September, 1931; Darling, *Punjab Peasant*, 67-9; Darling, *Wisdom and Waste*, 61-2, 75; G.G.B. Iver, *In An Indian District* (Lahore, 1919), 103.

18. A. Brandreth, *Report on the Settlement of the District of Jhelum in the Rawalpindi Division* (Lahore, 1865), 31-3; F.A. Robertson, *Final Report of the Revised Settlement of the Rawalpindi District in the Punjab, 1880-1887* (Lahore, 1893), 37-8, 40-1; *Rawalpindi DG 1907*, 45.

19. A composite quotation: the second sentence comes from Talbot, *Jhelum AR*, 26; the rest comes from Thomson, *Jhelum SR*, and refers to the Mairs, Kasars and Kahuts. Cf. Kitchin, *Gujar Khan AR*, 33; Talbot, *Chakwal and Tallagang AR*, 32.

20. Darling, Travel Diaries, 20 November 1931; Darling, *Wisdom and Waste*, 45-7, 49, 61-2, 65-6; *Attock DG 1907*, 72-4; *Attock DG 1930*, 85-8; *Jhelum DG 1904*, 100ff, 126ff; Thomson, *Jhelum SR*, 36-8.

21. *Attock DG 1930*, 85-8; *Rawalpindi DG 1907*, 188; S.S. Thorburn, commissioner, Rawalpindi, to under-secretary to the Government of the Punjab, 21 September, 1895, Proceedings of the Government of the Punjab in the Home Department, Judicial Branch, January 1899, nos. 1-51.

22. Mohammad Ayub Khan, *Friends Not Masters* (London, 1967), 2-3.

23. Darling, Travel Diaries, 22 November 1931; *Rusticus Loquitur*, 245-6, 299-306, 318; *Wisdom and Waste*, 40, 53, 68, 81-2; *At Freedom's Door*, 85-6. The *pirs'* conversion of their religious authority into political influence is discussed in Ian Talbot, 'The 1946 Punjab Elections', *Modern Asian Studies*, 14 (1980), 79ff, and David Gilmartin, 'Religious Leadership and the Pakistan Movement in the Punjab', *ibid.*, 13 (1979), 509ff.

24. J.A. Rahim, *Report of the Special Hajj Inquiry* (n.p. and n.d. but probably Delhi c. 1941), 11, 66-72, 156; Francis Robinson, *Atlas of the Islamic World* (London, 1982), 195; *Rawalpindi DG 1907*, 102-3; fairs and shrines are described in all the western Punjab DGs.

25. *Rawalpindi DG 1907*, 55ff; *1921 Census*, I, 258-61; Barry, *Attock AR*, 18; M. L. Darling, *The Punjab Peasant in Prosperity and Debt* (5th edn., Delhi 1977), 48-59, 216-7; Darling, Travel Diaries, 1-2 June 1931; Darling *Rusticus Loquitur*, 300.

26. Darling, Travel Diaries, 28 May, 1932.

27. Darling, Travel Diaries, 26 November, 1930, 10 October, 1931, 19 December, 1931; *Wisdom and Waste*, 110-1, 305-11.

28. Darling, Travel Diaries, 28 May, 1932.

29. *Report on the Administration of the Land Revenue in the Punjab*, 1889/1900-1939/40, statement varies; *Agricultural Statistics of the Punjab, Pakistan 1901-02 to 1946-47*, PBEIP No. 97 (Lahore, 1950), Table 49; Thapar, *Jhelum SR*, 10-15; Raja Hasan Aktar, *An Inquiry into the Mortgages of Agricultural Lane in the Pothwar Assessment Circle of the Rawalpindi District*, PBEIP No. 14 (Lahore, 1926), 15; Ghulam Yasin, *Economic Survey of Sagri: A Village in the Rawalpindi District, Punjab, Pakistan*, PBEIP No. 100 (Lahore, 1950), 69; Darling, *The Punjab Peasant*, 76–7; Darling, *Wisdom and Waste*, 51; Kitchin *Rawalpindi AR*, 19-20; Kitchin, *Murree and Kahuta AR*, 21; Kitchin, *Gujar Khan AR*, 35-6; Barry, *Attock AR*, 21-4; Barry, *Pindigheb AR*, 117-20; Barry, *Tallagang AR*, 12; Barry, *Fatehjang AR*, 22; Thapar, *Jhelum AR*, 19, 22–4; Thapar, *Chakwal AR*, 16–21; Thapar, *Pind Dadan Khan AR*, 25 and 'Government Orders', W. G. Bradford, *op. cit.*, para 13.

30. *Punjab Land Revenue Report, 1939/40*, Statement III; Thapar, *Jhelum SR*, 13–4; Thapar, *Jhelum AR*, 19, 22–4; Thapar, *Chakwal AR*, 16–25; Thapar, *Pind Dadan Khan AR*, 22–4; Chaudhri Sardar Khan, *Final Report of the Fourth Revised Settlement (1923-7) of the Attock District* (Lahore, 1928), 14; Barry, *Attock AR*, 22–3; Barry, *Pindigheb AR*, 19; Barry, *Tallagang AR*, 12; Barry, *Fatehjang AR*, 22; W.G. Bradford, *op. cit.*, para 13; Hassan Ali Syed, *Report on the Need and Supply of Credit in the Rural Areas of the Punjab*, PBEIP No.101 (Lahore, 1951), 45.

31. Cyril P.K. Fazal, *A Note on Sales of Land . . . 1922-23 to 1926-27*, PBEIP No. 23 (Lahore, 1931), 13; *Rawalpindi DG 1907*), 140-1, Kitchin, *Gujar Khan AR*, 35–6; Kitchin, *Fatehjang and Pindigheb AR*, 25; Robertson, *Rawalpindi SR*, 97, 99; Attock DG 1907, 166-7; Barry, *Attock AR*, 21-2; Barry, *Pindigheb AR*, 17-8; Barry, *Fatehjang AR*, 21; Talbot, *Chakwal and Tallagang AR*, 36; Thapar, *Jhelum AR*, 24; Thapar, *Chakwal AR*, 16-21; S.S. Thorburn, *Report on Peasant Indebtedness and Land Alienations to Moneylenders in Parts of the Rawalpindi Division* (Lahore, 1890), 242, 244, 252–3.

32. The annual *Reports on the Working of the Alienation of Land Act* (1900/1-1907/8) and the subsequent *Reports on the Administration of the Land Revenue in the Punjab* contain tables showing early tribal gains and losses via sales and mortgages.

33. Thomson, *Jhelum SR*, 100; Barry, *Attock AR*, 'Government Orders'.

34. *Attock DG 1930*, 192; Butler, *Attock AR*, 26-7; Kitchin, *Rawalpindi AR*, 19-21; Barry, *Fatehjang AR*, 16.

35. H. Calvert, *The Size and Distribution of Agricultural Holdings in the Punjab*, PBEIP No. 4 (Lahore, 1925), 16-7; *Proprietary Holdings in the Punjab—Their Size and Distribution*, PBEIP Preliminary Report for officia use only; (Lahore, 1939); *Report of the Land Revenue Committee* (Lahore 1938), Appendix 1; the relevant *District Gazetteers* (Part B) Table 38 (for full list of post-1931 gazetteers see my 'Handlist of the Settlement Literature'); Khan Ahmad Hasan Khan, *Census of India, 1931*, XVII, *Punja* (two parts, Lahore, 1933), Part II, Tables VII and X.

36. Darling, Travel Diaries, 8 September 1931; *Wisdom and Waste*, 44, 62-3, 71 *Rusticus Loquitur*, 179; Anand, *Soldiers Savings*, 16-20; Barry, *Attock AR*, 18

Cf. Charlotte V. Wiser, *Four Families of Karimpur* (Syracuse, New York, 1978), 51ff.

37. Darling, *Wisdom and Waste*, 62-3.

38. *Ibid.*, 43, 49, 71; April Darling, Travel Diary, 163-4; *Rawalpindi DG 1907*, 119-20; Kitchin, *Rawalpindi AR*, 27-8; Butler, *Attock AR*, 18; Barry, *Attock AR*, 18; Kitchin, *Fatehjang and Pindigheb AR*, 36; Thapar, *Jhelum AR*, 9-10; Thapar, *Pind Dadan Khan AR*, 13-5.

39. A composite quotation; the first part comes from Kitchin, *Rawalpindi AR*, 18; the last three sentences come from Kitchin, *Murree and Kahuta AR*, 7, 20.

40. Kitchin, *Murree and Kahuta AR*, 7, 19.

41. Kitchin, *Rawalpindi AR*, 29.

42. Kitchin, *Rawalpindi AR*, 11, 16, 41; W.G. Bradford, *op. cit.*; *1921 Census*, Part II, Table IV.

3. *Rawalpindi DG 1907*, 113, 127-9; Kitchin, *Rawalpindi AR*, 18, 28, 31-2; Malik Amanat Khan, *Rise of the Price of Bhusa in the Punjab*, PBEIP No. 95 (Lahore, 1949), *passim*. In 1944/5 the Military Department bought 94,000 tons of *bhusa* (mainly for its dairy farms), enough to make military purchases 'one of the major factors responsible for the abnormal rise in the price of *bhusa*'. At the time the price of *bhusa* was higher in Rawalpindi than in any other town in the Punjab (Khan, 14-15, 19).

4. *Rawalpindi DG 1907*, 119-20, 123-6, 131-2, 155-6; Kitchin, *Rawalpindi AR*, 27-8.

5. *Rawalpindi DG 1907*, 132-3; Kitchin, *Murree and Kahuta AR*, 39-40. Cf. tobacco in the Chhachh: *Attock DG 1930*, 182-3, 185; Barry, *Attock AR*, 47-9. The Chhachh plain in Attock was more extensive than the Pothwar plain in Rawalpindi, but it was less dependent on military patronage.

. *Rawalpindi DG 1907*, 143-4; Kitchin, *Rawalpindi AR*, 14-15; *Attock DG 1907*, 171ff; *Attock DG 1930*, 195-8; Barry, *Attock AR*, 13ff, 24; Barry, *Fatehjang AR*, 15-16; Barry, *Pindigheb AR*, 12-13; Thapar, *Jhelum SR*, 6; Talbot, *Chakwal and Tallagang AR*, 28; Thapar, *Chakwal AR*, 9-11; Thapar, *Jhelum AR*, 9-10; Thapar, *Pind Dadar Khan AR*, 13-15; R. Sykes, director of land records and agriculture to revenue and financial secretary to the Government of the Punjab, 13 December 1899, PR(R), January 1900, Nos. 8-10; A. M. Stow, *Cattle and Dairying in the Punjab* (Lahore, 1910), *passim*.

. *Rawalpindi DG 1907*, 146, 148-51; Robertson, *Rawalpindi SR*, 130-5; Brandreth, *Jhelum SR*, 37-8; *Attock DG 1907*, 171ff; *Attock DG 1930*, 199; Wace, *Punjab Colony Manual*, 132-49.

Rawalpindi DG 1907, 147; *Attock DG 1907*, 171ff; *Attock DG 1930*; 198-9; Barry, *Pindigheb AR*, 12-13.

Rawalpindi DG 1907, 72-4, 163ff; Kitchin, *Murree and Kahuta AR*, 7, 18-19, 23; Kitchin, *Rawalpindi AR*, 18; *Attock DG 1930*, 185; Barry, *Attock AR*, 15; Thapar, *Chakwal AR*, 9.

Rawalpindi DG 1907, 72-4; Kitchin, *Gujar Khan AR*, 36; Kitchin, *Murree and Kahuta AR*, 18-19; Kitchin, *Rawalpindi AR*, 18; *Attock DG 1930*, 60-1; Butler, *Attock AR*, 1-12, 27-8; Barry, *Attock AR*, 18, 24; Barry, *Fatehjang AR*, 24;

Barry, *Pindigheb AR*, 21-2; Barry, *Tallagang AR*, 14; Talbot, *Jhelum SR*, 9; Thapar, *Pind Dadan Khan AR*, 'Government Orders'.

51. *Rawalpindi DG 1907*, 245-9; Robertson, *Rawalpindi AR*, 174ff.

52. Table 1; *Rawalpindi DG 1893-4*, 193ff; *Rawalpindi DG 1907*, 172ff; Robertson, *Rawalpindi SR*, 179ff; Kitchin, *Gujar Khan AR*, 4-5; Kitchin, *Rawalpindi AR*, 6-7; *Jhelum DG 1904*, 211ff, 274ff; Thomson, *Jhelum SR*, 65ff; Thapar, *Chakwal AR*, 8-9; Thapar, *Pind Dadan Khan AR*, 12-13; *Attock DG 1907* 200ff, 267ff; Kitchin, *Fatehjang and Pindigheb AR*, 7-8; Barry, *Pindigheb AR* 11-12.

53. *1921 Census*, Part II, Table XVI B; *Rawalpindi DG 1907*, 245-9.

54. Rawalpindi Municipal Committee, *Rawalpindi Directory, 191*[illegible] (Rawalpindi, 1916), *passim*; *1921 Census*, Part II, Tables VIII, XI; Part I Subsidiary Table XII. For two 'sample' contractors, see 'The Mobilisation of the Notables', *infra*. The municipality spent more money on service (per capita) than any other city in the Punjab: *Annual Reports on the Working of Municipalities in the Punjab, 1890/1*.

55. *Rawalpindi DG 1907*, 249-52; J. E. Bartholomew, *Constable's Hand Atlas* [illegible] *India* (London, 1893), Map 30; *Murree Directory, 1894* (Lahore, 1894); 192[illegible] *Census*, Table XVI; Hari Kishen Kaul, *Report on the Summer Census* [illegible] *Murree, 1911* (Lahore, 1912); *Report on the Summer Census of the Punjab Hi*[illegible] *Stations of Simla, Dalhousie and Murree, 1921* (Lahore, 1922); E.B. Eastwick *Handbook of the Punjab . . .* (London, 1883), 253-4; L.F.R. Williams (ed.) *A Handbook for Travellers in India, Pakistan, Burma and Ceylon* (London 1965) 500-1. The Victorian fascination with technology and the lack of obviou[illegible] alternatives made Dyer's brewery a great tourist attraction.

56. *Rawalpindi DG (Part B) 1935*, Table 6.

57. Yasin, *Sagri*, xvi.

58. *Ibid.*, 81-2.

59. *Ibid.*, 15, 23, 25, 27, 31, 83-5, 133-6.

60. *Ibid.*, xii, 14.

61. *Ibid.*, 17, 133-6.

62. *Ibid.*, xiii.

63. *Ibid.*, xv, 21, 61, 78, 83-4.

64. *Ibid.*, 78.

65. *Rawalpindi DG 1893-4*, 206-8; *Rawalpindi DG 1907*, 8-12; Robertso[illegible] *Rawalpindi SR*, 148ff; Kitchin, *Final Report of the Revision of the Settlement* [illegible] *the Rawalpindi District in the Punjab, 1902-7* (Lahore, 1909), 4; Kitch[illegible] *Rawalpindi AR*, 1; Thomson, *Jhelum SR*, 10; Faqir Chand Arora, *Comme*[illegible] *by River in the Punjab*, Punjab Government Record Office Publicatio[illegible] Monograph No. 9 (Lahore, 1930), 20-3, 32-3, 40-45, 91, 94.

66. Arora, *Commerce by River*, especially 45ff, 66-7, 79-82.

67. D.C.J. Ibbetson (ed.), *Gazetteer of the Punjab: Provincial Volume, 188*[illegible] (Calcutta, n.d.), 195ff; *History of Indian Railways, 1923*, 143-71; *Rawalpi*[illegible] *DG 1893-4*, 208-10; *Attock DG 1907*, 200ff; Kitchin, *Fatehjang and Pindig*[illegible] *AR*, 7; *Jhelum DG 1904*, 212ff; *Report on the Internal Trade of the Punjab by* [illegible]

and River 1884/5, Statement II; H.C. Wylly, 'Some Strategic Railways on the North-West Frontier of India', *United Service Magazine*, 32 (1905-6), 556-62

68. *Rawalpindi DG 1893-4*, 210-13; *Rawalpindi DG 1907*, 176-81; Thomson, *Rawalpindi SR*, 68-9; Kitchin, *Gujar Khan AR*, 4; Kitchin, *Rawalpindi AR*, 5ff; *Attock DG 1907*, 202ff; *Attock DG 1930*, 185, 228-33; Kitchin, *Attock SR*, 4-5; Butler, *Attock AR*, 4-5; Barry, *Attock AR*, 14-15; Kitchin, *Fatehjang and Pindigheb AR*, 7; Barry, *Fatehjang AR*, 14; Barry, *Pindigheb AR*, 11; Thapar, *Jhelum SR*, 3; Thapar, *Chakwal AR*, 7-8; W. S. Dorman, *Road Development in the Punjab*, Punjab Public Works Department Papers No. 77 (Lahore, 1928); *Report of the Indian Road Development Committee, 1927-8* (Calcutta, 1928), 84; 'Punjab Provincial Report' in K.G. Mitchell and H. Kirkness, *Report on the Present State of Road and Rail Competition* (Calcutta, 1933). In 1929/30 the Punjab spent more than four times as much (per capita) on its roads as Bengal, and three times as much as the United Provinces. The impact of the army on the road network was most obvious in the two adjacent hill tehsils of Rawalpindi. Communications in Kahuta (which had no strategic importance) were 'the worst in the Punjab' (not a single track fit for wheeled traffic), while hardly a village in Murree was more than a few miles from a good road: Kitchin, *Murree and Kahuta AR*, 6. See also: *General Staff, India, Routes in the Rawalpindi District* (Calcutta, 1932), and *Military Report on the Rawalpindi District* (Simla, 1922), Chapter VII.

69. Kitchin, *Murree and Kahuta AR*, 7; Kitchin, *Rawalpindi AR*, 18; Barry, *Attock AR*, 14-15; *Report on the Season and Crops of the Punjab, 1908/9*, Statement VII; *Punjab Cattle Census (Livestock Census* from 1935), 1914, 1920, 1923, 1928, 1930, 1935, 1940 (all published in Lahore).

70. Mitchell and Kirkness, *Road and Railway Competition, passim;* Thapar, *Chakwal AR*, 7-8; Thapar, *Jhelum AR*, 7-8; Thapar, *Pind Dadan Khan AR*, 12-13; Ghulam Yasin, *Problems of Road Transport in the Punjab*, PBEIP No. 68 (Lahore, 1956), 7-10; Statistical *Abstract of British India, 1942/3*; Anand, *Soldiers' Savings*, 27, 29; Prasad, *Expansion of the Armed Forces*, App. 13; *Caste Return of the Army in India*, 1942; *Report of the Disposals Enquiry Committee* (New Delhi, 1947), 7, 18, 25-6, 33.

71. *1921 Census*, Part II, Table XXII. The annual *Reports on the Working of the Joint Stock Companies in the Punjab* listed the Express Cart Company and the Phoenix Carrying Company as having their headquarters in Rawalpindi before the First World War, the same reports give details of the big garages twenty years later. The army's workshops are marked on the 2" to a mile Survey of Pakistan maps of Rawalpindi. There is an interesting description of the East India Railway's workshop at Jamalpur in the Indian Industrial Commission's confidential *Inspection Notes, 1916-18*, 89-91, which are filed in the India Office Revenue Department Papers for 1915, vd. 851, no. 8417.

72. Compare *Prices and Wages in India*, 23rd issue (Calcutta, 1906), Table 51, with the *Seventh Report on the Wages Survey of the Punjab, 1943*, Table B; *Attock DG 1930*, 224-5; *Attock DG (Part B) 1933*, Table 28; *Jhelum DG 1904*, 135, 211-12; *1921 Census*, Part II, Table XXII; J. Coggin Brown and A. K. Dey, *India's Mineral Wealth* (3rd edn., Bombay, 1955), 338ff.

73. *Jhelum DG 1904*, 197ff. B.H. Baden Powell, *Handbook of the Economic Products of the Punjab* (2 volumes, Lahore, 1868-72), I, 27-34; E.E. Oliver, *Notes on Coal and Iron in the Punjab*, Selections from the Records of the Government of the Punjab, New Series XXI (Lahore, 1883), 7-9; Latifi, *The Industrial Punjab*, Appendix IV, 298-9, A.C. Badenoch, *Punjab Industries 1911-1917* (Lahore, 1917), 43-5; *1921 Census, loc. cit.*; Brown and Dey, *India's Mineral Wealth*, 59ff.

74. *Rawalpindi DG 1893-4*, 192-3; *Attock DG 1930*, 222-3; Baden Powell, *Handbook*, I, 20-22; Brown and Dey, *India's Mineral Wealth*, 85ff.

75. *Jhelum DG 1904*, 135ff; *1921 Census, loc. cit.*; F. Ashton, 'The Salt Supply of Northern India', *The Agricultural Ledger*, No. 13 of 1900, 130-8.

76. Latifi, *The Industrial Punjab*, 100-112; Badenoch, *Punjab Industries*, 20; *Report on the Working of Joint Stock Companies in the Punjab 1908/9*, Statement II. Cf. J.A. Grant, *Monograph on the Leather Industry of the Punjab* (Lahore, 1893), and Roshan Lal Anand, *Tanning Industry in the Punjab*, PBEIP No. 6 (Lahore, 1939).

77. Badenoch, *Punjab Industries*, 13-14, 34-5; *1921 Census, loc. cit.*; *Gurdaspur DG 1891-2*; 113.

78. Baden Powell, *Handbook*; B.H. Baden Powell, *Report on the Punjab Exhibition, 1881-82*, Selections from the Records of the Government of Punjab, New Series, XXII (Lahore, 1883); Ibbetson (ed.), *Gazetteer of the Punjab*, 143ff; Latifi, *The Industrial Punjab*; Badenoch, *Punjab Industries*; *Attock DG 1930*, 166-7, 174, 182; Barry, *Attock AR*, 7-9; *Prices and Wages in India*, 23rd issue (Calcutta, 1906), Tables 35 and 52; *Reports on the Season and Crops of the Punjab, 1908/9* and *1912/3*, Statement VI; *First Wages Survey of the Punjab, 1912*, Table B; *Seventh Wages Survey of the Punjab, 1943*, Table B.

79. *Ludhiana DG 1888-9, 157*; Latifi, *The Industrial Punjab*, 4, 44, 52-3; Darling, *Wisdom and Waste*, 184, 263. But cf. Thapar, *Chakwal AR*, 8-9.

80. *Rawalpindi DG 1893-4*, 207.

81. *Rawalpindi DG 1907*, 43-5, 197-200; Robertson, *Rawalpindi SR*, 40-; Kitchin, *Gujar Khan AR*, 35-6; Kitchin, *Murree and Kahuta AR*, 18-; Kitchin, *Rawalpindi AR*, 16-21; *Attock DG 1907*, 78-81; *Attock DG 1930*, 85-99; Butler, *Attock AR*, 9-10; Barry, *Attock AR*, 18, 21-4; Kitchin, *Fatehjang and Pindigheb AR*, 24-5; Barry, *Fatehjang AR*, 21-3, 32; Barry, *Pindigheb AR*, 29- 34; Thapar, *Jhelum SR*, 14-15, 17-19; Thapar, *Jhelum AR*, 13-14, 24-; Talbot, *Pind Dadan Khan AR*, 33; Darling, Travel Diaries, 1-2 June and 1 September, 1931.

82. *Rawalpindi DG 1907*, 139-43; Kitchin, *Murree and Kahuta AR*, 21; *Attock DG 1907*, 164ff; Barry, *Attock AR*, 21-4 and H. R. Calvert, commissioner Rawalpindi to financial commissioner, Punjab, 23 August, 1928, *Jhelum DG 1904*, 104; Brandreth, *Jhelum SR*, 30, 65, 96-8; Talbot, *Pind Dadan Khan AR*, 'Government Orders'. The two Pind Dadan Khan ARs show, with particular clarity, how the Muslim peasantry broke the Hindu moneylenders' monopoly of rural credit with the aid of their 'outside earnings' between the 1890s and the 1930s.

83. *Rawalpindi DG 1907*, 161; Kitchin, *Murree and Kahuta AR*, 7; Kitchin, *Rawalpindi AR*, 5, 18; *Attock DG 1930*, 185; Barry, *Attock AR*, 15, 19; Talbot

Chakwal and Tallagang AR, 26-7; Thapar, *Pind Dadan Khan AR*, 9.

84. April Darling, Travel Diary, 9-10, 43, 63-4; Darling, Travel Diaries, 8 September, 1931, 22 and 26 November, 1931, 11 December, 1931, 2 February, 1932; Ian Talbot, 'Deserted Collaborators: The Rise and Fall of the Punjab Unionist Party', unpublished typescript.

85. *Rawalpindi DG 1907*, 161, 191-3; Robertson, *Rawalpindi SR*, 84-5 and financial commissioner's review; *Attock DG 1907*, 217ff; *Attock DG 1930*, 60; Thomson, *Jhelum SR*, 52ff; Thapar, *Jhelum AR*, 38-9; Thapar, *Pind Dadan Khan AR*, 37-9.

86. Kitchin, *Gujar Khan AR*, 35-6.

87. Darling, Travel Diaries, 1929, page 12, 10 September, 1931, 18-19 December, 1931, 8 February, 1932, 12 March, 1932, 28 May, 1932.

88. Robertson, *Rawalpindi SR*, 37-8, 40-1; Kitchin, *Rawalpindi AR*, 16-8, 21; *Attock DG 1907*, 72-4; *Attock DG 1930*, 85-8; Thomson, *Jhelum SR*, 35; Darling, Travel Diaries, 9 and 13 September, 1931.

89. *Rawalpindi DG 1907*, 43-5, 63-6, 297-200; Robertson, *Rawalpindi SR*, 37-8, 80-2; Kitchin, *Murree and Kahuta AR*, 17-8; Kitchin, *Gujar Khan AR*, 26, 33; Kitchin, *Rawalpindi AR*, 8-10; *Attock DG 1907*, 37ff; *Jhelum DG 1904*, 89-93, 227-9; Brandreth, *Jhelum SR*, 29ff, 65, 96-8; Thomson, *Jhelum SR*, 26-90; Talbot, *Jhelum AR*, 26; Thapar, *Jhelum AR*, 12-4; Sir Lepel Griffin, *The Punjab Chiefs* (Lahore, 1865), 573-81; *ibid*, ed. C.F. Massy (2 volumes, Lahore, 1890; pedigree tables 1899), II, 319-23, 351-60; G.L. Chopra, *Chiefs and Families of Note in the Punjab* (2 volumes and appendices, Lahore, 1940), II, 280-8; Sir Denzil Ibbetson, *Punjab Castes* (Lahore, 1916; a reprint of the chapter on caste in the Report on the Punjab Census of 1881), 165-9; Johnson, *Rawalpindi War History*, 9.

90. Kitchin, *Murree and Kahuta AR*, 16; Johnson, *Rawalpindi War History*, 8.

91. Griffin, *Punjab Chiefs*, ed. Massy, II, 367-70; Chopra, *Punjab Chiefs*, II, 275-9; Johnson, *Rawalpindi War History*, 22ff (references to Sir Khem Singh's sons); *Report on Estates under the Administration of the Court of Wards, Punjab, 1940* (the 7,500 acre Kallar estate belonging to Sir Khem's eldest son, Baba Sir Gurbaksh Singh, was taken under the Court of Wards in 1932; the 4,250 acre estate belonging to his grandson, Baba Harbans Singh Bedi, was taken over in 1933).

92. Chopra, *Punjab Chiefs*, II, 302-5; Johnson, *Rawalpindi War History*, 22ff.

93. *The Rawalpindi Directory, 1916, passim; Court of Wards Report*, 1910 (for Hardit Singh) and 1940 (for Buta Singh); Johnson, *Rawalpindi War History*, 22ff. Cf. the irresistible rise of Tola Ram Singh, an Arora contractor resident in Campbellpur. He built a large part of the cantonment at Campbellpur, the waterworks at Rawalpindi, the high schools at Hasan Abdul and Kahuta, and so on. *Attock DG 1930*, 108.

6

TRIBESMEN, GOVERNMENT AND POLITICAL ECONOMY ON THE NORTH-WEST FRONTIER

R.O. CHRISTENSEN
University of Leicester

Traditionally the relations between the independent tribes of the North-West Frontier and the British-Indian government have been viewed largely in military and political terms. Much of the emphasis has been on tribal risings and their suppression, and almost nothing has been written about the economic aspects of the relationship. Although British policy on the North-West Frontier was concerned above all with problems of military strategy, it also had important consequences for tribal economic organisation. This paper shows how tribal political culture and the government's policy objectives—rather than conventional factors of production—led to changes in the tribal economy.

The tribes in question occupied a peripheral position. They were never incorporated into British India, and continued to live beyond the administrative border of the North-West Frontier, a border already roughly established when the British annexed the Punjab in 1849. This border defined not only a political-administrative division, but also an ecological and cultural division. Put broadly, the trans-border tribes were politically independent, possessed a mountainous habitat, and maintained a way of life based on the principles of the *Pakhtunwali* (the tribal code of honour). The cis-border tribes, on the other hand, were settled in that they were under government administration and were generally sedentary agriculturalists inhabiting the river basins of the region. They were also widely thought of as having lost many of the cultural traits associated with adherence to the *Pakhtunwali.*[1] In view of the independent tribesmen, the 'settled' tribes were no longer true Pakhtun, their way of life being very similar to that of the peasants of the Punjab.

The position of the trans-border Pakhtun tribes, like that of many other tribal societies, was economically and politically marginal.[2] Their territory was poor in revenue-yielding resources, relatively inaccessible to would-be invaders, and well-nigh ideal terrain for partisan guerrilla warfare. No government has ever attempted to establish its administration over the tribes, because of the high costs (fiscal and military) that would be incurred. Yet for governments of the region relations with the tribes have always been a matter of importance, partly because of the tribes' apparently warlike character, and partly because of the strategic position of their territory, which forms the mountain buffer separating Afghanistan from the plains of the Indus river system. Moreover, although the tribes have never been integrated politically into any state system, for a combination of ecological and political reasons most of them have come to be economically highly dependent on both the settled population and the government. Indeed, the position of the tribes may be described as one which combines political independence with economic dependence—a position which it has not always been easy for either the tribes or the government to maintain.

The relationship between the tribes and the government exercised a crucial influence over the processes of change in the tribal economy and society during the century of British frontier administration. This is not to argue simply that British policy caused whatever change occurred; but interaction with external forces—usually states—has been the main factor in generating change in tribal societies.[3] One prolific writer on the Pakhtun tribes has taken a quite different view. The anthropologist, Akbar Ahmed, has consistently argued that until very recently external government has had no impact on the socio-economic organization of the independent tribes. In the past, Ahmed maintains, tribal-governmental relations have served to reinforce the traditional tribal way of life expressed in the principles of the *Pakhtunwali.* It has only been since the early 1970s—as a result of policies pursued by the Pakistani administration and the opening up of employment opportunities for many of the tribesmen in the

Gulf—that change has become evident.[4] This argument assumes the existence of a static, ideal-type model of Pakhtun society which the tribesmen have maintained in the face of external forces.

Ahmed's view is not without substance. By the close of the British period the North-West Frontier was considered to be economically one of the most backward regions of India.[5] And there is little to suggest that there had been any fundamental change in the structure of the tribal economy in the previous century. But the absence of such a structural transformation does not mean that the socio-economic organization of the tribes was merely static. Certain important quantitative changes—notably the growth of population, income, commerce and employment opportunities—did occur during the nineteenth and early twentieth centuries, prefiguring those economic processes described by Ahmed as being of only very recent origin. If these changes failed to constitute development (in any sense of this problematic word), the explanation lies not in the lack of impact by the British government, but in the character of government policy and the way external forces were mediated by tribal values and political organization. In short, the backwardness of the tribal economy is largely a problem of political economy.

Ecology and Political Culture in Tribal Economic Organization

A common—and plausible—way of explaining tribal socio-economic organization is in terms of ecology. Indeed, the influence of the physical environment on tribal culture seems self-evident.[6] A rugged terrain, climatic aridity and a largely uncultivable land area have all been taken to account for the tribes' relative poverty, their dependence on the sedentary-agricultural population of the administered districts, their rejection of external government and their militant defence of their political independence. Thus a stereotyped picture has emerged of barren hills producing wild and predatory tribes in a state of permanent hostility towards the outside world.[7]

This rather oversimplifies matters. For one thing, the tribal areas of the North-West Frontier do not form a homogeneous physiographic entity. There are many variations in local ecological conditions, and associated with these are covariations in socio-economic organization. In the valley of Swat, for example, water for irrigation and fertile land have allowed the development of a fairly intensive agricultural economy; and unlike other tribal areas, Swat has always been a net exporter of rice, wheat, *ghi* and other foodstuffs.[8] Certain tribes, by virtue of their location on commercial routes, have specialised in the local or regional carrying trade. Others, again, have engaged in forestry, mineral extraction and small-scale manufacturing (notably firearms), depending on local environmental factors and resource availability. Insofar as ecology has shaped the tribal economy, it has been in the way the economic organization of particular tribes has varied with the ecological niche occupied.[9]

Nevertheless, some of the best known and most 'ideal-typical' of the independent tribes (these would include the Afridis, Mohmands, Orakzais, Darwesh Khel Wazirs and Mahsuds) do in certain aspects of their economy approximate to the stereotype. These tribes are generally engaged in both pastoralism and cultivation, activities which are mainly for subsistence and which account for most of tribal income. Several practise transhumance, migrating with their flocks and herds to upland pastures in the summer and back to lowland pastures in the cooler months. These migrations enable tribal members to avoid the sub-freezing temperatures in the mountains in winter and the intense heat of the plains in summer. Migration is also a way of making optimal use of scarce land resources, since it means that pasturage does not become over-grazed. Cultivation is generally dependent on rainfall, but in some places, where valleys open out to form small alluvial basins, irrigation is possible. The most important point about the economy of these tribes is its lack of self-sufficiency in subsistence requirements, and the tribes' consequent dependence on the outside world. The shortfall in tribal subsistence production is difficult to estimate, but it is likely that between one-fifth and one-quarter of tribal income had to be obtained from external sources. During the British period, large numbers of tribesmen spent at least part of the year engaged in petty trade or working as agricultural labourers in administered territory. Additional sources of income were provided by the government, as discussed below.

The popular view of the tribes as predators on the sedentary-agriculturalists finds little support. Only one or two tribes or tribal sections (e.g. the Mahsuds and the Zakha Khel Afridis) carried out raids with any regularity, and these raids usually had little economic significance, being acts of hostility towards the government rather than a means of securing an income. According to returns for the period 1920-21 to 1941-42 (the only years for which figures are available), the mean annual cash value of property stolen by the independent tribes on the entire North-West Frontier was less than Rs 57,000. This average conceals the fact that by far the greater part of the raiding in this period occurred during the disturbances following the third Anglo-Afghan war or was connected with the insurgency in Waziristan. In several years there were no raids at all in the most of the frontier districts.[10] In ecological terms, the relation of the independent tribes with the sedentary population of the administered districts has been one of the symbiosis or interdependence, rather than predation.

More generally, the relationship between ecology and economic organization is not quite as simple as it initially appears. Certainly, given a static and low-level agricultural technology, such factors as the availability of water and soil fertility set the limits of what is possible in the sphere of production. But within those limits, ecology is not the only determining factor. Political organization and the tribal value system have also played very significant roles in the deployment of resources. The absence of any centralized system of government among the tribes and the strongly-held desire to remain independent of external polities have given rise to and been reinforced by an ethic which stresses egalitarianism, self-help and the maintenance of honour, an ethic embodied in the *Pakhtunwali*. While it could be argued that these cultura features are closely related to ecological conditions, a more convincing approach is to treat them as independent variables influencing important aspects of tribal economic organizatio in their own right.

Political culture and the *Pakhtunwali* influenced the triba economy in two ways. First, tribal members were obliged to uphold group and personal honour. This in turn meant tha they had to possess adequate means of defence, since feud and other types of violent conflict were often intense an chronic. Consequently, resources were channelled toward the acquisition of arms and ammunition rahter than the im provement of productive capacity.[11] The prevalence of feudin

PHUKTUNWALI IS SELF-PERPETUATING, IF LEAVE SYSTEM YOU BECOME A VICTIM OF IT.

sucked labour out of cultivation. The man working his plot of land was an easy target; and common tactics in feuds were to burn the crops of an enemy or destroy his irrigation channels. According to one frontier official, Evelyn Howell, there existed in Tirah and Waziristan 'the traces of terraced fields . . . to show that once men grew corn where now there is no tillage'; a vivid testimony to the economic consequences of insecurity of life and property.[12]

The tribesmen's values and political culture also fostered an aversion to activities considered dishonourable and deviations from the ideals of conduct prescribed by the *Pakhtunwali*. To many tribesmen, such activities include both trade (the occupation of Hindu *banias*) and agriculture (the occupation of the sedentary population of the administered districts). The aversion to these activities was, of course, relative rather than absolute. Most tribesmen engaged in some form of agricultural activity for at least part of the year, and certain tribes have exploited their location by specializing in commerce. But those tribesmen who could afford to left such matters to others. Much of the trade in tribal territory was carried out not by actual members of the tribes, but by men of client status who (until 1947) were Hindus and Sikhs. And most menial tasks—such as the carrying of water, the gathering of wood-fuel and the cutting of forage grass—were left to women. The tribesmen who engaged in trade and cultivation rarely regarded them as full-time occupations; and the majority spent much of the annual economic cycle in under-employment.

Thus the low productivity of most of the tribal economy of the North-West Frontier was the outcome of the way in which available resources have—or have not—been used, as well as the initial poverty of resources; and this in turn was the result of the priorities established by tribal values and political organization. As one report put it:

> Unproductive though a great part of tribal territory may be under existing conditions, too much stress can be laid upon the economic factor (i.e. an unfavourable ecology). Its importance is we think greatly exaggerated, with picturesque legends of hungry hills that breed more than they can feed. But poverty has not prevented the tribesmen from paying fantastic prices for their armament or kept down the price of human life or of

> women in tribal circles. It is in fact only certain sections whom it has been literally true to say that they must raid in order to live.[13]

There could be no clearer rejection of the environmental determinists' explanation of tribal economic organization. The tribesmen's preference for investment in rifles rather than ploughs shows conclusively that the economy of the independent tribes has been strongly patterned by the high value placed on the defence of honour compared with the accumulation of wealth.

This cultural-ecological approach questions the conventional factor of production analysis of many economists. While land, labour and capital were in short supply on the North-West Frontier, factor availability does not provide an adequate basis for assessing actual or potential economic change and development. It is a far more fruitful line to examine the ways in which adaptation to ecological conditions and the political culture of the tribes have influenced the utilization of factors. Thus, the deployment of land as a productive factor was closely related to both specific environmental features and culturally-determined tribal preferences. Similar points can be made about the deployment of labour and capital. When considerations of honour and defence meant that labour was economically idle for much of the year and capital was directed to non-economic ends, there is little to be gained from regarding the tribesmen merely as members of that much-mentioned species *homo economicus*. This is not to suggest that they are entirely unresponsive to economic forces, but they are very much a political species as well.

The British Impact: Government Policy and its Economic Consequences

From the start, the British interest in the North-West Frontier was predominantly military-strategic. Throughout the century after the annexation of the Punjab at least a quarter of the strength of the Indian Army was stationed on the frontier, and the most conspicuous aspect of the British presence in the region was the establishment of a chain of cantonments and defensive posts within and just beyond the administrative border.

In fiscal terms it was always accepted that the North-West Frontier was and would remain a deficit region. The revenue yielded by the administered districts never remotely approached government expenditure on military supply, defence and related construction work (including roads and railways), tribal allowances and militia pay, and so on. This deficit expenditure undoubtedly had a considerable effect on the frontier economy. The establishment of British rule promoted growth in other ways. Much was made in official statements of the benefits resulting from the creation of more peaceful conditions on the frontier. While the economic side-effects of *pax Britannica* should not be exaggerated—tribal insurgencies continued right until the last years of British rule—the *pax* probably contributed to an expansion of cultivated area in the administered districts. More important was land revenue policy. Before 1849 the Sikhs claimed half the produce as revenue, and collected it through coercion. The British greatly reduced the demand, to a level below that in most other regions of India; and this low revenue pitch, together with the rise in agricultural prices, did much to bring about the growth of commercial farming in Peshawar and other districts.[14] Thus military expenditure and revenue policy stimulated the growth of trade and cultivation in British administered territory. There was no growth of manufacturing industry; what manufacture existed remained almost entirely of the domestic handicraft type.[15]

The British view of their impact on the independent tribes was that improving economic conditions on the frontier would play an important part in achieving the integration of the tribes into the life of the administered districts, and so reduce any threat that they posed to frontier security. In the mid-nineteenth century a policy of *laissez-aller*, of giving the tribes free access to markets in British territory, was regarded as sufficient. In 1852 Reynell Taylor thought it was

> far better that (the Wazir tribesmen) should wander through our well-stocked bazaars, talk with strange merchants, acquire a taste for clean clothes, roofed houses, and sweetmeats, and experience the advantages of a warm market themselves, by finding a ready sale for their own cattle, tobacco, and other hill produce, than that they should be shut up in the hills to gaze on the luxuriant but indifferently protected vallies (*sic*) of the plain,

> and with no better employment than to plan highway robbery and assassination, if not more active hostility.[16]

A few years later it was remarked of the Afridis that

> these mountain barbarians are beginning to be influenced by self-interest and civilization.[17]

> The wealth which has been thrown amongst these tribes by trade with us was unknown to them under Sikh or Dooranee rule.[18]

Whether the tribesmen themselves shared this mid-Victorian faith in the beneficial effects of commerce as an agent of peace and progress is doubtful. Certainly, the descriptive evidence suggests that there was a significant growth in trade between the independent tribes and the administered districts in the second half of the nineteenth century. But it is unlikely to have transformed tribal economic organization greatly.

The opening up of trading opportunities did not provide the tribes with a vent for surplus. Very little tradeable surplus existed. Although several thousand tribesmen sold such products of tribal territory as hides and skins, timber and firewood, and fruit and nuts, this trade was very small-scale and served mainly to enable the tribesmen to purchase foodstuffs and manufactures (particularly cotton cloth) not produced in tribal territory. With the exception of Swat, the main feature of tribal commerce was the net visible deficit with the administered districts.[19] Given the cultural and resource constraints, commercial growth failed to stimulate any noticeable movement of factors into production for trade. Nor can commerce be regarded as an important source of growth in tribal income. Trade probably accounted for no more than 5 per cent of total tribal income, and whatever growth occurred was more a symptom than a cause of improving income.

Market forces, then, provide only a partial explanation of the growth of the tribal economy during the British period. Yet growth there was. Perhaps the main indicator of this growth was the increase in the independent tribal population. This increase is quite impossible to measure with any degree of accuracy, since the census estimates of tribal population are based on little more than rough guesses by the frontier authorities. These estimates do, however, indicate a demographic growth in the tribal areas commensurate with that in the administered districts. In 1911 the population of the tribal areas was just over 1.6 million; by 1941 it had risen to almost 2.4 million.[20] In other words, over the century of British rule the tribal population approximately doubled. The natural rate of population growth may have been even higher, since in the second half of the nineteenth century large numbers of tribal families migrated to and settled in British territory.[21] This steady demographic increase could not have occurred without a corresponding increase in total tribal income.

A second indicator of the growth of income among the tribes was the increase in the quantity and the improvement in the quality of their firearms. A good rifle cost several years' individual savings, so the growth in tribal armament is an important symptom of tribal prosperity. In the mid-nineteenth century only a small minority of tribesmen owned firearms, and these were all smooth-bore muskets. A century later, over half the tribesmen were armed, mostly with high-velocity precision rifles.[22] This expenditure on more up to date weapons—probably the largest investment by the tribes—clearly demonstrates the precedence given to political over economic considerations. The intriguing question is: how could the tribesmen afford to expand and improve their arsenal, when their resource base was narrow, their productive technology was static, and their population was growing?

The answer is to be found largely in the character of the political relationship between the tribes and the government.[23] The most persistent problem which the British had to confront on the North-West Frontier was how to establish a stable framework for tribal management. The British needed to gain enough political influence among the tribes to obtain their co-operation in arrangements for frontier security—or at least, to prevent their hostility towards the government. The most important of the management techniques they employed was the provision of sources of income. Perhaps the best-known of these was the payment of allowances to the tribes which agreed to safeguard military-commercial routes (such as the Khyber) and protect parts of the frontier. These payments were often described by contemporaries as 'blackmail',

ARRANGED PARTNERSHIPS, NOT IMPERIAL DOMINATION ∴
PUKHTUNWALI COULD CONTINUE.

but they were a cheaper way of securing the frontier than the extensive use of military force in tribal territory. Whether the allowance payments had much impact on the tribal economy is doubtful. The total payments to the tribes in the 1930s—by which time the system had been extended to nearly all tribes—were less than Rs. 900,000 annually, and they can have formed only a small increment to tribal spending power. Their purpose had never been economic, but political: to purchase tribal goodwill, and in particular to win over tribal leaders to acceptance of government policy.[24]

The government made a far greater contribution to tribal income through the employment of tribesmen as soldiers in the Indian Army and as militiamen in the various irregular forces established on the North-West Frontier. This employment reflected a complementarity of interests. From the point of view of the tribes, it provided their members with an income, military training and an 'honourable' occupation. During the three decades or so before World War I, the Pathans (Pakhtun) became one of the most favoured of the 'martial races' of India. The figure for trans-border tribesmen serving in the Indian Army rose from less than 2,000 just after the second Anglo-Afghan war, to a peak of over 7,500 in 1915.[25] At the same time several frontier corps (the Khyber Rifles, the Tochi Scouts, the Kurram Militia, and so on) absorbed many thousand more tribesmen. Not all the earnings of these men were injected into the tribal economy, but the contribution of military income to tribal income was nevertheless considerable and probably accounted for most of the growth described. In the most heavily recruited tribes, the pay of soldiers and militiamen and the pensions of retired soldiers may well have constituted as much as a quarter of tribal income

This increasing dependence on military employment placed the tribes in a vulnerable position. An important part of their income had become contingent on their ability to persuade the government that it was worth obtaining their political goodwill through enlistment. During the First World War this arrangement broke down. Disaffection and dislike of trench warfare led to the desertion of many tribesmen and the discharge of many others. Former soldiers fought in large numbers on the Afghan side in the Anglo-Afghan war of 1919, and formed the core of anti-government dissidence among the

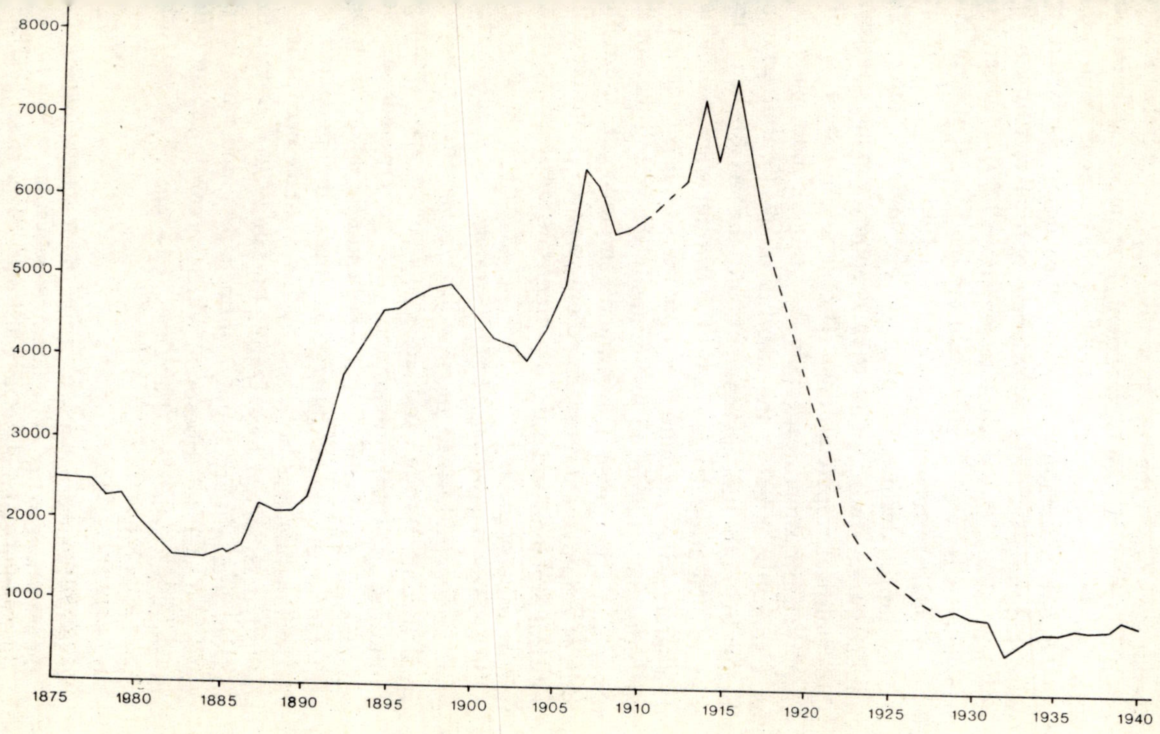
8000
7000
6000
5000
4000
3000
2000
1000
1875
1880
1885
1890
1895
1900
1905
1910
1915
1920
1925
1930
1935
1940

tribes in subsequent years. Enlisting the tribesmen ceased to have any political or military value: 'The presence of trans-border Pathans in the regular army is from a purely military point of view an embarrassment instead of a source of strength.'[26] Besides, financial retrenchment and the consequent reduction in size of the Indian Army greatly restricted the possibilities of re-opening tribal recruitment. By the late 1920s there were fewer than 1,000 independent tribesmen who were regular soldiers, and the figure did not pick up again until well into World War Two.

The rapid decline in military employment after 191 imposed great strains on the tribal economy and had consider-able political repercussions. The large numbers of un-employed tribesmen, especially the younger men, were seen as a standing threat to the stability of the frontier arrange-ments by both the government and the established tribal leaders. The irregular forces on the frontier were maintained as a safety-valve measure based on 'the simple economic pro-position that in order to live honestly the young men of the tribes must be given Government employment'.[27] But this form of employment represented only a partial solution to the political problem, and did not compensate for the sharp reduc-tion in military income.

Otherwise, the pre-World War I strategy was abandoned, even reversed. Instead of providing a significant share tribal income through military employment, as a means promoting political integration, the government devised schemes for employment that were conditional on the tribe acceptance of encroachment on their independence. Waziristan this was obtained by the military occupation strength of tribal territory. During the late 1920s road-building projects and military supply contracts provided work for the Wazir and Mahsud tribesmen, which, according to an offic-ally-inspired article in *The Times*, had greatly raised trib living standards:

> Instead of being content with maize and water and homespun, the clansman wants white flour, cigarettes, tea, silken *pugris*, good cotton cloth, elaborate waistcoats, better shoes; and his women—'What', said one despairingly, 'do they not want?'[28]

Rising consumer expectations solved no problems. By t

ECON. INDEPENDENCE ENSURED POL. IND. ∴ ENSURED PUKHTUNWALI, BUT HAD ECON. COSTS

mid-1930s the temporary boost to tribal income had come to an end, and the tribes of Waziristan had embarked on a full-scale insurgency under the leadership of the Faqir of Ipi. Elsewhere on the frontier, schemes to construct roads into tribal territory met with little success. When in the early 1930s Afridi leaders complained of the hardships being experienced by the tribe, the government responded with a proposal that recruitment into the Indian Army would be re-opened if a road suitable for military use were constructed into the heart of tribal territory. The proposal presented a difficult dilemma: should the tribesmen accept the offer of employment, and so compromise their political independence? or should they maintain their independence intact and suffer the economic consequences? Initially the proposal was accepted, and road construction began in 1935; but it had soon to be halted as tribal opposition grew.[29] In the last resort, the tribesmen set a higher value on political independence than on sources of income provided by government to limit that independence.

In the end, the course of relations between the tribes and the government revealed clearly the underlying weakness of the tribal economy—its lack of self-sufficiency and its failure to generate employment for a growing population. British rule stimulated few endogenous sources of growth among the tribes. Instead, the tribesmen had become increasingly dependent on the government for income and employment as part of a political bargain. After World War I the fragility of the bargain was exposed, as both sides came to realize the incompatibility of their respective political objectives. And the tribesmen, on their side, became conscious of their poverty in relation to the sedentary-agriculturalists, and of the welfare costs of maintaining their political independence.[30]

In the closing years of the British period the problem of tribal management was defined in slightly different terms. 'Like all political problems', Sir William Barton argued, 'the Frontier problem is largely economic.'[31] This perception of the problem was not new, but it led to a shift in emphasis. The official catch-phrase became 'peaceful penetration', and attention began to be given to the development of the tribes' subsistence economy and the improvement of their welfare. In the late 1930s schools and hospitals appeared in certain parts of tribal territory, inoculation programmes were introduced, and agricultural grants were made.[32] These measures, small in themselves, formed the start of what was intended to be a long-term policy of assimilation by raising economic conditions in the tribal areas. Development, as the 1946 five-year plan for the frontier explained, was at base a political exercise:

> the objective must be the ultimate development of the whole Tribal Areas to the same standards of civilization as those designed for India as a whole, in order to provide . . . security from tribal aggression.[33]

The difficulty was that the tribes were highly resistant to any policy perceived by them as a challenge to their way of life and political independence. If they accepted welfare measures, it was only on their terms:

> Although the tribesmen themselves often welcome the introduction of measures clearly designed to promote their own welfare provided that the cost of these is not charged to them, their instinct to freedom to manage their own affairs is strong, and much patient and persevering work will be required to win them from their own suspicions.[34]

By 1946, in any case, there were more urgent political problems to be dealt with, and the impasse on the North-West Frontier was left to the Government of Pakistan to resolve.

Conclusion

There are three general points to be made about the tribal economy of the North-West Frontier during the century of British rule. The first is that Ahmed's argument that tribal socio-economic organization was unaffected by government policy, though not altogether wrong, is nevertheless misleading. True, there was no transformation of the tribal mode of production. Technologically, pastoral-agricultural activities seem to have remained static; the growth of commercial links with the administered districts provided at most a weak stimulus to production; and there was almost no growth of manufacturing. But external forces did bring about change in other respects. The government provided the tribesmen with military employment and other sources of income which generated considerable growth in the tribal economy. This allowed a steady demographic increase and also a rise in consumption standards, although quite a large proportion of income growth went into arms expenditure. It is likely that the degree of economic interdependence of the tribes with the sedentary-agriculturalists grew appreciably.

Second, the pattern of and the constraints on change in the tribal economy have to be understood very largely in terms of two sets of political factors: tribal political culture and organization, and the policy objectives of the government. Adherence to the principles of the *Pakhtunwali* encouraged tribesmen to abstain from subsistence herding-farming (though ecological factors are also important in this respect), and diverted resources from economically productive uses to the accumulation of weaponry. The vigorous defence of political independence explains the rejection by some tribes of employment schemes that were conditional on their acceptance of the presence of external government in their territory. The British, for their part, provided them with a form of employment which they regarded as honourable. Enlistment as soldiers and militiamen was never regarded as an inefficient use of labour; it was considered an appropriate occupation for men whose martial skills would otherwise have been used against the government. But when, during and immediately after World War I, this arrangement collapsed, much of the political logic of the tribal recruitment policy was destroyed and tribal military income was sharply curtailed. The government provision of income to the tribes, in short, was a function of the assessment of its political value.

This leads to the final point, that the economic consequences of British policy towards the tribes have to be understood in the rather broader context of political priorities on the North-West Frontier. Insofar as the government had any interest in the economic condition of the tribes, it was only as an incidental aspect of the primary concern to achieve frontier security. Relations with the tribes were never perceived in any but political terms until the last decade or so of British rule. Equally, the level of tribal economic development was never an issue before the 1930s. The tribesmen themselves seem often to have made a virtue of their relative poverty, as a sign of their hardiness and their distinctness from the more prosperous sedentary-agriculturalists. Only in the late British period was the problem of relations with the tribes reformulated in a way which stressed the importance of economic conditions; and by then the political matrix of these relations, which largely determined the possibilities for introducing measures to improve tribal production and welfare, was too well-established to be dismantled. The problem of development is of very recent origin, and it is ahistorical to judge the course of change in the tribal economy and the impact of British policy by mid-twentieth century criteria.

NOTES

1. See Akbar S. Ahmed, *Pukhtun Economy and Society: Traditional Structure and Economic Development in a Tribal Society* (London, 1980), ch. 4 and *passim*.
2. Cf. Ernest Gellner, *Saints of the Atlas* (London, 1969), 2-3; also David M. Hart, 'The Tribe in Modern Morocco: Two Case Studies', in E. Gellner and C. Micaud (eds.), *Arabs and Berbers: from Tribe to Nation in North Africa* (London, 1973), 25 ff.
3. For an overview which cites a wide range of studies, see A.M. Khazanov, *Nomads and the Outside World* (Cambridge, 1984).
4. Ahmed, *Pukhtun Economy*, *op. cit.*, chs. 1, 3, 10, 11 and *passim*; also 'The Arab Connection: Emergent Models of Social Structure among Pakistani Tribesmen', *Asian Affairs*, n.s. vol. 12 (1981), 167-72.
5. See, e.g., (G.L. Mallam), *Five-Year Post-War Development Plan for the North-West Frontier Province and Tribal Areas* (Peshawar, 1946), 1-6.
6. See, e.g., David Dichter, *The North-West Frontier of Pakistan: A Study in Regional Geography* (Oxford, 1967), 3 ff.
7. For an early example of this view, see Richard Temple, *Report Showing the Relations of the British Government with the Tribes, Independent and Dependent, on the North-West Frontier of the Punjab, from Annexation in 1849 to the Close of 1856*, in *Selections from the Records of the Government of India* (Calcutta, 1856).
8. Capt. A.H. McMahon and Lt. A.D.G. Ramsay, *Report on the Tribes of Dir, Swat and Bajour* (1st edn. Calcutta, 1901; new edn. Peshawar, 1981), 49. See also Fredrik Barth, *Political Leadership among Swat Pathans* (London, 1959), 5-6, 79.
9. For a pioneering analysis, see Fredrik Barth, 'Ecologic Relationships of Ethnic Groups in Swat, North Pakistan', *American Anthropologist*, 58 (1956), 1079-89.
10. *Report on the Administration of the Border of the North-West Frontier Province*, 1921-22 to 1941-42.
11. Cf. Sir William Barton, *India's North-West Frontier* (London, 1939), 265.
12. Evelyn Howell, *Mizh: A Monograph on Government's Relations with the Mahsud Tribe* (1st edn. Simla, 1931; new edn. Karachi, 1979), 97.
13. *Report of the Tribal Control and Defence Committee, 1931* (Delhi, 1931), 10.
14. H.R. James, *Report on the Settlement of the Peshawar District* (Lahore, 1862) 56; E.G.G. Hastings, *Report of the Regular Settlement of the Peshawar District*

of the Punjab (Lahore, 1878), 188; *Report on the Administration of the North-West Frontier Province 1901-03* (Peshawar, 1903), 30.

15. *Census of India, 1921*, XIV, *NWFP* (Peshawar, 1922), 26; Mallam, *Post-War Development Plan*, *op. cit.*, 6.
16. R.G. Taylor, *District Memorandum: Derah Ishmael Khan*, in *Selections from the Records of the Government of India* (Calcutta, 1852), 83.
17. *General Report on the Administration of the Punjab and its Dependencies 1860-61* (Lahore, 1861), para. 164.
18. Note by Lt. Col. H.B. Edwardes, Commissioner, Peshawar Division, 19 March 1860, file of the Office of the Commissioner, Peshawar Division, no. XXXIV/F/8.
19. See, e.g., the statement on the trade between Peshawar District and neighbouring independent tribal areas in L.W. Dane, *Final Report of the Settlement of the Peshawar District* (Lahore, 1898), 21.
20. *Census of India, 1911*, XIII, (Peshawar, 1912) and *Census of India, 1941*, X, (Delhi, 1942).
21. See, e.g., D.C.J. Ibbetson, *Report on the Census of the Punjab Taken on the 17th of February 1881*, vol. 1 (Calcutta, 1883), 63, 86.
22. Annual *Statement of Fighting Strengths and Armament of Independent Tribes on the North-West Frontier*, 1907-47, compiled by the Office of the Chief Commissioner/Governor of the NWFP.
23. The term 'political' in this context has much the same meaning as that given it by British-Indian administrators, who, Macaulay remarked, 'always use the word "political" as synonymous with diplomatic'. Quoted in T.C. Coen, *The Indian Political Service* (London, 1971), 5.
24. *Report of the Tribal Control and Defence Committee, loc. cit.*
25. These figures are derived from the *Annual Caste Return of the Native Army in India* (title varies), 1874-1940. There is certainly some margin of error in the figures; the method of compilation seems to have varied over time also. The chart does, nevertheless, provide a fair guide to levels of tribal recruitment.
26. *Report of the Tribal Control and Defence Committee, op. cit.*, 55.
27. Report on the Administration of the Khyber 1920-21, in file of the Office of the Chief Commissioner, NWFP, no. 5/18 of 1921.
28. 'The Changing Frontier: Check to Wazir Blood-Feuds', *The Times*, 31 March, 1930.
29. *Report on the Administration of the Border of the North-West Frontier Province 1934-35* (Peshawar, 1935), 9-10.
30. See, e.g., Application by the Tribes of the Khyber Agency to the Governor, NWFP, 21 February, 1938, file of the Political Department, Civil Secretariat of the NWFP, no. 39/72 FRP.
31. Barton, *India's North-West Frontier, loc. cit.*
32. See, e.g., *The Border (NWFP) 1939-1940* (Peshawar, 1941), 23-25.
33. Mallam, *Post-War Development Plan, op. cit.*, 1.
34. *Loc. cit.*

7

IN SEARCH OF DOMINANT PEASANTS: NOTES ON THE IMPLEMENTATION IN BIHAR OF THE BENGAL TENANCY ACT OF 1885

PETER ROBB

School of Oriental and African Studies, London

The Bengal Tenancy Act of 1885 marks a point on which may be centred a discussion of agricultural property and production in nineteenth-century Bihar, the region for which the Act was originally intended.[1] This essay contends that the Act benefited tenants rather than landlords, against a background of economic change whereby the formal rent-receiving roles were losing out in comparison with more direct means of securing agricultural surplus, that is, through cultivation or non-regulated tenancies and share-cropping. The benefits of the Act were not shared equally by tenants because these economic changes also took place within the context of persistent norms and institutions, which marched with weaknesses in the Act.

These assertions partly qualify and partly endorse old ideas and new trends which may be generally subsumed under the head of 'arrested development'. The notion is of course chiefly concerned with industry and commerce. Where the countryside fits is less clear. But it has usually been thought, more or less vaguely, that revenue settlements and tenancy legislation hold the key. Two assertions command widespread assent. One is that the institution of landed property, as a commodity, acted as both a social solvent and a sump for capital. The other is that concentrations of agrarian power dispossessed and impoverished large sections of the rural population. In other circumstances such changes might have been regarded as painful but necessary accompaniments of industrialization, increasing agricultural productivity per capita and creating an industrial labour force. In colonial India, however, the wider economic transformation did not occur, and changes in the agricultural sector have been seen as an additional impediment to development. Not only was the economy 'arrested' in terms of manufacturing and trade, it was also 'distorted' in terms of agriculture and rural life. There is, however, little agreement and less clarity about the processes involved.

In Bengal the permanent settlement of 1793 has undergone many bouleversements in popular esteem, being variously regarded as a damaging and fruitless application of aristocratic prejudice, or alternatively, in its creation of a moderately taxed landed interest, as a model which other revenue systems might copy. Nowadays reactions are more uniformly hostile, perhaps because the areas to which the settlement applied have recently remained stubbornly poor and 'backward' in agriculture. Often the idea is that the settlement confiscated the quasi-property rights of cultivators, and encouraged their exploitation by layer upon layer of rentier classes. Economic development was stifled because on the one hand (after an initial upheaval in which 'traditional' families were replaced) the rent-receivers had easy profits without having to invest in agricultural improvement or even to maintain productivity.[2] On the other hand the peasants were impoverished, at the mercy of their overlords or the mahajan, unable to stimulate either agriculture or effective demand. In this context the tenancy legislation of the later nineteenth century was initially treated as a belated redressing of the balance. More recently, there has been a further refinement of ideas about the permanent settlement and a corresponding shift in interpretations of the Tenancy Acts. It is suggested that 1793 did not necessarily reduce old 'owner-peasants' uniformly to 'wretched tenants-at-will': there is now a substantial body of opinion which has found itself close to the verdict reached by W.W. Hunter on the basis of manuscript records and under the influence of the great rent law debates of the 1870s and 1880s, a verdict taken up in large part also by Baden-Powell.[3] On the other hand, the current views on the 1885 Act have effectively relocated the discarded generalizations about 1793. The consensus is growing that the Act extended to a middling class the benefits originally provided to the landlords, and thus progressively impoverished the majority. This school of thought points in particular to transfers of raiyats' holdings and a supposedly consequential increase in the proportion of landless labourers. The result is described as 'depeasantization', that is, a reduction in the proportion of the agriculturists engaged in family-farm production.[4] The analysis centres on land control, thus justifying and confirming the attention to tenancy legislation, and is complementary to the trade and occupation-centred theory of 'deindustrialization'.[5] Both processes allegedly swelled the ranks of agricultural workers. Thus, where once the product of British law and administration was a uniformly downtrodden peasantry, it is now being seen as a mass of bonded and landless labourers.

The question of whether such polarizations occurred cannot be resolved on a statistical basis: in 1900 as in 1800 some of the agriculturists were landless and some, effectively without land, were technically tenants. The factual miasma on which generalizations have been based is shown in two recent essays. One endorses the depeasantization thesis while admitting that it is impossible to show any increase in the proportion of landless labourers in the rural population;[6] the other remarks on the imprecision of the familiar assertions about 'subinfeudation' in Bengal.[7] There is a clear need, if attention is to shift to the 1885 Act, for its impact to be much better understood. The key features must be tenure and rent, at root the two means whereby there could have been a movement in land control within the peasantry. This paper considers these two aspects in turn.

Tenure among Bihari Peasants

One criticism of the 1885 Act was that it redistributed the boon of property, already carelessly bestowed on the landlords, to a middle stratum of peasants defined by larger-than-average holdings and occupancy status.[8] This broad explanation unfortunately bears no obvious relation to the status of tenants recorded under the Act. There is no correlation between occupancy right and size of holdings, and occupancy was recorded, in very different areas, for very large majorities of all tenancies. Why should a right apparently accorded to the many bring privileges only to a few? The means implied in some recent work is the disfunction of British categories. Contrary to the original intentions of the tenancy reformers, the 1885 Act gave privileges to individual 'tenants' rather than to the actual cultivator. As a result, the recorded 'occupancy holdings' were not uniform: some were very much larger than others. Codification in the context of such differences encouraged subletting and alienation, which in turn increased the disparities.[9] There has been no clear presentation of this case, in which, moreover, the instrumentality of the Act is not well distinguished from supposed underlying causes of stratification such as ecology and indebtedness. In particular, how does the mere codifying of pre-existing differences among peasants constitute a mechanism for 'depeasantization'?

The 1885 Act defined occupancy right as the 1859 Act had, with some important differences. The reformers concentrated on the need to avoid denials of occupancy right by manipulations of tenancy or records: they provided that a right of occupancy accrued, for any land in a village, to a tenant who had held land there for the qualifying period of twelve years. This was a legal rather than a practical innovation: a tenant who held some land over a long period already had occupancy in practice; he was, in the terminology of 1885, 'settled'. The Act therefore sought to define the legal incidents of existing practice, and to make it defensible in law. Most significantly it allowed the status to be independently established and recorded in a private or district settlement. Unlike any previous survey or regulation of rights in land in Bengal, this latter record distributed holdings according to what it defined as 'cultivating' as well as proprietary possession: 'cultivating' possession meant in effect management of agricultural production, by personal or employed labour. Several types of possession were defined, according to the legal status of the 'cultivator': holdings for zamindars, permanent tenure-holders and temporary lessees, for tenants of several kinds, and for sub-tenants. District-wide surveys started under the Act in the early 1890s in North Bihar.[10]

Two broad configurations were revealed in these surveys, one in which rent-receivers held relatively little land in relatively large holdings, and another in which rent-receivers held a quarter or more of all land but in holdings more nearly of the average size for the area. In the first variety were places, such as most of Champaran, where very large majorities of all holdings were leased from intermediaries and not the zamindar. Both varieties contained settled and occupancy holdings covering between 60 and 80 per cent of the cultivated area, and accounting for similar proportions of all holdings. Wide variations were found within this general pattern; on the other hand, the categories based on British legal terminology may well have overlain a social profile that was more similar across the region than it was made to appear.[11] The similarities suggest that there was throughout Bihar a small number of people who lived principally from rents, and large numbers who were dependent on moderate to small holdings, some of them held as tenants and some as zamindars. This position was codified after 1885; it was not the stratification into landlord and tenant which was supposed to have resulted from the permanent settlement. Clearly, settled raiyats survived the inimical laws of the earlier decades of British rule.

The record of rights, nonetheless, created an alternative view of the rural order, in which raiyats' 'property', the right to cultivating possession, was elevated to consideration alongside landlord's property, land ownership. Settlement *amins*, however 'corrupt and venal', were not local men, and were under the control of officials and rules imbued with the spirit of tenancy reform. They expected to identify as occupancy right the position in which they found the great mass of resident raiyats, and they did so, it seems, to an extent that the local *patwaris* would not.[12] The manager of Bettiah raj complained that the survey had assumed that raiyats held 'all the land measured to them as theirs of right', whereas (he said) hitherto occupancy rights had been unknown and the land was leased or cultivated at the zamindar's will.[13] The record of rights standardized the perceptions of the government and the law in a way which weakened the landlords' standing with these institutions and encouraged official intervention in rural life. The record of rights also provided a standard measure of lands, often the first exact measurement available.[14]

At first sight it would seem that such a change would benefit the landlord, as the discovery of 'excess area' led to the enhancement of rents. But in the longer term certainty was a disadvantage to those whose incomes rested in the collection of rent from regular tenancies. There are three main reasons. First, government and other external interference became far easier, and intervention was most likely to encourage the 'cultivating' interest: both officials and entrepreneurs considered the zamindari interest unproductive. Secondly the zamindar's power rested in part on a monopoly of knowledge, which these changes breached. The best-run estates could impose effective management over a multiplicity of subdivided tenant interests, because their complexity and ambiguity allowed them to be manipulated at will, with little hope of challenge or combination. Thirdly, rising agricultural prices imposed a continual pressure on landlord incomes wherever these were expressed in money terms, and one of the strategies adopted to combat this, in the later nineteenth century, was the attempt to extend the land which the zamindars kept 'in hand' (the *zerat*). The Hathwa raj made numerous such claims, even in respect of lands which had been passed down through several generations of intermediary leaseholders (*thikadars*) or tenants. The beauty of *zerat*, for the landlord, was that it avoided outside interference, maximized any benefits from competition for land, and allowed for flexible strategies on an annual basis. Such lands might be cultivated directly using hired labour, but often they were let out on short leases or capitalized through usufructuary mortgages. The government noticed the landlords' hostility to inquiries in the first quinquennial review of the 1885 Act. 'The effect of a survey and record', they predicted, '. . . would be to fix once and for all the area of the *zerats* and prevent extensions which are now wrongly made.'[15] At least such encroachment would be more difficult wherever it could be challenged, once relations in land were regularized and recorded.

As early as 1894, tenants as well as landlords were reported to be attending settlement proceedings patiently and the former to be keenly interested in receiving *parchas*, copies of the entries relating to different holdings. Often this eagerness succeeded a period of apathy, inspired partly by rumours sponsored by the zamindars. During Holi, in Muzaffarpur, new songs were sung celebrating the settlement.[16] Earlier intervention by the British had imposed an order from outside in the interests of proprietors, even when measures were gradually taken to protect tenants. This was true of the sale laws which encouraged the legal insecurity of most tenancies by treating agrarian relations on the basis of contracts between individuals; it was true of the partition of estates (or *batwara*) which, among the tenants, invariably raised rents as it divided holdings. The record of rights was more thoroughgoing and deliberately directed towards tenant rights. Its methods ensured that the influence brought to bear would be, locally, that established in the villages of settlement and cultivation, and not necessarily that which had previously been visible, the revenue-payers. The context was an attempt by rent-receivers to erode the security of tenure of settled raiyats, a process aided by rising prices, increased population and, some argued, the provisions of the 1859 Tenancy Act.[17] The record of rights reversed the law and in some situations also affected the practice, by strengthening the hand of the tenant. A pilot survey undertaken in Muzaffarpur in 1885-86 was found in the 1890s to have produced results that were incorporated in zamindars' *jamabandi* papers and then kept up-to-date, finding their way into the materials in use by the people to an extent not repeated in the records maintained by government.[18] The raiyat knew which holdings he cultivated; with a record he could produce evidence in a standard form which, at one time, had been admitted by all parties.

Many practical checks inhibit the impact of law and government in rural India, and the investment of official effort in the settlements did not influence behaviour uniformly. But the overall effect of the record of rights was to favour the tenant interest. Was there also a distortion between tenants? It seems likely. The basic unit of the survey was the true field or plot, held under a single title at a single rate of rent. This represented the probable unit of production, ranging in size from about one-third to one-half an acre. The unit of the record, however, was the holding, consisting on average of between three and seven plots. A judgment was required each time a holding was defined, in terms set by the 1885 Act. The holding was a collection of production units expressed through ownership and rent. Complexities of land use and land users may be lost in this transition. Moreover, many individuals had more than one holding and holdings in different categories, effectively dissolving the British categories. Again holdings within each category varied greatly in size.[19] Subtenancies too were likely to be under-recorded. The 1885 Act vested occupancy in the holder, not the holding, and this is likely to have encouraged the concealment of subordinate rights once the claim of a privileged raiyat was admitted.

particularly where part holdings were sublet to someone who was not himself a substantial tenant. The record was after all still only of a legal property, albeit that of cultivating possession. The occupancy category must include many tenants whose tiny holdings were insufficient to allow them a surplus and who had to work for richer villagers. The category presumably at the same time represented a smaller proportion of the population than of those whose interests in land were recorded. The tenancy legislation was intended to benefit actual cultivators, but political accident or expediency had conflated this cultivator with the resident raiyat and secured to the latter a quasi-proprietary right. There remained the potential for the separation of cultivation and ownership, yet the emphasis on giving rights to agricultural producers had obviated the need to scrutinize and regulate the relations between one tenant and another or between the owner of a cultivating right and the man who worked on the land. In the law these relations were largely ignored; in the record of rights they were virtually invisible.[20]

The effect of the record of rights on popular perceptions in ural areas also altered the balance of power in agrarian conlict. For the first time the government was seeking out a new lliance in the Bengal Presidency, and it was presenting a view f the rural order which was significantly different from that vhich existed. Less weight should be given to the operations f the courts and specific acts by district authorities; more veight should be given to generalizing activities of the execuive, as in the creation of the record.[21] Expectations may well ave been raised which affected transactions between and indeed among zamindars and raiyats, in instances which never ame to the attention of the courts.

Traditional forms of land control and land tenure were nultiple, various and ambiguous to the extent that eigheenth-century states found it impossible to enforce uniformity nd tended to incorporate in outward form what was still emi-independent in substance. British power did not at once ransform the situation. Yet multiplicity and ambiguity began be lost with the permanent settlement, a process that slowly ontinued with the recording of ownership in revenue papers, ales or resumption proceedings, and surveys of estate boundries. Such activities, and decades of administrative and legal ction, tended to make practice more regular, or rather to conrm with what was provided in regulations. Partition too marked a readiness to use British forms to adjust and record ownership. Thus divisions of ownership consequent upon inheritance and transfer were hardened, under the influence of more effective machinery for making all formal control in land individual, recorded and of one kind. The larger estates adjusted by avoiding partition after 1850. The Act of 1885 and the record of rights mark an extension of this process to occupancy raiyats. If reports are to be believed, very few of the transfers and mortgages of their holdings were recorded in the 1880s but almost all of them were by the 1920s.[22] Again, the average size of the holdings transferred was greatly reduced, partly because the larger transactions were more likely to be recorded earlier, partly because the average holding was becoming smaller, but largely because bigger holdings apparently came to be divided less frequently. Arguably, a reason for tenancies as for estates was that weaker holders were less able to stand out against the tendency inspired by administration and law. The result, in the absence of any other factor, would be developing polarization among landlords and raiyats. For the latter, the change would be most effective where one of the pressures for sub-division came from richer tenants, zamindars or creditors anxious to secure land.

Having said this, it is important to stress again how gradual the process was. Many features of the pre-existing, informal systems continued in existence after a century of British rule. In 1893-94 there were still almost 1300 boundary disputes to be resolved among the petty *maliks* of Muzaffarpur, where zamindaris were numerous and tenancies small. In Patna Division, too, of the two thousand or so raiyati transfers recorded each year in the later 1880s, only about five were of succession: heirs still expected to succeed without the benefit of official registration.[23] These differences in impact and the consequent survivals had major consequences, as will be shown later in this essay.

Nineteenth-century Rent Rates

The case for the oppression of the raiyats rests largely on a supposed increase in the burden of rent after 1793. Emotionally, the basis of the claim is that raiyats had been deprived of property, expressed particularly as the privilege of paying rent at a rate which the landlord could not change at will and which was not affected by competition and contract. For some scholars this has seemed enough.[24] Empirically, however, an absolute change of this nature is insupportable. There *were* customary ideas about rates of rent, some of which were still evident at the end of the nineteenth century. But each agricultural plot was subject to a recognized 'field rate' which varied from one plot to another whenever zamindari management was sufficiently close. (On large estates it tended to be merely the average of the rate for an entire holding.)[25] The endency of custom, as this information shows, was towards specific rather than general rates of rent—rents which changed in accordance with status, soil, crop, and supply and demand too. Average rent rates certainly differed from place to place and, less dramatically, between the different categories applied by the British; but the greatest variations were from village to village and holding to holding. There was no 'pargana rate' at the end of the nineteenth century, nor has anyone been able to demonstrate one in existence at any previous period. Theory and even state dictat may have called for it, but investigators repeatedly failed to find it. To consider that custom reinforced it, is, moreover, a gross misunderstanding of the nature and effect of Indian social norms.

Rent and other payments by cultivators rose in the eighteenth century, and economic considerations played some part in fixing the amounts. Moreover, despite the special pleading of certain protagonists in the great rent law debate, the intention of Shore and Cornwallis in 1793 (so far as they considered the question) was that rents should result from contracts between landlords and tenants: this was the essence of the *patta-kabuliyat* system and the provisions relating to tenants in the sales laws.[26] It is therefore not a sufficient condemnation merely to show that rents rose after 1793. It is necessary to measure the increase in real terms, per acre and per person.

Attempts to do so are fraught with difficulty. The *Cambridge Economic History* estimates that rents increased by between 60 and 200 per cent in the fifty years to 1890, and relates this increase to the proportionately smaller enlargement of the cultivated area.[27] This is not to say that real rents increased accordingly. Very many complications arise. There were changes in what constituted rent, in particular the consolidation of additional cesses (or *abwabs*) and varying abilities to impose them. There were changes in the manner of calculation or payment, as between produce and money rents, and within the former between *batai* (division) and *danabandi* (appraisement). Such changes may affect the real proportion of the crop made over by the cultivator. But in particular there were changes in the value of agricultural produce, and possibly in access to its benefits. Here polarization becomes essential to the idea of progressive impoverishment, for the later nineteenth century saw a shift in production towards higher-value crops, and a progressive though patchy improvement in agricultural prices, alongside fairly steady prices for other commodities.[28] The agricultural sector benefited; questions of productivity, population and entitlement need to be resolved before anything more precise can be said. In fact, with regard to rent, there is no way through such complexities, and we are unlikely to be able to generalize about the period as a whole. We can produce reasonably accurate averages, for the first time, only from the 1890s, and even these figures are open to interpretation. Some officials thought they vindicated the view that rents were intolerably high (the conclusion reached one hundred years before). Others professed themselves agreeably surprised to discover that rates in Bihar were after all moderate compared with those in neighbouring districts of Awadh.[29] Perhaps many observers considered the agricultural population of Bihar to be poor by Indian standards, and aware of the wealth of a few great landowners, assumed that rack-renting was the cause.

The issue needs to be approached differently. Why should real rents have risen? One reason might be demand. A hig revenue with regular *kists* (instalments) exacted after 1793 ma be a factor elsewhere, but will not explain the prominence of Bihar as an example of rural poverty—its landlords wer thought less hard-pressed than their fellows in Bengal—nc the alleged increases in rent later in the century when the re value of revenue payments gradually declined. On all-Indi and for that matter international comparisons (except for th remainder of the Presidency), it would be easier to argue th Bihar was poor because its agriculture was *lightly* taxed. Similarly, the beginning of extra taxation through governme cesses from the 1870s, though a significant departure, w more the occasion than the cause of extra rent demand Moreover, government demand must have been very patch in effect: the proper criticism of it in Bihar was not that it w high but that it was carelessly made, and this may have been a perennial feature in the region.[31] Again, the resumption of 'invalid' revenue-free holdings, completed by about 1850, undoubtedly had an effect on specific holdings, but there is no reason why it should have led to a general enhancement of rents.[32] It would naturally be related to a large decline in the proportion of rent-free holdings, once suggested to account for as much as 30 per cent of the cultivated area and nowhere above a half of that by 1900. (The other influences here would be the desire to increase rental incomes as prices rose, as an alternative to *pro rata* increases on rent-paying holdings, and the availability of other sources of supply for the services which rent-free holdings provided). The decline of rent-free lands increases the general significance of the recorded enhancement in rents per acre; it decreases the relevance of district-wide calculations on the basis of cultivated area. Finally, the very large expansion in the number of estates, through partition, may have represented a real growth in the number of rent-receivers, the product of formal registration and generational increase. On the other hand, partitions seem to have resulted in fewer co-sharers per estate, and by the later nineteenth century they were concentrated on small zamindaris, suggesting that families were seeking to preserve the larger estates at a size which would allow incomes based on rent: the growing numbers of very small estates implied increasing involvement in direct cultivation rather than an explosion of rent-receivers or 'sub-infeudation'. Moreover, numerous though partitions were, they did not affect all estates or areas. Conversely, increased rents were also found on great estates which avoided partition and were not subject to division at succession.[33]

Rising prices naturally generated pressure to increase cash rents, yet for much of the later part of the nineteenth century this pressure was mitigated by relative stability in outgoings. Neither this nor increasing numbers of rent-receivers seem clearly to have created a general demand for a higher proportion of agricultural surplus. What then of opportunity? It increased on some large estates, when they were controlled by the Court of Wards and management systems were reformed. Closer undivided supervision could pay dividends also on partitioned estates. The legal position strongly favoured the zamindar under the permanent settlement: measures such as the distraint of property for non-payment of rent weighed the balance heavily against the tenants, and official attempts to redress this balance were largely ineffectual before the presen century. This is not to say that law was very important. The permanent settlement vested much in the zamindar, but by the same token removed most of the direct agency whereby the influence of European concepts and practice would be felt Law was little used to increase rent. Landlords benefited from the assistance of the executive or the police *in extremis*, bu were mostly dependent on their own resources.

Pressure on the land is usually cited as allowing competitive rents. But Bihar's population raises further difficult questions of fact. There was a recovery from the losses of the catastrophic famine of 1769-70 which struck particularly at northern and eastern Bihar as well as some areas of western Bengal. The estimates of total population throughout the nineteenth century are, however, virtually useless. There are good reasons for suspecting that even the 1871 census may under estimate the totals for North Bihar by as much as 15 or even 20 per cent, an error which would account for much of the presumptive increase of the following three decades.[34] By the end of the period, reports state that land use had been maximized in most Bihari districts (implying a continual demographic rise over the preceding period); but the fact tha the verdict was untrue, in an absolute sense, is now demonstr able in the huge increase in rural population which occurred in the middle decades of the twentieth century. It is importan to remember how rhetorical was the assertion that condition had worsened over the nineteenth century, how dependent on notions of theoretical wrongs done in 1793, and how instru mental in the rent-law reforms being advocated. Even the worsening incidence of famine in the later nineteenth century was not an objective argument among officials and polemi cists, and does not itself prove a deterioration in underlying poverty.

Nonetheless, an important shift had occurred by the 1880s. In the eighteenth century, as Hunter alleges, there was a cer tain mobility of labour and tenantry because they were rela tively scarce.[35] Those who were willing and able to move could colonize abandoned or previously uncultivated land, on favourable terms. This fact does not always explain the differ ence between 'settled' and other raiyats and the rent each paid; much needs to be added about cultural and political restraints on movement, especially for high-caste agriculturists.[36] Yet there was certainly a chance for malcontents to seek out zamindars who were asking for lower rents to attract cultivators; and this 'colonizing' option was far less common in 1900 than 1800. It existed within Bihar mainly in Champaran, where it depended on a favourable man:land ratio but also on economic incentives. By 1900 another option was far more common than before: the situation in which zamindars sought raiyats who would pay higher than average rates. The reason was a less favourable man:land ratio, but also—and perhaps primarily, in the nineteenth century—the increasing opportunities to market higher-value crops. This option was expressed by filling in or dividing up underutilized villages. It must be taken into account in connection both with emigration—arguably related partly to a proportionately reduced demand for non-family labour with a decline of high-caste in favour of agricultural-caste production (a process of peasantization?)—and with the sub-division of holdings which represents in part the alienation of land to higher-paying tenants, and indeed concentrations of land in such hands, rather than a straightforward response to population increase.[37] To sum up, then, the mobile raiyat in 1800 might be one who paid a lower rent, for demographic and development reasons. In 1900, however, he was more likely to be one who paid a higher rent, the reasons being again demographic but also economic. The argument depends on a sufficiency rather than a rapid increase of population. It is very different from the idea of all tenants being rack-rented as their numbers inexorably grew.

The question, indeed, is not so much one of demand or opportunity but of incentive for increased rents. Results are bound to have been selective and conditional. The improvement in agricultural returns between 1860 and 1900 followed two or three decades of depressed prices for items of long-distance trade, and was interrupted by repeated crises of climate and production. The sequence of events would increase zamindari appetites; uncertainties of output would on the one hand damage the resistance of raiyats but on the other reduce the landlord's chance of actually receiving regular and general increases in rent. Above all, marketing for cash was still peripheral in terms of Bihari production and consumption. Those of whatever legal status who could sell their produce stood to gain; the zamindar dependent on rent had to exert additional pressure on such producers in order to enhance rents at comparable rates. Where payments were made in kind, the price inflation was disguised and even further efforts would be needed to increase the zamindar's portion or to reduce the share taken by labourers and artisans. In short, fortunes varied. Some zamindars would make the attempt to increase real rents in response only to pressing financial difficulties. In Bettiah, for example, rents were supposed to have been little changed until 1869 when a shortage of funds forced an effort: in the following years, allegedly, the 'controlling influence' of the great Bhumihar clans was mobilized to extort rack-rents, *thikadari* leases were auctioned to the highest bidders, and by these means the ignorant cultivators were prevented from acquiring a permanent interest in the land.[38] Subsequent rent rates on the estate, only two-thirds of those elsewhere in North Bihar, show this assessment to have been hyperbole; but the moral is plain: when rent rises depend on incentive, they will occur only where landlords are especially eager and effective.

Rent rates recorded in the 1890s cannot, in aggregate, reveal distinctions illustrating which social groups were benefiting and which were being oppressed. But they suggest that rents were higher where population was greatest, and even higher where zamindaris were small: they reflect the realities of demand and power. They show also that the legal categories of tenancy offer no uniform picture. So-called 'fixed-rate' tenancies were always more lightly rented than others, but not to the extent that would be expected given their supposed pedigree of having enjoyed unchanging rents since before 1793. Settled and occupancy rates were sometimes lower and sometimes higher than those of less privileged status. Sometimes non-occupancy and under-raiyats' rates were at a discount, because such people—little better than day-labourers, as one report had it[39]—needed to be attracted to underpopulated areas, or held inferior lands, on the better part of which they paid produce rents. At other times such tenants paid significantly higher rents, most notably on the crowded lands of Muzaffarpur.[40] The differences imply that the strength of zamindars or *thikadars* on large estates may have evened out the average rates for tenancies of different kinds, whereas on petty estates the occupancy tenants' average was reduced by the fact that village elites and successful cultivators (whose holdings appeared elsewhere among tenants' lands) were often returned as zamindars. The imperfections of the categories thus make the question of rents less amenable to analysis, as if it were not already complicated by the poor correlation between rents and productivity and the fact that weaker raiyats could pay more than stronger for land of similar quality.

The Tenancy Law and Rents

The *Cambridge Economic History* is fastidious but obscure in concluding that zamindars 'refined the existing machinery' in order to raise rents, and holdings became smaller and a section of the peasantry was forced into agricultural labour.[41] Other accounts are equally unclear while blaming the 1885 Act for codifying the occupancy right so as to encourage alienation and subletting, and thus contributing to a process whereby excessive demands in rent and especially debt led to higher proportions of *bargadars* (sharecroppers) and labourers in place of peasant family farmers.[42] Both of these apparently contradictory interpretations seem to agree that the tenancy laws brought benefits to some tenants, those who avoided the loss of their land and privileges, even though it was these, confusingly, who had the mortgageable property which was at risk through debt. Again, rent is clearly important, and particularly the differences between that paid on formal tenancies and what was extracted in irregular ways. A weapon of the economically successful among tenants was arguably the rent control provided in the 1885 Act; by the same token the weakness of other tenants might be traced to the effective lack of such privileges.

Yet the 1885 Act, a compromise between pro-raiyat and pro-landlord pressure, was never a charter for low rents. Common wisdom was that rents should be high but 'fair' in order that the raiyats might (in Woodburn's prim phrase) have 'impulses to industry and be relieved of the temptation to subletting'; alternative arguments were regarded by Ibbetson as 'vicious' and 'abominable' [43] The legislation provided for state regulation of disputed rents, a record, and restrictions on enhancement, particularly for settled raiyats; it was not to be expected that it would have immediate or specific impact. Until 1906, indeed, the civil courts allegedly ignored its provisions, such as those restricting rent increases for occupancy holdings to 12½ per cent at fifteen-year intervals.[44] The Act was irrelevant too in that its remedies for raiyats depended on their initiating civil actions, except for a few provisions whereby the aid of the executive could be invoked. Raiyats could deposit disputed rents with district officers, who could fine zamindars for refusal to issue receipts, and officials could be called in to divide or appraise crops where produce-rents prevailed; but British administration was ill-equipped for close and effective intervention, especially in the Bengal presidency. In the 1890s receipts were in evidence only on larger estates, and though officials were called in about 450 times a year over produce rents in the Patna Division, particularly in Gaya, they reported themselves pawns on the landlords' side in disputes little connected with rents, rather than instruments for securing fair rents for the raiyats.[45] The Act, in short, was likely neither to raise rents nor progressively to lower them.

Nonetheless, 1885 does mark a stage in the gradual pressure of the law towards regulation of tenancy and rents, and in this respect, again, the survey and record of rights were more significant than the Act itself.[46] Settlements were not imposed on individual zamindars to curb oppression—the first such case was not until 1910.[47] Nor was the settlement of government estates generally to the advantage of tenants: in the absence of specialist survey teams, the work could be rough-and-ready and sometimes resulted in additional power for village elites along with overall increases in rent.[48] The district-wide surveys, however, present what was for Bihar an unprecedented intervention in agrarian relations. Its effect too was at first sight to increase rents. On the great estates, initial hostility by the zamindars quickly gave way to attempts to use the occasion to increase rental incomes, and the demand per tenant. In Bettiah every raiyat was required, with the agreement of the settlement officer, to enter an agreement to pay in full at the existing rate per *bigha* for whatever land they were proved to hold, less 10 per cent: thus half of all tenancies were subject to increased demands on the ground of 'excess area', though the net increase in the total rental was extremely small. In the Hathwa villages in Saran district a smaller proportion of the tenants was also subjected to more significant enhancement. In such areas too the recorded increases may have represented a small proportion of the additional influence which the operations provided to the landlord.[49] The overwhelming majority of the applications for the fixing of fair rents (section 104 of the Act) were lodged by zamindars and European planters—in Muzaffarpur in 1894-95 only 9 out of 406 were tenants—and in the case of the planters almost two-thirds of the claims were very small and withdrawn before judgment: clearly they were devices to secure the tenants' acquiescence in indigo leases or other agreements. In the same way, and particularly in Muzaffarpur with its mass of petty estates, disputes over entries (section 105 of the Act) allowed zamindars to dispute issues which had never been contentious before.[50]

And yet the record of rights was not a straightforward invitation to increase rental incomes, let alone to increase rents per acre. In Muzaffarpur section 104 was used against just over one per cent of the tenancies; even under the influence of a large estate such as Hathwa the proportion reached only 20 per cent. (Champaran was a special case in that many tenants undoubtedly did hold larger areas of land than were recorded.)[51] Moreover, it was soon recognized that the means provided in the 1885 Act to justify increased rents were very nearly useless to the zamindars. Figures on prices were not available during the settlement; the power to enhance on the basis of 'prevailing rate' proved a dead letter (with the exception of some cases brought by the Hathwa raj) as the reformers had intended it to be; and if a zamindar went to court, there was the danger that the resulting rents would be declared fixed for a period of years.[52] Zamindars were generally better off using existing methods to enhance their rents.[53]

Very soon, however, the landlords and the local government in Bengal were complaining about the provisions of the law in regard to rent, as if they did indeed have practical consequences; and the number and vehemence of their representations imply that they were after all finding it desirable to use the courts.[54] Here too the settlement was important. The presumption of the operations was that existing rents were 'fair'. In the vast majority of cases the effect of the record was merely to establish what was payable. The effect on the future, however, was potentially to stabilize these rates. In a minority of cases, in which existing rents were disputed before the officials, the settlement established what should be paid. The prospective effect in these cases was apparently normative, particularly because in Bengal the rules provided for judicial procedure and not for the *ad hoc* and locally specific decision-making of the North Indian system.[55]

The eagerly-received *parcha* was thus, for the majority, a record of what they should pay, something which raiyats may not have generally known. The zamindars' *jamabandis* tended to be defective in this regard, as in distinguishing between dues of different kinds and payments of different years.[56] The position was worse in the case of joint proprietorships and joint tenancies. The uncertainty, except sometimes when co-sharers fell out amongst themselves, suited the landlords well, and particularly when they wanted surreptitiously to match their rents to rising prices. Real or notional arrears of rent were also useful, in the confusion of the estate records, for maintaining the zamindar's economic and social control. Loans advanced to cultivators and mixed in with the records of rent could serve the same purpose. The visits of the settlement team were designed to establish what each tenant paid to each zamindar. The British argued in the later nineteenth century, as some scholars do today, that custom had provided a check on zamindari power and extortions;[57] it is true at least that from the 1870s economic constraints on behaviour were changing and arguably were reducing the interdependence of each local community. In their place the British were seeking to introduce the protection of generalizing law. The diminution of ambiguity in rents as in land rights was part of this process.[58] Landlords were being edged, therefore, towards more formal means of control; twentieth-century reports remark on their acceptance of the tenants' right to transfer their holdings, subject to the tenant's payment of a transfer fee; they also draw attention to the virtual disappearance in some areas of landlords who lent to their tenants.[59] Such landlords were potentially vulnerable.

Certainty in rents would promote stability, but not necessarily standardization. In the Hathwa case the estate did not achieve a general enhancement of rents, though the officials believed this would have been permissible in view of the rises in prices and their belief that rates had not been increased for twenty years.[60] Rather the estate raised certain rents and recognized others as exceptions: the claim was that low rents were being raised to the average unless a discount was justified, as where cultivation was new or the land inferior. The explanation was invited by the 1885 Act and need not be taken too literally. It is hard to believe that concessions operated wholly on such objective grounds, for all that settlement officers' judgements implied a notion of a standard rate: this would indeed have amounted in the longer run to rent control rather than selective enhancement. In practice, however, rates of rent between villages and raiyats remained diverse, particularly where there were many small estates, but also (no doubt because of equivalent local bases of power) on the great zamindaris. It is tempting to think that rents in comparable areas were becoming more similar; in fact divergences were being entrenched.

So rent after the record of rights was still an instrument of differentiation among the raiyats. There were any number of important variables. Many rent agreements solemnized at the settlement were the outcome of old-fashioned duress. Many disputes merely continued earlier quarrels in which the 'richer class' of raiyats—as the Muzaffarpur settlement officer called well-to-do Bhumihars and Kayasths—were 'perfectly able to hold their own' against the petty *maliks*.[61] A raiyat who paid a rent calculated in money terms benefited from the erosion of his rent by inflation, and the commutation of produce rents was one indicator of the impact of the legislation.[62] In general, zamindari incomes from formal rents were limited rather than augmented by the record. Tenants with established privileges were protected from pressures tending to create tenants-at-will in practice as well as low, and able to maintain favourable (rather than low) rents. The Act was particularly obliging to middle-sized raiyats who encroached on their fellows: it gave them weapons against the zamindar which it denied to under-raiyats.

The 1885 Act proceeded from the belief that Indian society needed to be protected rather than reconstructed, and consequently that it was acceptable to attach occupancy right to raiyats rather than to the land and hence to those who actually worked it. This distorted its impact; understanding the record of rights makes this verdict even more plausible for Bihar. However, the impact was further qualified by pre-existing conditions. The society was one in which the larger social categories (of rent-receivers, surplus cultivators and those with insufficient land for subsistence) were fairly rigid and contained, while at the same time there was remarkable flexibility, in terms of land use, in the relative strength of families within the surplus category and the labourers, apparently because of rapid and even annual fluctuations of fortune (rather than Chayanovian family cycles).[63] The society was complex and various, therefore, but it was also integrated and interdependent and hierarchical. The changes discerned in the late nineteenth century seem, as a result, to have been unable to take either of two extreme forms. They could not produce a society wholly dominated by a few land controllers and traders leading to large-scale capitalist production; but nor could they transform the conditions and opportunities of the majority of the population. Rather benefits were captured by relatively large numbers of dominant peasants and brokers of various kinds, who already commanded appropriate resources and the existing points of exchange. By contrast, the 1885 Tenancy Act postulated essentially two classes, landlords and tenants. Being applied to a society made up of a multiplicity of linked sections, it had the result of encouraging only those of the tenants who were already advantaged. More extended marketing of crops, too, in a stratified society, did not open up general opportunities, but increasingly locked already subordinate people into systems of control. Thus the influence of both the state and economic change reinforced the same tendencies in the society.[64] It was hardly remarkable, therefore, that the record of rights tended to make definite and defensible the differences in status and privilege between the raiyats, and to benefit some of them against some of the zamindars, rather than to secure the supposed rights and well-being of the body of 'actual cultivators'.

Thirteen Villages of Muzaffarpur

Some indication of the raiyats who benefited, and the means and circumstances of their doing so, can be gleaned from a comparative study of thirteen villages in Muzaffarpur which were surveyed in both 1886 and a decade or so later during the district-wide settlement.[65] The sample is small but the data are interesting and relatively rare. The thirteen villages differed markedly in size, holdings per acre and so on. They ranged from those in which a body of maliks held a large share, to others where a single proprietor occupied relatively little land. Once again British terminology ignores similarities and conceals distinctions. The ten years between the surveys witnessed some remarkable change, but also strikingly different fortunes.

In aggregate, the number of zamindari holdings was greatly reduced; only two villages stood out against the trend, one because of a large increase in the area of *zerat* and the other due to sub-division among a large number of proprietors. At the same time there was an increase in the number of raiyati holdings, amounting to 12 per cent, along with a small decline in the area covered. The increase was unevenly distributed, though roughly related to villages in which the proportion of *zerat* had declined. There is no correlation to suggest that zamindars were dividing holdings in order to raise rents; nor is there any connection with the size of the average holding in 1885 or with stricter official definitions at survey. The explanation is that zamindars were consolidating holdings, and that raiyats were not. The increase in the area of *zerat* and in the average size of zamindari holdings bore this out.

More detailed examination, however, undermines these generalizations. Most of the increase in *zerat* in aggregate was achieved in only two villages, which in 1885 had stood at the bottom and in the middle of the range in regard to the landlord's share of the land. The former was the smallest of the villages; the latter one of the largest. The only other significant increase in *zerat* was in a third village which already had the highest proportion of proprietary land. The fortunes of different villages in fact reveal different management strategies: on the one hand increasing reliance on *zerat*, and on the other increasing dependence on rents. *Zerat*, as noted already, could be let out on short-term leases or cultivated directly; the latter was more likely where there was a large number of zamindari families. The letting put the land with raiyats whom the British categories ignored; cultivation might make for zamindars hardly to be distinguished from raiyats. Villages of both types were included among the thirteen. The alternative strategy, to increase the amount of raiyati land, was also to be found, and in some cases resulted in significant increases in income.

In aggregate too rents rose considerably over the ten years. These figures present the usual difficulties of interpretation, and do not show real outgoings. It is impossible to judge or explain variations in the absence of information about soils, cropping, irrigation and so on. The comparison is in each case merely with the recorded figures of ten years before. In detail, moreover, the picture is very different. In nine villages the raiyats paid more per acre. One very highly-rated village apparently experienced great pressure; it was perhaps engaged in profitable agriculture, even market gardening, in 1885. This and one other village with a large increase had been subject, moreover, to *batwara*; their rents bear out the reputation of such proceedings. Conversely villages with a multiplicity of zamindars tended to be little disturbed; least affected were four owned by more than one estate. And indeed several villages actually paid less per acre, or experienced very small increases. The decade was on the whole a good one for North Bihar, and prices rose. It is arguable therefore that about half the villages were paying a lower proportion of their crops by value to the landlord in 1895 than they were in 1885. It is tempting to believe that the record was holding down rents—at a time when on subjective evidence revenue officers were reporting a general and extortionate enhancement—but more probably the figures reveal the expected stickiness of rents. The main conclusion from the figures is that, in real terms, zamindars in these villages were not after all being very successful with rents, even though, in terms of the land they held, the proprietary interest was overwhelmingly strong.

It is interesting that the fortunes of villages varied. Most instructive, however, is that the fate of raiyats varied within each village. *In toto* nearly half of the holdings were enlarged, about one-third experienced no change in size, and the remainder lost land. The first of these categories was as large as 67 per cent of holdings and a greater proportion of raiyati land in one village; in another it was as little as 25 per cent. With the unchanging group, this section testifies to the effective security of tenure experienced by a majority of raiyats in respect of most of the land. It is unfortunately impossible to break down these categories into the legal heads employed at the settlement, but whether or not the two are identical it seems reasonable to call this majority 'settled', in that they had occupancy in practice. Their advantage was also expressed in one of two ways: either they held their land and resisted rent rises, or they enlarged their holdings and—without exception—on average paid higher rents. The latter group is of the greatest significance.

Except in one village, raiyats in this group had paid below the average rate in 1885; in some villages they continued to do so in 1895. Those who lost land had very often paid more originally but paid less per acre in 1895. The category may conflate some who paid at a higher rate for the same land with others who paid at the same rate for more land, but it does very strongly suggest that in many villages there were raiyats ready and able to take on increased area at higher rates of rent, and others who could or would not do so and who lost land as a consequence. As their rent rates were then reduced, it seems probable too that it was their better land which had been taken over. Moreover, turning to the average size of holdings, one finds once again that the group paying higher rents enjoyed fortunes quite against the trend. In some villages average holdings were becoming smaller; in others they were increasing or remaining unchanged. But the larger-than-average holdings, in almost all villages, were in the hands of raiyats whose rents were either raised or maintained. These raiyats thus were able to follow the example of the zamindars. There was one village where the so-called raiyats' holdings were mere pockets presumably allocated to servants and labourers, and where the *maliks'* interests were on average almost as small; but even in this village the average size of holding was doubled in the period. There were other, true exceptions, associated with *batwara* or increases in *zerat* (and presumably re-letting to cultivators or sharecroppers). But most zamindars were consolidating their holdings, on average, without much affecting the size of the raiyats'. It is possible that this indicates an increase in direct cultivation. It implies a benefit. It was one some but not all raiyats shared.

The conclusion for the thirteen villages is that only a minority of zamindars were able to gain land and to raise rents significantly in real terms. Most, however, were able to increase the average size of their holdings. The majority, then, may have been embarking on different, more direct means of tapping agricultural surplus, as rental incomes proved less elastic than those from production. One result was that a majority of raiyats experienced little change, except those in the minority of villages whose zamindars had the power to increase their *zerat*. In some villages raiyats whose position was unchanged constituted a majority; and in some of these, but not all, these people were apparently privileged, judging from rent rates and average sizes of holdings. A more clearly advantaged group was those raiyats who gained land at the cost of higher rents. This section seems likely to have included successful agriculturists but also those managers and brokers of surplus within the village, the dominant peasants.

There is no way of knowing, from these data, whether the changes were cyclical or secular; they are likely to have been both. The advantaged group may have been composed of different families at different times; changes in the average size of holdings may subsume temporary circumstances and family cycles. On the other hand, within the averages, there were bound to be even larger or stronger raiyats—with the kinds of variation visible between zamindars—for whom the changes represented a progressive strategy of commanding the most valuable resources, in this case larger holdings because of the increasing value of agricultural production. We have already identified such people at the theoretical level, and there is ample evidence of their existence in reality. Some of them enjoyed collective advantage, as when raiyats were known for resisting their landlord, even the government; more significant, however, were others who, often by their outside contacts, were able to assume control over fellow villagers. Details of maladministration on government estates in this period offer many instances in which enterprising, opportunist individuals or families succeeded in dominating villages.[66] Such people were typical, not perhaps in their opportunism, but in filling a role which was to be found in villages throughout Bihar.

The officials concluded that the answer, on government estates and generally, was a record of rights, to secure that 'artificial thing', tenant right.[67] But if its effect was at all to harden and perpetuate the differences in society, then it must have worked to the further benefit of those who, in the thirteen villages, were taking progressive advantage of the changes in landholding, the hidden category as it were within the section of raiyats who were gaining lands at higher rents. The mechanism was not purchase at this stage, and indeed the statistical evidence for an increasing number of sales, even in the twentieth century, does not entirely justify the emphasis which has been placed upon it.[68] (Much of the increase was in registration; in any case numbers as a proportion of holdings were always small.) The weapon was apparently a willingness to pay higher rent, at least during the nineteenth century. The suggestion is that the holdings of petty raiyats were being sub-divided, and amalgamated with those of the more successful. If a record of rights made tenancies more definite, moreover, this process would gradually be accelerated, because sub-division would have been encouraged through the normal pattern of inheritance and partition; only the strong would be able to resist this impoverishment, and the gap between them and the remainder, widening already as they retained a larger share of the profits of marketing crops, would be further increased.

Such polarization was not of course produced by the Tenancy Act or any single official policy. The Act and particularly the record of rights, as they came to have some effect, worked on existing inequalities, which they did nothing to reduce, and which they allowed to harden. The influence of economic change on persistent institutions and attitudes was another potent factor in the equation. None of these trends is very happily described as 'arrested development'. The emphasis is rather on the specific impact of policies, as of other influences, on an existing society. That society was extremely various in detail, but also had certain prevalent and resilient features. Thus tenancy laws could modify without transforming. British rule was not applied to a *tabula rasa;* Bihari society was neither egalitarian before 1793 nor uniformly depressed by the permanent settlement. European concepts of class and property, in the latter case particularly arguments about value, combined with notions of moral economy and village community to obscure the inherently divided and stratified nature of Bihar, where structures ensured redistribution of resources and hierarchies were buttressed by complex concepts of differentiation. Thus, in 1885, when the 'boom of property' was extended, in theory, from landlords to cultivators, in practice it proved an additional benefit to individuals who were already well-placed. It revolutionized neither property nor production, but helped produce and then fix the kinds of changes visible in the thirteen villages.

Trade offers a metaphor for the continuities contained within the process of change in the later nineteenth century, a process in which it was of course a most important factor. Cultivators had always been involved in exchange: between rich and poor in villages, between wet and dry lands, between rent-payers and receivers, between areas of specialist production, between country and town. In Bihar, as in many other places, such exchanges, when not between superiors and subordinates and hence subsumed under the dominant culture's preference for gifts, tended to be mediated through a variety of hands or separated over time. The payment of advances of cash, food or seed was a characteristic means of stimulating production for sale; the tendency was to capture the producer rather than to compete for production. A *jajmani* system is a similar mechanism for services and labour. In Bihar these features were still very apparent in the later nineteenth century, and as much in the new industries based on European capital, such as opium and indigo, as in the predominant rice trade or for oilseeds and other long-traded commodities. It is extremely hard to establish the extent to which the substance as well as the form of such institutions persisted over time, but that is immaterial to our present purpose of establishing the existence of controllers and intermediaries and their continued role under conditions of growing trade and commercial agriculture. It may be of course that they were the more secure because much of Bihar and a majority of Biharis did not attract large inward trade although providing commodities for export: methods appropriate to the extraction of 'surplus' thus continued to be preferred to methods appropriate to the generation of consumption. In such a case, it is inevitable that as the volume of trade increased, its benefits grew but continued to be concentrated on those who were strategically placed within existing systems. And as the number and range of exchanges grew, without transforming the manner in which they were conducted, it follows that the role of exchange in reinforcing control and in promoting hierarchies would be, if anything, enhanced. On the one hand one has, therefore, the *jeth raiyats* of Champaran who became indigo planters' *amins*; on the other hand one has the chorus of allegations about the burgeoning exactions based on debt, which indeed was often substituted for money from the point of view of the cultivator at the end of a line of intermediaries who delivered his crop into the market. So it was also, as the property right was individualized and made more secure.

There were some interlopers, but mostly the hierarchies and intermediaries worked within village society. Thus a numerous section of the rural population benefited as opportunities grew; the section can be described by caste, tenure or some other particular resource but can only be defined as those who commanded their own production and controlled others. The British did not identify them, except occasionally to record some indigenous term, meaning in effect the dominant ones. Hence tenancy laws were but clumsily directed. However, as the dominant were themselves of diverse kinds it was possible to give advantages to one role over others, as the record of rights did in shifting the balance in favour of tenants over landlords.[69] The more formal their means of control, the more susceptible rent-receivers were to economic and political change; some raiyats, like some intermediaries, could benefit from being exempt from interference but able to manage their own and their fellows' land and produce.

A FUCKING USELESS

Glossary

abwab	cess
amin	surveyor, agent
batai	a rent based on division of the harvest when a fixed proportion is due to the landlord
bargadar	sharecropper
batwara	partition of an estate in revenue records
bigha	unit of area: 1600 square yards (subject to local variation)
danabandi	a rent based on appraisal of the standing crop
jamabandi	the accounts and records of a village or estate
jajman	patron: a landlord or cultivator who employs client labourers or artisans
jeth raiyat	chief tenant
kabuliyat	counterpart to a lease
kist	instalment
malik	landowner (whether or not revenue–paying)
parcha	copy of an entry in a record of rights in land
patta	lease
patwari	accountant
raj	an estate practising primogeniture and not held in severalty
thikadar	fixed–term intermediate tenure–holder
zerat	'home–farm' lands: the part of his estate which a landowner claims for his own cultivation (as opposed to *raiyati* land).

Abbreviations

CEHI Dharma Kumar, ed., *The Cambridge Economic History of India* Vol. 2 (Cambridge 1983).

PCR Records of the Commissioner of Patna Division, Bihar State Archives, Patna. Citations give *basta,* collection, file and year in that order.

PSS Asok Sen, Partha Chatterjee and Saugata Mukherji, *Perspectives in Social Sciences 2. Three Studies on the Agrarian Structure in Bengal 1850-1947* (Calcutta, 1982).

R&A Proceedings of the Government of India in the Revenue and Agriculture Department, National Archives, New Delhi. These records have been seen in file volumes, and references include 'keep-withs' (not available in London). Citations give department, branch, series, number, month and year in that order 'Dep.' is Deposit series; 'Rev' Revenue Branch.

NOTES

1. A small part of this essay summarizes the paper presented at Heidelber in July 1984; other, larger sections were included in a paper read at S Antony's College, Oxford, in March 1985. I am grateful to participants o these occasions for their comments. My chief debt, however, is to Cliv Dewey whose suggestions on an earlier draft persuaded me to recast an widen the scope of the essay. General background will be found in th relevant Settlement Reports, beginning with Stevenson-Moore's o Muzaffarpur, which is the most useful; but in particular the accounts c the implementation of the record of rights are based on the annual Re ports on the Settlement Operations in Bengal, from 1891-8, in R&A. Sepa rate references will not be given to these materials. For an introduction t the 1885 Act see Dietmar Rothermund, *Government, Landlord and Peasant i India: Agrarian Relations under British Rule, 1865-1935* (Wiesbaden, 1970).
2. I have advanced a similar argument in 'State, Peasant and Moneylende in late Nineteenth-century Bihar' in *Rural India. Land, Power and Socie under British Rule,* ed. Peter Robb (London, 1983). For the eighteent century see Ranajit Guha, *A Rule of Property for Bengal* (Paris and Th Hague, 1963).
3. See *CEHI,* 86ff.; W.W. Hunter, 'A Dissertation on Landed Property an Land Rights in Bengal at the end of the Eighteenth Century' in *Bengal M Records* Vol. 1 (London, 1894); B.H. Baden-Powell, *Land-Systems of Britis India,* Vol. 1 (Oxford, 1892), 398-442 and 500-640. The most interestin recent examination is Ratnalekha Ray, *Change in Bengal Agrarian Socie* (New Delhi, 1979).
4. See Binay Bishen Chaudhuri, 'The Process of Depeasantization in Beng and Bihar, 1885-1947', *Indian Historical Review,* II (1975). The argument that some peasants but in the main non-cultivators gained the land lost b small-holders through indebtedness and land transfer. For a recent appl

cation of these ideas see *PSS*, for example 10, 21, 28, 114-22, 146-63 and 231-3. See also *CEHI*, ch. VI.

5. Daniel Thorner, 'De-industrialization in India, 1881-1931' in Daniel and AliceThorner, *Land and Labour in India* (Bombay, 1962); A.K. Bagchi, 'De-industrialization in Gangetic Bihar, 1809-1901' in *Essays in Honour of Professor S.C. Sarkar*, ed. Barun De, (New Delhi, 1976) and 'De-industrialization in India in the Nineteenth Century', *Journal of Development Studies*, XII (1976). See also the debate in *Indian Economic and Social History Review*, XVI, (1979); and Partha Chatterjee 'Agrarian Relations and Politics in Bengal: Some Considerations on the Making of the Tenancy Act Amendment 1928', Centre for Studies in Social Sciences Occasional Paper 30 (Calcutta, 1980).
6. Willem van Schendel and Aminul Haque Faraizi, *Rural Labourers in Bengal 1880-1980* (Rotterdam, 1984), 5-6, 21, 27-40. At page 40: 'The proportion of labourers declined, if anything.' The unreality of some data on this subject is shown by the 1891 census which gives figures of around one per cent for field labourers in North Bihar; estimates at settlement show that between one-fifth and one-third of agriculturists had insufficient land to support themselves, and perhaps half of all families could not avoid some labour for others.
7. M. Mafakharul Islam, 'Some Aspects of the Problem of Subinfeudation in Undivided Bengal', *Indian Economic and Social History Review*, XX (1983).
8. Rothermund, *op. cit.*, 21, 28, 40, 96, 104, 109, 113 and 185.
9. See Asok Sen in *PSS*.
10. For the origins of the inclusion of a settlement procedure in the Act see R&A Rev A16-46 July 1883, especially C.L. Tupper, 'Memorandum on the Rent Question in Behar', 20 October, 1881.
11. Two principles of analysis are being contrasted here: the settlement and categories based on source of income. Some officials also referred to two main classes: rent-payers and rent-receivers including raiyats (see PCR 355, 15/3 1891-2) which might imply those who controlled production or distribution and those who provided the surplus or their labour. None of these categorizations was to be found uniformly.
12. This argument, too complicated to detail here, is based mainly on a comparison of returns made by patwaris and those made by *amins*. See also R&A Rev A73-4 October 1894 and B3-4 December 1898.
13. Gibbon to Champaran Collector, 7 January, 1892, PCR 355, 15/4 1891-2.
14. Just as the institution of landed property occurred in law more absolutely than in practice, and needed a variety of administrative acts to reinforce it, so tenant rights depended on such support in order to evolve outside the statute book.
15. R&A Rev A17 February 1893.
16. See for example Bengal Revenue resolution, 30 May 1894, R&A Rev B3-4 May 1898, B17-18 January 1897, A21-3 July 1904. One result was that collections of contributions to costs were better than expected; see R&A Rev A10, 11 & 14-15 February 1897, A15-18 March 1896, B36 April 1897.
17. Members of the Rent Law Commission thought the 1859 Act reduced security of tenure by defining (that is, limiting) the right to it.
18. In common with other arguments below, this qualifies the suggestion that even the record of rights had little result because ignored in the

courts (in regard to rent, until legislation in 1906; see Rothermund, *op.cit.*, 104-5 & 107-8). The area contained a 'mass of involved coparcenary tenures' and changes in government records were numerous; in sixteen villages entirely new *khesras* were needed. Growing awareness and the importance of the record-making are perhaps indicated by the disputed entries, over 25000 in Muzaffarpur in 1893-4, covering 241 out of 712 villages and 368217 out of 487099 fields. For an investigation suggesting a lack of zamindari interference after the survey see R&A Rev A1-2 August 1901. These points also diminish the damage done by the failure of plans to maintain the records (see for example R&A Rev A40-5 March 1895 and A26-31 July 1913).

19. In one Bettiah village 153 raiyats held 2.3 *bighas* on average, but 42 held less than one, 19 held 5 or more (8 of these 9 or more and one over 17); PCR 355 15/4 1891-2. In Muzaffarpur the average raiyat had two holdings.
20. It was thus—in part a matter of terminology—that Ibbetson could state that the proportion of protected tenants was very much greater and the protection much stronger in Bengal than elsewhere in India: R&A Rev A28-9 December 1902.
21. See note 18. Compare the 1920s when commutation of produce rents was sought not so much for financial independence as for 'taming' the landlords; *CEHI*, 130.
22. Inquiries in selected villages in Hajipur in 1898 showed 14 per cent of holdings transferred since settlement (6 per cent by succession); in another case, of 200 transfers, only 21 had been registered; R&A Rev B3-4 May 1898. For the later period see *Report of the Bihar and Orissa Provincial Banking Enquiry Committee 1929-30*, Vol. 1 (Patna, 1930). Figures on partitions are available in R&A in annual Revenue Administration Reports.
23. R&A Rev A17 February 1893 and B17-18 January 1897.
24. See for example Upendra Narain Singh, *Some Aspects of Rural Life in Bihar. An Economic Study, 1793-1833* (Patna, 1980) and also *PSS*, 3.
25. See PCR 357, 15/1 1892-3. The plots were virtually invariable, unlike holdings; hence the importance to the record of the *khesra*, the field number.
26. See for example [R.H. Hollingbery], *The Zamindary Settlement*, 2 vols. (Calcutta, 1879), the Report of the Rent Law Commission (Calcutta, 1880), and Ripon's despatch of 1882 in R&A Rev A16-46 July 1883.
27. See *CEHI*, 124-43 (138 for estimates of rent). The following discussion will not seek to disentangle the large and separate question of produce rents which prevailed in South but not North Bihar, taking different forms with varying implications (*CEHI* at page 124 is somewhat misleading and incomplete). By 1900 the main point is that zamindars preferred produce rents often in effect to secure unregulated rather than regulated tenancies, and *zerat* rather than raiyati land.
28. *CEHI*, chs. IV and XI. Sen claims that in eastern India rice was some 30 per cent dearer in 1900 than 1887; *PSS*, 111.
29. See R&A Rev B17-18 January 1897.
30. For a version of this argument see Peter Robb, 'State, Peasant and Moneylender'. A contrary argument is that by acquiescing in rural stagnation, landlords became hard-pressed (see *PSS*, 111). How then is one to interpret the expansion of cultivated area and cash cropping? Eric Stokes'

explanation is far more convincing; see *CEHI*, 36-68.

31. See for example Francis Buchanan (Hamilton), *An Account of the District of Shahabad in 1809-10* (reprint, Patna, 1934), 351-2.
32. I have considered this in an unpublished paper, 'The East India Company and the Peasants of Bihar', given at a seminar in the School of Oriental and African Studies in 1978.
33. This discussion is indicative not exhaustive. As will be shown below, the question is further complicated by the doubt over what constituted rent: another way of saying that it was often uncertain. For example, were illegal cesses less common because of the impact of official and legal bans, or more common due to increases in zamindari power and possibly some decrease in alternative income such as that from ground rents in markets or tolls on trade and communication?
34. This argument extrapolates from the results of MacDonnell's checks on the census figures in Darbhanga. See W.W. Hunter (ed.), *A Statistical Account of Bengal*, vol.XIII (London, 1877) 31-6.
35. See note 4.
36. See Aditee Nag Chaudhury-Zilly, *The Vagrant Peasant: Agrarian Distress and Desertion in Bengal 1770 to 1830* (Wiesbaden, 1982).
37. This point will be elaborated below.
38. Hunter, *Statistical Account*, XIII, 256-7 and 283-4.
39. Such was the Muzaffarpur Collector's view in 1891: almost all raiyats had occupancy rights, the exception being a few who were 'scarcely anything but day labourers'; PCR 355, 15/3 1891-2.
40. Almost complete figures for average rent rates in the Reports on Survey Operations by 1898 may be summarized thus:

	Muzaffarpur		*Saran*		*Champaran*	
Holding	Rs/acre	Rs/cult. acre	Rs/acre	Rs/cult. acre	Rs/acre	Rs/cult. acre
Fixed rate	3/6/4	3/14/-	3/8/-	3/13/9	1/1/6	1/4/2
Settled, occupancy	3/15/9	4/5/5	3/14/6	4/1/-	2/0/3	2/3/5
Non-occupancy	4/13/9	5/1/6	3/10/7	3/13/2	1/15/5	2/3/11
Under-raiyats'	4/15/9	5/4/5	3/15/6	4/0/11	1/9/2	1/10/8

41. *CEHI*, 175.
42. In *CEHI* the engine for change is unclear, and perhaps is intended to be merely demographic. In *PSS* the role of the 1885 Act is on one hand to provide raiyats with mortgageable property. Hence it disadvantaged those with occupancy by tempting them into debt and leading to the alienation of their land. On the other hand the Act allowed subletting and unregulated rents or terms. Hence it disadvantaged 'true cultivators' who did not have occupancy, making those who did into a newly-secure class. The inter-regional variations in landholding, moreover, are explained by differences in the severity of debt, largely for ecological and marketing reasons, a view which further confuses the assessment of the Act and is in any case ahistorical—regional differences being of very long standing and not shown here to have arisen in the later nineteenth century (but see note 45).

43. R&A Rev A22-3 November 1896.
44. Rothermund, *op.cit.*, pp. 104-5 and 107-8. See also note 18.
45. R&A Rev A17 February 1893; see also A17-18 January 1897. There were some differences in the use of the law: distraint by zamindars was most common in Bihar (Patna Division accounting for 48 per cent of all applications in the Presidency in 1889-90), whereas deposit of rents was used more by tenants in Bengal proper; see R&A Rev A8 November 1885. Such differences, which also occurred in the reactions to the record of rights, are indicative of regional and local variations, important in assessing change. The 'salience of diversity' has recently been developed into a major theme in a study of South India, and is as applicable elsewhere; see David Ludden, *Peasant History in South India* (Princeton, 1985).
46. J.H. Kerr told Minto: 'experience shows that this [record] is the only true remedy, and far more effective than isolated suits brought by individual raiyats or executive interference between landlord and tenant'; note kept with proceedings of the Government of India in the Home Department, Political Branch, A33-5, May 1908.
47. R&A Rev A15-16 May 1910.
48. Careless methods and rent increases are illustrated for Shahabad and Gaya in PCR 359, 17/9 and 30/9 & 12 1893-4; 361, 30/1 1894-5; and 366, 30/14 1896-7. See also R&A Rev A15-18 March 1896.
49. On Hathwa see R&A Rev A17 February 1893 and B17-18 January 1897. Already in 1887-8 Saran accounted for 853 out of 874 applications for enhancement in Patna Division, including claims for wells built with Opium Department advances.
50. A breakdown of over a thousand objections in 1898 showed just over half referred to possession and just under half to rent; of the former two-fifths were by landlords against raiyats, a quarter by raiyats against landlords and one-seventh by raiyats against raiyats; R&A Rev B3-4 May 1898.
51. This assessment allows for the confusion of earlier measurements and the use of a smaller *bigha* at the settlement. See R&A Rev B17-18 May 1897 and B3-4 May 1898. For other districts, which were similar, see R&A Rev A21-3 July 1904.
52. See R&A Rev A21-2 February 1896, A15-30 January 1897, and C1 December 1895. Ibbetson was here speaking for the framers of the 1885 Act, whose attitudes he did largely share. On prevailing rate see M.N Gupta, *Land System of Bengal* (Calcutta, 1940), 207. Excess area was also interpreted restrictively at survey and proved difficult for landlords to prove in court because of the development of case law. A contrary argument was that the 1885 Act distinguished between fixed-rate and settled raiyats, allowing the latter's rents to be raised (see Board of Revenue to Government of Bengal, 30 April 1892, R&A Rev A17 February 1893). In practice it probably helped prevent the raising of fixed-rate rents!
53. Raja Pyari Mohan Mukherji, R&A Rev A17 February 1893.
54. See note 50. Earlier, zamindars had objected to government scrutiny; see a petition against the record of rights, R&A Rev B24-8 May 1892.
55. On the other hand, before a draft record was formally published, disputes were dealt with summarily, though strictly this was illegal; R&A Rev A21-2 February 1896. Even so, the officials were applying the principles of the pro-peasant school, to the extent (the Government of India com

plained) of settling rather than recording rents: R&A Rev A73-4 October 1894, and see also A22-3 November 1896. These arguments undermine Rothermund's; see notes 18 and 44.

56. See for example records in one Bettiah village which did not show area, rates per plot, type of soil and so on, but only totals per holding; PCR 355, 15/4 1891-2, including note by Finucane, 24 November 1891.
57. For explanations of the differing awareness of the 1885 Act in different districts, see R&A Rev A17 February 1893 (report by the Patna Commissioner).
58. This argument bears on the one discussed in note 18.
59. On landlords' earlier opposition to raiyati transfers see R&A Rev A3-22 November 1898, A56-8 January 1895 and A17 February 1893.
60. The comparison was with records made under the Court of Wards.
61. See Peter Robb, 'Hierarchy and Resources: Peasant Stratification in late Nineteenth-Century Bihar', *Modern Asian Studies*, 13 (1979).
62. Though in Patna Division total applications rose from 5 in 1886-7 to 154 in 1889-90, there was little commutation in the earlier period; see R&A Rev A17 February 1893 and *CEHI*, 142-3. Of course produce rents might not be wholly immune to the impact of regulation on the ideas of cultivators' 'rights'; see also *CEHI*, 128-9.
63. See note 61.
64. A brief return to these themes will be found at the end of this paper, but fuller treatment is in Peter Robb, 'Law and Agrarian Society in India: The case of Bihar and the nineteenth-century tenancy debate', *Modern Asian Studies*, 22 (1988).
65. This section is based on the Annual Report on the Settlement Operations in Bengal, 1895-6. See also above note 18.
66. See note 48.
67. R&A Rev A9-11 June 1909; the phrase is J.H. Kerr's (one-time Settlement Officer in Darbhanga). He assumed, that is, that tenancy was created by British law.
68. See Chaudhuri, *op. cit.* In the villages discussed in this section many transfers of property were at the initiative of the landlord, and the most common transaction recorded was of mortgage with possession; few were sales despite signs that the price paid for occupancy holding was increasing. Of the mortgages 89 were to lawyers, 746 to moneylenders and 6153 to raiyats; the moneylenders were likely to be most often raiyats too, as mahajans from bazars tried to avoid taking over land for cultivation. In Champaran a survey of 391 villages showed in addition migration from one to another, when a raiyat took up a small holding to escape his debts. Proprietary rights were also sold: a study of 194 villages in Muzaffarpur showed 607 transfers affecting 7 per cent of the area: 72 per cent to landlords, 16 per cent to raiyats, 10 per cent to moneylenders and 2 per cent to lawyers. The price paid was remarkably uniform. Most interesting of all perhaps was another study of 1269 villages in the same district, which showed 8083 transfers, 14 per cent by sale, 85 per cent by mortgage (representing about 4 per cent of all holdings—again only mortgages with possession were recorded), but of these very many were of part-holdings only: in the case of sales this was true for over half, and with mortgages for over 70 per cent. In the light of the 13 villages discussed in detail, the

changes seem thus to be largely by mortgages of parts of holdings, or by landlords who were able to oust one tenant in favour of another. Changes in holdings were not new. It was normal for under-raiyats to hold land for short periods at high rents (except in Champaran where low cash rents were common in such circumstances) and for occupancy raiyats to cultivate for a year or two the lands of a neighbour who had more land than he wished to cultivate directly. The pattern in the 13 villages and the corroboration from other studies may however have represented a secular trend whereby the advantages of the well-to-do section, to be found everywhere, were increased.

69. See note 64. Since this paper was written, Sugata Bose, *Agrarian Bengal: Economy, Social Structure and Politics, 1919-1947* (Cambridge, 1986), has argued that credit was the key to agrarian structure and change, but also that rent was *becoming* less important than the management of cultivation as a means of extracting surplus. This paper finds the latter also true for Bihar from the later nineteenth century, but assumes that, though credit always mattered for social control, its importance grew in the twentieth century, after the weakening of state and legal support for rent-receivers (other than raiyats), improving of the hand of settled tenants, shifts in land control, and the differential benefits of expanding trade. See also Partha Chatterjee, *Bengal, 1920-1947. The Land Question* (Calcutta, 1984). Another recent study of connections between British law and socio-economic conditions, in deltaic Bengal, is Sirajul Islam, *Bengal Land Tenure. The Origins and Growth of Intermediate Interests in the 19th Century* (Rotterdam, 1985).

8

EXCHANGE DEPRECIATION AND ECONOMIC DEVELOPMENT: INDIA AND THE SILVER STANDARD, 1872–1893

B.R. TOMLINSON
University of Birmingham

The great controversy over the consequences of the decline in the gold price of silver was the nineteenth century equivalent of the contemporary debate about the practicability and desirability of a New International Economic Order for the world's monetary system. The disparity in exchange rates and domestic prices in silver and gold standard countries that opened up from the mid-1870s onwards attracted a good deal of theoretical and practical attention, a major focus of which was on the relative costs and benefits that this brought for industrial countries (on gold) and primary producers (on silver). For British observers this debate often concentrated on a discussion of the fortunes of Britain and India, at a time when the exchange between them was subject to more severe disturbances than had ever been known before.

Recent academic discussions of the silver standard, and of later episodes of currency depreciation in debtor countries, have often argued that a depreciating exchange can bring significant benefits to developing economies, at least at times of falling international prices. By securing price advantages for exportables over imported goods, currency depreciation is thought to secure advantages that outweigh the exchange costs of shifts in the external terms of trade and of the servicing of foreign debts. Cheapening exports, or maintaining local returns to exporters despite declining international prices while making imports more expensive, can sustain incomes earned by the production of primary produce, while also acting to further the process of import-substituting industrialisation.

In such ways, it has been argued, the declining silver standard of the late nineteenth century provided a satisfactory adjustment mechanism for certain primary producers faced with threats of increased competition in domestic and foreign markets caused by the expansion of the international economy. Most important here were the disproportionately large productivity changes that favoured the industrial countries and those agricultural exporters best able to make use of empty lands, new systems of transportation, and capital-intensive techniques of production. In the case of India, however, there were many complicating factors which, as we shall see, make clear judgements such as this extremely difficult.

India was the largest economy in world trade based on a silver standard before 1900. The analysis of the effects of her currency system in the last quarter of the nineteenth century has often been overlaid by other political and economic issues, notably the related, although distinct, question of the developmental effects of an export surplus. This concern with unilateral transfers of Indian goods is easy to understand since under the Company's rule they had been encouraged as a way of transferring capital out of India, and of enabling Leadenhall Street to repatriate a profit on its Indian operations. After 1858 this system was apparently maintained by the Secretary of State's direct participation in the foreign exchange market. The sale of Council Bills, bills sold in London for sterling (gold) and met in India by rupees (silver) to finance the India Office's current expenditure on goods, services and debt charges in Britain, bulked large in the running of India's foreign exchange system, and in the minds of its critics.

Council Bills were sold to those who wished to export goods from India. The amount of bills offered each year was determined by the size of the Secretary of State's expenditure in Britain (before 1900 Council Bills were not sold simply to meet demand for private remittances and hence to 'facilitate trade', as later commentators put it). The exports that were bought with the proceeds of these bills were not balanced by the import of goods to India; they were met instead by rupees raised in taxation in India that were then used to redeem the bills presented there, balancing the sterling that had been received in London for the Secretary of State's expenditure.

Council Bills were in effect the means of remitting Indian revenue for expenditure in London. The form of that remittance was as unrequited exports of Indian produce, and it was this that focused contemporary concern about the system. Of India's export earnings from merchandise between 1872-73 and 1893-94 of £1369.9 million, £812.7 million (59 per cent) was met by the import of goods, £294.3 million (21 per cent) by the sale of Council Bills and £173.8 million (13 per cent) by imports of treasure. Of the trade surplus in goods of £555 million over these 22 years, 54 per cent was balanced by the sale of Council Bills, and 32 per cent by the import of treasure [Banerji (1982): Tables 34 & 40A)]. It was the size of the transfers made through Council Bills that suggested to some that these transactions were a means of engineering a 'drain of wealth', with exports as the enforced payment of 'tribute' to India's foreign rulers.

The settlement of a relatively large proportion of India's international account each year by the sale and purchase of Council Bills was a new phenomenon of the period after 1865. With this system in operation it could be argued that the true contact point of the rupee with gold lay here, not via the price of silver bullion. As Figure 2 (at end of paper) makes clear, there were considerable annual fluctuations in the cross-rate between the rupee exchange in sterling and the London price of silver. Thus it was tempting, for observers of the international monetary system with an Indian perspective, to reject the conventional wisdom that the downward floating rupee exchange was caused by the decline in the gold price of silver after 1873 which resulted from changes in the supply of the two metals. Many Indian experts (Lord Farrar, for example) attached a good deal of importance to the role of remittances in disrupting the course of exchange and prices, some even going so far as to argue that the world price of silver itself was determined by the value of the rupee, and that this in turn was directly linked to the volume of sales of Council Bills.

Since Council Bills were sold to meet the Secretary of State's contractual obligations in England, their volume was not directly related to the state of trade or the exchanges. When bills were offered, exporters in India had to calculate at what price they would be able to sell their goods on world markets, given that domestic prices were rising faster than foreign ones. In practice the volume of supply of Council Bills in sterling was influenced by the rate of return in rupees that Indian exporters were prepared to accept for their sterling expenditure. If, for the sake of argument, the Secretary of State offered Council Bills at £100 for Rs. 1,000, but exporters calculated that they required an exchange rate of £ 1 = Rs. 15 to make a profit, then they would force the price of a £100 bill down to £66.66. Therefore the Secretary of State would have to sell one and a half times as many bills as he had estimated to raise the sterling needed to meet his commitments.

Given that the Secretary of States's exchange dealings were by far the most visible part of India's international adjustment mechanism, it is easy to see how this mechanism was thought to push the price of the rupee downwards. Many contemporaries believed that any such fall would also serve to depress the gold price of silver bullion, of which India absorbed about one-third of world production in any year, and for which she was always the largest single market in the world. Thus a decline in the rupee exchange could depress the world price of silver, encourage its export to India, and hence swell Indian currency stocks. A rise in circulating currency could, in turn, push up prices in India, thus requiring a further fall in the exchange in the form of cheaper Council Bills to enable local goods to sell abroad. Since the Secretary of State's demands were fixed in sterling, the lower the exchange rate the more bills had to be offered, and the more bills were offered the greater the downward pressure on the exchange.

These arguments are interesting, but extremely difficult to test. Working from the annual data on the price of silver, the rupee exchange rate, the volumes of trade and of Council Bill sales, and price fluctuations, it is not possible to confirm them, as Figures 2 through 4 demonstrate. In general, the rupee exchange rate was slightly above the price of silver, which is not suprising since Council Bills could command a premium because they meant remitting without having to handle imports. Yet the annual fluctuations in the volume of Council Bills alone does not seem to provide a good explanation of the rupee's variations against silver (it is difficult to investigate the nature of forward exchange markets since monthly and weekly data are hard to obtain, especially for the price of silver).

The most sophisticated and plausible explanation of short-term fluctuations in the exchange is that provided by Atkinson. On the basis of monthly rupee and silver prices for 1891 Atkinson argued that the Council Bill mechanism tended to fix the lower point of the exchange, while the price of silver determined the upper point (although he did not note that 1891 was one of the rare years when the rupee exchange was falling faster than the silver price). While bills would normally command a premium over silver, Atkinson argued, in times of disturbance the bill exchange rate would lead silver prices downwards and lag behind any upward movement. Because Council Bills had to be sold irrespective of price, the exchange rate they represented had to fall with any exogenous fall in the gold price of silver, and sometimes the bill exchange rate would fall faster than the silver price because it was also sensitive to rises in domestic prices in India and falls in the gold price of goods on world commodity markets. When the price of silver rose for reasons unconnected with the rupee, the Council Bill rate of exchange would also follow in a lagged manner because competition for bills would become more intense as the import of silver bullion became less profitable. Thus equilibrium through the exchange mechanism was never possible: price rises were cancelled out by depreciation, depreciation caused further price rises. While at some times a weak exchange was associated with rising domestic prices and falling imports, and a strong exchange with less rapid price increases and rising imports, at other times these 'normal' relationships were reversed.

The inflow of treasure, especially silver bullion, to South Asia was another important feature of the Indian monetary system in our period. Silver was the basis of the domestic currency, with open mints until 1893. Thus some silver had to be imported to increase currency for transactional purposes at a time when commercial agriculture was spreading rapidly under the stimulus of railway building and export demand. It is worth noting that although the world gold price of silver was falling in this period it was not falling any faster than any other gold price, and so it is hard to sustain the argument that the world was somehow acquiring India's exports cheap by paying for them with a devalued commodity.

The strain on the metallic coinage was made more intense by the extremely restrictive and conservative nature of the banking and paper money policy followed by the Government of India after the mid-1860s. The best estimates available suggest that five-sixths of the silver imported between 1861 and 1895 was coined, and that over 80 per cent of this coinage passsed into active circulation (which included short-term hoards). Atkinson's careful estimates, and those of other authorities in the 1880s and 1890s, such as Barbour, suggested strongly that by the mid-1880s rupee prices were rising, in part, because of excess circulation of coin. While rainfall remained the most important single influence on the course of Indian prices, with drought and famine almost solely responsible for the first upward surge of domestic prices in the late 1870, by the mid-1880s the steady rise in the price curve could better be explained by redundancy of currency.

Domestic prices in India were rising at a time when they were falling in most of the rest of the world. Clearly, one effect of the decline of the rupee exchange was to make it possible for the gold prices of India's exports to fall in common with world trends, while allowing domestic prices to rise. In addition, the internal price of India's exportables and importables (or of agricultural and industrial goods) began to diverge markedly. While agricultural prices rose and then fell sharply in the late 1870s, and then rose again more gradually from the mid-1880s non-agricultural prices fell slightly over the period. As Figure 1 demonstrates, by the mid-1890s agricultural prices were about 40 per cent above their 1873 levels while non-agricultural prices were at par. Between 1873 and 1893 the terms of trade for agriculture improved in 13 years and worsened in 8 with a net improvement of 66 percentage points overall. There was, however, no simple relationship between Indian domestic prices and export performance. This was partly due to the peculiarities of the exchange system, and partly to the fact that levels of international demand for many Indian goods depended not so much on their prices as on the availability of other sources of supply. As Atkinson demonstrated, the volume of Indian wheat exports varied in accordance with output in Europe and North America, rather than wih the gap between Indian and world prices. For this reason it is difficult to sustain arguments that one effect of the depreciating exchange was to scour out foodgrain exports that would otherwise have gone to meet home demand.

It seems possible that the course of rupee prices was simply part of a classical balance of payments adjustment process. If prices rise in a bullion standard country, especially one with open mints and a metallic coinage, as a result of the coinage of bullion imported to meet a trade surplus, the obvious inference is simply that the adjustment process for a surplus country is at work, tending to raise prices and lead to equilibrium. But the nature of the balance of payments data available to us makes it extremely difficult to uncover the nature of any adjustment process that may have been taking place in the case of India. As Table 1 demonstrates, the most recent and complete reworking of the balance of payments figures suggests that India was suffering from an overall deficit, rathar than a surplus, during the 1870s, 1880s and 1890s. Banerji's calculations show clearly that there was a current account deficit in every year, and that known capital account items converted this into an overall surplus only rarely (thus raising the intriguing possibility that the decline in the exchange rate of the rupee was, in part, a consequence of a persistent and unadjusted structural balance of payments problem).

The whole issue of interpreting India's balance of payments position, in this and later periods, is complicated, in reality, by the definitional problem presented by the import trade in 'treasure'. Most analysts have simply followed the Government of India's accounting practice here in regarding these as part of the import trade in commodities. Yet while a small proportion of annual imports of gold and silver were required for industrial purposes, the bulk was used as transaction coinage or was 'saved' in the form of hoarded coin, bullion and jewellery. If the treasure imports are removed from Banerji's balance of payments figures then the smaller current deficit is cancelled out by known capital imports in almost every year until the 1890s. It could be said, therefore, that India was running a surplus on goods, services and capital combined, which she was liquidating by importing the medium of mass savings in the form of bullion.

The existence of open mints until 1893 confuses the conceptual issue of the nature of India's bullion imports still further. As Adams and West discovered, no simple statistical relationship can be established between the annual fluctuations in the volume of silver imports and increases in money supply, suggesting that the interaction between changes in income, expenditure and savings (in hoards that may not have been sealed off from the rest of the economy as completely as has often been supposed) was a complex one. Clearly, the period of open mints coincided with a time of rapid commercialisation which brought a need for large amounts of transactional coinage, but ownership of rupees even for transactional purposes may also have been symptomatic of rising wealth in at least some parts of the producing economy. Whether such indications of rising wealth can also be taken as evidence of the existence of an overall balance of payments surplus is a much more open question.

The position of India as one of the largest trading economies in the world with a depreciating currency attracted a good deal of attention from contemporary economists, both amateur and professional. Amateurs were mostly concerned with what the Indian example had to teach for the embattled cause of bi-metallism, while professional interest centred on what adjustment effects the falling exchange caused in the domestic economy. Here the main focus of attention was on the behaviour of prices. Alfred Marshall, the most rigorous of the professional economists interested in Indian matters, always argued most strongly that any apparent price advantages to be gained from the depreciation of the rupee were illusory. In his evidence to the *Gold and Silver Commission*, and elsewhere, he enunciated a strict purchasing-power-parity theory of exchange-rate determination, arguing that domestic prices were bound to rise fairly rapidly to balance out the effect of a falling exchange, and stressing that in the interim exporting interests could gain only at the expense of labour and capital as a whole.

Economists and economic historians have, more recently, focused further attention on the price movements which are the key to Marshall's arguments. India's subsequent monetary history, especially the tight money policies that seemed inevitably to accompany the maintenance of a high, fixed exchange parity in the late 1920s, made many local commentators anxious to establish that the floating, depreciating rupee of the late nineteenth century had brought positive and peculiar advantages. A good deal of evidence was therefore put forward to suggest that, although Indian prices rose in the

.870s, 1880s and 1890s, such increases did not keep pace with he depreciation of the currency against gold, and that there- ore real benefits accrued to the economy as a whole. Some evidence to support this position can be obtained from Figure 1, but all Indian price data, and especially that from this period, must be used with caution and care. The major influ- ence on domestic prices, apart from rainfall, may well have been the progress of railway building. This had the effect in India, as in North America, of slightly depressing port prices (which form the basis of the data in Figure 1), but of consider- ably raising interior prices as the depressive effects of local gluts were outweighed by the expansionary effects of external demand. While it is true that, over time, one effect of railway building was to unify prices in the various inland markets, and to link these more closely to those of the port cities, this process was far from complete by the mid-1890s, especially for ndia's newly expanding export crops such as wheat.

Overall, perhaps, the phenomenon of the silver standard upee in the late nineteenth century deserves to be demystified. In the first place, the influence of monetary matters in determining the structure and development of the ocal economy was weaker than has often been assumed. Furthermore, the peculiar financial arrangements associated with colonial rule during this period had rather less effect on he local monetary system than many contemporaries believed. Yet the monetary issues that are raised by this episode still require analysis. Here it seems that silver bullion mports and domestic price increases may well best be explained as part of a classical adjustment process for a bullion-standard country with a trade surplus. But such adjustment could never be fully effective for a number of reasons. In the first place, the exchange rate could be forced downwards by large Council Bill sales (as may have happened n 1891); secondly, the exogenous decline in the gold price of silver limited the extent of any rise in the rupee exchange so long as open mints meant that silver imports could pass directly into circulation as coin. To complicate matter still further, the rate of change in production and transportation meant that any adjustment mechanism based on expectations of equilibrium would be hard to detect or analyse.

The broader consequences of this unadjusted exchange rate egime may be of more general interest. Here two broad trends can be seen which have a wider significance. Firstly, the period saw a considerable internal transfer of resources from taxpayers to producers. As the exchange rate fell, so the rupee costs of the Home Charges (most of which were fixed in sterling) rose and new taxes had to be imposed to meet them. Rs. 5.5 million a year was added to the tax bill from the mid-1880s onwards, in addition to steady increases in the staple land tax. But while increases in land revenue and rents lagged behind prices in general, taxes on urban incomes and consumption rose at a time when non-agricultural prices as a whole were not rising, and when the internal terms of trade were turning decisively in favour of the rural sector. Central government tax revenue rose from Rs. 374 million in 1872 to Rs. 501 million in 1893; over one-third of this increase came from non-agricultural taxation such as income-tax, excises on consumption, etc. During this period total taxes rose by 34 per cent, agricultural prices by 44 per cent and taxes on agriculture by 23 per cent [Fowler Committee: Appex. II nos 52]. It is hardly surprising that the principle of 'no taxation without representation' led in this period to the rise of urban-based nationalism profoundly critical of the fiscal consequences of colonial rule.

A second major effect of exchange instability may have been to limit the penetration of the domestic economy by external agencies. Contemporaries were convinced that uncertainties about the exchange acted as a disincentive to British capital to invest in India. While we may doubt that massive amounts of British money might ever have been forthcoming for long-term investment in India whatever the exchange regime, there may be something in this point. More important may have been the way in which fluctuations in the silver rupee increased the perceived risks even of short-term capital transfer. It is striking that exchange banks and import/export firms prided themselves on withdrawing balances from India at the end of each trading season, and on minimising exchange risks by limiting asset holding in India. The possibility of exchange rate instability may have added significantly to the barriers of risk, uncertainty and imperfect information that inhibited the activities of foreign firms in the up-country domestic economy of production and exchange.

The most obvious lesson of India's experience on a declining silver standard is that an unadjusted, downward-floating exchange system can give substantial help to agrarian economies in escaping from constraints imposed by technical advances elsewhere (even when faced by high foreign exchange commitments for debt servicing and the like). The late nineteenth century was a time of declining gold prices for primary produce; had India been on a gold standard it is not clear that her exports could have remained competitive without forcing down domestic wages to below subsistence levels (given the lack of unutilised resources or factors of production in her economy). Even with the cushion of a depreciating exchange Indian exports were only competitive, arguably, thanks to agricultural wage rates that were not substantially above subsistence levels in many cases. Since the monetary system presided over by the colonial government was so inflexible, with no central bank and little provision for seasonal currency or a fiduciary issue, the expansion of commercialisation that took place would not have been possible on a gold basis either. Without India's ability to earn an export surplus on visible trade it is hard to see how the superstructure of colonial rule could have been maintained.

Yet it is almost equally obvious that the substantial help that the Indian economy obtained from the depreciating silver rupee was secured at a cost. The succour of a declining exchange benefited the rural sector almost exclusively, and resulted in a transfer of resources to agriculture and a stimulus to the system of petty commodity production that, in the long run, has proved inadequate to the needs of the domestic economy as a whole. The implication is that downward floating only produced palliatives, while at the same time it increased barriers to change by underlining the status and position of current producers, thus increasing conservative welfare-type pressures on future policy.

Perhaps, in the end, the most severe pressure which maintaining a depreciating exchange rate regime with high fixed foreign currency costs imposed was on government itself. While the Government of India was always just about able to overcome the internal and external transfer problems associated with a silver currency in the late nineteenth century, and still had enough power at the end of the period to close the mints and adopt an active policy, others were less fortunate. Governments less able to tax at home and borrow without supervision abroad, such as the Ch'ing Empire in China, found that exchange depreciation with high gold costs could lead to increased external pressure and renewed domestic revolt. Exchange depreciation alone did not provide a satisfactory means of adjustment to changes in the international economy for those facing major structural problems coupled with institutional inadequacies. Indeed, it may even have served to make them worse in the absence of any action to tackle them directly.

NOTE ON SOURCES

There is a mass of contemporary opinion and evidence on the silver standard and its problems, in India and elsewhere, in the reports and appendices of four major committees of enquiry set up by the U.K. Government: *Parliamentary Select Committee on Indian Currency and the Depreciation of Silver* (1876-8); *Royal Commission on Recent Changes in the Relative Values of the Precious Metals* (1888) [Gold and Silver Commission]; *Report of the Indian Currency Committee* (1893) [Herschell Committee]; *Report of the Indian Currency Committee, 1898* [Fowler Committee]. Other useful contemporary accounts of the Indian case are F. J. Atkinson, 'Silver Prices in India', *Journal of the Royal Statistical Society* (1897); D. Barbour, *The Theory of Bimetallism and the Effects of the Partial Demonetisation of Silver* (London, 1885); Lord Farrer, *Studies in Currency* (London, 1898); reprint, New York, 1968); Dadabhai Naoroji, *Poverty and Un-British Rule in India* (London, 1901). Marshall's views on India are conveniently collected in *The Official Papers of Alfred Marshall*, ed; J. M. Heynes (London, 1926) and *Memorials of Alfred Marshall*, ed. A. C. Pigou (London, 1925).

More recent accounts of the period and its issues, for India and elsewhere, include: J. Adams & R. Craig West, 'Money, Prices and Economic Development in India, 1861-95', *Journal of Economic History* (1979); B. R. Ambedkar, *The Problem of the Rupee* (Bombay, 1923); S. Ambirajan, *Political Economy and Monetary Management, India 1766-1914* (New Delhi, 1984); Amiya Kumar Bagchi, 'Anglo-Indian Banking in British India: From the Paper Pound to the Gold Standard', *Journal of Imperial and Commonwealth History* (1985); A. K. Banerji, *Aspects of Indo-British Economic Relations, 1858-1898* (Bombay, 1982); A. Krishnaswamy, 'Marshall's Contribution to Indian Economics', *Indian Journal of Economics* (1942); A. Krishnaswamy & V. G. Edelberg, 'Measuring the Power of an Undervalued Currency to Stimulate Exports', *Review of Economic Studies* (1937-8); Michelle B. McAlpin, 'Price Movements and Fluctuations in Economic Activity', in *The Cambridge Economic History of India*, vol. II, ed. Dharma Kumar (Cambridge, 1983); B. Narain, 'Exchange and Prices in India, 1873-1923', *Weltwirtschaftliches Archiv* (1926); D. Rothermund, 'India's Silver Currency, 1876-1893', *Indian Economic and Social History Review* (1970); C. F. Diaz-Alejandro, 'Latin America in Depression, 1929-39', *The Theory and Experience of Economic Development*, ed. M. Gersovitz *et. al* (London, 1982); J. B. Nugent, 'Exchange-Rate Movements and Economic Development in the Late Nineteenth Century', *Journal of Political Economy* (1973); L. B. Yeager, 'Fluctuating Exchange Rates in the Nineteenth Century; the Experience of Austria and Russia', *Monetary Problems of the International Economy*, in ed. R.A. Mundell & A.K. Swoboda (Chicago, 1969). Other statistical data have been taken from Reserve Bank of India, *Banking and Monetary Statistics of India* (Bombay, 1954).

TABLE 1: BRITISH INDIA; BALANCE OF PAYMENT ON CURRENT ACCOUNT, 1869/73 — 1894/98
(£ millions, quinquennial averages)

	Balance Merchandise Trade	Treasure Imports	Balance Visible Trade (1 + 2)	Home Charges	Other Invisibles	All Invisibles (4 + 5)	Balance of Payment of Current Account (3 − 6)
	1	2	3	4	5	6	7
1869/73	+ 22.6	− 8.4	+ 14.2	− 8.8	− 15.6	− 24.4	− 10.2
1874/78	+ 21.0	− 6.4	+ 14.6	− 9.3	− 18.0	− 27.3	− 12.7
1879/83	+ 23.8	− 7.1	+ 16.7	− 10.7	− 17.7	− 28.4	− 11.7
1884/88	+ 23.8	− 9.2	+ 14.6	− 12.3	− 18.0	− 30.3	− 15.7
1889/93	+ 25.2	− 9.7	+ 15.5	− 13.5	− 19.4	− 32.9	− 17.4
1894/98	+ 20.7	− 5.6	+ 15.1	− 13.9	− 18.9	− 32.8	− 17.7

Source: Banerji (1982) Tables 34 & 40A.

Figure 1 : INDIAN PRICES (WEIGHTED INDICES), 1872-1893
(1873 = 100)

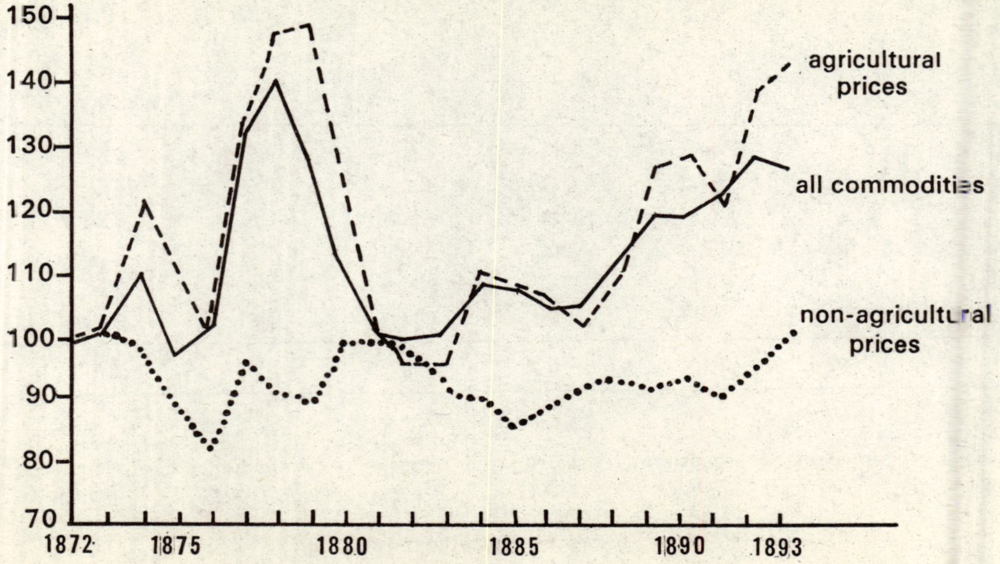

Source : McAlpin (1982), Appendix Table 11A. 1, Cols. 1-3

Figure 2 : RUPEE EXCHANGE (COUNCIL BILL RATE) AND LONDON GOLD PRICE OF SILVER, 1872-1893 (ANNUAL AVERAGES) (1872=100)

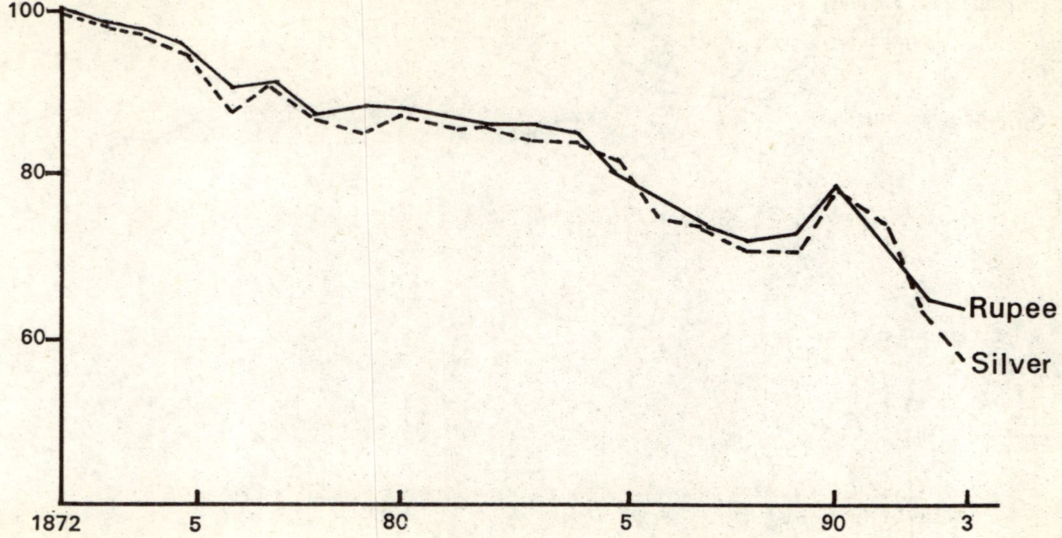

Source : Banerji (1982), Statement III; Indian Currency Committee (1898), Appendix II, no. 12.

Figure 3 : VALUE OF INDIAN TRADE AND REMITTANCES, 1873-1893 (in £ millions)

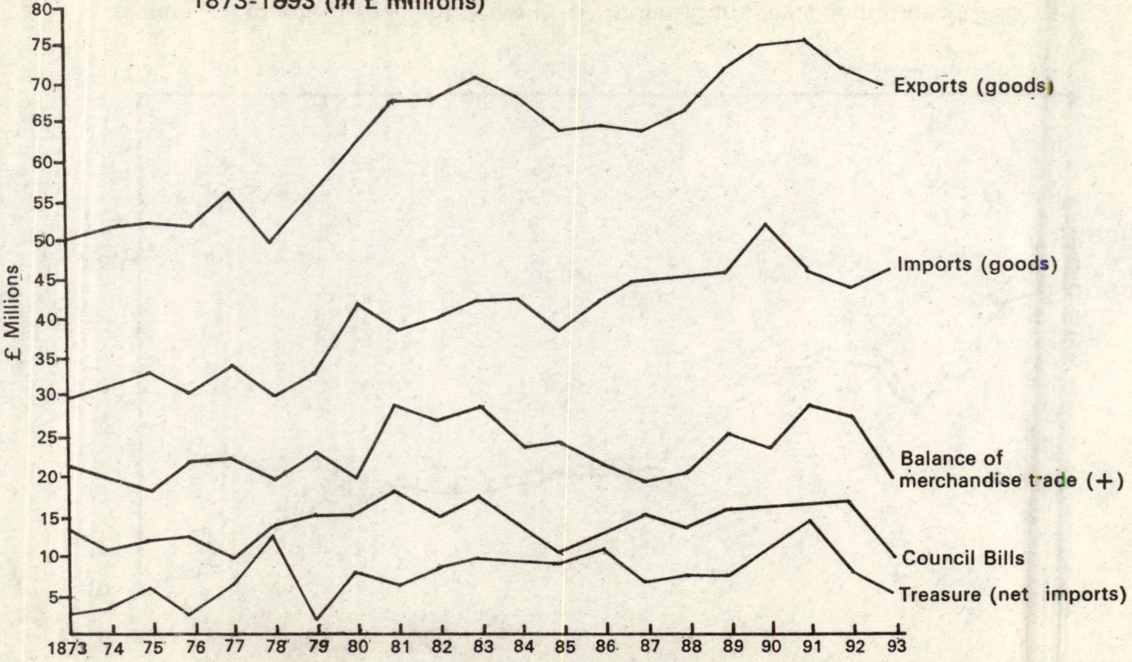

Source : Banerji (1982), statements I, II, IV, IX

PART IV
AGRICULTURAL GROWTH AND AGRARIAN STRUCTURE

9

CLASS AND ECONOMIC CHANGE IN CENTRAL INDIA: THE NARMADA VALLEY 1820–1930

CRISPIN BATES
Churchill College, Cambridge

This paper is part of a larger work whose purpose is to question the relative importance of changes in social structure and economic activity, the availability of natural and human resources, and the impact of colonial rule in allowing, encouraging, or positively restraining economic development in different areas of the British-ruled Central Provinces and Berar. It is the intention to derive from this conclusions that may be of relevance in the formulation of contemporary development policies. A valuable tool in the course of this study has been the concept of the agro-economic zone, which has been used as a unit of political economy. The geographical limits of these zones are illustrated in the accompanying map. In the course of the research startling differences have emerged between the class structures and different trajectories of development followed by each zone. In turn this has raised important questions about the role of dependency in the analysis of class, and the relationship between class, or the social relations of production, and the process of economic change.

The Narmada valley wheat zone, the subject of this paper, is just one of the agro-economic zones of central India, but it presents a classic example of how economic 'growth' can occur in the absence of 'development'.[1] The arrested nature of development in the Narmada valley was partly an effect of colonial rule, but colonial rule was only one of the number of factors that shaped the contrasting patterns of growth and surplus distribution to be found in central India. Equally important were the pre-colonial history, class structure and ecological characteristics of each of the agro-economic zones. As important as the class structure within zones was the relationship between them, since inequalities between regions encouraged interdependence and inter-regional exploitation in a variety of forms.

The British first took over the administration of the Narmada valley in 1818, and the early years of their rule saw the desolation and depopulation of the region under an oppressive system of land revenue collection. Land was abundant and labour at a premium, but in the mid-1830s the British determined to reverse this situation for reasons of financial and political expendiency. The *malguzars* (the revenue farmers of the former Maratha system) were pushed steadily to the Furej and in the revenue settlements of the 1860s they were given exclusive rights of ownership over most of the land. Land revenue was then collected solely from this class at a reduced rate. The *naqdi,* or substantial, cash-paying tenants (similar to the *mirasdars* of western India) were guaranteed occupancy rights and large holdings at fixed rents. The remainder of the tenants were left entirely at the mercy of the *malguzars,* who could dispose of the land however they liked. Adjacent forest areas were reserved exclusively for the use of the government. The tribal populations of these tracts were caught in between, cut off from any possibility of settling in the lowlands, and forbidden rights of ownership or allowed only very limited rights of occupancy, in their former homelands.

There thus developed a regional division of the classes, with capital owners being confined largely to the centre of the valley and a sizeable portion of the labouring population residing in the less fertile lands and in the hills. In the long term, big tenants and *malguzari* landlords were able to take advantage of their control of the land and the availability of cheap migrant labour. They established a symbiotic relationship with firms of exporters such as Vale, King and Co. and Ralli Brothers, who began sending their agents into the Narmada valley in the middle of the nineteenth century. International demand and the opening of the railway to Bombay meant that valuable surpluses could easily be extracted from this grain-rich country, and small fortunes were quickly made. The development, however, was forced and immature, being based principally on the super-exploitation of labour rather than the capitalization ot assets, and by the early 1890s a crisis in production had become apparent which was compounded by the catastrophic impact of successive monsoon failures at the turn of the century.

If this brief history were to be viewed from a neo-classical or purely ecological perspective the shades of emphasis would change markedly. In the process, important questions would go unanswered such as, why was there no 'trickle-down' in income distribution, why did poverty, low wages and indebtedness persist (and even increase) on such a vast scale, and why did the economic development of the Narmada valley fail to become both progressive and self-sustaining? In particular, why was this system of economy so susceptible to external shocks and so incapable of adaptation without a major loss of output? Ecological and conventional neo-classical economic arguments give only partial and unsatisfactory answers to these questions.[2] By concentrating on the class structure of the Narmada valley, this article sets out to address these issues and attempts to discover the role played by class in the heydays and, importantly, in the ultimate failure of the wheat boom of the late nineteenth century.

THE CENTRAL PROVINCES AND BERAR circa 1900

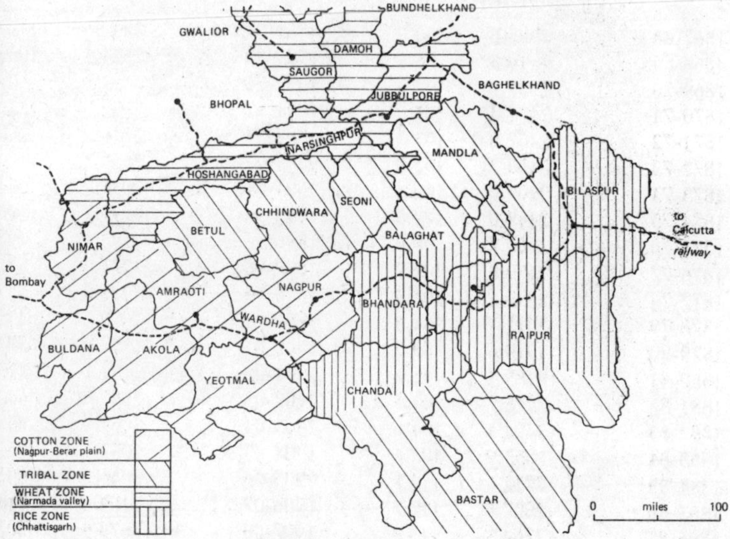

Trade and Agricultural Growth

The growth in agricultural production in the Narmada valley is illustrated by the statistics given in Table 1 which shows the total area under the principal crop in all of the wheat-growing districts. Land in parts of the adjacent tribal districts of Betul, Chhindwara and particularly Seoni was increasingly turned over to wheat cultivation during the colonial period, often by encroaching land-grabbers from the valley. For this reason the wheat acreages in these districts have been included in the totals for the Narmada valley. The object of the table is to illustrate the development of production for the purpose of trade. Aggregated simply for the districts of the wheat zone, the resulting trends, shown by the accompanying indices, illustrate more accurately the actual experience of the region than if I had reproduced official aggregates based on administrative divisions or calculated for the province as a whole. Though they involve much less trouble, official aggregates such as these disguise the regional character of economic growth.

TABLE 1

ACREAGE UNDER THE PRINCIPAL CROP IN THE WHEAT ZONE

	'000 Acres	Indices		'000 Acres	Indices
1867-68	2385.6	100.0	1888-89	2742.6	115.0
1868-69	2114.3	88.6	1889-90	2524.5	105.8
1869-70	2333.2	97.8	1890-91	—	0.0
1870-71	2471.4	103.6	1891-92	2699.3	113.1
1871-72	2467.6	103.4	1892-93	2818.9	118.2
1872-73	2453.3	102.8	1893-94	2668.7	111.9
1873-74	2405.6	100.8	1894-95	2037.2	85.4
1874-75	2447.0	102.6	1895-96	1645.4	69.0
1875-76	2380.7	99.8	1896-97	1185.1	49.7
1876-77	2439.8	102.2	1897-98	1277.3	53.5
1877-78	2595.1	108.8	1898-99	1521.0	63.8
1878-79	2011.4	84.3	1899-1900	1078.5	45.2
1879 80	1919.6	80.5	1900-01	1370.9	57.5
1880-81	2185.1	91.6	1901-02	1722.1	72.2
1881-82	2476.7	103.8	1902-03	1582.8	66.3
1882-83	2494.4	104.6	1903-04	2065.9	86.8
1883-84	2555.9	107.1	1904-05	2057.6	86.3
1884-85	2712.6	113.7	1905-06	2046.5	85.8
1885-86	2807.5	117.7	1906-07	2169.9	91.0
1886-87	2764.3	115.9	1907-08	1678.9	70.4
1887 88	3062.8	128.4	1908-09	1598.6	67.0

09-10	1781.7	74.7	1930-31	1807.6	75.8
10-11	2130.6	89.3	1931-32	2016.3	84.5
11-12	2217.5	93.0	1932-33	2108.3	88.4
12-13	2281.9	95.7	1933-34	2163.7	90.7
13-14	2083.1	87.3	1934-35	2269.0	95.1
14-15	2000.3	83.8	1935-36	2107.1	88.3
15-16	2003.0	84.0	1936-37	2008.0	84.2
16-17	2216.8	92.9	1937-38	2110.3	88.5
17-18	2321.7	97.3	1938-39	2125.9	89.1
18-19	1766.4	74.0	1939-40	2056.6	86.2
19-20	2077.3	87.1	1940-41	1996.0	83.7
20-21	1822.0	76.4	1941-42	1760.5	73.8
21-22	1655.2	69.4	1942-43	1520.3	63.7
22-23	2030.3	85.1	1943-44	1607.8	67.4
23-34	2156.8	90.4	1944-45	1532.9	64.3
24-25	2176.3	91.2	1945-46	1540.4	64.6
25-26	2256.8	94.6	1946-47	1693.3	71.0
26-27	2335.7	97.9	1947-48	1031.5	43.2
27-28	2342.2	98.2	1948-49	1111.9	46.6
28-29	1831.5	76.8	1949-50	1533.9	65.1
29-30	1718.7	72.0	1950-51	1675.8	70.2

ote: See appendix for sources.

The statistics on the acreages under different crops are one f the more reliable indicators of the state of the agricultural conomy produced by the colonial administration. Estimates f total output are more arbitrary, as although figures on the verage yield of different crops are available, these are elatively unhelpful unless combined with the *annewari* stimates made annually by village *patwaris* indicating the uality of the harvest. Although acreage statistics are derived om similar sources, they were nonetheless verified by easurement at each settlement, as well as by occasional spot hecks in between. By contrast, the science of estimating the rop outturn was nowhere near so well developed. Since they epended on a subjective comparison between the current eason and that which had preceded it the estimates are quite seless as a means of indicating long-term trends, though they etain some value as a measure of short-term fluctuations. Iultiplying acreage by yield estimates to calculate statistics of otal output only tends to compound the errors inherent in eir compilation.[3]

Immediately striking is the increase in wheat cultivation up 1887-88, and rapid decline to a fairly stable plateau after 392-93. Annual fluctuations in yields and acreages overlaid this pattern before and after these dates, but the scale of th reduction after 1892-93 clearly marks a qualitative transforma tion in production. This transformation is all the more strikin when the wheat acreage is compared with the gross cultivate acreage in the wheat zone (Table 2). Once again, 1887-8 marks the peak year in wheat production, with over 53 pe cent of the gross cultivated acreage occupied by this crop Eight years later only one third of the area was cultivated wit wheat; by 1909-10 little more than one quarter of the gros cultivated area was under wheat, and by 1947-48 less than 1 per cent.

TABLE 2

PRINCIPAL CROP AS PERCENTAGE OF GROSS CROPPED AREA IN THE WHEAT ZONE

	%s	Indices		%s	indic
1867-68	46.9	99.2	1897-98	28.6	60
1868-69	42.7	90.4	1898-99	33.4	70
1869-70	45.0	95.2	1899-1900	26.2	55
1870-71	46.0	97.5	1900-01	30.1	63
1871-72	46.7	99.0	1901-02	35.2	74
1872-73	45.4	96.1	1902-03	31.0	65
1873-74	46.3	98.0	1903-04	40.2	85
1874-75	47.2	100.0	1904-05	40.2	85
1875-76	45.2	95.8	1905-06	39.4	83
1876-77	45.4	96.1	1906-07	40.6	86
1877-78	46.1	97.5	1907-08	35.5	75
1878-79	36.8	77.9	1908-09	31.6	66
1879-80	34.2	72.3	1909-10	28.0	59
1880-81	37.9	80.3	1910-11	32.8	69
1881-82	42.3	89.5	1911-12	33.6	71
1882-83	42.5	90.1	1912-13	35.2	74
1883-84	43.2	91.5	1913-14	34.5	73
1884-85	51.3	108.6	1914-15	30.7	65
1885-86	51.5	109.0	1915-16	30.0	63
1886-87	49.7	105.3	1916-17	32.9	69
1887-88	53.5	113.3	1917-18	36.8	77
1888-89	50.4	106.6	1918 19	29.0	61
1889-90	47.0	99.5	1919-20	33.2	70
1890-91	—	0.0	1920-21	31.3	66
1891-92	51.1	108.2	1921-22	27.6	58
1892-93	51.1	108.3	1922-23	32.5	68
1893-94	49.5	104.9	1923-24	34.7	73
1894-95	37.4	79.2	1924-25	34.2	72
1895-96	33.1	70.0	1925-26	35.4	75
1896-97	27.5	58.1	1926-27	36.5	77

927-28	35.6	75.4	1939-40	31.7	67.1
928-29	27.5	58.3	1940-41	30.4	64.3
929-30	27.1	57.4	1941-42	27.6	58.4
930-31	27.7	58.6	1942-43	24.0	50.8
931-32	30.8	65.2	1943-44	24.2	51.2
932-33	32.3	68.4	1944-45	23.8	50.3
933-34	32.1	67.9	1945-46	24.5	51.8
934-35	34.3	72.6	1946-47	26.7	56.5
935-36	32.3	68.4	1947-48	17.0	36.0
936-37	30.1	63.7	1948-49	17.3	36.5
937-38	31.7	67.1	1949-50	24.0	50.8
938-39	32.0	67.7	1950-51	26.3	55.8

'ote: See appendix for sources.

Taken district by district, the figures are in some cases even nore striking. In 1887-88, in Hoshangabad for example, wheat ultivation was 53 per cent up on the level in 1867-68, while he area under cotton, rice, sugarcane and other foodgrains vas halved. In Narsinghpur, 1867-68 saw an abundant wheat rop, so 1887-88 was only 12 per cent up on this, but rice ultivation fell by half, cotton fell to less than half its former evel, and sugarcane production dropped to 25 per cent of its evel in 1867-68. Since sugarcane required the best soil and ntensive cultivation and was the most expensive crop to pro-luce, the fall in the area under cane from 7,800 acres to 1,600 icres in Narsinghpur and Hoshangabad combined marked a :lear diversion of capital resources. Meanwhile, wheat pro-luction peaked in 1887-88 with a total of 969,400 acres being levoted to the crop (including mixtures of wheat and gram). 3y 1894-95, however, only 689,800 acres were under wheat in he two districts; by 1909-10 only 465,100 acres; and by 1942-43 only 366,800 acres. Significantly, there was no increase in sugarcane cultivation,[4] the principal increases taking place in he area under gram, fodder, and the cheap, inferior food-grains such as *juar*, *kodon* and *kutki*.

In Jabalpur, the 1887-88 peak was marked by a 32 per cent ncrease in wheat acreages compared with 1867-68, after which the cultivators fell back on the production of rice, gram and other pulses. In Saugor and Damoh the wheat acreage ncreased from 681,400 acres to 884,100, before falling to 465,900 in 1894-95. There was a slow recovery thereafter, though once again *juar* and fodder tended to become relatively more important. In Betul, Seoni and Chhindwara much smaller acreages of wheat were involved, but a similar ebb and flow was to be seen, with *kodon* and *kutki* (grains commonl associated with tribal modes of cultivation) being the mos common resort as the popularity of wheat declined.

Wheat cultivation had begun to increase in the 1850s wit the growth of demand from Malwa, followed by a deman from cotton-growing tracts for foodgrain as land formerl devoted to food crops was taken over by cotton during th period of the American civil war. Thus despite the completio of the Great Indian Peninsula Railway through the Narmad valley in 1870 there was no sudden increase in demand an the acreage under wheat did not expand dramatically overa until after 1880-81. The statistics on exports by rail (Table 3 show a very gradual increase in exports before that in respons to a slow rise in price.

TABLE 3

WHEAT EXPORTS BY RAIL
(five-year averages)

	Maunds (in 000s)	Rupe (in 000
	C.P. only	
1866-71	495	1,48
1871-76	1,461	3,4
1876-81	3,641	6,5
	C.P. & Berar	
1881-86	8,406	15,73
1886-91	8,254	19,08
1891-96	4,925	18,37
1896-1901	1,359	4,37
1901-06	3,221	9,27
1906-11	1,459	5,13
1911-16	4,058	15,22
1916-21	2,806	13,05
1921-26	2,472	13,74
1926-31	1,478	7,99
1931-33	1,392	4,49

Source: Central Provinces, Berar, and Central Provinces & Berar, *Reports o Trade and Resources* and *Reports on Railborne Traffic*.

Note: The figures before 1903-04 include trade *between* the CP and Berar.

The key year was 1876-77, when wheat first surpassed cot- ton as the province's most valuable export crop. That year alsc saw a considerable leap forward in the acreage under wheat ir

Narsinghpur. The expansion in Hoshangabad started earliest of all, in 1868-69, Narsinghpur leapt forward in 1876-77 (excluding the poor monsoon seasons of 1878-79 and 1879-80), while Jabalpur was a late starter in 1884-85. This expansion in cultivated acreages and the areas under wheat went ahead without any upsurge in population growth to consume the increased output. Although Harda town in Hoshangabad (population 13,945 in 1891) came to have a larger population than the district capital as a result of its strategic position in the wheat trade, the population of the district as a whole registered little change before the 1880s. In neighbouring Narsinghpur district, the population increased by only 8 per cent between 1881 and 1891, and actually declined in the Narsinghpur tahsil.

The growth of the export trade was given its first fillip by the abolition of an export duty in January 1873 (which amounted to three annas per maund), an all-round reduction in freight rates of 30 per cent, the abolition of certain terminal charges, and the opening of the Suez Canal.[5] At an all-India level, retail prices rose in fits and starts, climbing at times to sudden peaks, such as one in 1878, a scarcity year, when the price was 79 per cent above the 1873 base. Bombay wholesale prices were more steady, but reached a clear plateau of around Rs. 3.70 per maund between 1888 and 1895 (see Table 4).[6] The relative price of gram and barley and other substitute *rabi* crops could greatly influence the production of wheat.[7] This relationship ran clearly in favour of wheat in the Bombay wholesale market in the late nineteenth century, a trend which was sharply reversed in the 1890s and persisted in this form until the end of the First World War.

Of greater importance to Narmada valley cultivators was the trend in local prices. Before the opening of through rail communications, it was said that the prices at Hoshangabad 'were often arbitrarily fixed by a ring of dealers, the demand not being large enough to induce outside competition'.[8] Settlement officers at this time compiled local price indices on the basis of *malguzars'* and grain-dealers' account books. Between 1851 and 1855, wheat sold on average for one rupee per maund in Hoshangabad, gram for Rs. 0.60 per maund, and between 1856 and 1860 wheat sold for only Rs. 0.92 per maund on average. Over 1861-65 the average price of wheat was

TABLE 4

INDEX NUMBERS OF THE AVERAGE PRICE OF 'KHANDWA' WHEAT IN THE BOMBAY WHOLESALE MARKET, 1867-1931

(1873 = 100 = Rs. 3.68 per maund)

1867	99	1899	107
1868	112	1900	109
1869	107	1901	107
1870	114	1902	96
1871	57	1903	91
1872	87	1904	91
1873	100	1905	92
1874	76	1906	99
1875	73	1907	94
1876	75	1908	137
1877	99	1909	144
1878	115	1910	119
1879	134	1911	101
1880	114	1912	106
1881	79	1913	110
1882	90	1914	124
1883	90	1915	149
1884	72	1916	126
1885	69	1917	131
1886	89	1918	215
1887	97	1919	241
1888	103	1920	191
1889	100	1921	199
1890	92	1922	346
1891	98	1923	221
1892	113	1924	213
1893	100	1925	218
1894	99	1926	216
1895	104	1927	243
1896	97	1928	228
1897	154	1929	279
1898	153	1930	221
		1931	165

Source: Index Numbers of Indian Prices, 1861-1931 (Delhi, 1933), Table VI.

Rs. 1.91. A shortage of rain over central India as a whole in 1868-69 helped a further rise in wheat prices, leading to a quinquennial average of Rs. 2.65 per maund in 1866-70. The price of gram rose too, but always remained slightly lower.[9] Another peak occurred in 1878-79 due to famine in north India and a local attack of blight. Normally though, the local wholesale price of wheat ranged only just over Rs. 2.5 per maund, peaking at Rs. 3 in 1888-89 and just over Rs. 3 again in 1891-92. The average price quoted for Hoshangabad between 1886 and 1890 was Rs. 2.6 per maund and was closely matched by the average rates fixed by panchayats of *malguzars* and tenants at the same time for converting grain rents into cash rents in Narsinghpur.[10]

None of these price rises was spectacular enough on its own to account for the increase in wheat production, and the changes in price correlate imperfectly with the increases in crop acreages and the statistics on trade. Furthermore, it is difficult to account for the onset of a decline in the wheat trade come the 1890s, or its continuation, by reference to price changes alone since local prices were consistently reaching much higher levels, peaking at Rs. 3.5 or Rs. 4 per maund in the post-famine period between 1900 and 1917.[11] These and many other factors determined the profitability of wheat cultivation, but profitability, in the strictest terms, was only one of a number of factors determining the actual pattern of peasant production.

Initially, much of the increase in exports recorded by rail was simply the result of the reorientation of trade which had formerly gone by road. Not until 1889 was Saugor connected to the railway, but before then the improvement of the road connecting Saugor to Kareli railhead in Narsinghpur meant that a great deal of traffic that had formerly headed northeastwards towards Mirzapur now came onto the line. The construction of the Indian Midland Railway connecting Hoshangabad and Bhopal in 1882 added further to rail traffic. The pack-bullock trade all but disappeared and there occurred a decentralization of trade, with grain dealers establishing themselves at each railway station, as well as at the large markets of Harda, Seoni, and Itarsi in Hoshangabad.[12] Produce from Seoni district also headed south by road to Nagpur for export.[13] In Hoshangabad there were 17 stations and here, and in neighbouring Narsinghpur and Jabalpur districts, there was hardly a single village of any importance situated more than twelve miles from a station.

The relatively low price of Narmada wheat and the improvement in communications induced Ralli Brothers and at least eight other European firms to send their agents into the valley to buy up the *pissi*, or soft white wheats grown here. These wheats mixed well with European-produced grains and were ideal for export.[14] Locally, it was always *juar, kodon, kutki* and the hard wheats that were consumed and the *pissi* wheat used to be sold at a discount of 8 to 10 per cent, but with the growth of European demand this situation was reversed and *pissi* wheat became valued at least 12 per cent higher than the hard *jalalia* or *kathia* varieties after 1877.[15] As a result, the proportion of U.K. wheat and flour imports supplied by India rose from 5 per cent in 1880 to 16.7 per cent in 1886, and the Central Provinces provided the lion's share of the grain.[16] Only in 1871-72, a year of abundant harvests and low prices, did the first reports come from the Jabalpur division of exports of Narmada wheat being made to England by Messrs. nicol and Co. of Bombay,[17] but by 1888-89 the trade had reached its height. That year the failure of the Russian harvest and bad crops all over the rest of Europe forced European demand to a peak, and the Central Provinces exported a total of 7,106,760 cwt to Bombay and Calcutta ports, the nearest rival being the Punjab, with an export of 3,090,676 cwt.[18]

A key role in the growth of this trade was played by the European traders working in league with local *mahajans*, who amassed bulk supplies of the grain and transported it to Bombay. An asset was the low freight charges, which amounted to less than 22 per cent of the Bombay retail price from Saugor, and were lower still for the rest of the valley.[19] Besides the European merchants, there were also the travelling agents of the Bhattia firms at Bombay and the Marwari grain-dealers who bought and exported on receipt of telegraphic orders from Bombay.[20] Collectively they were known as the *pakka arhatiyas* or wholesale merchants of the trade. Unlike in the Bombay Deccan, Hyderabad and Berar, the *kachcha arhatiya*, or small commission agent, a source of finance to both cultivator and village *bania*, was less important. In the Narmada valley wheat trade, the big wholesale merchants bought directly from the local *ganjes* or wholesale markets (otherwise known as *golas* or *handis*) and the itinerant trader buying at *hats* or periodic markets or in the villages was a feature confined largely to Chhattisgarh and the remoter districts of the tribal zone.[21]

Forms of Surplus Appropriation

One source suggests that in Hoshangabad district, in the centre of the Narmada valley, the wheat boom was primarily the result of the *malguzars* of the valley engaging in direct cultivation.[22] Yet it is arguable that class differentiation within these tracts was more acute than elsewhere in central India at the time, and that differentiation on a *regional* scale played a more important role in fomenting the wheat boom of the 1870s and 1880s. The key to the continuance of the trade was the very low cost at which *mahajans, malguzars* and the cultivating elite were able to amass a marketable surplus, by using cheap tribal labour and by raising rent, debt and other charges on their tenants and sub-tenants. These methods allowed a brief period of very rapid growth, but ultimately led to a precipitate collapse of the wheat economy at the end of the century.

The exploitation of unprotected tenants can be shown by an analysis of the impact of British settlement policy and by reference to the available statistics on land-holding. Taking a closer look, it is apparent that the class of the substantial tenantry, descended from the *naqdi* of the early nineteenth century, was as important in terms of production as the *malguzars*. The absolute occupancy area, or at least the area held under this right, covered 25 per cent of the total occupied area in Hoshangabad in the early 1890s, a larger proportion than anywhere else in the Central Provinces. The *malguzars* cultivated only 21 per cent of the area. A similar class of substantial tenants was important elsewhere in the Narmada valley. In the *haveli* lands between the Narmada and Hiran rivers in Jabalpur district, there were said to be a great many substantial Brahmin tenants with large holdings, cultivated by means of farm-servants (*halwahas*).[23] One of Stokes' sources reports that two-thirds of the total net income (after payment of the government revenue) of Hoshangabad *malguzars* came from the profits reaped from direct cultivation, but this diverts attention from the amount of land sublet by this class of privileged tenants. Furthermore, the concealment of subletting was general by the 1890s for fear that subtenants might claim occupancy rights and because, if the high level of sub-rents paid were uncovered by settlement officers, this would almost certainly lead to an enhancement in the revenue demand. In Narsinghpur, in fact, twice the amount of *malguzari* home-farm land was found to be leased (16 per cent) than in Hoshangabad (8 per cent), and the 1925 revenue administration report states that 30 per cent of the occupied area was actually cultivated by subtenants in Hoshangabad. Much of this area was undoubtedly contained in the larger holdings, and it would be difficult to maintain that subletting on this scale had only sprung up after the turn of the century.

On average, subtenants on the *malguzars' sir* land in Hoshangabad were reportedly paying Rs. 3.66 per acre by the 1890s, or more than double the rate paid by ordinary tenants, whose rents, in turn, had been jacked up by 102 per cent by the *malguzars* over the previous 30 years. In Narsinghpur, 2,434 out of 19,823 acres of *malguzari sir* land rented out was leased on a 50:50 sharecropping basis, known as *batia*. J.B. Fuller thus concluded that the strength of the *malguzars* of the Narmada valley was exceptional and that 'they have been able to divert to themselves the profits of a large proportion of their ryots by rack-renting, pure and simple, such as is rarely practised elsewhere'.[24] Absolute occupancy tenants, in contrast, had suffered only a 4.1 per cent increase in their rent rate per acre over the 30 years since the first settlement in Hoshangabad. This increased both the prosperity of the absolute occupancy tenants as a class, as well as the value of their land as an investment. Hence the appearance that 'in many villages there are now absolute-occupancy tenants who are tenants only in name, being moneylenders who have purchased holdings, and who lease them out again at high rents to cultivators'.[25]

In this respect, government reports and accounts based upon them are victims of a delusion that the agrarian economy actually functioned according to official writ. Officials preferred to think that the family farm was strengthened by the operation of tenancy laws, but in fact they were widely circumvented, and English law remained an alien imposition, just as it does today. The growing use of *nazranas* (gifts and gratuities) and other irregularities as a means of evading tenancy legislation means that the amount of sub-tenancy reported in official sources is probably a marked underestimate. Thus:

> of late years, instances have occurred in Harda of peculiar transactions affecting occupancy rights. In some cases *malguzars* have

> sold at high prices pieces of land with the occupancy status and a low rental to moneylenders and others desiring an investment. Other cases have occurred in which *malguzars* have given to their relations vacant holdings together with the status of an occupancy tenant. This transaction is in most cases only a nominal one, made by some astute *malguzar* in order to prevent the acquisition of tenant-right by the real cultivator, who thus only becomes a subtenant of his relation, and also in order to keep off the record the real rents paid by these cultivators and so exclude them from the [taxable] assets of the village.[26]

There was also in Saugor, the case of the *galliya* serf, the cause of some official dispute, who was described as follows:

> many a moneylending *malguzar* in this district deliberately refrains from rent enhancement. When his operations have extended far enough he reduces his tenants to the position of *'galliyas'*, a term used locally to denote these cultivators who hand over the whole of the produce (*gulla*) of their land to the *malguzar* in satisfaction of debt. It is obvious that when this condition of affairs exists the *malguzar* is getting all he possibly can out of the land. The rent is an unimportant item.[27]

Nazranas were noticed to be generally prevalent after the second settlement. They usually took the form of premia paid to a landlord on the lease of a holding, representing the capitalized difference between the actual and the so-called economic rent of the holding. Alternatively the term referred to consent-money paid to the same person on the transfer of a holding from one tenant to another.[28] The average *nazrana* paid at the time of the 1913-18 settlement of Hoshangabad worked out at approximately Rs. 14 an acre, or about 10½ years' rental. In the Harda tahsil, tenants stated that they typically paid from Rs. 25 to Rs. 30 an acre, and from Rs. 30 to Rs. 40 for the very best quality land. An examination by the settlement officers of the accounts of certain *malguzars* revealed that they received Rs. 60,668 as consent-money on the transfer of 16,428 acres (rental Rs. 21,975) from tenant to tenant, giving a total income of Rs. 12 lakhs from *nazranas* against an average rental demand of Rs. 10.5 lakhs per annum. To this total, the settlement officer considered that 33 per cent might be added to account for concealment, giving a total amount paid equivalent to more than one and one-half times the annual rental demand of the district. The sum paid to the *malguzar* might be considered as capital invested in land and interest allowed on it at 8 per cent, thus giving a further supplement to income totalling Rs. 172 lakhs.[29] Overall, the income from *nazranas* was 166 per cent on top of that from rents *per se*. If then we assume that something like a modest 30 per cent of home-farm land was sublet (instead of the figure of just over 8 per cent cited for Hoshangabad), then the income from direct cultivation is comparatively unimportant. In addition, there were the *khot*, *batai* and *taksim* forms of charging rents which did not always find adequate reflection in the statistics. The *khot* rent was a fixed grain payment which had started in the Harda tahsil (where it was extremely common), and had spread right up the valley by the early 1890s, the Jabalpur equivalent being the *bhag* rent.[30] A variation on the *khot* system was known as *taksim*. In one example, a tenant was found to have sublet 108 acres, supplying twelve bullocks for the ploughing, a subtenant doing all the work and bringing with him a further four cattle:

> when the crop was reaped, the tenant took grain to the value of Rs. 375 *plus* the seed sown and all the costs of cultivation. The grain that was left was then divided, twelve-sixteenths going to the tenant and four-sixteenths to the subtenant, who must have realised little more than *coolie*-hire out of the transaction.[31]

The share-crop tenure known as *batai*, as found in Narsinghpur, was common elsewhere in the Narmada valley. The custom was that the landlord gave the land and advanced the seed while the tenant supplied bullocks and labour. After the crop was reaped, the seed equivalent was returned to the landlord with interest at 50 per cent, the hired labour employed in reaping and the dues of the village servants were paid, and only then was the balance of the crops divided equally between the landlord and the cultivator.

The most notorious landlords in Hoshangabad were those of the Harda tahsil. Overall, they enhanced rents by 133 per cent during the course of the first settlement and in some villages, such as the Pokharni group, the ordinary rent-rate was trebled, rising from Rs. 1.26 to Rs. 3.46 per acre. Rents in kind were sometimes forced even on occupancy tenants amounting to three maunds to the acre (worth at least Rs. 7), a sum which had to be paid, regardless of the quality of the harvest.[32]

Antagonism between landlord and tenants was high in this tahsil, but things could hardly have been any better in neighbouring Narasinghpur district if the statistics on litigation contained in the Central Provinces administration reports are to be believed. A common ruse here was for *malguzars* systematically to levy rent instalments in advance of the due date and well before the harvest, forcing tenants into rapidly mounting arrears, so that each year they had to surrender their entire crop to him.[33] This sort of deeply exploitative relationship between landlords and their tenants was the rotten core that lay behind the superficial abundance of the Narmada valley economy.

Indebtedness and the Credit System

Debt was especially important and was another form of surplus appropriation that yielded far greater returns than direct cultivation. The price of wheat seed was high and tenant cultivators traditionally borrowed seed at the beginning of each season, paying it back again with interest. The custom was widespread and became more so as the market price of wheat increased. Moneylenders, *malguzars* and the agents of Bombay trading firms saw this as an important means of gaining a greater share in the crop. J.B. Fuller commented that this business was far more lucrative to a *malguzar* than any rent enhancement.[34] Even the smaller wheat tracts of western Bilaspur were exploited in this fashion, with Bombay agents based in Jabalpur advancing money to cultivators in order to gain a lien on the next harvest's produce.[35] In the Narmada valley the forestalling of crops in this fashion was uncommon simply because the moneylending *malguzar* was already in there first.[36] The Dufferin enquiry of 1888 revealed that out of 46 tenants in Hoshangabad only 12 were out of debt. The remaining 34 owed in aggregate Rs. 18,300, a sum four times the rental charge on their land. The high price of wheat meant that interest on these grain loans, formerly 25 per cent per annum, was now sometimes charged at 50 per cent for six months. Two typical suits were for the recovery of grain to the value of Rs. 990 and Rs. 2,940 on original loans amounting to Rs. 60 and Rs. 140. The situation was similar in Narsinghpur and Jabalpur, and out of 920 tenants questioned in Saugor and Damoh only one-fifth were found to be out of debt.[37]

The quantity of this debt was less important than the unique fact that a larger proportion of the debt than perhaps anywhere else in India at the time consisted of loans of seed grain, repaid in kind at harvest end, with interest. In 1937 it was estimated that 40 per cent of the cultivators habitually borrowed all their seed grain, a further 20 per cent needed to borrow between 20 and 30 per cent of their requirements, and 10 per cent usually stored all they needed, but occasionally had to borrow whenever there was a shortfall in the harvest. By contrast, in Bihar, cultivators were thought to retain enough to meet all their own seed requirements, and in the surplus areas of the Punjab (for example, in the Canal Colony zone around Lyallpur) more than 83 per cent did so. In Bombay Presidency, Gujarat and the Carnatic most wheat cultivators kept their own seed and only 5 to 25 per cent of the remainder borrowed. Only in Hyderabad and parts of Baroda and the poorest parts of the U.P. did cultivators traditionally part with all their crop and borrow seed grain for the next year's harvest. The Narmada valley, however, had a lower population density and produced abundant surpluses and yet the majority still borrowed their seed grain. Furthermore, unlike in the Deccan and elsewhere, where the small village *bania* or shopkeeper was the usual resort for loans of seed grain, in the Narmada valley 60 per cent was borrowed from *malguzars* or large landlords, 35 per cent from other large cultivators, and only 5 per cent from the village *bania*.[38] This phenomenon could be traced back to the importance of the *mahajan-malguzar* in first settling the region in the early nineteenth century and it gave such individuals, and the more substantial tenants, a directing control over the means of production far in excess of what is suggested by the raw statistics on landholding or rents. This control was of crucial importance during the boom years of the wheat trade.

Further down the Narmada valley from Saugor and Jabalpur, as many as 62 per cent of the *malguzars* (in Hoshangabad) were free of debt, large debts only being held by those who could afford them, according to the Central Provinces provincial banking survey conducted in the late 1920s.[39] Relative to the value of estates, *malguzari* debt in Narsinghpur and Hoshangabad was small. A substantial number of tenants here were also free of debt, but there were more hopelessly indebted here than anywhere else in central India. Over the vheat zone as a whole there was some of the largest propor-ions of the tenantry involved, all but a third on average, and a arger portion of debts in Narsinghpur and Hoshangabad were ncurred for the repayment of earlier debts, hinting that the narked differentiation among the tenantry in terms of in-lebtedness here was no recent phenomenon. Most of this debt vas unsecured (83 per cent on average over the zone as a vhole) suggesting, again, a concentration of debt amongst the inprotected subtenants and ordinary tenants, and that the arge amount of *malguzari* debt in no way threatened their andholdings.

Between 1873 and 1874, the first statistics compiled on the roblem of landlord indebtedness concluded that over a third f proprietary heads of ancestral estates were in debt, 13 per ent owing a sum equivalent to more than five years' revenue, nd that overall 9 per cent of estates had been transferred to ew proprietors since settlement. By 1888, 19 per cent of *ialguzari* land paying land revenue was found to have been ermanently transferred.[40] In Banda and Hatta tahsils of augor and Damoh districts, over 27 per cent by area had een transferred; in Murwara tahsil of Jabalpur district, over 0 per cent; in the Ramgarh tahsil of Mandla district, very early 27 per cent; and reputedly 25 per cent of Narsinghpur ahsil and just under a quarter of the Seoni tahsil of Ioshangabad district. The district commissioner of Narsingh-ur also estimated that, apart from the fifth of the area of the istrict actually transferred, another fifth was either mort-aged, or had been saved by being taken under the manage-ient of the government Court of Wards. Of the total land evenue alienated by 1888, the largest proportion going to noneylenders' was in Narsinghpur and Hoshangabad. How-ver, the significance of all this was debatable since census tatistics suggested that half the moneylenders in the province ad interests in land, and that half the persons who owned nd in addition to other occupations were moneylenders.[41]

In Jabalpur, Saugor and Damoh, the long-standing in-ebtedness of many small *malguzars* (resulting from the exces-ve revenue demands of the early nineteenth century),[42] and ie number of tribal *malguzars* still surviving in the 1860s, ieant that the substantial *mahajans*, or moneylenders-cum-rain dealers, had a firm grip. There was a high rate of transfer f village ownership to, as well as between, members of this class over ensuing decades. In Jabalpur, 16 per cent of villages in the district were transferred between first and second settlements; in Saugor, 34 per cent, or a total of 750 mahals, the principal losers being the 'small farmers' who had 'overdrawn their credit'. The Kurmis here lost 39 of the 154 villages in their ownership between 1867 and 1909.[43] The number of villages held by tribal (mainly Gond) landlords also fell, totalling over 90 in the late 1880s but only about 25 (or 1 per cent of the total) in Saugor district by 1911-16. In Damoh, the tribals held 6 per cent of villages in 1867 and less than only 4 per cent by 1909, whilst the much larger Gond population of Jabalpur held only just over 16 per cent of the total number of villages in the district by 1907-12. The principal gainers were the *banias* and Brahmin *mahajans*. Saugor district was typical in that the *banias* held 250 villages at the second settlement of the district and 441 by the third settlement. In Damoh they increased their share from 9 per cent of the total to 15 per cent between 1869 and 1908, the Brahmins increasing their share from 15 per cent to 20 per cent.

The Mahajans

So it was that in the Khurai tahsil of Saugor district, five big moneylenders came to hold between them shares in 189 villages, equivalent to 131 whole *mahals*, or one-quarter of the entire tahsil. Diwan Bahadur Seth Bullubhdas of Jabalpur held a *chaurasi* of approximately 100 villages, Shrimant Seth Mohanlal of Khurai held approximately 50, and the heirs of Rai Sahib Seth Mohanlal of Roanda, Nathuram Singhai of Bina-Etawa and Seth Khetsingh of Khurai each held more than 20 villages.[44] But these transfers in Khurai really marked the failure of the grain-dealing and moneylending business of the 1880s and 1890s. Before him, Seth Bullubhdas' uncle, Raja Gokuldas, had built up a veritable empire based on moneylending and grain-dealing, in which his landholdings represented but a fraction of his investments. Seth Khet Singh, Shrimant Seth Mohanlal, Seth Birdichand of Rahatgarh and the firm of Seth Karakmal of Ajmer were small but still substantial rivals of the same period.[45] In Damoh, it was the Pawar-Banias who generally held sway, a prominent Bania landowner being Seth Sukhdeo Munim, agent of the firm of Raghunath Das Hamir Mal of Ajmer.[46] In Jabalpur district, the Murwara tahsil was a 'happy hunting ground' for the Bania *iahajans* based here and in neighbouring Bilheri, one Ram Jaik acquiring a total of 23 villages.[47] The largest share of this rade was held by the *mahajans* who had settled in the district arlier in the nineteenth century. Foremost amongst their umber was Rao Bahadur Biharilal, a Bhargava Brahman, who n addition to his moneylending business acquired an estate f 43 villages. The original representative of the family settled n the district in 1820 and was appointed *khazanchi* of three istrict treasuries, as was his son Biharilal, until 1866, after which the business expanded still further, the family helping) establish a branch of the Bhargava Commercial Bank at abalpur in 1893.[48]

Amongst the Bania *mahajans* both here and lower down the Jarmada valley, the Marwaris took pride of place, and foremost mongst their number in the second half of the nineteenth entury was Raja Gokuldas of Jabalpur, who by 1905 held approximately 30 villages in Narsinghpur tahsil, 10 or 12 in adarwara tahsil, a *chaurasi* of 76 villages (increased to 89 by 912) in Mandla district, and another *chaurasi* (this time of 25 llages) in Wardha district. He also left a total of 158 villages Jabalpur district itself to his son Jiwandas when he died in 908. His nephew Ballubhdas held a substantial number of llages as well, principally in Saugor, as did Gokuldas himlf. In Narsinghpur, Gokuldas held the large villages of ichai and Srinagar, the latter since before 1866. Both were rmer *pargana* headquarters. By the end of the century Raja okuldas held the mortgages of many other properties as well, cluding one among the leading Gond estates which had llen under the management of the Court of Wards by this ite, which contained 84 villages. Gokuldas' estates algether contained some 800 villages covering a total of 63,000 res of land.[49]

More important than Gokuldas' landholdings was the grain ealing and moneylending business he conducted through an tensive network of approximately 300 shops which he held attered throughout the Central Provinces. Like other *ihajans* he moved into industrial undertakings at the end of e century, setting up the Perfect Pottery Works in Jabalpur d the Gokuldas Ballabhdas Spinning and Weaving Mills in 85 (employing 700 workers, with 277 looms and 15,208 indles). His family was also a shareholder in the Sakchi Iron e company, founded in 1907 by the Tatas and others to mine in the Satpuras, and set up numerous cotton ginning and pressing factories scattered throughout the Central Provinces and Berar.[50]

As a result of these fantastic concentrations of wealth, 13 per cent of the landholding body of the Jabalpur district held more than 70 per cent of the land as early as 1870. The income-tax levied on these men (supposedly 3.1 per cent) raised an income for the government equivalent to nearly a twentieth of the total land revenue of the district.[51] As with other *mahajans,* the origins of the Gokuldas fortune lay in moneylending and grain-dealing, the unprecedented rise of this particular family firm marching hand in hand with the wheat boom of the 1870s and 1880s. It crumbled just as swiftly under the combined pressure of agricultural depression after 1900 and the extravagance of his heirs, and Ballabhdas was forced to mortgage all his lands in the Central Provinces in 1914.

In Narsinghpur district the principal *mahajans* were the Oswal Marwari banias and the Singhpur Kalars, who owned about 30 villages. Richest of all, according to the Central Provinces provincial banking report of 1929-30, was Rao Sahib Seth Laxminarain of Gadarwara. During the course of the first regular settlement a total of 164 villages, 19 *mahals* and 66 shares were transferred in this district, most going to the moneylending classes.[52] The principal losers, as elsewhere in central India, were the tribals. In Narsinghpur, the proportion of villages held by Gonds fell from 19 per cent to 13 per cent, and it was said that 'but for government protection and management of the estates of large Gond landlords they would now have scarcely a village left'.[53] In Hoshangabad, the proportion of Gond villages fell from 25 to 18 per cent between 1865 and 1908, only the 'Rajputs' doing equally badly, falling from 14 to 7 per cent (but then their numbers may have included a number of Raj-gond *thakurs*). Figures given in the 1891-98 settlement report for Hoshangabad give added confirmation. Here the number of villages held by tribal and pastoral peasants are shown to have fallen, as did that held by Hindu agriculturists, whereas the number held by 'non-agriculturists' rose from 26 to 32 per cent.[54] Besides Raja Gokuldas of Jabalpur, important recipients were Hari Bai (widow of Seth Narbada Prasad of Gadarwara) who owned 26 villages, Seth Ghasi Ran (her father-in-law) who had a similar estate, and the heirs of Ganesh Pandit, who acquired a total of 25 villages n the second half of the nineteenth century. Rai Bahadur Seth Tikaram, a Marwari and proprietor of Singhpur, also ran an xtensive moneylending business.[55] Thus it was said that there is hardly a single moneylender in the Hoshangabad listrict who is not a landlord, and many of the landlords, even of agricultural castes, combine the business of a money and grain-dealer with that of a cultivator'.[56]

It was no coincidence that the most infamous landlords of Hoshangabad were mainly absentee, residing away from their states in the Harda tahsil and living in the towns of Timarni and Harda, a centre of the wheat trade. All were simultaneously moneylenders dealing in grain, the wealthiest being he Shukul family, while amongst others we may mention Sukhdeo Seth (owning 27 villages in Harda tahsil and Nimar listrict combined) and Nandram Brahman of Magardha (who owned three), though the true power of this class is difficult to stimate, since large firms sometimes operated under different names as landowners and moneylenders.[57] As always, the key to success in the most important wheat producing tracts ay not just in the exploitation of *malguzari* lands but the use of xtortionate loans (as seen in the Bordha and Charwa tracts) nd rack-rents of one sort or another in order to gain control over the annual wheat crop produced by the weaker enantry.[58] Having gained control of this surplus the *mahajan*, andowner or substantial tenant could play the market and at he same time extend his moneylending business and the oans of seed grain, which promoted the rapid extension of wheat cultivation.[59]

he Super-Exploitation of Labour

ndebtedness among the landlord class often represented a nere shuffling for position and the continued agglomeration f land by the landlord-moneylending elite. Not only did they hen profit by the rents and other payments in kind that they were able to extort from the tenantry, but on the land they hose to cultivate themselves they were also able to benefit rom the availability of cheap, tribal labour. While the overall osts of direct cultivation increased by something like 80 per ent between the first and second settlements of Hoshangabad, and 98 per cent by 1907,[60] the price of labour was the one tem that declined. Thus in eastern Hoshangabad, the reaping of the spring harvest was done on contract at the rate of eigh *kuros* of mixed grain for every five acres reaped in 1863-64, bu by 1893-94 the rate was only six *kuros* (108 lbs). According t one source, only four acres were reaped at this rate, bu another gives the *mani* (meaning an area of five acres) as th basis for comparison, whilst a large portion of the grain wag was still made using inferior grains, such as *juar*, which ha not risen in price as much as wheat. Grain payments t ploughmen fell too, whilst cash payments generally failed t keep up with the overall rise in prices.[61] In Narsinghpur i 1893 the general price rise since 1860 was estimated at 83 pe cent, but the general opinion of the cultivators was that grai wages had remained static. By the 1890s the reaper invariabl received one bundle out of every twenty cut by him, wherea formerly the custom was to give two bundles of grain pe diem, irrespective of the amount cut, and although the reape was not always successful in insisting on this rate in the 186(he did not tend to work so fast.[62] In Damoh in 1906 it was sai that grain wages had not changed within living memory, apa from when grain prices were high, when they tended to b substituted for cash. In real terms this represented a decreas in the rate of payment.

Even the most exaggerated estimate of the cost of labou 26 per cent of the total value of the harvest in Narsinghpur i 1907, was still remarkably low in view of the increase competition for labour by then from the cotton zone and th recent impact of famine on the death rate. According to th Datta report this is supposed to have raised the nominal wag of agricultural labour in the Central Provinces from virtu stasis to a level 55 per cent higher overall between 1894 an 1907, and real wages by nearly one-third (25 per cent in Bera over the same period.[63] Notwithstanding Datta, howeve local evidence for the Narmada valley suggests that wage actually fell in the years immediately after the famine and onl returned to their former level a few years later under the pres sure of demand from the neighbouring cotton tracts. Thus th rates paid for reaping in eastern Hoshangabad worked ou according to one estimate, at one sheaf in twenty before th famine, but afterwards this fell to one in thirty and then onl gradually rose to one in twenty again.[64] Further corroboratic of these trends is available from estimates of the wages able-bodied agricultural labourers in the Jabalpur distric which were made for every month in the years between 1873 and 1927. These also suggest a decline in wages in the mid-1880s which ran right through to 1907. Only then did the increase noted by Datta begin. But wages were still lower than in the late 1870s, when they had ranked equal with the best rates being paid in the cotton tracts of Khandesh and Berar.[65]

The explanation for these low wage levels at a time of rapid growth in the wheat economy in the late nineteenth century lay in the availability of cheap and plentiful supplies of labour, a large part of it migrating from the nearby tribal districts of the Satpuras. Whilst the super-exploitation of lesser tenants lay at the core of the wheat economy, this bountiful supply of cheap labour was the leaven which spurred its growth. As late as 1927, long past the heydays of the wheat trade, the total number of migrants flocking into the valley to assist in the harvest operations was estimated at 120,000 while the census of 1921—which was conducted in mid-March and caught a number of districts only at the beginning of the wheat harvest—recorded 18,812 migrant labourers (or *chaitharas*, as they were known) in the Hoshangabad district and 14,862 in Jabalpur; 1921 was a poor year for wheat, but the migrants still amounted to 22 and 13 per cent of the labouring populations of the two districts, respectively. It can be imagined how much higher these figures would have been at the peak of the harvest period in the mid-1880s, when wheat exports were more than three times as high and wheat acreages 35 to 40 per cent greater in extent.[66] This remarkable phenomenon helps explain how the cultivated acreage and the level of export managed to expand so dramatically at the time when population levels were low and, in some cases, even declining. Thus in Hoshangabad, the gross cultivated areas increased by 45 per cent between 1863-64 and 1892-93, and wheat exports carried by rail from the district tripled, but the density of population, only 118 per square mile in 1872 and 106 per square mile in 1881, was still only 115 per square mile by 1891. At the same time, there is evidence of only a slight increase in the local force of agricultural labourers as a proportion of the total population before the turn of the century. Overall, the number of permanent labourers accounted for 13 per cent of the population, compared with more than 33 per cent in the Nagpur-Berar Plain.[67]

The Collapse of the Wheat Trade

Various reasons have been put forward for the failure of the wheat trade and undoubtedly the explanation lies in a combination of several factors. However, the timing of this decline is important. After the peak year of 1888-89 the quantity of wheat exported declined by 43 per cent from an average of 8,139,000 maunds over the previous eight years to a figure of only 4,613,000 maunds in 1889-90. Only one more year of major exports followed and that was in 1891-92, when 8,693,000 maunds were exported, but then the average price offered was 16 per cent up on the figure for 1889-90 owing to the failure of Russian wheat and rye harvests and the generally poor quality of European crops. For the next two years only just over five and one-half million maunds were exported, a catastrophic decline then occurring in 1894-95. The main cause of this was excessive rain commencing in the autumn of 1892 which brought in its wake a severe attack of rust (a fungus disease) in the Narmada valley. Rust attacked the crop with even greater ferocity in 1894-95, resulting in a crop yield 37 per cent down on the average of the preceding eight years.[68] By then, stocks had been used up and the decline in exports was dramatic. A shortfall in rain the following year and severe drought in 1896-97, and again in 1889-1900, dealt the final *coup de grace*, after which trade never fully recovered.

A quick glance at Tables 1, 2 and 4 reveals that the decline in the wheat economy cannot be blamed entirely on the succession of poor harvests. The wheat acreage in the wheat zone reached a maximum in 1887-88, after which a gradual decline occurred, upset only in 1892-93, presumably in response to the high prices of the preceding year. Hoshangabad and Narsinghpur, in particular, showed a steady decline. The international demand for Indian wheat disappeared in 1893, owing to competition from cheap Argentinian wheat in European markets.[69] However, at Rs. 2.25 per maund, the price was no lower locally in 1893-94 than it had been in 1887-88, when total wheat exports were 40 per cent higher, whilst the Bombay wholesale (*khandwa*) and all-India retail prices also remained firm.

The thesis that the relative price of other *rabi* crops was primarily responsible for fluctuations in the wheat acreage might appear substantiated by the marked increase in the acreage under gram after 1890-91 in Hoshangabad, Narsinghpur, Saugor, Damoh and Jabalpur.[70] This increase had, however, been going on for a number of years in response to declining yields resulting from the continuous cultivation of wheat, year in year out, without irrigation, manure, rotation or fallowing. The technique was to mix wheat with a nitrogen-releasing leguminous crop, such as gram, from which it was easily separated. The mixture (known as *birra*) had the effect of maintaining a higher outturn than the cultivation of wheat alone.[71] The greater amount of virgin land in the Hoshangabad district meant that the technique was less necessary, the wheat-gram area only increasing from 13,854 acres to 107,213 acres between first and second settlements, compared with an increase in the pure wheat acreage from 455,193 to 517,314 acres.[72] In Narsinghpur, on the other hand, cultivation was exceptionally dense, 94 per cent of the total occupied area in the Harrai and Mekh-Chhindwara *haveli* village groups being under cultivation. As much as 75 per cent of the cultivated area in some villages in this district as well as Hoshangabad district was covered in wheat. As a consequence, wheat was seldom sown by itself, being nearly always mixed with gram, which accounted for about 18 per cent of the seed sown on average. This mixture resulted in a crop, 85 per cent of which was pure wheat, the outturn being at the rate of about 700 lbs of wheat per acre.

In Jabalpur district and the eastern *haveli* of Narsinghpur, the embanking of wheat fields was another tactic adopted to help retain moisture, discourage weeds (particularly the dreaded *kans* grass) and erosion, and to maintain yields.[73] Such techniques were preferred to fallowing as this allowed *kans* to gain a hold, and once this had occurred it was almost ineradicable. The difficulty was that embanking and the continuous cultivation of wheat and gram brought with it the danger of rust (fungus disease) to which both crops were prone, particularly when grown in exhausted soil and in damp conditions. The seeds of disaster in the 1890s were thus being sown at the very height of the wheat boom in the previous decade.

Nonetheless, the boom in wheat cultivation was not purely a response to technical conditions of soil fertility and the improvement in communications. The *social* relations of production were equally important in creating an exportable surplus of grain, and the onset of decline in the wheat economy of the Narmada valley was not simply the effect of weather, price, or the over-exploitation of the soil. It was also the result of the super-exploitation of the cultivating classes themselves. A major factor here was the cost of seed-grain. In a report on the abatement of land revenue in Hoshangabad district submitted in 1901, C.E. Low commented that 'many tenants are too poor to sow their own holdings', their only chance of getting seed being to sow the holdings of well-to-do absentees on a crop-share basis, a phenomenon he described as being on the increase. He also noted that it was not easy to distinguish the deterioration caused by high rents from that caused by bad seasons.[74]

One bad season alone would be enough to break a severely pressed tenant and if his land fell out of cultivation through his inability to borrow the funds to finance the next year's sowing, *kans* would inevitably take over and deterioration set in. This seems to have been precisely what happened in a number of instances. Poverty also encouraged the cultivation of *juar* and gram, the seed-grain for which was much cheaper than that of wheat.[75] The Chief Commissioner, D.C.J. Ibbetson, writing in 1899, was also of the opinion that deterioration in the Jabalpur and Hoshangabad districts had more to do with exorbitant levels of rent than harvest failure.[76] East of Seoni tahsil a great number of fields were found to be out of cultivation and were white with *kans* grass, 15 per cent of Hoshangabad tahsil and 11 per cent of Sohagpur tahsil being covered in *kans* in 1898. The situation was similarly bad in Jabalpur, an abatement of 28 per cent on the land revenue demand in certain villages there being allowed in 1900. Strenuous efforts were made by settlement officers to arbitrate the reduction of rents as well.[77] The settlements broke down entirely in Hoshangabad and Damoh, rent increases of more than 33 per cent above the level ascertained at the second settlement being banned in all the deteriorated villages of the former district.

Saugor, Jabalpur and Narsinghpur saw a spate of land transfers as indebted petty landowners defaulted in their repayments to the *mahajans*. Totalling all the shares transferred, approximately 40 per cent of all the villages in Jabalpur were transferred between 1889-90 and 1907-08, and in Narsinghpur approximately one-third of all the villages between 1894 and

1904.[78] Jabalpur (34%), Damoh (31%), Saugor (21%) and Narsinghpur (17%), in that order, also had the greatest number of tenants in straitened circumstances, hopelessly indebted or dependent on the extra income they received from selling their labour (described by settlement officers as class D and E tenants, the latter, rather more dramatically by the Jabalpur Settlement Officer as 'absolutely broken down and living from hand to mouth').[79] To cope with this problem, efforts were also made to introduce the programme of debt conciliation first proposed by J.B. Fuller for the Saugor district in 1894.[80] Government officers there had run into opposition from Raja Gokuldas and they did so again, indirectly, when conciliation proceedings were commenced in Hoshangabad district, where Marwari creditors, many in turn financed by Gokuldas, refused to participate.

Greater success was had in Damoh in 1901, where a total of 507 *malguzars* and *patidars* and 8,724 tenants were dealt with, leading to the remission of a total of Rs. 28,000 of debt (though much of this was irrecoverable in any case).[81] Khurai tahsil in Saugor was finally resettled in 1900-01 with a reduction of 57 per cent in the revenue demand and corresponding reductions in rents and debts in 400 out of 548 villages (the remainder being held by Gokuldas).[82] The total claims dealt with here amounted to Rs. 526,677 (more than half of which was owed in grain), out of which nearly two-thirds were remitted, a total of Rs. 8 lakhs being remitted over the district as a whole. In Hoshangabad, creditors were finally persuaded to write off Rs. 12.5 lakhs of debt and the government itself remitted a total of Rs. 62 lakhs in revenue demand.[83]

The Central Provinces administration was partly responsible for precipitating the crisis in production in the Narmada valley, by its singularly inappropriate timing in introducing increases in the land revenue demand in the early 1890s, despite the concern then being expressed about the perilous condition of the lesser tenantry upon whom these increases were likely to have been passed given the prevailing state of agrarian relations. Thus in Hoshangabad an 87 per cent increase in the revenue demand was attempted, only to be hastily cut back with the onset of famine. Elsewhere in India, the official reaction to famine and agricultural depression was usually a temporary remission of land revenue, the advance of *takavi* loans (mainly confined to ryotwari areas) and the

wheat seed was usually drilled, requiring only around 50 lbs of seed per acre on average. The field was also usually ploughed several times and levelled before sowing, and this despite the generally high cost of labour here.[89] The costs of freight and shipping were no more expensive in the Punjab than for central Indian wheat, but the Punjab enjoyed the advantage of massive state-funded irrigation projects and effective co-operative credit and sale societies. The Narmada valley had nothing to compare with this. Narmada wheat, indeed, had not merely failed to improve but had actually deteriorated in quality and could no longer guarantee shippers a regular supply. So it was that, one by one, the trading firms withdrew their agents and, apart from a brief resurgence during the First World War, the trade declined to a mere trickle, at a quarter of its former level in the boom years of the 1880s.

The decline in trade can thus be seen to have been merely a part of a general decline in the wheat economy. Significantly, what were thought to be the richest villages in Hoshangabad were also the slowest to recover in the years after the famine. Population levels generally stagnated and the price of land fell from speculative levels as high as 36 times the level of land revenue in the 1880s, to a low of only ten times the land revenue by 1902.[90] In terms of rupees per acre the price was virtually stagnant from 1888 right through to 1909. The gradual rise thereafter seems to have been largely due to inflation and the declining relative weight of the government revenue demand. This was by contrast with the cotton zone, where the price of land showed marked fluctuations, quite independent of the general trend in prices or the pressure of the government demand (see Figures 1 and 2). The dramatic escalation in rents of the 1880s and 1890s in the Narmada valley also ceased, and after 1915 the proportion of the total occupied area held by the *malguzars* of the wheat zone began to decline, from 22 per cent in 1884-85 to 16 per cent by 1945.

Apart from the Jabalpur district, there was practically no increase in the number of ploughs to be found, and in the ratio of plough cattle to ploughs (a useful indicator of capital formation in rural areas), a gradual decline is noticeable in nearly all the districts of the wheat zone between 1885-86 and 1925-26. This ratio was 4 : 1 at its peak in Hoshangabad in 1895-96, and 2.9 : 1 by 1925-26, a trend not helped by another scarcity and water shortage in 1920-21. By contrast, plough cattle to plough

URE 1: *AVERAGE PRICE OF LAND IN PRIVATE SALES AS A MULTIPLE OF THE LAND REVENUE CHARGE (five year moving averages)*

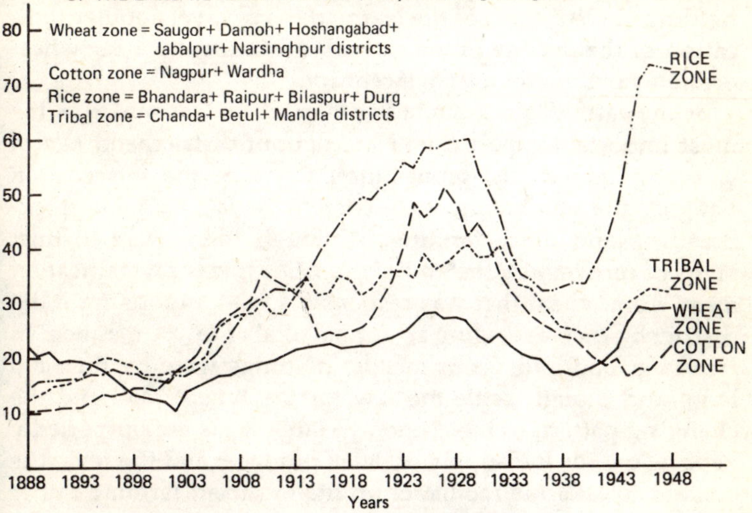

URE 2: *AVERAGE PRICE FETCHED BY LAND IN PRIVATE SALES IN RUPEES PER ACRE (five year moving averages)*

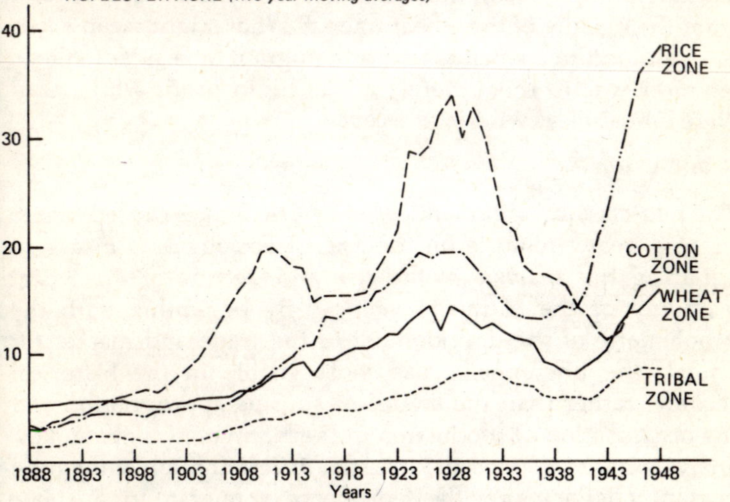

Source: Proprietary mutation statistics given in the annual *C.P. Land Revenue Administration Reports.*

rates in the Berar districts to the south typically ranged between six and eight to one throughout most of this period, the quality of these cattle being generally much higher as well. Finally, there was a noticeable increase in the fragmentation of holdings in the north of the Narmada valley, yet another indication of the decline in the extensive, monocultivating wheat economy of the previous half century.

By the early 1920s, gram rather than wheat was said to be the most important export from Narsinghpur district, and *rabi til* was edging out rust-prone linseed among the oilseeds. In Saugor, the cultivators were content to fall back on stock-breeding and dairy farming. Although there were distinct signs of recovery by the end of the 1920s it was diversification away from wheat that was responsible, *ghee* exports from the district by then averaging an annual total of 45,000 maunds. In Hoshangabad and Seoni tahsils, holdings were by then too large and plough cattle too few for the type of soil and the changing pattern of the economy: 'large areas are purportedly kept fallow for the supply of dairy produce; and the tenant is content to take his moderate profits of mixed farming rather than work his land fully'.[91] As might be expected, the substantial landholders of this district seem to have suffered least from the decline of the wheat trade.[92] What might mean a loss of livelihood to a small tenant or a migrant or resident village labourer was to them merely a decline in profit which they were more or less willing to accept.

Conclusion

The neo-classical arguments used by Eric Stokes caused him to place a heavy reliance on the role of ecology as a means of squaring his analysis of the rise and decline of the wheat economy of the Narmada valley.[93] By beginning with the problematic of the development of the trade and market for wheat (the phenomena also most visible in the historical record), rather than the modes of surplus appropriation and the organisation of production in the Narmada valley, Stokes' analysis understressed the unusual differentiation among the peasantry of the region, the dependence on migrant tribal labour and the internal contradictions in the economic development that resulted. Similar shortcomings are noticeable in other works. Dharm Narain, for example, notes a poor correlation between wheat output and price levels in the Central Provinces between 1900 and 1936, but has no satisfactory explanation for this phenomenon.[94] R.P. Gupta, in his detailed study of shifts in relative prices and cropping patterns in Madhya Pradesh in the 1950s, also notes the poor price responsiveness of the central Indian peasant, but is at a loss to explain this.[95] My intention here has been to redress this balance in the conviction that the social relations of production, and features such as the unequal regional division of labour encouraged by colonial rule, played an important role in both fomenting and stymying economic development in central India in the late nineteenth century. These factors are at least as important a condition of economic change as are the logical (but not easily demonstrable) possibilities opened up by the growth of the market economy. They must also form an important element in any explanation of the more recent failures of the Green Revolution in this region. To what extent these structural elements in the economic history of the colonial period have persisted into modern times, and the effects they may have on the cultural and political life of the region, are topics that require further and more detailed research.

APPENDIX

NOTES ON TABLE 1 AND 2

CROP ACREAGE STATISTICS

Sources: *CP Annual Administration Reports 1867-68—1890-91; CP District Gazetteers, volume B, 1891-92—1908-09: CP and Berar Season and Crop Reports 1909-10—1950-51*

Notes: The data for the wheat zone have been summed from district statistics as follows:

WHEAT ZONE = Betul + Chhindwara + Damoh + Hoshangabad + Jabalpur + Narsinghpur + Saugor + Seoni districts

Gross Cropped Acreage (GCA) statistics for each district were not always available and often inaccurate, so these have been recalculated from the available data for each district. A certain amount of under-renumeration probably occurred before 1909/10 (particularly in the more backward districts), which would affect the GCA totals, but I have not massaged the statistics with weightings in order to compensate for these shortcomings. The arguments of the paper are based on manifold changes observable in the data and these are well beyond most conceivable margins of error. After 1909/10 the very small acreages under miscellaneous food and non-food crops, fibres other than cotton, condiments and spices, maize, ragi, barley and bajra have been excluded from my data base. Similarly, the small area given under 'miscellaneous crops' for the CP districts between 1884/85 and 1889/90 has also been excluded. None of these omissions makes any significant difference to the GCA totals. The wheat area includes the area sown with a mixture of wheat and gram known as *birra*. Current fallows have been excluded from the GCA totals.

Whenever a complete run of data for all the districts of the wheat zone is not available a blank space has been left in the table. In calculating the indices in Table 2, the year 1874-75 was chosen as the base (instead of 1867-68) simply in order to improve comparability with data available for other agro-economic zones.

Further computations on the basis of these data are currently being undertaken.

Abbreviations

The research for this paper was conducted in the Madhya Pradesh Central Record Office, Nagpur, the Agro-Economic Research Centre in Jabalpur, Cambridge University, and the India Office Library, London. All records referred to are from the Nagpur archives except when preceded by 'IOR', when they are from the India Office Records. Other abbreviations used are as follows:

C	Commissioner
CCCP	Chief Commissioner of the Central Provinces
CP	Central Provinces
CPPBECR	*Central Provinces Provincial Banking Enquiry Committee Report* (Nagpur, 1929-30)
CPR	Central Provinces Revenue, Agriculture and Commerce Proceedings
CPSSR	Central Provinces Survey and Settlement Records, 1821-1874
DG	District Gazetteer
GCA	Gross Cultivated Acreage
GI	Government of India

I	Letters to the Government of India (from the CP secretariat)
Comps.	Central Provinces Revenue Department Complications, 1859-93
	Settlement Report

NOTES

See the pap:r by C. Simmons in this volume.

Some of these arguments, together with more realistic hypotheses, are to be found if E.T. Stokes' masterly work, *The Peasant and the Raj: Studies in Agrarian Society and Peasant Rebellion in Colonial India* (Cambridge, 1978) chapter 8.

This is the only reasonable conclusion that can be drawn after the valiant but inconclusive efforts of Blyn, Islam *et al.* to calculate complex output series from the available statistics. In the case of the CP there is the added difficulty that I have found no continuous series of *annewari* estimates for all districts of the CP before 1891 comparable to those used by Blyn after that date, apart from figures available for the years 1867-68 to 1882-83 found in the administration reports. See G. Blyn, *Agricultural Trends in India, 1891-97: Output, Availability and Productivity* (Philadelphia, 1966) and M.M. Islam, *Bengal Agriculture 1920-1946: A Quantitative Study*, (Cambridge, 1978). M.B. McAlpin in *Subject to Famine: Food Crises and Economic Change in Western India, 1860-1920* (Princeton, 1983) employs just the sort of aggregations I would take issue with, and although she attacks the reliability of yield estimates the nonetheless gives them an important and extremely suspect role in her analysis as an indicator of mortality. See my review in *Modern Asian Studies* (1985), 866-871. Satish Mishra has admirably analysed much of the literature on yield statistics in his Ph.D. thesis 'Patterns of Long-run Agrarian Change in Bombay and Punjab, 1881-1972' (University of Cambridge, 1981). I have also been strongly influenced by the conclusions of Sumit Guha and the cautionary comments on official statistics made by Clive Dewey. See Sumit Guha, *The Agrarian Economy of the Bombay Deccan, 1818-1941* (Delhi, 1985), and C. Dewey, '*Patwari* and *Chaukidar*: Subordinate Officials and the Reliability of India's Agricultural Statistics' in *The Imperial Impact: Studies in the Economic History of Africa and India*, ed. C. Dewey and A.G. Hopkins London, 1978), 280-314

This was a general phenomenon, the consequence of competition from mports from the United Provinces and Bombay. See IOR, J.B. Fuller, Off. Director of Agriculture to CCCP, 22 August 1883, *Sugarcane Report for he Year 1882-83*.

See *Report on the Trade and Resources of the CP* (hereafter *CP Trade Report*), 875-76, 18, and *Report on the Marketing of Wheat in India* (Delhi, 1937), 48.

ndex Numbers of Indian Prices, 1861-1931 (Delhi, 1933), plus annual ddenda.

Report on the Marketing of Wheat in India.

Hoshangabad SR, 1891-98, 12.

Hoshangabad DG, 164-65.

Narsinghpur SR, 1885-94, 22.

11. It ought to be noted that these local prices, averaged over the year, we usually calculated from *kusba* or market town prices. In a developed di trict like Hoshangabad this was probably not a bad guide, but harve prices in the villages could be much lower. The reverse might also be t case. Thus in Sambalpur district, while the average village price of ri attested between 1886 and 1888 was 35 to 40 seers per rupee, the *kusba* bazaar rate at which grain could be sold was 18 to 25 seers due to combination of the *banias*. In Jabalpur though, the difference betwe village and bazaar rates was thought to have narrowed from plus 100 p cent (1861-63) to plus 12 per cent (1887-92). A similar trend was appare in Nagpur, where the discrepancy only amounted to 34 per cent in 186 70 and 14 per cent by 1886-90. This greater conformity in prices w largely caused by the export trade. See J.B. Fuller, Memo. on Prices a Rents, 18 February 1892, CPSSR, bundle 3/1/1892/147. The local pric quoted here have been compiled from official series published in the *Administration Reports* for 1867/8-1900/01, volume B of the *District Gaz teers* for 1900-1909, and the *CP Season and Crop Reports* after 1904/05. Th quoted after 1904/05 purported to be harvest prices representative of t whole district, but it is to be doubted that the method of compilation degree of error changed very much.
12. *Hoshangabad SR, 1891-98*, 10
13. *The Wheat Production and Trade of India* (Simla, 1879)
14. See *CP Land Revenue Administration Reports* for *1886-87* and *1888-89*, sta ment D; G. Evans, *Varieties of Wheat Grown in the C.P.*, (Nagpur, 1908) 2 *The Wheat Production and Trade of India* (Calcutta, 1883), 91; LGI, J. Chisholm, GI, Department of Revenue, Agriculture and Commerce, September, 1877, Memo on Wheat Cultivation and Exportation; *CP La Revenue Administration Report, 1883-84*, 5; also *Hoshangabad SR, 1891-* 26, which describes 80 per cent of the wheat area as *pissi*.
15. *The Indian Wheat Trade* (Calcutta, 1893), 90-91. LGI, J.B. Fuller, 2 Octo 1882, Report on Wheat Cultivation.
16. George Watt, 'Wheat', vol. 6, part II of the *Dictionary of the Econo Products of India* (Calcutta, 1889), 88 and 108-9.
17. *CP Revenue Administration Report, 1871-72*, 25.
18. George Watt, *Dictionary of the Economic Products of India*, vol.6, part 108-9 and 101.
19. *Report on the Marketing of Wheat in India* (Delhi, 1937), Chapter IX a Appendix XLVIII.
20. *The Indian Wheat Trade* (Calcutta, 1893), 302.
21. *Report on the Marketing of Wheat in India* (Delhi 1937), Chapter V and *Revenue Administration Report, 1877-78*, 9.
22. *Hoshangabad SR, 1891-98*, 61, cited in Stokes, *The Peasant and the op. cit.*, 258.
23. *Jubbulpore SR*, 1886-94, 23.
24. J.B. Fuller, *Review of Progress in the Central Provinces in the last 30 years, of the Present and Past Condition of the People* (Nagpur, 1892), 45.
25. *Hoshangabad SR, 1891-98*, 33-34.
26. *Hoshangabad SR, 1891-98*, 34.
27. *Saugor SR, 1887-97*, 42. CPSSR, Bundle 143/7-1904/2/5-7. M.W. F Strangways, C of Jubbulpore, commented on the moneylending firm

Raja Gokuldas: 'it is generally found that in villages held by this firm the actual pitch of rent makes little difference, the tenants being for the most part hopelessly indebted to the firm for seed grain and on other accounts'

8. *Hoshangabad SR, 1891-98*, 33-4.
9. *Hoshangabad SR, 1891-98*, 39.
0. See *Jubbulpore SR, 1886-94*, 38 and *Jubbulpore SR, 1907-12*, 30. Thakur Hanuman Singh of Barwara, a large landlord in Jabalpur, owning 54 villages, was actually said to have taken to leasing the right to collect his *bhag* rents to speculative middlemen at the end of the nineteenth century. See also *Damoh SR, 1888-89*, 22. Gond cultivators here often paid up to one-third of their crop in *bhag* rents, as well as paying in kind for the bullocks they borrowed in order to cultivate.
1. *Hoshangabad SR, 1913-18*, 30.
2. *CP Revenue Administration Report, 1889-90*, 7.
3. J.B. Fuller, *Review of Progress*. See comments on this in *Narsinghpur DG, 1971*, 282.
4. J. B. Fuller, *Review of Progress, 41*.
5. See also RD Comps. 1888-89, no. 237(a): Indebtedness of Proprietors and Land Transfer in the CP, J.B. Fuller to GI, 25 July, 1888.
6. J.B. Fuller, *Review of Progress*, 47.
7. See the *(Dufferin) Enquiry into the Condition of the Agricultural Classes of India* (Calcutta, 1888).
8. *Report on the Marketing of Wheat in India* (Delhi, 1937).
9. See *CPPBECR*, 104-5, 119, 122, and 125.
0. *Selection of Papers on Agricultural Indebtedness*, vol.I (Simla, 1898), 73. The 1873-74 statistics are cited in full by Peter Harnetty in Table 5 of his paper ' "A Curious Exercise in Political Economy": Some Implications of British Land Revenue Policy in the Central Provinces of India, 1861-c.1900', *South Asia*, 6(December, 1976), 14-33.
1. According to the census of 1891, 20 per cent of the 32,685 individuals recorded as 'moneylenders and pawn-brokers' *over the province as a whole*, combined this occupation with land owning, and 30 per cent held tenant land. On average, 5.6 per cent of all 'non-agriculturists' combined their principal occupation with some form of landowning, compared with only 4 per cent of agriculturists (including field labourers). See *Census of India, 1891*, vol. 2, Table XVIIC, 266.
2. See, for example, *Jubbulpore SR, 1886-94*, 24.
3. *Jubbulpore DG*, 190, *Saugor DG*, 33.
4. Also well known were Ajmullah Khan and Sir Kasturchand Daga, who bought the Kesli *tappa*, see *Saugor SR, 1911-16*, 7 and 9.
5. *Saugor SR, 1887-97*, 43.
6. *Damoh SR, 1866*, 21 and para 29.
7. *Jubbulpore SR, 1886-94*, 21-2, and *Jubbulpore DG*, 145.
8. *Jubbulpore DG*, 138.
9. See Jiwanchandra Mukerji, *Biography of Raja Gokuldas* (Jabalpur, 1929), and *Services of the late Raja Gokuldas and his family to the Government and the Public* (privately printed copies of letters and official commendations, dating from the late nineteenth century, published c.1920-25). This latter source makes it clear that Gokuldas lent money to nearly every encumbered zamindar to be found in the Narmada valley in the last two decades

of the nineteenth century, as well as eminent individuals such as Si Rao Holkar and the Maharaja of Jodhpur. The decline of the fami fortunes and their move into politics is charted by Gokuldas' grands Govindas, in his three volume autobiography, *Uthal-Puthal Ko Yug*. further details, the readers is referred to P.F. McEldowney's 'Colo Administration and Social Developments in Middle India: the Cen Provinces 1861-1921', (Ph.D. thesis, University of Virginia, 19 Chapter eight gives an excellent account of Raja Gokuldas, based pa on the above-mentioned sources. Peter Harnetty also describes the pa lel fortunes of a number of 'banker-zamindars' in his paper 'The La lords and the Raj: the Malguzars of the Central Provinces, 1861-19 (presented at Jawaharlal Nehru Memorial Library, Delhi, in March 19 Other sources I have used include *Jubbulpore DG*, 143-44, and *Mandla S*

50. See *Jubbulpore DG*, 143-44; Frank Harris, *J.N. Tata: A Chronicle of His* (Delhi, 1958), 191, and *Wardha DG*, 84 and 144.
51. *CP Revenue Administration Report, 1870-71*, 49.
52. *Narsinghpur SR, 1885-94*, 28.
53. *Narsinghpur DG*, 122.
54. *Hoshangabad SR, 1891-98*, 34.
55. *Narsinghpur SR, 1885-94*, 28.
56. *Hoshangabad SR, 1891-98*, 34.
57. Peter Harnetty cites the case of Mukhundran Sukal and others in footr 64 of his paper 'A Curious Exercise of Political Economy'.
58. *Hoshangabad SR, 1913-18,* 30.
59. *CP Revenue Administration Report, 1884*, 5.
60. *Hoshangabad SR, 1891-98*, 3 and *Hoshangabad DG*, 177
61. See *Hoshangabad SR, 1913-18*, 21ff, *Hoshangabad DG*, 169-172 *Hoshangabad SR, 1891-98,* 30. One *kuro* was equal to 10-16 *seers* (a *seer* be 2.14 lbs).
62. CPSSR, Bundle 11/8/1893/147/(16)/9410. Preliminary Report on Gadarwara tahsil in Narsinghpur district.
63. *Narsinghpur DG*, 131, and K.L. Datta, *Report on the Enquiry into the Ri Prices in India*, 5 vols. (Calcutta, 1914), 25, 215 and 235.
64. *Hoshangabad DG*, 171-2
65. These statistics are available from the CP administration reports, series of *Prices & Wages in India* and vol.B of the *Jabalpur DG*.
66. *Royal Commission on Agriculture in India*, (London, 1927), vol.VI, 5; *Ce of India, 1921*, vol.XI, part I, 12.
67. *Hoshangabad SR, 1891-98*, 11. Further details on migration, labour and occupational evidence afforded by the Census reports are to be foun C.N. Bates, 'Regional Dependence and Rural Development in Cer India: the Pivotal Role of Migrant Labour,' *Modern Asian Studies*, 1 (1985).
68. *CP Trade Report, 1894-95*.
69. See *CP Trade Reports* for *1894-95* and *1895-96*
70. The Jowar (Juar) acreage increased in Seoni, Betul and Chhindwara, this was a *kharif* crop and therefore not directly substitutable.
71. *Narsinghpur SR, 1885-94*, para. 32.
72. *Hoshangabad SR, 1891-98*, 26.
73. *Narsinghpur SR, 1885-94*, 13, and *Narsinghpur DG, 1971*, Chap. IV, 125f

74. CPSSR, Bundle 115/2/1901/1/1&2. Abatement of Land Revenue in Hoshangabad district. Report submitted by C.E. Low, 14.3.1901, 7ff.
75. A settlement officer of Saugor regarded the fact that in 1893-94 541,000 out of 1,036,000 acres were sown with wheat and its mixtures as a serious threat: 'The great rust of 1893-94 inaugurated more enlightened methods; not indeed because the faults of the existing system were recognised, but, as contemporary records clearly show, because shortage of seed grain made wheat cultivation on the old scale impossible'; this shortage was also engendered by poverty. See CPSSR, Bundle 268/1911/21-16/20. Forecast report of Saugor resettlement by G.L. Corbett, Assistant C, 31 Oct 1910.
76. CPR, January-April 1900, no. 6, R.H. Craddock to GI, 12 February, 1900, enclosing Note by CCCP on revision of Hoshangabad Settlement, 24 June 1899, IOR.
77. CPR, May-August 1900, no. 4, Craddock to C of Jubbulpore, 4 June 1900 and January-April 1901, no.1, Craddock to C of Settlements and Agriculture, 2 April 1901. According to the *Central Provinces Provincial Banking Enquiry Committee Report*, two-thirds of farm land in the Narsinghpur district was still infested with *kans* as late as 1929. See *CPPBECR*, IV, 852.
78. *Jubbulpore DG*, 190; *Narsinghpur DG, 1971*, 171.
79. *Jubbulpore SR, 1912*, 3; *Damoh SR, 1908-13*, 19; *Saugor SR, 1911-16*, 35; *Narsinghpur SR, 1923-26*, 61.
80. CPSSR, Bundle 46/1/1895/2/127-130. J.B. Fuller to CCCP, 19 July 1894 and Bundle 143/7/1904/2/5-7, Memorial from the Firm of Raja Gokuldas, Rai Bahadur Ballabh Das and Seth Jiwan Das, Bankers, Jubbulpore, 13 October, 1903.
81. CPR May-August 1901, no.7, F.A.T. Phillipps, Off. C of Narmada to CCCP, 20 July, 1901, and January-April 1902, no.1, R.H. Craddock, Off. C of Nagpur to CCCP, 3 January, 1902, IOR. On the operation of the CP Debt Conciliation Boards in Balaghat and Bhandara districts, Parliamentary Papers, LXX (1902), 539.
82. CPSSR, Bundle 128/1/1902/2/15, Papers on Conciliation and abatement proceedings in Khurai tahsil, Saugor.
83. *Saugor SR, 1911-16*, 36; *Hoshangabad SR, 1913-18*, 4. See also *CPPBECR*, 149-50.
84. *Damoh SR, 1908-12*, 20.
85. *Report on the Marketing of Wheat in India* (Delhi, 1937), 23, and G. Blyn, *Agricultural Trends in India, 1891-1947: Output, Availability and Productivity* (Philadelphia, 1966), 200.
86. *Jubbulpore DG, 1971*, 205.
87. *Saugor DG, 1967*, 158 and 146; *Report on the Marketing of Wheat in India* (Delhi, 1937), 48.
88. D. Clouston, *The Organisation of the Department of Agriculture*, Department of Agriculture Bulletin no.13 of 1921 (Nagpur, 1922).
89. A. & G.L.C. Howard, *Wheat in India, its Production, Varieties and Improvement* (Calcutta, 1909).
90. *Hoshangabad SR, 1891-98*, 36.
91. *Narsinghpur SR, 1923-26*, 32; *Saugor SR, 1911-16*, 2; *Hoshangabad SR, 1913-18*, 18.
92. Despite the evidence of deterioration, the third settlement of

Hoshangabad district still revealed a total of 31 per cent of the tenants in class B (that of the substantial or well-to-do tenantry) and a further 50 per cent in class C, thereby confirming the general character of the social differentiation we have observed in the development of the Narmada valley. See *Hoshangabad SR, 1913-18*, 28-9.

93. Stokes, *The Peasant and the Raj, op. cit.*, ch. 68.
94. D. Narain, *Impact of Price Movements on Areas under Selected Crops in India, 1900-1939* (Cambridge, 1965), 152-154.
95. R.P. Gupta, *Agricultural Prices in a Backward Economy* (Delhi, 1973).

10

THE IMPACT OF THE INTERWAR DEPRESSION ON AGRICULTURE IN THE BOMBAY PRESIDENCY: A CASE OF FURTHER ARRESTED DEVELOPMENT?

NEIL CHARLESWORTH
University of Glasgow

The depression of the interwar period stands as a great crisis amidst British India's otherwise undramatic economic history. As is well-known, from 1929 a deep-seated agricultural depression coincided with the world financial collapse and the primary producing economies like India experienced a slump in prices, following on the instability of the 1920s.[1] Within the space of five years after 1928-29 the value of India's foreign trade was very nearly halved and recovery thereafter was sluggish and restricted.

In the historical pattern of India's 'arrested development' this depression could be ascribed a key role. It is notable that the immediate transfer of a major international crisis to India, on the scale that occurred in 1929, was a new phenomenon. The previous 'Great Depression'—that of 1873–96—was admittedly a less violent event, but still there had been a sustained fall in world agricultural prices. However, India's internal economy remained relatively insulated. The only marked decline in crop prices came temporarily in the 1870s and there was never any serious loss of foreign trade values. Partly, internal prices held up because the impact of the depression was counterbalanced by the inflationary effect within India of the steady devaluation of the rupee between the 1870s and the 1890s.[2] Yet the situation also suggests that, at the price level, India was not yet fully incorporated with the Western-centred international economy. With transpo imperfections, world prices were still transmitted to ma villages in a variable, protracted fashion and could anyway b countermanded by local market influences. By 1929 th cushioning effect was far weaker. The Indian peasant, as mu as the bosses of the export houses, was thrust to the forefro as a prominent victim of depression.

This has further implications. The Indian locality had b come more fully integrated with the international economy the very time, after 1914, when the latter had become so mu more unstable. An optimistic, diffusionist view of India economic development down to 1929 would have to argue th extending commercial agricultural production for wor markets had proved stimulatory and generally beneficial ar that more rapid growth and change was inhibited only by lac of capital, climatic and ecological difficulties and mark imperfections. Yet, if so, the interwar depression must stan as a devastating blow at the process. The prices of India major crop exports like cotton slumped with particul violence. Traditional balance of payments relationships we disrupted as India, always regarded as a sink for precio metals, exported gold on a large scale. Indian development- however one views the normal vitality of the process—wa surely newly arrested.

These notions are supported by the existing speciali studies of the depression, which emphasize the profoun impact on the Indian agrarian economy and society.[3] All soci groups apparently faced distress. The landlords and rich peas ants were squeezed by sharply falling cash crop prices, bu they found it difficult to retrench quickly and their cultivatio costs usually remained high. For the poorer peasant th burden of agrarian indebtedness became more oppressive an short-term credit was very difficult to obtain. Agrarian protes increased, often, in the circumstances, involving new cross currents of inter-peasant conflict.[4] The only productiv dimension lay in the very mobilisation of resources away fron the depressed agricultural sector: some argue that muc capital, hitherto heavily committed to the land, rural money lending and cash crop trade, was now diverted to busines and industry in the market town and the city.[5] Even so orthodox views maintain that India's industrial developmen remained disappointing during the 1930s.[6]

Our objective will be to examine the impact of the depression on agriculture in the Bombay Presidency and to test here the existing interpretative notions, by focusing on the twin themes of cropping patterns and the fortunes of differing peasant social groups. Then, the eventual aim will be to locate the agricultural depression and its implications within the broad set of problems of India's arrested growth under British rule.

The Context of the Depression

Firstly, though, what was the general condition of Bombay agriculture in 1929? The most notable of the long-term trends shaping agrarian society was the pronounced acceleration of population growth in the interwar period. Western India had proved a prominent victim of India's great era of high mortality crisis between 1890 and 1920. The famines of the late 1890s and the influenza epidemic of 1918 caused such large numbers of deaths that the Bombay Presidency's total population rose from 18.5 millions in 1901 to only 19.3 millions by 1921, an increase of just over four per cent.[7] Thereafter, however, in the absence of any serious crisis, the rate of population growth became quicker and more consistent and the Presidency's population rose by over 13 per cent between 1921 and 1931, from 19.3 millions to 21.9 millions.[8]

At the same time the vital process of expansion in land under cultivation was losing momentum. The statistics on land acreage indicate that the Bombay Presidency's gross cultivated area stood at around 24 million acres in the first years of the twentieth century, rising to just over 27 million acres by the early 1920s and about 29 million acres by the mid-1930s.[9] At this point, though, a ceiling was reached and very little further expansion occurred during the late 1930s. This suggests that, whilst the rate of extension of cultivation fully matched population growth into the early 1920s, it lagged thereafter. By 1930, certainly productivity improvements on land already under cultivation would have been necessary to maintain per capita standards. This fits with George Blyn's presentation of the agricultural statistics, indicating that per capita production of foodgrains was deteriorating by the interwar period in Bombay[10]—though the acreage statistics

Official orthodoxy argued that the cash crop producer experienced a massive blow, whilst the subsistence cultivator and, especially, the labourer were much much less adversely affected. As early as 1922-23, a downswing in the prices of all the leading crops except cotton was alleged to have produced 'a rise in the prosperity of the labouring classes in the rural areas' whilst most employers of labour 'suffered badly': 'this fact may lead to very marked economic changes in the near future, the exact nature of which it is difficult at present to forecast'.[13] With the onset of the depression the changes were apparently accomplished. By 1930-31 conditions for labourers were 'especially good' because 'while prices have greatly fallen the reduction in the rates of wages has been relatively small. . . . The class of the agricultural population which has suffered most is the big cultivator employing hired labour on a large scale in producing his crop . . . especially . . . the Deccan Canal Irrigator and the cultivator of commercial crops like cotton and groundnut'.[14] This seemed logical, at least for the peak of the depression between 1929 and 1931. As prices started to fall and then slumped dramatically in the space of a few years, it does seem unlikely that employers could have forced down wages as rapidly and consistently as the general decline in prices demanded. Real wages for labour, as in the industrial West, therefore rose, in the short term anyway. This was regarded as economically harmful since, with the rise in real wage costs, 'agriculture cannot hope to be as remunerative as it has been for the past twenty years'.[15] Similarly, the balance of the relationship between landlord and tenant might have shifted significantly against the landlord. The key influence here was the relative scarcity of cash rents in the Bombay Presidency. As Sykes the Bombay Governor argued, 'where there is a crop share system, and this prevails to a fairly considerable extent in this Presidency, the tenant class have no great difficulty but the landlords are hard hit':[16] clearly the value of the produce the landlord received was dropping.

In the longer run, commercial agriculture and its adherents may also have been adversely affected by differential price movements. The price collapse, across the deepest trough of the depression, was severe in all crops. Table 1 shows that prices of jowar, the leading millet foodgrain, were halved in Sholapur District in the relatively uncommercialised east Deccan famine tract. However, these and the other food crop ices did stabilise during the course of the 1930s. Export crop ices seemed more volatile and, in particular, slumped badly ıring the downswing of the late 1930s: prices of Broach tton in fact reached their lowest ebb in 1938-39. The ıenomenon is explicable. The depression of 1929-32 was fficiently traumatic to rule all prices even in the more olated markets, but in the long run foodgrain prices were aped by other local influences too. Thus in a relatively poor strict like Sholapur significant numbers of poor peasants d labourers needed to buy food to supplement subsistence eds and hence levels of local demand, especially with pidly growing population, acted as some countervailing rce to international trends. This would explain why jowar ices at Sholapur and other foodgrain prices held up in the e 1930s. Export crops, however, including here Ahmedabad ıeat as well as Karad groundnut and Broach cotton, ntinued to be dominated by international overproduction d the further dip in world prices in the late 1930s.

In addition, commercial farmers were financially squeezed rough one significant imposition. The burden of land venue charges in Bombay Presidency must have increased ırkedly in real terms over the depression. Table 2 gives tails on the land revenue demand and actual collections. The mbay revenue system allowed for 'suspensions' and also al 'remissions' of land revenue in unfavourable circumsıces and, as the figures show, these were steadily granted a moderate scale. Yet, during the depression, the revenue ministration firmly set its face against concessions on the ounds of falling prices and demand: the revenue report on Central Division of the Presidency for 1933-34, for ample, boasted that 'no remissions were granted on account the slump in prices'.[17] Instead, standard practice was folved and suspensions and remissions given for crop failures ked to climatic and ecological factors, particularly during poorer years of the late 1930s. Furthermore, political resistce to land revenue payment during the depression was ak and officialdom itself seemed surprised how 'although prices have fallen the agriculturists paid the land revenue t down for collection . . . without undue pressure'.[18] The cially divisive impact of the events of 1929-32 was probably cause. Political unity between peasant groups in western lia was fractured during the early 1930s as the gloomy tone of the Maharashtra Congress' Peasant Enquiry Committe Report of 1936 conceded.[19] The Bombay revenue administra tion could now recover some of the initiative it had lost wit the humiliation of the Bardoli campaign of 1928. The consequ ences are clear from Table 2. Levels of land revenue collectio were barely affected by the depression. They held up in abso lute terms and the real burden on individual payers must hav increased significantly. This, of course, hit only the owners o land and further discriminated against them and not tenant and labourers.

TABLE 2

LAND REVENUE, 1926-27–1938-39

(Note: Figures are for the 'Bombay Presidency Proper' (excluding Sind) rupees)

	Original Revenue Demand	Suspensions, Remissions & Previous Collectionns	Actual Collections Realised
1926-27	4,49,39,143	58,08,614	3,90,78,445
1927-28	4,53,45,438	31,67,239	4,20,35,856
1928-29	4,37,90,996	39,27,923	3,94,33,990
1929-30	4,36,26,495	51,15,189	3,76,92,791
1930-31	4,53,25,325	60,74,669	3,90,67,096
1931-32	4,57,82,685	65,52,831	3,94,67,096
1932-33	4,64,42,361	62,27,759	4,05,52,496
1933-34	4,55,39,241	62,72,694	3,94,22,161
1934-35	4,39,96,975	76,59,564	3,54,67,122
1935-36	4,60,24,846	58,13,932	4,10,91,349
1936-37	4,40,11,436	83,09,849	3,60,43,211
1937-38	4,65,39,312	1,02,13,204	3,65,93,997
1938-39	4,63,27,078	88,29,298	3,75,77,797

Source: *Annual Land Revenue Administration Reports of the Bombay Presider* (Bombay, 1928-40), Appendix 1.

All this, then, provides a powerful case that the depressic and its legacy proved a great watershed in the history western Indian agrarian society. The landlords and the ric peasants, so often seen as the beneficiaries of econom change over the British period, were apparently the ve groups most adversely affected. The main victim of tl depression as portrayed in the Bombay official literature is stereotype of a big rent-receiving and labour-employing landlord. These certainly did exist in many regions of the Presidency but the problem is that the typicality of actual tenures by the interwar period was much less rigid and clear-cut. Many peasants owned some land, rented more and perhaps even engaged in part-time labouring activities. Hence even the major commercial producer may not have been so disadvantaged in some of the roles he played. In particular, in regions like south Gujarat and the Deccan canal tracts those who had rented extensive areas of land to expand commercial activities now probably enjoyed declining rent levels, for the evidence suggests that even cash rents fell substantially.

Nevertheless, the onset of much lower prices in 1929-31 undoubtedly did gravely affect commercial farmers. Many growers of cash crops, as might be expected, initially tried to expand production to maintain their incomes but this of course increased their labour costs and hence the real wages received by labourers, whilst exacerbating the price problem by flooding the market. The phenomenon had already occurred in cotton cultivation. The price boom in the commodity reached its peak in 1924, but then came the first abrupt fall: by 1926 prices in Bardoli taluk of south Gujarat, for example, were under half the level of two years previously.[20] Meanwhile cotton cultivation had continued to extend rapidly, passing, as we have seen, the 5 million acres mark for the whole presidency for the first time in 1925-26. There is little doubt that, under these conditions, labourers in the cotton growing areas had enjoyed a notable improvement in their relative position whilst land owners, with no quick price recovery, had further committed themselves to a now less profitable enterprise. In similar vein, an investigation into sugarcane cultivation on the Poona canal tract revealed that the value of the crops fell short of total costs in many cases in 1925-26 and 1926-27.[21] It seemed that 'the cane-growers on the canals are running their businesses at a loss nowadays. This is because the prices of gul have fallen very low, while the costs have remained high on account of the high price of labour'.[22]

This evidence about trends already in progress in the middle 1920s highlights one vital aspect of the depression in the Bombay presidency. Whilst the major collapse in prices occurred between 1929 and 1932, a difficult period of complex economic and social change was already in process and cultivators were having to make adjustments. Furthermore, the official comments about the difficulties of commercial farmers and the relative advance of labourers are made most fully about the period between the mid-1920s and 1931. This raises the possibility that there was a two-stage, short-term and long-term impact to the agrarian depression with a divide around 1931 and 1932. In the short term cash crop producers undoubtedly suffered severely but to discuss the continuing effects in the 1930s we need now to widen our focus.

An obvious mechanism is to examine the long term crop acreage statistics. One might have expected, with the differential price trends and the social indicators we have noted, a steady movement to the foodgrains during the 1930s, especially when population pressure on subsistence added additional motive. In fact, no such overall pattern seems to have occurred and the foodgrains did not noticeably increase their share of the land. In 1922-23 all the cereals and pulses combined covered 18.6 million acres out of Bombay's gross cultivated area of 27.7 million acres, or 67 per cent. By 1938-39 they mustered 19.4 out of 29.7 million acres, 65 per cent of the total. This trend was reflected within the individual cultivation of jowar and bajri, the main millet crops of the Deccan, and of rice in the Konkan coastal strip.

Although the commercial crops in overall terms maintained their share of the land, there were sharp individual variations. Cotton experienced what might be seen as the natural reaction to its large price falls. Cultivation dropped from the 5 million acres peak of 1925-26 to 4.7 million acres in 1928-29 and then slumped sharply to 3.8 million acres in 1932-33 before tailing away still further to 3.6 million acres in 1938-39. Yet some other cash crops apparently extended their acreages markedly across the depression. Sugarcane cultivation, a special case admittedly because it benefited from substantial protection, continued to expand with only a short-lived decline in the mid-1920s. Its total acreage in the Bombay Presidency, standing at 58,000 in 1922-23, had risen to 73,000 by 1938-39, an increase of 25 per cent. Tobacco experienced a boom during the 1930s. Its pre-depression peak was the 114,000 acres of 1924-5, but by 1938-39 tobacco cultivation covered 153,000 acres, a rise of over 34 per cent. Groundnut cultivation extended considerably during the 1920s to around one million acres in 1928-29 and maintained these levels throughout most of the peak depression years before experiencing a further expansion during the late 1930s. Individually, these obviously were less important crops than cotton, but their history does not suggest that a broadly-based crisis of commercialisation emerged out of the depression. In this context, too, it is notable that wheat, the foodgrain with the most extensive market, expanded its acreage more than the millets. And even, on reflection, the fate of cotton was not as dramatic as might have been expected. The falls in cultivation were large but they came after a great period of expansion after the First World War so that cotton cultivation in the Bombay Presidency by 1939 had merely returned to the levels of the early years of the twentieth century.

Commercial agriculture, therefore, reacted in a very diffuse way to the depression. What accounted for the variations? At the general level they can be explained in terms of the opportunities available in different markets. Crops like cotton which were highly dependent on international markets were the most severely affected. The boom in cotton cultivation in Gujarat and parts of Maharashtra in the ten years before 1925 depended much on increasing demand from the Japanese cotton industry. This slumped as the Japanese mills experienced the first severe effects from the depression and then made an impressive recovery based on more extensive use of the longer staple American cotton. Other commercial crops, though, particularly where linked to local industry, could expand on the basis of home demand in the more autarkic climate of the 1930s. Sugar is a well-known example here. Its linkage effects in the Bombay Presidency were less striking than in the UP but, even so, a number of small new sugar refineries opened in the Deccan during the early 1930s, particularly in Rahuri taluk of Ahmednagar District.[23] In Gujarat, tobacco formed another classic example of a crop sustained by home demand and local refining skills.

This line of explanation only dominates at the broadest Presidency-wide level. Below this, in the districts, the detailed trends in cropping patterns were more complex and cultivators seemed to be switching between different crops for diverse reasons. A good illustration of the subtlety of reactions comes in the East Khandesh district. This was traditionally a major centre of cotton cultivation but, as Table 3 shows, a series of shifts in cropping patterns occurred during the 1930s.

Amidst the trough of the depression between 1929 and 1932 cotton cultivation contracted and land was switched to food-grains or left fallow. Then in 1932-33 acreage under ground-nuts leapt substantially and 'the sowing was extended to deep soil lands' which had traditionally grown cotton.[24] This surge of groundnut cultivation is the more curious because at the same time in Satara district, the leading centre for groundnut production in western India, the acreage under the crop was declining.[25] Yet the shift was short-lived. Cotton cultivation in East Khandesh soon recovered at the expense of groundnuts and by 1935-36 the extent of cotton acreage was little lower than pre-depression levels.

TABLE 3

CASH CROP CULTIVATION IN EAST KHANDESH DISTRICT, 1928-29 – 1935-36 (Acres)

	Extent of land under	
	Cotton	Groundnuts
1928-29	790,406	350,833
1929-30	736,269	351,603
1930-31	668,076	363,553
1931-32	651,988	361,401
1932-33	589,527	421,929
1933-34	637,660	337,550
1934-35	687,006	227,819
1935-36	744,057	217,325

Source: *Annual Land Revenue Administration Report of the Bombay Presidency 1931-32* (Bombay, 1933) 39; *1935-36* (Bombay, 1937) 39.

How do we explain such patterns? The simple answer is continuous reaction to the vagaries of local price trends. For all the dominating force of the international depression, prices still varied significantly from district to district and thus, for example, jowar prices in July 1932 were 20 per cent lower in Ahmednagar compared with Poona and more than 4 per cent lower again in Sholapur.[26] Hence groundnut prices may have remained higher in East Khandesh District than in Satara District, for certainly the main official explanation for the East Khandesh groundnut boom emphasized that 'though the price of groundnut also was low, the fall was small as compared with that in the price of cotton.'[27] Yet price responsiveness does not entirely explain the East Khandesh phenomenon. The marked recovery of cotton in the mid-1930s took place conspicuously at a time when 'the rate of cotton in East Khandesh remained practically unchanged' whilst groundnut still 'fetched a good price'.[28]

Cultivators faced intense problems over economic calculations in the depression. Prices were so volatile and unpredictable that organised reaction to them, in terms of choice of crop sown, was very complex and difficult. Prices in the sowing season were no sure guide to harvest prices. Hence in East Khandesh the agricultural season of 1934-5 saw 'very low' cotton prices over the latter part of 1934, 'a welcome rise by the middle of January 1935' and then 'a sudden drop in March 1935'.[29] Peasants may have been strongly price-responsive in approach but the frequent mismatch with actual price trends, evident in East Khandesh, may simply reflect the difficulties of being right in the unstable circumstances. The official reports are littered with accounts of failed calculations. In 1934-35 again, groundnut prices in one taluk of Satara District seemed to be rising markedly and peasants 'held back their crops in the hope of large profits . . . however, the demand for the article fell with the result that those who harvested their crops late or held them back had to suffer'.[30]

Yet episodes like this themselves pointed the dangers of too slavish a reaction to short-term prices. The situation might suggest that entirely different calculations became paramount during the depression, calculations about the ease and costs of cultivating different crops. Baker, thinking along similar lines, has argued in Madras for 'a transfer of acreage from crops that were relatively cheap to produce, such as groundnut and local cotton, to crops that required more expensive inputs such as good quality cotton, sugar, spices, fruit and vegetables'.[31] Bombay was different. Here, perhaps because of more established industries in sectors like cotton or as a result of a commercial farming system rather less 'under the control of the oligarchy of village leaders',[32] the cheaper crops held up. Indeed, it might well be argued that in western India economies of cost proved the key mechanism whereby commercial agriculture rode the depression.

The groundnut story is one clue. Unlike in Madras, groundnut cultivation did not decline during the depression and indeed in 1932-3 proved a valuable reserve for many East

Khandesh cotton farmers. The special value of groundnut was that it was cheap and easy to grow: 'it requires less rain than cotton, is not subject to many deteriorating causes which may affect cotton and so is more certain to give a satisfactory return . . . it ripens early and can be sold in October and so brings in money much sooner than cotton'.[33] With these qualities it was a particularly economical crop for commercial farmers at the climax of a severe depression. Before 1929 it can be argued that many Bombay cash crop producers had acquired comparatively high cultivation costs. It had made sense, as prices had steadily increased, to maximise production without too meticulous an investigation of outlays. Thus, on the Deccan canal-irrigated lands, 'during the boom period when the prices of gul were most alluring, the tendency of sugarcane cultivators was to get the maximum outturn, spending more money on manuring and labour'.[34] This approach had helped to create the improved conditions for labourers about which there is such widespread comment in the Bombay revenue papers even in the early twentieth century. It also ensured that the initial impact of the depression on the big commercial landowner was disastrous, particularly where he reacted by trying to increase production in a still more profligate manner. Costs came down at best only 'slightly', whilst the fall in the value of commodities was 'relatively much greater'.[35]

In the long term, though, there was no panic retreat from commercial crops into the foodgrains because this was not necessary. Instead, the retreat could be made into methods and types of commercial agriculture which were cheaper and, in particular, less labour-intensive. This helps to explain the Presidency-wide trends in the cultivation of various crops. Cotton cultivation declined overall because the largest cotton producers in Gujarat and the southern districts of Maharashtra enjoyed limited opportunities for adjustment within cotton cultivation and therefore switched crops. Jan Breman gives an excellent example of the process in south Gujarat: the agrarian elite in his villages turned, in particular, to the tending of mango trees, which required relatively little labour.[36] As a result, they were able to strengthen their hold over the village and increase the economic divide between themselves and the *halis*, the farm servants and labourers who traditionally worked for them.

Elsewhere, however, entire shifts in cropping patterns were

unnecessary. Sugarcane cultivation, for example, had experienced a rapid growth in costs before the depression. These had reached as much as Rs. 1,000 per acre per year on some Deccan canal plots by 1925-6,[37] but retrenchment was clearly possible. Most plots on the canal lands were tiny, only one or two acres in size, and more intensive work by the family might diminish cash costs significantly. The same logic would apply to the tobacco-growing small-holders in areas like south-eastern Kaira (Kheda) District in Gujarat. Equally in East Khandesh the return to cotton cultivation may have followed a shake-out of labour and a retrenchment on costs. In general, where commercial agriculture rested mainly on intensive cultivation of small units of land, as it did in western India with sugarcane, tobacco and some types of cotton, considerable economies to counteract price falls were possible. Greater use of family labour would also be an option encouraged by demographic trends. Accelerating population growth, created as it was by declining mortality rates, would have increased availability of adult labour to most peasant farms by the 1930s.

This hypothesis has important social implications. With the land revenue squeeze, labour costs were everywhere the largest and most obvious expenditure on which economies were available. The inference is that, whilst in the short term the depression severely afflicted the landlord and rich peasant, its more long-term and substantive impact was to weaken the ability of labourers and the poor to earn good wages. By the last years of the early twentieth century commercial expansion in Bombay Presidency, many of the richer agricultural producers were retreating from day-to-day involvement in cultivation, preferring leisure and social position to maximum efficiency within the family budget. The depression arguably drove them back to greater use of their own, and family, labour. But if this, for the rich peasant, was a social and cultural loss, the main economic consequences would be lower wages and loss of opportunities for those who sought labouring work. The largest contraction in commercial cultivation occurred in the crop cotton, where fixed demands for additional labour at times like harvesting were especially great. By December 1931, therefore, the Bombay government was already arguing that a significant change had occurred: 'as compared with two years ago wages in rural areas have now fallen by 22 per cent.[38] At the same time credit was contracting making it more difficult for the poor to borrow. As with Baker's Madras, renewed social stratification may well have been the long-term legacy of the depression to Bombay agrarian society.

Conclusions

In reviewing the depression, it is impossible to deny its role as a major crisis for the Indian agrarian economy. It introduced a sharply changed relationship with the external world, identified by officialdom as the general 'lack of purchasing power among the cultivators'.[39] The credit contraction affected all groups adversely. In western India dislocation was intense in the first stage of the depression down to 1931: commercial agriculture was severely affected and deep-seated social changes seemed in train. In the second stage, however, from about 1932 the agricultural theme was adjustment and adaptation. Retrenchment occurred and there were subtle shifts rather than the major reorganisation of cultivation patterns.

During the 1930s, then, the most striking feature in the Bombay Presidency is the relative imperviousness of the agricultural economy to revolutionary change. Given that the depression *did* genuinely create large dislocations in some other sectors, notably in India's foreign exchange reltionships, this finding reasserts the value of concepts like dualism and distinctions between the formal and informal economy, along with the notion that the long-term impact of the international economy on India was actually to strengthen the divide. Aginst the vast size, weight and stability of the traditional agricultural economy, external pressures for change, even when in the shape of a massive international depression, *were* weak. The commercial agriculture sector in a province like Bombay by the interwar period was too institutionalised to be subject to swift and radical change.

Since, then, commercial agriculture did not experience a fundamental structural decline in Bombay Presidency, it is hard to see that there was any justification for a decisive intersectoral shift of resources. The cotton industry did diversify into a wider range of upcountry centres in western India, but insofar as new capital resources were involved they were probably the already more mobile funds of Marwaris and Gujaratis rather than capital of explicitly agrarian origin. In

Bombay resources remained tied up on the land, underpinned by the continued demand for it as an asset as well as the adaptability of commercial agriculture. This contrasts with the situation in some other developing economies. In Soviet Russia, for example, there was unquestionably a large transfer of resources out of agriculture to pay for very high rates of industrial investment.[40] In Japan, agriculture was devastated by the dramatic collapse in the international price of silk, hitherto consistently the country's leading single export and buoyed up in the 1920s by the favours of Western fashion designers. Japanese agriculture was further afflicted by intense competition for the home market in rice from the imperial possessions of Taiwan and Korea.[41] Here then was a genuine agricultural crisis. Capital left agriculture and the desperate quest of peasants to supplement incomes drove down wages and labour costs. Whatever the massive social problems involved, these processes were at the heart of Japan's successful recovery in the 1930s. The developments we have outlined in Bombay agriculture and its adaptability in the face of the depression therefore help to explain why industrialisation was not stimulated so strongly in the India of the 1930s as in some other developing economies.

This leads to a final point which can be deduced from the reaction of Bombay agriculture to the depression. We began by emphasizing the interwar depression's novel role as a major international crisis immediately translated to the Indian scene, but paradoxically its long-term impression in western India was less radical and deep-seated than nineteenth century influences. It was the international economy through the American civil war cotton boom of the 1860s which had first greatly promoted western India's agricultural export economy. As Harnetty has shown, the response to international price trends was then swift and close.[42] Now developments in the world economy were acting as a depressant but the outcome was not so great a permanent change in cultivation patterns as in the 1860s. The forces which had been a genuinely dynamic element in the nineteenth century liberal economy were in this way stultifying and losing their power to determine events on the ground. Commercial agriculture in Bombay by the 1930s had become predominantly another device in the peasant struggle to adapt and survive and to gain in the manoeuvres for social position between richer and poorer peasants. This signified that it would never now spontaneously transform the rural economy of western India.

Glossary

bajri	millet foodgrain
gul	sugar
halis	hereditary labourers in south Gujarat
jawar	millet foodgrain
kharif	autumn crops or season
rabi	spring crops or season

NOTES

1. For a general discussion of the phenomenon, see C.H. Lee, 'The Effects of the Depression on Primary Producing Countries', *Journal of Contemporary History*, 4 (1969) 139-55; C.P. Kindleberger, *The World in Depression 1929-1939* (Stanford, 1973).
2. For a discussion of price trends in the late nineteenth century, see Michelle McAlpin, 'Price Movements and Fluctuations in Economic Activity (1860-1947)', ch. 11 of *The Cambridge Economic History of India*, vol 2, ed. Dharma Kumar (Cambridge, 1983). On the impact of rupee depreciation, see John Adams and Robert Craig West, 'Money, Prices and Economic Development in India', *Journal of Economic History*, 39 (1979), 55-68.
3. See, for example, the work of C.J. Baker, particularly 'Debt and the Depression in Madras 1929-1936', in *The Imperial Impact: Studies in the Economic History of Africa and India*, eds. Clive Dewey & A.G. Hopkins (London, 1978) and *An Indian Rural Economy 1880-1955: The Tamilnad Countryside* (Oxford, 1984). The other leading authority is Dietmar Rothermund. See especially his 'Agrarian Distress in India 1930-1935', in *The Indian Economy Under British Rule and Other Essays* , ch. 7 (New Delhi, 1983).
4. Jacques Pouchepadass deals with this aspect well in his 'Peasant Classes in Twentieth Century Agrarian Movements in India', ch 9 of *Peasants in History: Essays in Honour of Daniel Thorner*, ed. E.J. Hobsbawm *et al.* (Calcutta, 1980).
5. These views are suggested in the cited works of C.J. Baker and the important study by B.R. Tomlinson, *The Political Economy of the Raj 1914-1947* (London, 1979).
6. See, for example, A.K. Bagchi, *Private Investment in India 1900-1939* (Cambridge, 1972). The Indian literature contrasts with the general thesis that industrialisation was quite sharply stimulated in most less developed countries during the depression. For this argument, see C.J. Lee, 'The Effects of the Depression on Primary Producing Countries'.
7. *Census of India, 1931,* Vol VIII, Part 2, *Bombay Presidency* (Bombay, 1932), Table 2.

8. *Ibid.*

9. See the *Annual Crop and Season Reports of the Bombay Presidency*, Appendix A. All subsequent references to crop and acreage statistics, where not explicitly stated, come from these reports.

10. George Blyn, *Agricultural Trends in India, 1891-1947: Output, Availability and Productivity* (Philadelphia, 1966), 100.

11. For a wider discussion of this phenomenon and its implications, see my 'The Origins of Fragmentation of Landholdings in British India: A Comparative Examination', ch. 7 of *Rural India: Land, Power and Society under British Rule*, ed. Peter Robb (London, 1983).

12. *Crop and Season Report 1930-1*, para 43.

13. *Crop and Season Report 1922-3*, para 24.

14. *Crop and Season Report 1930-1*, para 44.

15. *Annual Land Revenue Administration Report of the Bombay Presidency, 1930-31* (Bombay, 1932), 45.

16. Sir Frederick Sykes to Lord Willingdon, Viceroy, 20 Dec 1931, Sykes Papers, vol.38, India Office Records.

17. *Land Revenue Report 1933-4*, 23.

18. *Land Revenue Report 1932-3*, 36.

19. The report conceded that 'the peasant cannot spontaneously respond to the call of the Anti-Imperialist struggle': *Report of the Peasant Enquiry Committee of the Maharashtra Provincial Congress Committee* (Poona, 1936), 91.

20. R.S. Broomfield and R.M. Maxwell, *Report of the Special Enquiry into the Second Revision Settlement of the Bardoli and Chorasi Talukas* (Bombay, 1929), Appendix A.

21. P.C. Patil, *Studies in the Cost of Production of Crops in the Deccan No. 1: Crops in the Neighbourhood of Poona*, Department of Agriculture Bulletin No. 149 of 1927 (Poona, 1928), 6.

22. *Ibid*, 8.

23. *Land Revenue Report 1932-3*, 40.

24. *Ibid*, 39.

25. *Land Revenue Report 1932-3*, 39.

26. *Land Revenue Report 1934-5*, 47.

27. *Land Revenue Report 1931-2*, 39.

28. *Land Revenue Report 1935-6*, 39.

29. *Land Revenue Report 1934-5*, 42.

30. *Ibid.*

31. C.J. Baker, *An Indian Rural Economy 1880-1955*, 164-5.

32. *Ibid*, 166.

33. *Land Revenue Report 1932-3*, 39.

34. P.C. Patil, *Studies in the Cost of Production*, 8.

35. *Ibid*.
36. See Jan Breman, *Patronage and Exploitation. Changing Agrarian Relations in South Gujarat, India* (Berkeley, 1974).
37. P.C. Patil, *Studies in the Cost of Production*, 6.
38. Sykes to Willingdon, 20 December, 1931, para 6, Sykes Papers, Vol 3B.
39. *Crop and Season Report 1938-9*, para 35.
40. There has, it is true, been an attack on this notion following the work of the Soviet historian A.A. Barsov. Yet Barsov's statistics, with their high assessments of capital formation, seem to show that industrial workers paid for the industrial investment *as well as* the agricultural sector. For the figures and a sympathetic assessment, see Michael Ellman, 'Did the Agricultural Surplus Provide the Resources for the Increase in Investment in the USSR during the First Five Year Plan?', *Economic Journal*, 85 (1975), 844-63.
41. For a recent introductory source on interwar Japan, see Takafusa Nakamura, *Economic Growth in Prewar Japan* (New Haven, 1983).
42. Peter Harnetty, 'Cotton Exports and Indian Agriculture, 1861-1870', *Economic History Review*, 24 (1971), 414-29.

11

CANAL MANAGEMENT AND AGRICULTURAL PRODUCTION IN THE UNITED PROVINCES

IAN STONE
Newcastle Polytechnic

Canal irrigation schemes are generally assumed to make a positive net contribution to the level and stability of agricultural output. In the doab which lies between the Jumna and the Ganges in western Uttar Pradesh the easily applied perennial supplies of canal water made the more intensive use of land possible by widening the range of feasible crops, releasing labour and cattle from working wells, reducing crop failures and improving the cultivators' operational flexibility.[1] Thus the spread of canal irrigation within the doab, to dry areas as well as those with well irrigation, at an average rate approaching 50,000 acres per year between 1860 and 1920, plainly made a major contribution to the growth of output over the period, particularly with regard to valuable crops like wheat, sugarcane, indigo and cotton.

Despite their impact on output, the canal schemes consistently underperformed in the sense that their incremental contribution to yields and total output value was below the theoretical maximum that could have resulted from the quantities of water entering the system. This has been a particularly important theme in the discussions on agricultural development since Independence. Estimates vary, but it is commonly suggested that the proportion of optimal output actually achieved is as low as 50 per cent.[2] Considerable attention has been directed towards increasing the utilisation of existing systems as a more cost-effective way of expanding output than building new schemes.

There are many influences which depress the output

achieved per cu sec (cubic feet per second) of water entering a canal system. Beyond such ubiquitous factors as imperfections in credit, land and commodity markets and the inadequacy of agricultural support services—all of which limit the cultivators' ability to make the most of the resources available to them—canal water was wasted *en route* to the peasant's field and was ineffectively utilised—even by the low standards of peasant farming systems—on its arrival. Supply characteristics were important in this respect. The poor timing and inadequate quantity of water supplies limited obtainable yields, and risk-averse cultivators—unable to predict the quantity of water likely to be received or the time intervals of waterings—chose second-best production options, planting less valuable crops which were certain to survive water shortages.

Some of the uncertainty over water supply was the direct result of the nature and scale of the canal projects themselves. As works of engineering the British schemes had technical and operational limitations. A notable example is the uncertainty which arose because the Ganges Canal had only temporary headworks at Hardwar. From the date of its opening in 1854 right through to 1922 this canal, irrigating 1.25 million acres annually, relied for its cold-season supply upon a series of hastily erected *bunds* which diverted the falling river supply towards the intake. These were often washed away, interrupting supplies for weeks together while the *bunds* were replaced. Even when full supplies were flowing within the system, water still had to be distributed to different branches taking off from the main canal, and then into the numerous distributaries which fed the water-courses of the irrigators. By 1920, the linked Upper and Lower Ganges systems consisted of 1,230 miles of main channels and 6,400 miles of distributaries. Understandably, such a system placed immense demands upon information flows and posed formidable problems of co-ordination, which were exacerbated by the numerous leaks, silt build-ups, and sudden demand changes. A variety of technical improvements—telegraph lines, escape facilities, link channels which permitted the transfer of supplies, and the eventual remodelling and systematic calibration of the network of channels—gradually made the system's operation less cumbersome and imprecise; but a certain amount of unreliability at the divisional or local level was inevitable for technical reasons alone, and the problem persists to this day.

This paper examines the evolution of schemes like the Ganges Canal, showing how the technical and physical aspects of canal building interacted with institutional and managerial arrangements to affect the conditions of supply of a vital agricultural input.

Design and Control of each Scheme

The design and management of the early schemes were understandably crude. In the development of the Jumna canals (from the 1820s) and the Ganges Canal (from the early 1830s) military engineers, with little practical experience to guide them, experimented with designs and methods of operation within the tight and fluctuating bounds of ordinary expenditures drawn from each year's revenues. Scarce engineering skills and capital resources were mostly absorbed by the construction of the main channels. Little time and few resources were devoted to the distribution of the water, and the Canal Department encouraged local individuals and cultivator groups to arrange for the construction and maintenance of channels to their villages. They were also expected to manage the supplies themselves.

At first, on the Eastern Jumna Canal, no government distributaries existed at all, and cultivators' watercourses were fed directly through simple cuts in the canal banks. This unsatisfactory arrangement was subsequently replaced by a system whereby irrigators paid the department the cost of constructing their *kolabas* (outlets) and a rudimentary distributary network. This system was less than ideal, since many purchasers were individual speculators who claimed proprietary rights to the water supply only to resell it to the irrigators at higher rates.[4] Eventually, the Irrigation Department accepted responsibility for the installation and maintenance of the outlet, as well as the construction and upkeep of a distributary network feeding the outlets; private rights over the outlet and the use of water did not arise. Villagers, either individually or through representatives, applied for *kolabas* which were granted fairly indiscriminately, with little control over numbers per village or their position and size. The villagers then arranged the construction of the *guls* (watercourses) among themselves. Unless the village channels were strikingly wasteful of water and poorly maintained, the engineers did not interfere. *Kolaba* owners established the rotation of turns *(warabandi)* when water was flowing. Such matters were to remain strictly outside the jurisdiction of the canal establishment.[5]

The initial operation of the canal system was thus conditioned by the fact that cultivators were assigned a large role in the construction, operation and management of the distribution network. With few exceptions, the system wasted water in poorly aligned, ill-maintained and environmentally disruptive channels. Because the department's distributary network was itself grossly defective, the 'open flow' concept on which the channels were supposed to operate was seriously undermined. Engineers envisaged a fixed discharge flowing continuously through uncontrolled outlets, reaching the fields via a hierarchy of progressively smaller channels, whose dimensions were calibrated so as to balance available supply against expected local demand. In practice, villages and irrigators high in the hierarchy of channels took water according to their needs, depriving users further down the system. The permissive policy of granting *kolabas* on demand was a major reason why these favoured villages could expand their use of canal water at will. The simple act of clearing silt from *guls,* which was usually done in well-placed villages only in years of high demand for water, increased their drawing power and added to the plight of the villages further down the system when they needed water most.

Although officials intended to give an important place to famine protection in the design of earlier canals, the location of the distributaries tended to favour the best-developed villages rather than the outlying and more sparsely populated areas. This situation suited the Canal Department because the backward areas were less lucrative sources of revenue and were more expensive to supply.[6] A reorganised administrative structure and the acceptance of new financing provisions in the 1860s led to a re-examination of the role of irrigation, particularly in relation to famine protection. Colonel Richard Strachey, the first Inspector-General of Irrigation, played an important part in establishing a principle which was to be extremely influential in determining the character of canal irrigation throughout northern India. A policy was adopted of "extending irrigation generally and so far as possible in a manner that shall to the utmost guard against the worst effects of severe drought". Canal policies were oriented towards spatial rationing, rather than a compact system providing reliable and substantial supplies for a narrow zone of intensively irrigated cultivation.[7]

Henceforth the physical design of the distributary network would be based on the premise that "a certain normal standard or proportion of irrigated area should be claimable by every district to which water can be given". This normal standard was set very precisely at 42.5 per cent of the culturable area of each village. Only villages where the existing well area fell below this percentage were to be given canal water, and then only that amount sufficient to bring irrigation up to the 42.5 per cent level. In practice it proved impossible to adhere to these guidelines and villages were often able to irrigate considerably in excess of this area. A significant principle had been established, however: equity was to be an important aspect of distribution and as many villages as possible were to be served with the aim of enhancing protection rather than production.

This concern for protection led to the installed capacity of schemes being set above the minimum recorded river supply levels for the *rabi* season. An average minimum rather than an actual minimum was taken as the lower limit, on the grounds that to restrict capacity to the minimum *rabi* supply would correspondingly reduce utilisation of the ample *kharif* supplies. Since it was thought that *kharif* irrigation was likely to be used to protect food and fodder crops, the policy was felt to be justified. Thus, the Upper Ganges Canal was given an installed capacity of 8,000 cu secs, when the river supplies had been known to fall during the *rabi* to 6,000 cu secs. Occasional shortages of *rabi* supplies were therefore built into the system.[8]

These decisions posed considerable managerial problems for the Canal Department. Without the power to intervene in distribution beyond the initial outlets, engineers had to devise ways of rationing supplies, not only to serve the villages the system was being extended to cover, but also to enable them to distribute the available water more evenly so as to improve the wildly fluctuating service to downstream users. The built-in periodic shortages merely aggravated the problem.

Limitations on Control through Pricing

One way in which the rationing of supplies might have been

achieved was through pricing. The *form* of pricing and the level of charges might have been used to influence the way in which water was used and to assist in its distribution according to accepted principles. For some years considerable attention was given to the possibility of introducing a system of charges based on the volume of water consumed. The champions of volumetric sales argued that it gave cultivators an incentive to reduce waste and maximise output per unit of water. Experiments based on a version of the *modulo magistrale*, in use in Lombardy, were conducted on the Ganges Canal in the 1860s.[9] Here, and subsequently elsewhere, the experiment was deemed unsuccessful. It proved practically impossible to devise a sluice which gave a uniform discharge into a village channel when there was variation in the distributary water levels. Not only this, but the modules silted-up, were far from tamper-proof, and irrigators were uneasy at having to estimate water volumes when carrying out irrigation.[10]

There was considerable official enthusiasm in the 1860s and 1870s for an alternative system involving sale of water by contracts, which was also similar to a method currently in use in Italy. This system possessed certain attributes of volumetric charging. Under it, an irrigating community which signed a three-year contract received a reduction of around one-sixth on the average annual sum paid as crop-acre water rates over the previous five years. Those accepting the contract could irrigate freely according to their needs, subject only to the size, number and position of the outlets remaining the same. This obviously reduced administrative costs (particularly the measurement of irrigation) and gave an incentive for users to minimise waste and allocate water among crops according to its most productive uses. There is evidence that the system had precisely that effect; but it was a cause of conflict among the irrigators, since the stronger cultivators gained more than the weaker ones, who still had to pay their share of the costs. While there were villages controlled by moneylender proprietors who were happy to continue with the scheme, in the more numerous and egalitarian *bhaiachara*, or coparcenary, villages clashes between the shareholders over dividing the gains made the scheme unpopular and the contracts were not renewed.[11]

The result was a reversion to the crop-acre system of charging for water. A rate per unit area was levied which varied according to the category of the crop grown in that season. The use of this rather than the volumetric system meant that the cultivator, once he had decided upon the crops he wished to irrigate, faced a fixed charge regardless of the quantity of water he used. He could not divert some of the water designated for his maturing indigo crop to perk up a nearby field of *jowar* without running the risk of his action being noted by a canal official and his having to pay a full crop rate in addition. He was, however, able to treat irrigation in fields for which he had already taken water as a fixed cost: he could go on applying water, as long as it was available, up to the point at which its marginal product, fell to zero. The water would have had a higher marginal return in other fields or villages, but for cultivators with good supplies, there was no incentive to incur the costs of applying water more efficiently and without waste. Similarly, cultivators in any way unsure of their future supplies applied more water during their turn than was consistent with realising high yields, thus achieving some protection against losses should subsequent supplies be delayed or scanty. Such risk-averse behaviour was permitted by the fact that, under the existing price system, the extra water cost the cultivator nothing. It did, however, involve social costs in that it contributed to the uncertainty of supply for other producers lower down the line.

The *level* of water rates was not used to ration canal supplies either. The rates were set very low from the outset, to encourage peasants to go to the trouble of bringing canal water to their fields and substituting canal for well water.[12] There were advocates of higher rates in the Revenue and Irrigation Departments, and the Government of India pressed for increased charges (so that the profits of productive canals could be used to finance more protective works).[13] The provincial government, however, successfully resisted enhancements on the ground that the low water rates had been taken into account in rent agreements, and that the returns from canal irrigation were now effectively and inextricably entangled with the revenue system. To increase users' rates would, it was argued, undermine the position of the occupancy tenants in the canal zones. Since the occupancy tenants were too important, politically, to be offended, change was confined to the introduction (as in Punjab) of an 'owner's rate' levied on landowners in newly-irrigated villages.[14]

There were other reasons why water rates were not used as an active tool of control. High rates would, for one thing, have conflicted with the policy of spreading canal water over large areas. Low rates permitted canal water to be used at the margins: in areas of poor soil; by peasants with limited resources; and where the unreliable supply might make its use unprofitable. Attempts to increase rates on sugarcane irrigation brought forth organised and effective opposition from the Zamindars' Association. For these reasons the water rates remained low. Canal water was underpriced in relation both to the cost of irrigating from wells and to the value of the commercial crops it helped to raise. Indeed, as a proportion of the value of irrigated crops it became cheaper over time. The price of wheat tripled between the mid-1860s and 1920 but the flow water rate for the crop less than doubled, while the costs of lift irrigation increased by only one-third. The charge for flow irrigation on an acre of sugarcane was Rs. 7.5 (Rs. 3 for lift) on a crop frequently worth over Rs. 150. Canal water was an extremely valuable commodity for those who could get hold of it; excess demand was inevitable. Effectively, the benign pricing strategy meant that canal water had to be rationed through administrative and bureaucratic channels and technical controls.

Control through Bureaucratic Intervention

When officials in the Canal Department sought to control the distribution of canal supplies during the second phase of canal expansion (from the 1870s to 1890s) they came into conflict with the best-placed villages, where an initial oversupply of water had created water-intensive systems of cultivation. The numbers and intake capacities of *kolabas* had to be reduced so as to curtail the profligacy with which upstream villages used canal water. The larger privately-owned distributary channels were taken over and improved by the department. Along the length of these and other distributaries the supplies were improved by removing dams put there by cultivators wishing to increase their supplies, by more effective silt clearances, and by the systematic use of *tatils* (outlet closures), the most significant of the changes. Such closures were imposed in rotation upon the outlets of users in the upper sections of distributaries, so as to allow supplies to pass down to villages further along. The time limit these closures imposed upon irrigators forced cultivators to make economies.[15]

The Canal Department fought some of its keenest contests with the indigo planters, particularly the Europeans. Their dye output depended on the extent and success of the local indigo crop, so they cultivated good relations with the local engineer or exploited the antipathy which frequently existed between revenue and irrigation officials as a means of drawing attention to supply problems.[16] They also pursued compensation claims against the canal authorities for crops allegedly damaged by supply failures and intimidated or bribed the local canal employees. Less organised and less influential users were unable to exert the kind of pressure which improved the reliability of supplies.

In the struggle over access to water at the local level, the role of the subordinate officials became increasingly important. Supervision of officials operating at the subdivisional level by the executive engineer and his one or two assistants was necessarily minimal. The engineer was responsible for the irrigation of perhaps 200,000 acres from 600 miles of distributaries. The local administration was in the hands of the *ziladar*, who was assisted by suboverseers. He supervised the work of the measuring *amins* and the patrols, or *chaukidars*. The latter were each assigned six or seven miles of distributary along which they regulated the supplies of water to the villages and user groups, recorded and reported gauge levels, and noted down the fields and crops in receipt of water.

It was always possible for officials at this level to engage in petty corruption. The falsification of irrigation returns, reporting cultivators for breaches of canal regulations and interrupting the supplies of canal water, gave these officials plenty of opportunity to exact payments from cultivators. Such activity was rife, particularly in areas where water was generally in short supply. The opportunities to engage in such practices increased markedly when the authorities attempted to extend control over the distribution of water by enhancing the supervisory role of subordinate officials. Not surprisingly, an investigation into allegations of corruption made by A.P. Webb, a *zamindar*, in his 1878 pamphlet, 'Irrigation Topics',[17] found that 'very considerable gratuities are given systematically to all classes of canal subordinates, sometimes in kind and sometimes in money. It is feared not even the *ziladars* are exempt, and . . . the Deputy Magistrate could not have been ignorant.'[18] *Ziladars* on the Eastern Jumna canal commonly received *faslana* (harvest payments) at a rate per *kolaba* or per *bigha* of irrigation, with additional payments for such considerations as arranging for timely first waterings. *Chaukidars* received goodwill payments and further sums for allowing access to water during *tatils*.

The canal authorities were particularly embarrassed at the extent of the corruption revealed by the investigation, because revenue officers were already critical of the Irrigation Department. Nonetheless, it is important to set the corruption in context by asking what effect it had upon the supply of canal water to irrigators. The fact is that formal intervention by the subordinate establishment, particularly in relation to the use of *tatils*, destabilised supplies to villages which had been able to rely on reasonably full irrigation. *Tatils* were designed to restrict the time available for irrigation in upstream villages and reduce the drawing power they enjoying through deepening their water channels or irrigating at night. It was an important assumption lying behind the system of rotating closures that the water supply in distributary would remain roughly constant. In fact, given the crude and poorly-maintained channels typical of the time, this was anyting but the case. Frequently, low supply coincided with the open period allocated to outlets along a distributary section. Since compensatory irrigation was prohibited by departmental regulations, even villages well-placed within the system could find their irrigation severely disrupted. The *chaukidar* was able to supplement his monthly pay of Rs. 5-7 by simply opening these outlets out of turn and allowing irrigation at night.

There was an understandably close connection between the level of payments (in *faslana* and for *tatils*) and the wealth and style of cultivation of different villages. Villages near the distributary head normally expected full supplies and they engaged the services of local canal employees to ensure that attempts to spread the water along the distributary did not affect the quantity of water needed for their intensively cultivated fields. They could afford to pay heavily for such services because the actual water rate was so low and were prepared to do so because they could only commit themselves to large areas of input-intensive crops if they could rely on the water supply. The heaviest payments on the Eastern Jumna Canal came, predictably, from sugarcane villages.[19]

To these villages the existence of this informal market for water was of considerable benefit.[20] Overall, it produced more positive than negative effects. Inasmuch as the purchase of *tatils* raised the marginal cost of canal water applications and embodied time limits there was an incentive to economise on water use. Illegal payments decreased with the distance along the distributary and were seldom made at the tails. The lower villages, although they exhibited much less reliance upon canal water than those above them, used what water they could obtain with great care, constructing elaborate *kiari* (field compartment) systems and carefully maintaining, and even lining, their watercourses. The increased supply they received as a result of intervention activity was thus efficiently deployed.

Technical Improvements and Centralised Control

The irrigation authorities resorted to centrally controlled technical methods to reduce the discretionary role of the canal establishment in the day-to-day distribution of canal supplies. Engineers were convinced that even within the existing open-flow design of the system, refinements, properly maintained, could provide a larger and more evenly distributed supply. In practice, despite the fact that such investment in project refinement is relatively cheap and quick-yielding compared with outlay on new works, it was still difficult to wrestle sufficient funds for the proposed wholesale remodelling. Nevertheless, the third main phase of irrigation management was heralded by the commencement, in the 1880s, of a systematic and carefully integrated programme of remodelling the canal distribution network.

The whole purpose of this scheme was to reduce waste and facilitate the maximum area of irrigation per cu sec entering the system, whilst in the process dispensing with the need to apply *tatils* within individual distributaries. The latter were enlarged so that they could be run full in alternative weeks rather than continuously; moreover, their dimensions were calibrated at intervals according to the outlet capacity so that the water flow was more closely related to the drawing power of the various villages along the line. Distribution control now lay more decisively with the executive engineer, who determined whether an entire distributary was in flow or not. Tail villages almost invariably increased their irrigation as a result of these adjustments, not so much through depriving upstream villages of their supplies as by the speedier overall execution of irrigation and the reduction of losses through waste, percolation and evaporation. Irrigation expanded in most villages, while the system became more flexible in responding to abnormal local demand.

Following the greater integration of the four main doab canal systems, including the installation of supply-switching facilities, the remodelled network of the early 1900s used its core supplies with much greater efficiency. Nevertheless a basic doctrine had not been lost sight of: water economies resulting from technical improvements ultimately took the form of extended irrigation coverage. The aim of improving famine protection on a spatial basis, together with the Canal Department's wish to increase its direct revenue, pushed the reach of the canal outwards. This effectively ruled out the use of these technical refinements for ensuring reliable supply and thus more concentrated and intensive irrigation. In 1900, when the Chief Engineer was involved in discussions over whether it was wise, given the existing severe water supply constraints, to proceed with a new distributary on the Agra Canal, he tellingly insisted, "we must make the distributary first and then find water for it. It is in my opinion advisable to give as many villages as possible the benefit of a share of irrigation, even if the present supply is thereby reduced".[21] This basic principle of distribution thus continued to exert its influence over the character of canal irrigation in the doab and elsewhere.

Increased flexibility and technical sophistication lay behind the expansion in the doab's normal canal irrigated area from 1.6 million acres in the 1880s to 2.6 million in the late 1890s. The core supply had not notably improved; water was simply being applied more thinly. The refined system still failed to provide more reliable supplies. Villages at the tails were confident of some supplies during dry periods, but they could not rely on the timing or the quantity. Evidence given to the 1927 Commission on Agriculture confirms the continued existence of supply problems.[22] Disruptions through silt build-ups and distributary closures still worried irrigators at the tails, while villages at the heads could increase their supplies at will. The effect, inevitably, was that cultivators looked to crops and varieties which could withstand conditions of water-stress, and sacrificed output to security.

In the 1870s, the Director of Agriculture in the United Provinces , E.C. Buck, remarked that agricultural conditions had been less studied than engineering requirements by the canal administration.[23] The same sentiment was expressed in 1917 in an article by the respected agricultural scientists, A. and G. Howard.[24] In the intervening four decades the canals had been painstakingly reconstructed from the inside. Technical performance and managerial control had been enhanced. But they still failed to operate in a way which showed, in the Howards' words, 'a proper appreciation of the needs of the crops irrigated'. In the circumstances this should not really surprise us: the engineers had to operate huge and unwieldy systems; they were supposed to provide famine protection above all other considerations; and there were political constraints upon pricing and zoning initiatives, and on direct intervention beyond the outlets. The canal system in the doab *did* prove itself effective in combating drought, and if it fell short of achieving overall optimality in output terms, in its maturer stages overtly wasteful use of the water was not a great problem.

Despite the imperfections of the system, high cultivation was possible in a substantial proportion of villages, either because of their favoured position within the distributary network, or through the continuing use of wells as a supplementary source of water supply. It was common for officials to note the large number of carefully maintained but rarely used wells in canal villages, and the fact that new wells were forever being constructed alongside the canal distributaries. In the early days, canal officials regarded wells as a potential threat to their revenue, and went to considerable lengths to get cultivators to abandon them altogether; in fact, such wells were used to provide the timely applications of water necessary for high yields. They did not, when used in this manner, tie up resources of men and cattle for long periods, as was the case when cultivation was solely reliant upon this form of irrigation. A similar situation exists today in many areas of northern India, where the basic low-cost supply of water is obtained from the canal, and additional (and often, when using HYVs, crucial) applications are derived from private tubewells. Such use of complementary technologies results in significant improvements in yields, since it is possible to control both the timing and quantity of water applications.

This use of supplementary tubewell irrigation is necessary because the basic features of the canal systems have remained unchanged in the post-Independence period. Attempts at improving the operation of the systems have focused primarily upon physical and organisational refinements beyond the outlet. Interestingly, as Robert Wade has pointed out, the World Bank, which is especially influential in matters of irrigation development, has recently shifted its policy on irrigation towards increasing the flexibility of the main system supply.[25] In particular, the Bank is seeking to ensure that supplies available from each outlet can be varied over the course of a season in line with the needs of the crops. In a period when agricultural performance has been dominated by the development of crop strains which are characteristically more sensitive than *desi* varieties to the timing and quantity of water applications, this is understandable. Yet, to the extent that such a policy involves using rotational distribution methods rather than those of continuous flow, the historical experience of canal development in the United Provinces indicates that there are important questions to be faced, including the problem of exercising effective supervision over a system in which local-level discretionary control is re-introduced.

Glossary

amin	suboverseer, subordinate official
bhaiachara	coparcenary tenurial form in which the revenue demand is apportioned among village proprietors on some principle other than ancestral shares, usually on the basis of cultivation
bigha	unit of area; the standard revenue bigha in the NWP was five-eighths of an acre
chaukidar	watchman, patrol
desi	indigenous
faslana	charge realised at harvest time
gul	village watercourse
jowar	species of millet
kiari	field compartment made up of low earthen ridges
kolaba	irrigation outlet serving village or part of village
tatil	periodic closure of outlets on a section of a distributary
warabandi	list of days or part-days on which each cultivator is permitted to take canal water
ziladar	subordinate official; head of local branch of canal administration

NOTES

1. In the period under review the doab contained four major irrigation systems, the Upper and Lower Ganges Canals, the Eastern Jumna Canal and the Agra Canal.
2. G.P. Chapman, 'Underperformance in Indian Irrigation Systems: The Problems of Diagnosis and Prescription', *Geoforum*, 14 (1983), 267-75.
3. To the extent that, since the 1930s, electricity generation facilities have been embodied in irrigation schemes, further supply uncertainties arise due to periodic conflict between power product and irrigation provision.
4. For details, see L.A.S. Porter, *Final Settlement Report of the Saharanpur District* (Allahabad, 1891), 12.
5. Because water distribution beyond the outlet was a matter handled by the irrigators, information on distribution practices is sparse in official reports. There is, however, a useful collection of replies by district and canal officers to a questionnaire on water-course management in the Proceedings of the Government of the North-Western Provinces in the Public Works Department, Irrigation Branch [hereafter NWPPW (I)], July 1873, no. 27.
6. This aspect of canal system design is discussed in greater detail in my book, *Canal Irrigation in British India: Perspectives on Technological Change in a Peasant Economy* (Cambridge, 1984), 73-80.
7. NWPPW (I) Jan 1869, no. 33, Col. R. Strachey, 'On the Principles to be followed in determining the capacity of the Irrigation Canals of Upper India; in regulating the distribution of the available water supply to the districts through which a canal passes, and to villages or individual cultivators; and in assessing the charge made for the water supplied for irrigation'.
8. *Ibid*.
9. Based on a study visit by a canal officer in the early 1850s; R. Baird Smith, *Italian Irrigation: A Report on the Agricultural Conditions of Piedmont and Lombardy*, 2nd edn. (London, 1855), vol. 1.
10. For details, see *Papers on the Revenue Returns of the Canals of the North-Western Provinces*, 1860-1 (Roorkee, 1861), 25-6; and A. Swinton, *Report of the Committee on the Ganges Canal* (Roorkee, 1867), 23.
11. These experiments are detailed in canal revenue reports, extracts from which are included in Parliamentary Papers (hereafter PP) 1881, LXXI, *Further Report of the Indian Famine Commission, with Proceedings, Evidence and Appendices*, Pt. III, Appendix V. See also, NWPPW (I) June 1873, nos. 1-11.
12. The structure of occupier's rates from 1845, and their movements over time, are detailed in *Report of the Irrigation Rates Committee, United Provinces* (Lucknow, 1939), 12-24.
13. PP 1865, XXXIX, *Resolution by the Government of India Public Works Department Relative to the Canals of the North-Western Provinces*, 543.
14. For a typical exchange between central and provincial governments on

this issue, see proceedings of the Government of the North-Western Provinces & Oudh in the Revenue Department (hereafter NWP&OR), November 1879, nos. 3-24; also, *Report of the Board of Revenue on the Revenue Administration of the North-Western Provinces & Oudh, 1880-1* (Allahabad, 1882), 26.

15. For technical details, see R.B. Buckley, *The Irrigation Works of India and their Financial Results*, 2nd edn. (London, 1905), 282-4.
16. Some of these conflicts are examined in Stone, *Canal Irrigation in British India*, 209-13.
17. Reprinted verbatim in NWP&OR, Oct. 1879, no. 62
18. Conclusions of J.H. Fisher (Meerut Collector) and Maj. C.S. Moncrieff (Superintending Engineer, Eastern Jumna Canal), NWP&OR, Oct. 1879, no. 49. See also, nos. 35 and 52.
19. *Ibid.*, no. 49.
20. With regard to corruption, there are interesting similarities of experience between nineteenth century irrigators in UP and those in modern-day south India (described in Robert Wade's article, 'The System of Administrative and Political Corruption: Canal Irrigation in South India', *Journal of Development Studies*, 18 (1982), 287-328), where a system of rotational irrigation is widely practised. The greater prevalence of illicit revenue-raising by canal officers on the south Indian canals is at least partly due to differences both in crops grown and the availability of alternative irrigation sources. In the north-western canal zone, farmers are generally less dependent on canal supplies because their main crops require less intensive irrigation and are more tolerant of shortfalls in water supply than the paddy crops on the South Indian canals, and because of their greater access to groundwater supplies (wells and tubewells).
21. Proceedings of the Government of the United Provinces in the Public Works Department, Irrigation Branch, February 1903, no. 2, S. Preston, 'Project for Nandgaon Distributary, Agra Canal', 18 January 1900.
22. *Royal Commission on Agriculture in India, Evidence*, Vol. VIII (London, 1927), 672-4.
23. NWP&OR, January 1879, no. 92.
24. A. & G. Howard, 'The Irrigation of Alluvial Soils', *Agricultural Journal of India*, XII (1917), 199.
25. See R. Wade, 'The World Bank and India's Irrigation Reform', *Journal of Development Studies*, 18 (1982), 171-84.

12

TRENDS IN CROP PRODUCTION IN THE UNDIVIDED PUNJAB: A REASSESSMENT

M. MUFAKHARUL ISLAM
University of Dhaka

In discussing the performance of the agricultural sector in British India and its different regional units, it has been usual for commentators to treat Punjab as an exceptional case. This is understandable, for Blyn's study on the subject, which is still the only one of its kind, shows that there was a marked disparity between the Punjab and India as a whole or any other individual province. While all crop output remained almost stagnant in British India (0.37% year) from 1891/92 to 1946/47, in the Punjab it increased by 1.57 per cent. During the same period population increased at the annual rate of 0.67 per cent in India and 0.93 per cent in the Punjab. The disparity was even more marked in foodgrains output (0.11% in India as against 1.1% in Punjab). The nearest growth rate in all-crop output achieved in any province (Madras) was 0.98 per cent per year.[1] The Punjab's performance has suggested to several commentators that the foundation of the present-day Green Revolution in the two parts of the divided province was laid during the last half century of colonial rule. According to Clive Dewey:

> If one superimposes a map of agricultural India today on a map of Indian agriculture in 1900, one finds that the areas in which the Green Revolution is currently acclaimed—the Punjab and Gujarat—are those in which agricultural growth was always most pronounced. . . . Development economists, when they attribute the Green Revolution to the second five year plan, run a certain risk in ignoring this historical perspective.[2]

This contention may well be justified, but the present paper argues that the Punjab's performance in crop production may not have been as spectacular or as dramatic as Blyn's pioneering work would lead one to believe.

The 'Undivided Punjab' treated in this paper (i.e. the British province as it was constituted in November 1901) differs from Blyn's 'Greater Punjab' in as much as it includes the North-West Frontier Province (N.W.F.P.). This may not mean a significant difference in the trend rates, however, for in 1901 the cropped area of the N.W.F.P. only accounted for eight per cent of the total cropped area of the Punjab and the N.W.F.P. taken together—and it is likely that this weight declined in the subsequent years.

Blyn's Data Base and his Method of Adjustment

The need to reassess Blyn's study arises from the defects of his data and still more, the defects of the procedure he employs in estimating the production of certain crops not reported in his sources till 1911/12. The crop statistics are available from four main sources: *Punjab Revenue* (later *Land Revenue*) *Administration Reports, the Agricultural Statistics of India, Estimates of Area and Yield of Principal Crops in India* (henceforth *Estimates*) and the *Season and Crop Reports*. The *Revenue Administration Reports* contain district-wise data on individual crops from 1870/71 onwards. From 1887/88 a second set of data on the area under cultivation and production of wheat, cotton, indigo, mustard and sesamum is presented in separate appendices for the province as a whole. The sources and the method of collection of these two sets of data are not mentioned in detail but it is pointed out that the data in the first set are based on village papers and those in the second taken from the final forecasts. The first set is also available in the *Agricultural Statistics* from 1884/85. The second group of statistics on acreage and output of certain crops is published in the *Estimates* (as also in the *Agricultural Statistics*) from 1891/92. The number of crops covered in this series increased over time as follows: sugarcane 1898/99, barley, bajra, maize, jowar, gram 1911/12, linseed 1912/13, tobacco 1926/27 and rice 1939/40. The publication of the district acreage statistics (i.e. in the first set) in *Revenue Administration Reports* ceased in 1901/02, but the *Season and Crop Reports* took their place. Two mportant changes were introduced in this series from 1906/7. Firstly, district data on the production of the following rops were presented: wheat, rice, jowar, maize, barley, gram, otton, rabi, oilseeds and sugarcane. Secondly, the acreage lata referred to the areas sown with a crop (not harvested as n the past).

Blyn estimates the trends in cropped area, yield per acre and production on the basis of the data furnished in the *Estimates* i.e. those for the province as a whole based on final fore-casts).[3] Only the acreage data of bajra, gram, barely, maize and ice (which are not reported in this series) are said to have been collected from the *Agricultural Statistics* and the figures for hese crops are riddled with anomalies. Firstly, data on wheat acreage (as available from the *Estimates*) for the Greater Punjab differ considerably from those based on village papers in the first set of *Agricultural Statistics and Revenue Administration Reports*. The acreage data on wheat for the Punjab proper also differ from those given in the *Season and Crop Reports* from 1901/02. Again, the statistics on wheat production in Punjab proper as presented in the *Estimates* differ from those in the *Season and Crop Reports* from 1906/07. The discrepancy between the two series continues till 1922/23. Part of the difference in the acreage data during the period 1893/94 to 1905/06 was due to the fact that the data in the *Estimates* refer to the area sown whereas those in the other set apply to harvested area. Secondly, Blyn's data on sugarcane and cotton acreage and output do not agree with those available in the *Estimates* (Appendix A). The discrepancy continues till 1922/23 in the case of cotton and 1911/12 in sugarcane. Moreover, although Blyn estimates the trend rates of sugarcane from 1891/92, acreage and output data are not furnished before 1898/99. It is possible that he makes some adjustments in the data relating to sugarcane and cotton, as he does in the case of rape and mustard, but the specific procedure is not spelt out.[4]

The fact that Blyn's data are not comparable over time is a more important drawback. Acreage data of wheat and mustard relate to the harvested area prior to 1893/94 and sown area for all the subsequent years. For all other crops, up to 1905/06, the acreage statistics are those on area harvested and those of the subsequent years relate to sown area. Statistics showing the areas over which the harvest failed are not available for individual crops before 1906/07. But if we proceed on the basis of the proportion of total, failed area, for the period 1896/97 to 1900/01, it would appear that the acreage data are about 20 per cent lower for wheat and mustard during the first two years, and for all others crops during all the years up to 1905/06. This implies that Blyn's study overestimates the rates of change in crop acreage during the first two reference decades.

The same contention applies to trend rates for the output of minor cereals. Blyn estimates the output of gram, bajra, maize and barley for the period of 1891/92 to 1911/12 on the basis of the yield per acre of 'similar crops'. Crops taken as similar are, respectively, wheat, sugarcane, and sesamum.[5] Such a method overestimates the rates of change in the production of these crops in two ways. Firstly, as Blyn himself points out, irrigated area under these crops did not increase as much as the irrigated area under wheat.[6] Secondly, the acreage data of gram, barley, maize and bajra relate to those on harvested area prior to 1906/07 and sown area in the subsequent years, although the acreage data of wheat and sesamum are those on sown area for the entire period from 1893/94. This means that the output of gram, barley and maize is estimated at a lower level prior to 1906/07 because the yield per acre of wheat and sesamum is lower than it would have been if the 'failed' areas had been excluded. It is difficult to get any idea of the underlying trends in yield per acre, but if we go by the proportion of 'failed area' mentioned earlier, it would appear that production figures of these crops for the years prior to 1906/07 are about 20 per cent lower. Again, this would imply a certain degree of overestimation in the percentage rate of change.

Overall, it would appear that Blyn's study exaggerates the Punjab's achievements in crop production during the first two decades. If we compare rates of increase during these years with the subsequent reference decades (Table 1) we reach the same conclusion. Weather conditions were very unfavourable in 1891/92 and 1896/97 and exceptionally unfavourable in 1899/1900, but Blyn's study shows that the annual rates of increase in crop production were the highest during these early years. The last decade witnessed considerable increase in area sown with high yielding varieties, a phenomenal increase in the price level and the 'Grow More Food' campaign, but production—according to Blyn—increased at less than 2.0 per cent per year. Thus, the height of the trend rates of the first two decades is in doubt, not only because of he nature of the data on which it is based, but also because it s inconsistent with the rate of change in the subsequent ears.

Revised Trend Rates

As mentioned earlier, the *Season and Crop Reports* contain data n the cultivated area of each crop from 1901/02 and the roduction of all important crops (wheat, barley, bajra, rice, naize, rice, gram, oilseeds, sugarcane, and cotton) from 906/07 onwards. This series has several advantages over the *stimates.* Firstly, the method of estimating crop acreage and utput and the agency responsible for preparing the estimates emained more or less the same over the entire period. econdly, cropped area, yield per acre and total out-turn are hown under two heads: irrigated and unirrigated. Thirdly, e statistics are furnished for every district, thus making it ossible to get some idea of regional variations in the per- ormance of the agricultural sector. Fourthly, there are no gaps n the data except in the case of tobacco ouput. Finally, the *eason and Crop Reports* make it possible to include two crops owar and rice) excluded in Blyn's study. In other words, the tatistics available from this series should give us a better view f agricultural trends in the Punjab than the alternatives used y Blyn.

Average annual rates of change in crop acreage, yield per cre and crop production estimated on the basis of data avail- ble from the *Season and Crop Reports* are presented in Table 2. The nethod of crop aggregation and the weights given to indi- idual crops are the same as in Blyn's study. The methods of stimating the trend rates are also similar.[7] But the results are uite different. We get much lower rates of increase in food- rains output and its two determinants: cropped area and ield per acre. The rate of increase is a little higher in non- oodgrains, but for all crops taken together the average rate of hange as estimated by Blyn is reduced by nearly half. Conse- uently, population growth is shown to have exceeded crop roduction.[8] The disparity widens in the case of food produc- on. Such lower rates of change in all-crop output estimated n the present paper strengthen the contention that the inclu- on of the data for the period 1891/92–1905/06 introduces an pward bias in the performance of the crop production sector

TABLE 1

PERCENTAGE RATES OF CHANGE ESTIMATED BY BLYN

Crops	1891 to 1900	1896 to 1905	1901 to 1910	1906 to 1915	1911 to 1920	1916 to 1925	1921 to 1930	1926 to 1935	1931 to 1940	1936 to 1945	Average
Area											
FG	00	2.74	2.98	1.08	– .10	.45	– .03	– .08	– .14	1.82	.87
NFG	1.92	3.35	1.85	– .11	0.32	2.71	1.35	.72	1.12	– 1.19	1.20
All	.36	2.81	2.88	.94	.07	.82	.17	– .02	.13	1.47	.96
Yield											
FG	.77	1.72	– .01	– 1.28	– .18	.17	– .39	.84	1.21	.23	.31
NFG	– .87	– .14	1.43	1.65	1.92	.55	.20	3.37	1.03	2.20	1.13
All	.57	1.71	0.21	– .63	.34	.45	– .29	1.97	1.64	.28	.62
Output											
FG	1.06	4.12	2.92	– .16	– .05	– .60	– .61	0.56	1.23	2.50	1.10
NFG	2.07	3.72	3.68	1.88	2.15	3.34	.26	3.02	3.24	.69	2.40
All	1.20	3.89	3.08	.52	.56	1.26	– .39	1.73	1.86	1.98	1.57
Population	.70	.30	– .09	– .09	.37	1.58	1.29	1.94	1.59	1.58	.93

Notes: FG = foodgrains; NFG = non-foodgrains; All = All crops.

Source: George Blyn, *Agricultural Trends in India, 1891-1947* (Philadelphia, 1966), Appendix Table 5B, 332.

in Punjab agriculture. Further evidence reinforcing the same contention is provided by the remarkable similarity between these trend rates and the average of those estimated by Blyn for the seven reference decades beginning 1906/1916 (Table 2). Non-foodgrains output seems to have expanded at a faster rate when we base our estimates on the data available from the *Season and Crop Reports*, but despite this the rate of increase in all-crop output is a little lower than that estimated by Blyn.

TABLE 2

AVERAGE ANNUAL RATES OF CHANGE

Crops	Area			Yield			Output		
	a	*b*	*c*	*a*	*b*	*c*	*a*	*b*	*c*
AC	0.43	0.51	0.96	0.36	0.54	0.62	0.79	1.10	1.57
FG	0.31	0.43	0.87	0.11	0.01	0.31	0.42	0.41	1.10
NFG	1.08	0.70	1.20	1.55	1.56	1.13	2.64	2.10	1.40
MC	0.26	—	—	0.00	—	—	0.26	—	—
Wheat	0.36	—	—	0.28	—	—	0.63	—	—

Note: AC = All crops; FG = Foodgrains; NFG = Non-foodgrains; MC = Minor cereals (Jowar, Bajra, Gram, Barley and Maize); Trend rates under (*a*) are those estimated in this paper, those under (*b*) refer to the average of the rates estimated by Blyn for the decades beginning 1906·1916, while those under (*c*) are his estimates for the entire period 1891/92—1946/47.

Obviously this pattern implies that in the present paper foodgrains have more weight than in Blyn's study. This difference may be due to two factors. Firstly, Blyn does not seem to include rice and jowar in the foodgrains category. Secondly, it is possible that the inclusion of the N.W.F.P. in his study further increases the weight of the non-foodgrains.

Reliability of the Estimated Rates of Change

Should the trend rates presented in this paper—or any other paper—be taken seriously? If the range of error in the relevant statistics did not remain uniform over time, reliable trend rates cannot be estimated. Clive Dewey has argued that this was the case in the Punjab. He concedes that area statistics are generally reliable, but contends that it is questionable whether the degree of underestimation in the yield statistics did remain constant. He suggests that the subjectivity of the agricultural statistics induced conservatism, leading to an increase in the degree of underestimation, so that the growth of agricultural output was greater than Blyn supposed.[9] A detailed discussion of the questions which have been raised in the debate[10] is beyond the scope of this paper, but if we consider some of the more relevent facts the rates of change may not appear to be grossly underestimated.

Among the inputs which cause or facilitate improvement in crop yield significant progress was made in the Punjab in respect of two: irrigation and improved varieties of seeds. Irrigated area under the crops included in this study expanded at 1.2 per cent per year and, during the decade 1937/38-1946/47, total irrigated area accounted for 52 per cent of the total cropped area in the province. Secondly, improved varieties of wheat, cotton and sugarcane were evolved at the research centres, and the area sown with these seeds expanded rapidly from the 1920s. Thus, in 1938/39, about half of the wheat area, 64 per cent of the area under sugarcane and, in 1945, 70 per cent of the cotton acreage were sown with these seeds.[11]

Such impressive gains in irrigation and the use of new seeds naturally create the expectation that the rate of improvement in yields per acre should be higher than those estimated in this study, especially in the case of foodgrains. There were however, certain developments which probably had adverse effects on crop yields during the period under review. Firstly, soil fertility may have been affected by the fact that the proportion of land annually left fallow to enable it to recover its productive power decreased over time.[12] Secondly, working in the same direction was another development more serious in nature: the problem of water logging in the irrigated tracts of the province. In 1946/47 it was found that 2.3 million acres, or 24 per cent of the area under canal irrigation were affected by waterlogging in the thirteen districts of the Pakistani Punjab.[13] Thirdly, the proportion of land cultivated by the sharecroppers or tenants-at-will increased from 32 per cent in 1890 to 48 per cent in 1932,[14] and this is likely to have increased in the subsequent years. As Clive Dewey has argued, cultivation by such tenants may not necessarily have reduced efficiency,[15] but contemporary observers were almost unanimously of the view that tenants-at-will cultivated less efficiently than owners.[16] Fourthly, almost all the improved cottons were valued for the better quality of their staples rather than their higher yields. Moreover, the quality of the new seeds deteriorated after several years' use.[17] Finally, it was estimated that whereas the number of ploughs per 100 acres remained constant (at eight) the number of plough-cattle declined (from 19 to 14) during the period 1904 to 1935.[18] This suggests that the intensity of ploughing declined or at best remained constant over time.

If these facts are borne in mind, it is difficult to believe that the annual rate of improvement in cash crop yield was an underestimate. Indeed, we might even suggest that if there is an error at all, it is on the side of overestimation. In this connection it may be mentioned that the entire area under oilseeds continued to be sown with traditional seeds. Moreover, there was little expansion of the area under the American varieties of cotton during the first fifteen years of the period under review.

With regard to the foodgrains, virtually nothing was done to evolve new seeds for pulses and minor cereals like bajra, maize, gram and jowar. Nonetheless, the irrigated area under cereals and pulses expanded at 1.0 per cent per year, and during the last decade accounted for 40 per cent of the total area under these crops. Yield per irrigated acre was considerably higher than yield per non-irrigated acre. We should then expect a better rate of improvement in the yield of these crops. One would tend to take the same view if only the trend in wheat yield is taken into consideration. Irrigation acreage under this crop increased by 0.82 per cent per year and, as mentioned earlier, by the late 1930s about 50 per cent of the wheat area was sown with HYV. Still yield improved by only 0.28 per cent per annum. Should it then be suggested that the margin of error in foodgrains yield increased over time? Or should we attribute the relative stagnation in yield to the possibility that the adverse factors mentioned above operated more than proportionately in the case of foodgrains? Obviously nothing definite can be said on these questions. Perhaps, some allowance has to be made for a certain degree of underestimation in foodgrains yield rate, but it is clear that the adjusted rate of increase in all-crop output would not be as high as 1.57 per cent per annum. In this connection it may be mentioned that very little progress was made in the use of HYV of wheat during the first two decades.

To summarise and conclude, given the nature of the crop statistics of the first two reference decades and his method of estimating the crops not reported in the *Estimates*, Blyn's study exaggerates the rate of crop production in Punjab during these years, and this, in turn, introduces an upward bias in the time trends for the entire period, 1891 to 1947. This presumption is strengthened by the rates estimated on the basis of crop statistics available from the *Season and Crop Reports* for the period 1906-1947. It is possible that these statistics under-estimate the foodgrains output rate of increase, but the under-estimation is not likely to be very marked.[19] It is, therefore, doubtful whether the performance of Punjab's agriculture during the last half century of colonial rule was as dramatic as we generally suppose.[20]

APPENDIX A

CROP STATISTICS FROM DIFFERENT SOURCES

Years	*Wheat*		*Cotton*		*Sugarcane*	
	a	*b*	*a*	*b*	*a*	*b*
1891	7768	6224	547	540		
1892	8646	7123	582	948		
1893	9717	8265	1005	1125		
1894	9264	8052	1164	1161		
1895	7094	6893	1170	1177		
1896	6792	6584	1064	1128		
1897	8872	8013	1070	789		
1898	7942	7729	759	988	417	351
1899	5953	6366	763	145	380	344
1900	9810	8766	1134	1080	370	355
1901	6671	7227	988	1027	406	352
1902	7730	6995	1203	1194	361	309
1903	9567	7766	1185	1205	376	321
1904	9414	7712	1502	1698	382	326
1905	10388	8572	788	2020	181	173
1906	9647	9100	1261	1413	279	278
1907	7393	8272	1318	1474	394	392
1908	8397	9002	1448	1562	369	366
1909	8676	9142	1277	1436	417	404

Contd

910	8885	9981	1250	1385	400	387
911	9726	11018	1463	1582	298	285
912	8767	9309	1443	1575	367	360
913	8473	9588	1825	2053		
914	9915	11336	1688	1857		
915	8992	10246	827	902		
916	9467	10737	1074	1163		
917	9926	11271	1643	1800		
918	7684	8536	1418	1555		
919	8813	9953	2071	2269		
920	7751	8781	1957	2142		
921	8789	9981	1149	1239		
922	9620	10870	1273	1417		

otes: Data under (*a*) are those available from *Land Revenue Administration Reports* prior to 1901/02 while those under (*b*) are taken from the *Estimates*. For the period prior to 1901/02 the statistics relate to the Greater Punjab and those for the subsequent years are for Punjab proper. As mentioned in the text, statistics on sugarcane acreage are available in the *Estimates* from 1898/99. After 1922/23 there is no difference in the two sets of statistics for wheat and cotton. In the case of sugarcane the statistics are the same from 1913/14. All figures are in thousand acres.

NOTES

1. George Blyn, *Agricultural Trends in India, 1891-1947. Output, Availability and Productivity* (Philadelphia, 1966), 99 and 119.
2. Clive Dewey, 'The Agricultural Output of an Indian Province: The Punjab, 1870-1940' paper presented at the Institute of Commonwealth Studies. See also Xinru Liu, 'Small Land-holdings in the Punjab: The Historical Perspective', *Punjab Past and Present*, XVI-II, 32 (1982).
3. Blyn, 40.
4. *Ibid.*, 58.
5. Statistics on jowar and rice production in Punjab are not presented by Blyn in his Appendix Tables. This implies that they are not included in his study. However, he mentions that estimated rice yield is based on wheat, *op. cit.*, 216. This would mean that rice production figures have been estimated by him for almost the entire period, because the relevant data were not reported in the *Estimates* before 1939.
6. Blyn, 216-219.
7. In this paper trend rates are estimated by fitting an exponential equation of the type $\log Y = a + bt$.
8. Blyn's figures (Appendix Table 5B, 332) suggest that population in Greater Punjab increased by 1.2 per cent per year during the last seven reference decades beginning 1906-1916.

9. Dewey, 'Agricultural Output', 2.

10. Clive Dewey, 'The Agricultural Statistics of the Punjab, 1867-1947', *Bulletin of Quantitative and Computer Methods in South Asian Studies*, no.2 (March, 1974); '*Patwari* and *Chaukidar:* Subordinate Officials and the Reliability of India's Agricultural Statistics' in *The Imperial Impact: Studies in the Economic History of Africa and India*, ed. C. Dewey and A.G. Hopkins (London, 1978); S.C.Misra, 'On the Reliability of Pre-independence Agricultural Statistics of Bombay and Punjab', *Indian Economic and Social History Review*, XX (2) (1983); and C.E. Pray, 'Accuracy of Official Agricultural Statistics and the Sources of Growth in the Punjab', *Indian Economic and Social History Review*, XXI, (1984).

11. For wheat and sugarcane see *Report On the Operations of the Department of Agriculture, Punjab* (annual) 1938/39, 71 and 77. For cotton see William Roberts and S.B.S. Kartar Singh, *A Text Book of Punjab Agriculture* (Lahore, 1947), 437.

12. Fallow land declined by 0.5 per cent per annum during the period 1912/13-1935/36. For details see Hirashima Shigemochi, *The Structure of Disparity in Developing Agriculture* (Tokyo, 1978), 34.

13. Punjab Board of Economic Inquiry, *Agricultural Statistics of the Punjab, Pakistan* (Lahore, 1950), 14-15. Out of the total waterlogged area 13 lakh acres were being cultivated.

14. Dewey, 'Agricultural Output,' 9.

15. *Ibid.*, 10.

16. Thus, according to H. Calvert, 'These tenants (at-will) generally take less care in preparing the land for crops, plough it less often, manure it less and use fewer implements upon it than owners.' For details see his *Wealth and Welfare of the Punjab* (Lahore, 1936), 206. The same view was taken by D. Milne, Director of Agriculture, Punjab. For details see *Report of the Royal Commission on Agriculture in India*, vol. VIII, *Evidence taken in the Punjab* (London, 1927), 189.

17. Milne's testimony to the Royal Commission, *ibid.*, 242. See also T.G. Kessinger, *Vilyatpur 1848-1968* (New Delhi, 1979), 120.

18. Board of Economic Inquiry, Punjab, *Agricultural Statistics of the Punjab, 1901-02 to 1935-36* (Lahore, 1937), 27.

19. Growth rates of agricultural output in Punjab have also been estimated by Chander Prabha, 'District-wise Rates of Growth of Agricultural Output in East and West Punjab during the pre-partition and post-partition Periods' *Indian Economic and Social History Review*, VI (1964) and Raj Krishna, 'The Growth of Aggregate Agricultural Output in the Punjab,' *Indian Economic Journal* (December, 1964). Chander Prabha uses data from *Season and Crop Reports* for the period 1906/07-1945-46 and arrives at an annual growth rate of 0.92 per cent. The growth rate estimated by Raj Krishna (for the period 1913/14-1945/46) is 1.1 per cent per year.

20. This paper arises from my current research on the impact of irrigation on crop patterns and tenurial relations in undivided Punjab (1887-1947) and my earlier examination of the crop statistics of Bengal. For the latter see my *Bengal Agriculture, 1920-1946: A Quantitative Study* (Cambridge, 1978).

PART V

INDUSTRY AND LABOUR

13

'DE-INDUSTRIALISATION' IN NINETEENTH-CENTURY INDIA: THE TEXTILE INDUSTRY IN THE MADRAS PRESIDENCY, 1810–1870

KONRAD SPECKER
University of Zurich

Nationalist historians have seized on the decline of the traditional textile industry as proof of India's arrested economic growth under colonial rule. Lancashire cotton fabrics first deprived Indian weavers of their overseas markets, then competed with them in the home market. As a result, redundant textile workers were forced to seek employment within the primary sector, leading to an oversupply of labour in agriculture. That there was such a process of 'de-industrialisation' leading to 're-ruralisation' was challenged by M.D. Morris in the 1960s. He asked for more statistical evidence on the market for textiles in India, and suggested that increased demand might have absorbed the growing imports without depressing the demand for domestic fabrics. He also argued that imports of mill yarn strengthened the competitive position of the Indian weavers.[1] This paper re-examines this well-established controversy in the light of the structural changes which took place in the traditional textile industry in Madras between 1810 and 1870. It discusses the concept of 'de-industrialisation', to see whether the assumptions on which it is based are compatible with the situation in the south; and it explores the fate of the weavers. How did they adapt to the new dispensation? Did they become more mobile? What happened to their standard of living? And how did they fit into the emerging colonial mode of production?[2]

'De-industrialisation'

'De-industrialisation' implies that a preceding process of industrialisation has been halted or reversed, or that, at the very least, the incentives to industrial development have been nipped in the bud. There were two levels of textile manufacturing in pre-British India: one, scattered all over the country, produced coarse cloth for local consumption, the other, more specialised, wove high-quality cloth for export and the indigenous elite.[3] It is difficult to see the seeds of an industrial revolution at either of these levels of production. The weavers producing fine cloth in the better organised sector were dominated by political magnates or groups of merchants whose response to bottlenecks was to expand the labour force or intensify its exploitation; there was no question of technological innovation, substantial fixed capital investment, or improvements in organisation except for the purposes of control. Weavers, it is true, occasionally deserted one patron for another; and they worked for other customers in secret, but this 'tactical mobility' posed no threat to the traditional system; if anything, it was the element of flexibility which allowed it to survive until the East India Company stopped exporting Indian textiles and started undermining the purchasing power of the indigenous elite by monopolising the land revenue. There was, in short, no cessation or reversal of a long-term process of industrialisation; only the disruption of a handicraft sector whose principal customers were a class of alien traders and a parasitic elite.

Foreign Trade

Only a small proportion of India's aggregate output of textiles was ever destined for export, and foreign trade mattered less in Madras than elsewhere. The weavers of Gujarat supplied most of the subcontinent's cotton exports in the seventeenth century, and Bengalis took their place over the ensuing hundred years.[4] When the industry lost its export markets, the contraction of demand went much further much faster in Bengal. Textile exports from Madras remained on a relatively high plateau between 1820 and 1838, averaging Rs. 6.7 million a year (See Figure 1). There were considerable short-term fluctuations, mainly due to local crises; but a steady secular decline only set in the late 1830s.[5] By 1864/5 cotton textile exports were down to Rs. 1.6 million. Then, in the last quarter of the century, this decline was reversed. Indian emigrants, mostly in Ceylon, constituted a growing export market for Madrassi fabrics; and a brisk demand developed for Lancashire cottons which were imported via Bombay and dyed in Madras before being exported again. This recovery, however, was swamped by the growth of primary produce exports. Cotton textiles accounted for 38 per cent of the presidency's exports in 1805, 8 per cent in 1858/9, and 3 per cent in 1880/1. Raw cotton, skins, coffee and rice were the new staples which stole the textiles' thunder. Over the same period, Lancashire cotton goods flowed into Madras, but on a smaller scale and at later dates than Bengal (See Figure 2). Madras's imports only reached 10 million yards in 1859/60, whereas imports into India as a whole stood at 100 million yards twenty years earlier. But the 8 per cent of India's cotton imports which entered the subcontinent via Madras still accounted for two-fifths of the presidency's import trade and 30 per cent of the presidency's consumption in the 1860s, peaking at 50 per cent in the last quarter of the century. By then, Lancashire's penetration of the South Indian textile market was probably close to the all-India average, but it was still far from uniform. There were 'protected' regions and 'protected' products which the debate on de-industrialisation, relying on aggregate statistical evidence, overlooks.[6]

FIGURE 1. EXPORT OF COTTON FABRICS FROM MADRAS AND BENGAL, 1800/1-1890/1. (MILLION RS)

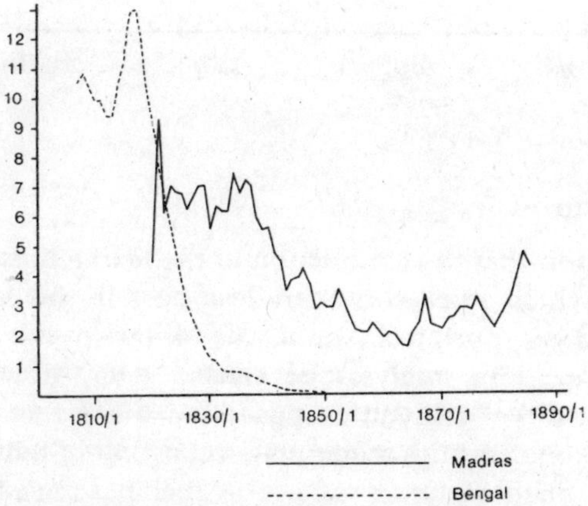

Figure 2 : IMPORTS OF COTTON TEXTILES INTO INDIA

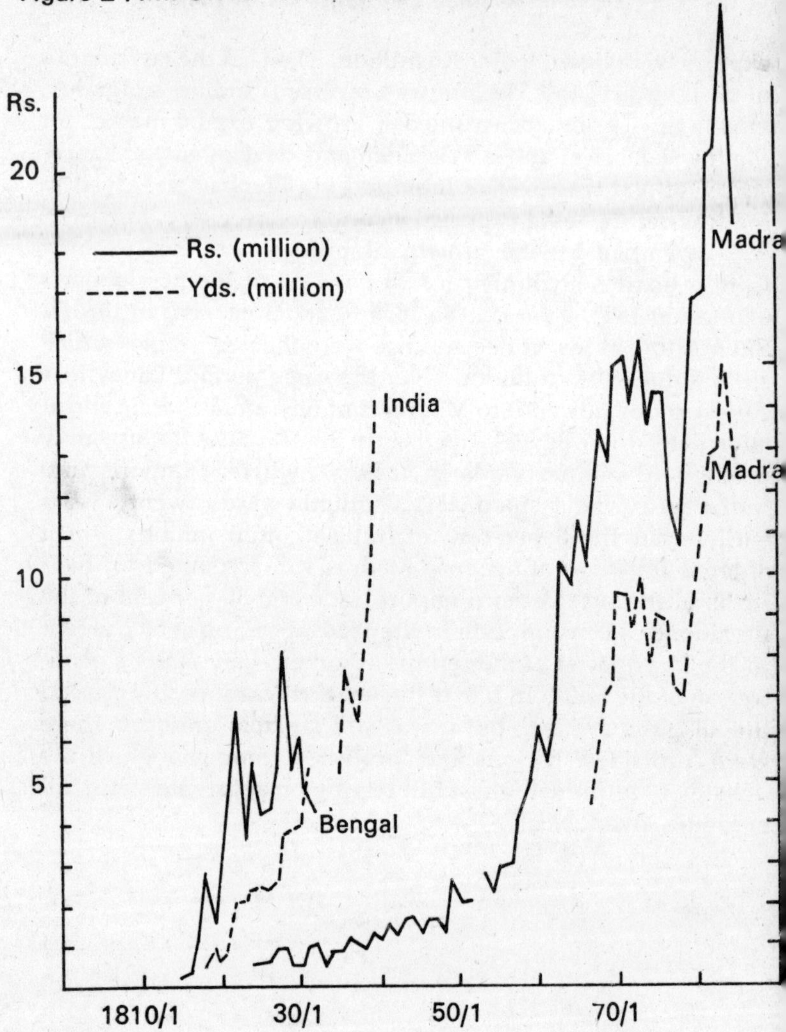

Employment

The notion that the contraction of the textile industry released labour which swelled the landless class in the contryside has received support from apparent shifts in the occupational structure.[7] The analysis of census data, however, cannot surmount the difficulties posed by the existence of mixed occupations and the inadequate reporting of female and child labour. Such statistics as are available suggest that after a period of stagnation the number of textile workers went up after 1881, without keeping pace with the growth of population as a whole. Comparisons of the occupational structures of the various districts under the Madras administration in 1856/7 and 1871 reveal that in the districts with the highest proportion of textile workers there was an average increase of seven per cent in the share of agricultural employment. Though in the long term there was a relative increase in the importance of agriculture for employment there was no constant or absolute shift of labour out of the textile industry into agriculture. The only absolute shifts which did occur were primarily due to short-term crises such as famines. Of course, underemployment may have been an increasing problem; degrees of employment are not revealed in this data. Twomey's claim that there was a loss of three and one-half million full-time jobs as a result of imports between 1850 and 1880 is based on a number of obvious miscalculations. He counts spinners as if they were full-time workers, ignores variations in labour input according to the quality of the product, puts his estimates of per capita cloth consumption too high, ignores the possibility of increases in consumption and posits a complete loss of employment for the unfortunate workers instead of intensifying underemployment. Even Twomey admits that his estimates are based upon such arbitrary assumptions that the loss of jobs could be anywhere between two and six million.[8]

Looms, Prices and Yarn

The only data available on long-term changes in the textile industry are incomplete counts of looms. Their reliability is an unknown quantity; they say nothing about the intensity with which the looms were operated; and they give no indication of the number of weavers per loom or the number of dependants per weaver. Nevertheless, they are the only statistics available, and they may indicate some trends (See Table 1).

In Madras the counts suggest an increase in the number of looms of 20 to 25 per cent between the late 1850s and the early 1870s, with a further increase of about 7 per cent thereafter (see Table 2). An analysis of the data according to the quality of output of the looms reveals that the weavers concentrated on the production of coarser cloth as a consequence of the

TABLE 1

NUMBER OF LOOMS IN THE MADRAS PRESIDENCY 1819/20—1843/4

		Masulipatam	*Malabar*	*Trichinopoly*	*Canara*	*Cuddapha*	*Nellore*	*Sub-division of Nellore*	*Guntur*	*N. Arcot*
	1819/20									
	1820/21									
	1821/22	7500			400	22300	8100[3]			5100
	1822/23	8400			350	23700	8500[3]			5700
F	1823/24	8100			350	24100	9000[3]			5400
	1824/25	8400			350	19800	8100[3]	4000		3300
F	1825/26	8800			350	18900	7300[3]	4100		3400
	1826/27	9000			350	20700	7800[3]	4100		4000
	1827/28	9300			600	21900	8500[3]	4200		4400
	1828/29	9600			600	23400	9100[3]	4500		4700
	1829/30	9800			600	25100	9400[3]	4600		5000
	1830/31	9800			600	25800	9900[3]	4900	12400	5300
	1831/32	9400						4900	12000	5400
F	1832/33	8200		7300				4600	8700	5300
F	1833/34	3700						2100	4400	4200
	1834/35	4100						2700	4600	5500
	1835/36	4800						3100	6100	5200
	1836/37	5500						3500	7400	5600
	1837/38	6050						3700	8300	5900
F	1838/39	6300						3800	7850	6100
	1839/40	6000						4000	7900	6200
	1840/41	6300	3700[1]				4600[4]	4100	8100	6400
	1841/42	6500	4100[1]				5500[4]	4200	8100	6300
	1842/43	6700	4300[1]				5600[4]	4100	7800	6300

	1820/21					17800			
	1821/22	8500		7800		18500		3800	
	1822/23	8700	9100	8100		19200		3800	
F	1823/24	8400	9500	7500		18200		3300	
	1824/25	6400	9400	7200	6700	18100		3800	
F	1825/26	6700	8700	8000	7200	18900		3800	
	1826/27	9300	9000	8300	12000[6]	19000		3900	
	1827/28	9700	13300	9100	11900	19200		3900	
	1828/29	10100	14400	12100[5]	11700	19400		3900	
	1829/30	10200	14100	12600	11500	21100		3900	
	1830/31	9700	13800	12800	11300	21000		3900	19700
	1831/32		13800		10500[7]	21000			
F	1832/33		13800		8900	20500			
F	1833/34		13500		7400	18400			
	1834/35		13100		8600	17800		3900	
	1835/36		13500		9800	18900			
	1836/37		14400		11300[8]	20100			
	1837/38		14900	15600	11900	22700			
F	1838/39		15400	14900	11400	22100			
	1839/40		15700	14400	10700	21500			
	1840/41	11700	16100	14800	10100	22400			15800
	1841/42	11800	16200	14600	10900	23500			17100
	1842/43	12100	16400	15100	11600	23700		5400	17100
	1843/44	11000	15900	14500	12100	24200			17700

[1] Immigration from Cochin and discovery of looms that have been worked "secretly".

[2] Increase due to more complete inquiry and to division of families.

[3] Decreases due to poverty of weavers who abandoned their trade. Increase due to the return of weavers and to the installation of new looms as a consequence of favourable demand.

[4] Three new taluks included for the first time.

[5] The factory of the East India Company was abolished in 1821/2. The increase is probably due to the addition of looms which had been in the Company's service and became liable to the loom tax.

[6] Former East India company's looms now liable to the loom tax.

[7] 'In almost all the villages . . . it will be observed that the effect of the loss of English trade in and soon after 1830, developed itself . . . chiefly . . . at the time of the abolition of the factories in the diminution of the numbers of houses, weavers and looms.' (Collector, Rajamundry to Board of Revenue, *Board of Revenue Proceedings*, 27 January, 1845)

[8] Includes the old zamindary of Pellapore for the first time.

Notes 1-8 are drawn from the remarks of the collectors who submitted the figures on the number of looms to the Board of Revenue. F = Famine.

Sources:

Letters from:
- Coll. Trichinopoly to BR, 6.4.1833, BRP 15.4.1833, IOR R/298/73, S. 3695.
- Coll. Canara to BR, 20.8.1832, BRP 3.9.1832, IOR R/298/51, S. 8787.
- Coll. Cuddapha to BR, 16.5.1832, BRP 24.5.1832, IOR R/298/43, S. 5006.
- Coll. Nellore to BR, 28.7.1832, BRP 13.8.1832, IOR R/298/49, S. 7768ff.
- Coll. Tinnevelly to BR, 29.5.1832, BRP 11.6.1832, IOR R/298/44.
- Coll. S. Arcot to BR, 10.8.1833, BRP 22.8.1833, IOR R/299/11.
- Coll. Tanjore to BR, 20.11.1844, BRP 28.11.1844, IOR R/305/27, S. 16367.
- Coll. S. Arcot to BR, 30.7.1844, BRP 5.8.1844, IOR R/305/16, S. 10200.
- Coll. Bellary to BR, 31.7.1844, BRP 8.8.1844, IOR R/305/16, S. 10288ff.
- Coll. Malabar to BR, 19.8.1844, BRP 29.8.1844, IOR R/305/18, S. 11531.
- Coll. Guntur to BR, 28.8.1844, BRP 5.9.1844, IOR R/305/19, S. 11761.
- Coll. Nellore BR, 14.9.1844, BRP 23.9.1844, IOR R/305/20, S. 12537/43.
- Coll. Cuddapha to BR, 18.9.1844, BRP 23.9.1844, IOR R/305/20, S. 12547.
- Coll. N. Arcot to BR, 2.10.1844, BRP 25.1.1844, IOR R/305/21, S. 13004.
- Coll. Coimbatore to BR, 8.11.1844, BRP 7.10.1844, IOR R/305/27, S. 16125.
- Coll. Tinnevelly to BR, 29.10.1844, BRP 7.11.1844, IOR R/305/24, S. 14952.
- Coll. Masulipatam to BR, 31.1.1845, BRP 10.2.1845, IOR R/305/39, S. 1852.
- Coll. Rajamundry to BR, 15.1.1845, BRP 27.1.1845, IOR R/305/38, S. 1147.
- Coll. Cuddapha to BR 17.7.1845, Moturpha Proceedings No. 58.
- Coll. Trichinopoly to BR, 16.5.1844, Moturpha Proceedings, No. 100.
- Coll. Chingleput to BR, 9.2.1832, BRP 14.5.1832, IOR R/298/42, S. 4742-6.
- Coll. Chingleput to BR, 23.1.1844, BRP 29.1.1844, IOR R/305/4, S. 3823.

District	Number of looms 1856/7 — 1860/1 (average)			Number of loons at work 1869/70			Difference	
	Urban	Rural	Total	Urban	Rural	Total		+
Ganjam	757	3735	4492	1227	6080	7307		2815
Vizagapatam				234	33770	34004		
Godavery	919	10456	11375	762	14676	15438		4063
Kistna	4081	10640	14721	4321	15319	19640		4919
Nellore	762	12327	13089	836	13893	14729		1640
Cuddapha	258	19173	19431	256	18450	18706	725	
Bellary	4975	12099	17074	9077	14216	23293		6219
Kurnool	446	7536	7982	759	13706	14465		6483
Chingleput	2612	5596	8208	2800	6181	8981		773
North Arcot	7948	12123	20071	4886	10151	15037	5034	
South Arcot			12882	3414	6079	9493	3389	
Tanjore	6479	10266	16745	5421	9221	14642	2103	
Trichinopoly	330	4722	5052	534	6204	6738		1686
Madura				3808	9745	13553		
Tinnevelly	7460	6579	14039	9463	14586	24049		10010
Coimbatore	1801	10349	12150	1562	11651	13213		1063
Salem	6840	8228	15068	9614	9367	18981		3913
South Canara				69	1978	2047		
Malabar	75*	4882	4957	162*	4742	4904	53	
Total			204623	59205	220015	279220		

Source: Letter from BR to Government, 28.6.1871, BRP 28.6.1871, IOR Madras Proceedings Vol. 359, S. 4729.

*Including looms installed in the weaving establishments of the Basle Mission.

pressure caused by imports.[9] The process of displacement i the cotton textile market is not so much 'horizontal', as th nationalists claim, but 'vertical', crossing the whole range products. The shift towards coarser cloth heightened th weavers' dependence on the local market exposing them more frequent gluts and more prolonged underemploymen because demand for the coarsest cloth was hardest hit by th collapse of set popular purchasing power during famines ar depressions. The violent short-term fluctuations in th number of looms show just how vulnerable weavers were economic crises.[10]

Prices of indigenous textiles fell some 30 to 40 per cen before the middle of the century, at much the same rate as th simultaneous fall in food prices, which helped the weave adjust their cost of production. But the more dependent the became on cheap food, the more weavers suffered whe agricultural prices rose in the second half of the century. The were particularly vulnerable to high food prices because the grew no crops. In fact, foodstuffs absorbed 80 per cent of the expenditure.

The imports of Lancashire yarn made very little differenc The price of cloth fell faster than the price of yarn, and larg quantities of Lancashire yarn only became available after th disintegration of the weaving sector. When machine-mad yarn was used extensively towards the close of the century usually came from Bombay Mills. Imports accounted fo almost 40 per cent of total yarn consumption in Madras i 1870, but imported yarn was only used in certain areas fo certain products. Localities close to major sea ports or majo trading routes tended to use imported yarn to manufactu higher-quality cloth. Lancashire yarn was too fine for coa cloth; only the Indian mills produced coarse yarn in sufficien quantities; and local yarn spun by family members remaine more profitable. Local yarn was superior with respect t durability, washing and dyeing. Despite the occasional prefe ence for Lancashire yarn for the warp, its use was to restricted to give the weavers much relief. There was n alternative to shifting towards coarse cloth and lowerin production costs.

Mobility

Labour was mobile enough in the traditional textile industry

/eavers migrated in response to political instability, :onomic crises or the growth of new markets, with the East ıdia Company's demand constituting the largest single ıagnet. In the nineteenth century, however, mobility became .most exclusively a matter of economic pushes, and occupa- onal mobility became dominant. Weavers moved into other ccupations, working as carriers or traders as well as agri- ıltural labourers. Two important changes increased the 'eavers' mobility after the cessation of the East India ompany's investments in textiles: their emancipation from ›rced labour and the beginnings of organised emigration verseas. The demand for contract labour which followed the ɔolition of slavery gave an immense impetus to organised nigration from India, and weavers joined these emigrant ows. They were not, however, fit for work on plantations and equently returned to their places of origin. Shifts into local griculture were generally responses to some local crisis, 'pically a famine. The producers of coarse cloth were more ulnerable to such crises, so the long-term shift towards the roduction of coarser cloth increased the amount of mobility ue to short-term fluctuations. But there was no long-term and ›nstant shift of labour from the textile sector into other fields f employment, particularly agriculture, as the changes in the umber of looms have shown. The industry lost labour in a eries of irregular pushes.

The American cotton famine of 1860 to 1865 was a new kind f crisis. It hit the weavers by depriving them of a crucial ıput, whereas famines deprived them of a market. As a result f the scarcity of cotton and yarn the number of looms at work ell, and many of the looms which remained in use were nderutilized. In the North Western Provinces the number of ›oms fell by 25 per cent between 1860 and 1863. But the differ- nces between various districts were striking. High prices led › a shift in demand towards cheaper coarse cloth, and those 'eavers who could obtain raw cotton made record profits.)thers found new employment in agriculture, particularly in rowing cotton at inflated wages.[11]

.nalytical Implications

he textile industry in nineteenth-century Madras needs to be ut into an alternative perspective. The traditional notion of the substitution of cheap imports for local cloth overlooks th observed shift in the quality of output. This does not mea that Indian textile manufacturing was not displaced; but th displacement was a vertical product-specific one. The declin of the old elite and the cessation of the East India Company investments did affect some textile centres seriousl especially along the Coromandel Coast. But in other are there was no far-reaching destruction of indigenous weavin except for short-term fluctuations; the number of looms he up remarkably well. Underemployment was, however, on th increase; the quality of the weavers' output went down; the was a serious deterioration in their standard of living, exce in a few fortunate enclaves; and the industry's survival was tribute to the lack of more lucrative employment opportu ities.

VERTICAL ANALYSIS OF THE TEXTILE SECTOR: CHANGES IN SUPPLY BEWEEN YEARS x, y, z

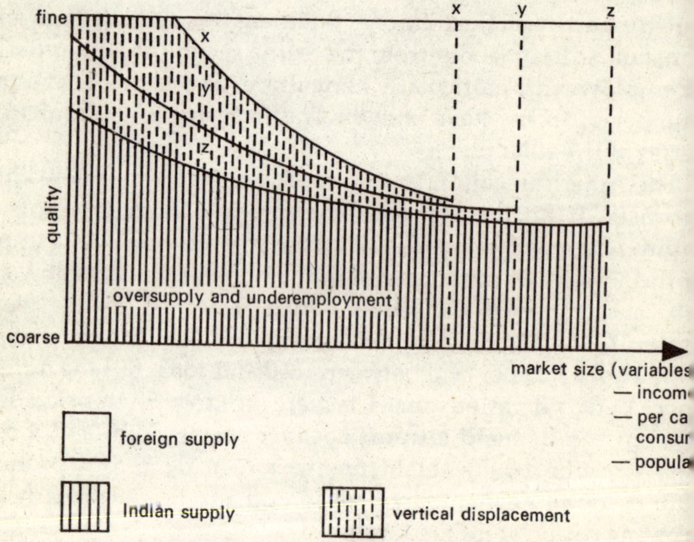

The model is purely schematic. Proportions are not to be taken as real. Enclaves of textile manufacturing with particular conditions of demand and producing special qualities are omitted for reasons of clearness. This, however, does not affect the general character of the structural changes taking place on the Indian textile market.

3 levels:

short-term crisis (famines/epidemics): changes in demand

short-term crisis in the world market (cotton famine): scarcity in input

long-term crisis (integration into the British world economy): vertical displacement, deteriorating working and social conditions increasing liability to short-term fluctuations

NOTES

1. M.D. Morris, 'Towards a reinterpretation of nineteenth century Indian economic history', *Indian Economic and Social History Review*, 5(1968). See also: J.G. Borpujari, 'The British Impact on the Indian Cotton Textile Industry 1757-1865' (Ph.D. thesis, University of Cambridge, 1969), and D.B. Mitra, *The Cotton Weavers of Bengal 1757-1833* (Calcutta, 1978). K.N. Chaudhuri, 'The Structure of Indian Textile Industry in the Seventeenth and Eighteenth Centuries', *Indian Economic and Social History Review*, 11(1974), and *The Trading World of Asia and the English East India Company 1660-1760* (Cambridge, 1978) has given a detailed survey of pre-colonial textile manufacturing in India. There are also some analyses of single issues like demand, occupational structure and employment: M. Desai, 'Demand for Cotton Textiles in Nineteenth Century India', *Indian Economic and Social History Review*, 8(1971); A.K. Bagchi, 'De-industrialization in India in the Nineteenth Century: Some Theoretical Implications', *Journal of Development Studies*, 12(1976); M. Vicziany, 'The De-industrialization of India in the Nineteenth Century. A Methodological Critique of Amiya Kumar Bagchi', *Indian Economic and Social History Review*, 16(1979); A.K. Bagchi, 'A Reply', *Indian Economic and Social History Review*, 16(1979); M.J. Twomey, 'Employment in Nineteenth Century Indian Textiles', *Explorations in Economic History*, 20(1983). The debate has led to a consensus that research has to be region-based but scholars have so far concentrated on Bengal. The *Cambridge Economic History*, vol.2 (Cambridge, 1983) covers all-India, but there is no overall interpretation and the analyses of the regional economies remain isolated.
2. This paper summarises the main findings of my Ph.D. thesis on the textile industry in the Madras Presidency; see K. Specker, *Weber im Wettbewerb. Das Schicksal des südindischen Textilhandwerks im 19. Jahrhundert*

(Wiesbaden, 1984). The main sources are the Madras Board of Revenue Proceedings containing reports from District Collectors.

3. C.A. Bayly distinguishes three 'levels of activity': (1) The production in the villages dominated 'by the conditions of the peasant economy around it'; (2) The intermediate level of cloth manufacture for the local military and political elite, being most' responsive to political change'; (3) the weaving of high quality cloth for export by the Company and for aristocratic consumption. C.A. Bayly, *Rulers, Townsmen and Bazaars, North Indian Society in the age of British expansion, 1770-1870* (Cambridge, 1983). This does not induce me to abandon my own two levels of production: Bayly's three level model is just a further differentiation of elite consumption.
4. Regional shifts in trade went along with changes in the quality composition of the exports (Gujarat: coarse cloth; Bengal: fine cloth), with the increasing control of European trading companies over Asian trade, and with India's integration into the European world trade system. New foreign markets emerged along with these shifts, which were favoured by the high level of mobility of commercial capital.
5. The figures on the value of textile exports have to be related to the general fall in prices for agricultural products as well as textiles in the first half of the century. However, this does not affect the general pattern. The differences between Madras and Bengal were not structural but purely quantitative.
6. It has to be remembered that imports were not distributed evenly all over the subcontinent. Due to regional and product-specific variations, imports had a closely circumscribed impact on specific parts of the market. It is in this context that the contradictory contemporary statments on the destruction of the traditional textile industry have to be understood. Though Twomey emphasizes the regional impact of the decline of Bengal textile exports between 1790 and 1830, he goes on estimating the loss of employment between 1850 and 1880 as a consequence of foreign penetration of the Indian textile market on an all-India level only.
7. See Bagchi, 'De-industrialization in India in the nineteenth century'.
8. Twomey, 'Employment in Nineteenth Century Indian Textiles', 37-57.
9. See Specker, *Weber im Wettbewerb*, chapter 5.1.
10. The shift in the quality of output resulted in a decreasing value of indigenous products, making more people dependent on a smaller income. Further, the proportion of the cost of raw materials was higher in the case of coarse cloth than in that of higher quality fabrics.
11. P. Harnetty, 'Cotton Exports and Indian Agriculture, 1861-1870', *Economic History Review*, 24(1971), 427.

14

THE RECRUITMENT OF AN INDUSTRIAL LABOUR FORCE THROUGH INTERMEDIARIES: A COMPARATIVE STUDY OF THE COTTON TEXTILE INDUSTRY

RICHARD NEWMAN
University College, Swansea

The recruitment of an industrial labour force is one of the problems which every society has to solve as it enters upon the early stages of industrialization. The method it adopts can have repercussions which extend far beyond the boundaries of industry itself. Recruitment procedures affect the movement of population from country to town, the reverse flow of earnings from town to country, the adaptation of traditional skills and by-employments into the new structure of manufacturing and the economic, social and political character of working-class areas in the cities.

Industries in many parts of the world have chosen to recruit their workers through intermediaries, men who are engaged by the management to stimulate and control the flow of labour into the factories and who are paid accordingly. In the Indian context, the intermediaries about whom there is the most information are the jobbers of the Bombay cotton mills. Morris has looked at the effect of a jobber recruitment system on the costs of production, I have examined the contribution of jobbers to the organisation of strikes and the evolution of trade unions, and Chandavarkar has explored the role of jobbers in the socio-political networks of the Bombay suburbs.[1] We also have details about jobbers in mills elsewhere in India and there is evidence to show that recruitment through intermediaries was widespread in coal mines, construction and many other industries.[2] Such practices were not confined to India. There are numerous examples of labour contracting described by Chesneaux in his study of the Chinese working class and there are many parallels in Japan.[3] In particular, the cotton mills of China and Japan, major competitors of Bombay in Asian markets, generally relied upon intermediaries for the recruitment of a workforce.

There were more than superficial similarities among the smokestacks, spinning rooms and weaving sheds of Bombay, Shanghai and Osaka. All were examples of late industrialization; in each case, the mills were an imported technology at an advanced stage of development. Until the First World War, the majority of mills were of British design and equipped with British machinery; British experts advised on their construction and frequently travelled out to Asia to manage them. The workforce, who were mostly young men and women of peasant background, moved directly from field to factory with few, if any, transitional stages of industrial development to accustom them to a new environment and a strange routine. These circumstances have coloured interpretations of the recruiting system. The use of intermediaries has sometimes been seen as a form of exploitation by entrepreneurs of the imperial powers who were eager to obtain local labour at the cheapest rate and with the minimum of obligations towards its welfare.[4] In cases where Indian and Chinese entrepreneurs adopted the same system as the foreigners, socio-cultural explanations have been used; because of the linguistic and regional diversity of India and China, millowners and millhands were often separated by more than the usual differences between capital and labour.[5] For the same reasons, since the criteria for employment were not imposed directly by the management and the millhands had some freedom to develop their own network of connections with the intermediaries, the recruiting system has been seen as an outgrowth of social traditions and rural, pre-industrial relationships.[6] More recently, historians have argued that the system of recruiting through intermediaries was the outcome of rational economic decisions by the employers about the costs of management and the labour requirements of the textile industry at a particular stage of its development.[7] These interpretations are not mutually exclusive or even clearly distinguishable from one another. There is, for example, the fact that what is felt by workers and employers to be socially desirable may, in the end, be economically rational as well if it reduces discontent and contributes to a more settled and productive workforce. A comparative analysis of recruitment can help to throw light on the interplay of motives behind the use of intermediaries in the textile industry and on the relative success of each country in creating an urban labour force.

The origins of the jobber system in Bombay are obscure. They are usually attributed to the British mill staff, who found the language and customs of the workers incomprehensible, but it is probable that they owed as much to members of the Parsi community who were prominent in the cotton industry as native assistants to the British managers and supervisors, as technically-qualified workers such as engineers and as pioneering entrepreneurs.[8] They had long controlled the city's first reservoir of industrial skills, the dockyards, and when cotton mills were established some of the Parsi technicians transferred to them, taking leading workers whom they could trust to recruit and control the rest of the workforce. British managers would not have been surprised by these arrangements, coming as they did from Lancashire, where overlookers had a similar combination of powers over ordinary workers.[9] Once established, the jobbers justified their continued existence, at least in part, by bridging the socio-cultural gap between management and men, assessing applicants for jobs, putting together compatible gangs of workers and providing a channel of communication on the factory floor. Even Indian-owned mills required their services because the workers were drawn from a multiplicity of castes and villages, mostly in the Marathi-speaking areas, while the owners and managers were generally members of the urban, Gujarati-speaking trading communities.[10] As late as the 1960s, a whole generation after the introduction of a decasualisation scheme, mill managers in Bombay were accustomed to taking their jobbers with them to the mill gates and following their advice in hiring replacements for absentees.

The first successful Japanese mills began work in the early 1880s, more than twenty years after the mills in Bombay. At first the Japanese mills do not seem to have had much difficulty in finding labour; the Japanese population was mobile, a large proportion of it had become detached from its rural background by repeated migrations from town to town and a work-force could easily be recruited from the urban poor.[11] Within a few years, however, the mills found themselves relying more and more upon young peasant girls who had to be specially recruited from the countryside. There were a number of reasons for this. Textile wages were low, consistently lower than in other industries and occasionally lower than wages in agriculture;[12] pirating of partially-trained labour was a universal problem in Japanese industry, so it suited the textile companies to employ raw peasant girls with no urban connections;[13] and working conditions in the mills were known to be harsh and strict. Textile work may also have been generally identified with women. Cotton spinning, silk reeling and handloom weaving were traditional by-employments for women in Japanese villages and the first modern expansion of textile production, the rapid growth of silk reeling in small country workshops during the 1870s, was also identified with a female labour force.

A professional recruiting system was in full swing by the 1890s. Agents toured the countryside, hunting out impoverished peasant families with teenage daughters and winning them over with glowing accounts of factory work and conditions. Girls were usually signed up on contracts of two or three years' duration and the families received a down payment equal to about three weeks' pay and a promise of regular remittances from the girls' wages. The recruiter was paid a commission of between four and six yen for each girl and had the opportunity of earning a small additional amount each month for maintaining communication between parents and daughters.[14]

The scramble for labour was such that areas close to the mills were quickly stripped of their potential recruits. Labour became even harder to find as the truth about factory conditions became widely known and the mill girls returned to their villages sick, undernourished, disillusioned and sometimes sexually abused.[15] As early as 1897 the Osaka mills were sending their agents as far south-west as Kagoshima and the Tokyo mills were reaching out to the north-east coast, a pattern of recruitment that was to persist until at least the 1950s.[16] Even such far-flung islands as Hokkaido and Okinawa were culled for recruits. One observer in the early 1920s reported that 'if a man has a daughter, no matter if he lives in the remotest inland village, he will have five or six recruiting men visiting him every day. They call on him not only at home but in the fields if he is working there. Some people have been driven to put notices at their doors with the statement: "No daughter for factory work in this house!", to keep off the importunate recruiters'.[17]

Early in the twentieth century the government and the employers tried to reform the recruiting system. The larger cotton mills divided up the country districts between them and each took its designated recruiting area under direct control, putting in a company representative to build up contacts with peasant families.[18] The millowners hoped that a greater sense of kinship would develop between company and worker and that this would be reinforced by the improvements that were being made to factory conditions. The government was also taking action, first through prefectural regulations and then through a national ordinance issued in 1924. The undisciplined rabble of recruiters, some 52,000 strong by 1922, could now be made to conform to minimum standards or suffer disqualification. Nevertheless, by 1932 there were still 4,000 recruiting agencies at work for the larger cotton mills alone.[19]

The Japanese recruiter was clearly very different from the Bombay jobber. The recruiter worked in the country districts; he had no duties inside the mill either as a supervisor or a production worker, and his loyalties to management and worker were of the most tenuous kind. The jobber, in contrast, seldom went into the villages to recruit. The flow of migrants into Bombay was normally quite sufficient to provide the mills with all the labour that was needed. Once the jobber had been appointed to his position in the mill hierarchy, word of his influence began to circulate from city to village, from brother to brother and from one villager to another until the trickle of job seekers had swollen to a steady stream. A pool of substitute workers (or *badlis*) was accumulated in the same way. *Badlis* had to demonstrate their loyalty to the jobber by giving him presents and performing various services for him and each morning they would assemble at the mill gate in the hope of being selected to replace an absentee, thus acquiring the skill which would help them to win a permanent position. The jobber also had important duties on the factory floor. For the management, he kept discipline, gave training and, in some departments, worked at the machinery as well; for the mill-hand, he was a leader and spokesman. The jobber's interest lay in maintaining a delicate balance between the interests of management and labour. If he showed too much favour to one, the other might disown him, his influence with both would evaporate and his livelihood would disappear.[20]

The jobber was not paid a commission for his recruiting; neither was he a genuine sub-contractor, except in the most peripheral of the mills' activities.[21] Both he and his men were on the muster roll of a mill and were paid directly by the management at advertised rates. He did, however, receive unofficial monthly payments, known as *dasturi*, from the workers who were dependent on him. These have been seen as outright bribes or as a means by which the managers shifted the costs and risks of recruiting away from themselves and on to the jobbers and workers, but the token nature of *dasturi* payments makes it more likely that they were symbols of a dependent relationship from which the workers hoped to benefit generally.[22] Whatever the nature of *dasturi*, the fact that there was no parallel to it in Japan shows that the Japanese recruiter aroused much lower expectations among his clients.

The first cotton mills in Shanghai were launched by Chinese entrepreneurs in the years 1888-1893 and several British, American and German mills were established after restrictions on foreign investment were lifted in 1895. The Japanese entered Shanghai industry after the turn of the century by buying up existing mills rather than building new ones, but they later shared with Chinese entrepreneurs the credit for the very large expansion of textile manufacturing during and after the First World War.[23] It is possible that Chinese recruiting practices were affected by the systems used in other countries, though it is difficult to prove. Japanese-owned mills in Shanghai do not appear to have used the Japanese system of recruiting until the later 1920s, but Chinese-owned mills employed many Chinese technicians who had been trained in Japan and may have been influenced by what they had seen of Japanese recruiting practices.[24] There is also the possibility of Lancashire overlookers and Bombay jobbers being a distant influence on the organisation of British-owned mills. Nevertheless, it is certain that no foreign influences were as important as the indigenous ones.

By the 1920s three rather different recruiting systems can be found in Shanghai.[25] The British put everything in the hands of a Chinese compradore; he hired the foremen, who then hired and paid the workers. The Chinese-owned mills had no need of a compradore and they paid their workers directly, but foremen were still responsible for recruitment. The Japanese also used foremen at first but in the mid-1920s they tried to change to a system in which personnel officers chose recruits on the basis of aptitute for a period of formal apprenticeship. This innovation undermined the established position of the foremen and caused much bitterness and several strikes.

Beyond each foreman stretched a chain of connections (*guanxi*) linking the mills with their recruiting areas in the Shanghai suburbs or in the distant parts of Jiangsu province. Nobody could get a job without *guanxi* that led eventually to a foreman. 'Almost always these connections were made through networks reflecting kinship relations or ties between people from the same native place' and since local groups were readily distinguishable by dress, dialect and behaviour, social clusters were formed on the factory floor and in the slums and shanty towns that fringed the industrial areas.[26] 'Job allocations depended at least as much—if not more—on social networks among women workers as on the policies and preferences of managements.'[27] As in Bombay, an informal recruiting system allowed primordial social structures to accommodate themselves to technologically-determined working patterns.

The chain of connections that stretched from foreman to countryside was one that was increasingly forged by contractors. This was the aspect of Chinese recruiting that most closely resembled the system in Japan and some commentators have attributed its use in Shanghai to the Japanese. In fact, this does not seem to have been the case. Contract labour was rare before the mid-1920s, even in Japanese-owned mills, and it was common thereafter in the mills of the nationalities, whether the managers were progressive or backward in the conduct of their business. The emergence of contracting at this point was due to a combination of circumstances. Bad harvests in parts of the hinterland coincided with the expansion of the cotton industry in Shanghai and some of the early peasant migrants saw that they had an opportunity of making a profit for themselves by returning home and recruiting their fellow villagers for work in the mills. The millowners needed a steady supply of new labour for the employment policy they were pursuing: their aim was to reduce the proportion of male workers, who were often militant and relatively expensive to employ, and replace them with low-wage female labour. Another important factor was the increasing influence of secret societies, such as the notorious Green Gang, to which most of the mill foremen and labour contractors belonged. Control of the labour supply was a source of profit and power, a reward which the gangs had extracted from the employers in return for their help in crushing the strikes and insurrections of 1925-27.[28]

Out in the villages, the contractors behaved very much like their Japanese counterparts. They concentrated on large impoverished peasant families and used a mixture of lies, promises and cash advances to persuade teenage daughters to enter industrial work. Back in the city, however, the girls were not handed over to a mill company, as they were in Japan. They remained the contractor's responsibility; the contractor had to persuade a mill foreman to give them work or alternatively find them less remunerative jobs in the silk filatures or less savoury employment in the brothels and bars. Girls usually contracted their labour for a three-year period. During this time they made over their wages to the contractor, who paid their families in annual instalments and fed and housed the girls in Shanghai, keeping the balance of their earnings as his profit. When the contract labour system was at its height in the 1930s there were about 5,000 contractors with almost total power over the livelihood and well-being of 80,000 workers, or two-thirds of the female labour force.

Superficially there may be certain similarities between industrial recruiting practices and the organisation of labour in pre-industrial times, but no clear line of continuity can be found in any of the examples under discussion. Labour contracting had a long history in China in occupations such as mining and agricultural labour, and, in the particular case of Shanghai, it is possible to trace a line of development from the guilds of boatmen and porters on the Grand Canal to labour contracting in the docks,[29] but the absence of specific references to labour contracting in the cotton mills before about 1925 would seem to indicate that its modern usage was due largely, if not wholly, to modern causes. Labour in Japan had become very unstable by late-Tokugawa and early-Meiji times, he old forms of long-term service and apprenticeship having roken down under the impact of rising wages and the urgeoning demand for industrial skills.[30] Concepts of loyalty nd patronage nevertheless survived as ideals and were xemplified to some extent in the role of foreman in early Meiji ndustry and the *oyabun-kobun* relationships that governed ecruiting and deployment in mining and construction work. apanese cotton mills exemplified the unstable aspects of the abour market rather than the paternal ones and it was not ntil the early twentieth century that paternalism came back nto vogue as a carefully-contrived solution to particular abour problems. Even then, the recruiters had little contribu-on to make to it since their contact with the workers was so rief. In India also, there was no real counterpart in pre-ndustrial society to the jobber's multifaceted role. Recruiting ystems in each country's mills were new creations. Their esemblance to the social structures of the past came from the act that they used many of the same human ingredients: etworks of kin, caste or clan, concepts of loyalty and defer-nce to employers and the age-old need to contribute to the amily income.

Indeed, it was the character of the workforce in the cotton nills and the nature of the demand for industrial employment nat influenced the recruiting systems more than anything lse. In China and Japan the textile labour force was largely emale: in Japanese spinning and weaving mills in 1922 it was 8 per cent female and in Chinese mills in 1930 it was 62 per ent female, rising to nearly 73 per cent female in Shanghai.[31] Iost of these women were young. Surveys carried out in apan in 1897 showed that 42 per cent were between the ages f 14 and 20 and 16 per cent under 14; the average age of a ecruit was only 19.[32] A survey of four mills in China, one in hanghai and three elsewhere, showed that the proportion of vorkers under 20 was usually about 60 per cent.[33] These girls ad come into the cotton mills to supplement the family ncome. Some of them came from families which regarded and spinning and handloom weaving as their traditional by-mployments but were now unable to compete with factory-nade products. Some were the daughters of migrant families vho would take low-paid jobs in any part of the urban conomy. In the days before labour contracting, many of the hanghai millhands were of these two types. A large number, and in Shanghai an increasing proportion, came from poor peasant families desperate to reduce the burden of population on the land and to find additional income of any kind. The recruiting contractor, with his cash advances and his promise of placement in an urban job, was an ideal solution to their problems. Some of them regarded their financial embarrassment as temporary and had the girls' wages earmarked for a particular purpose, such as the education of a son. The girls themselves usually had dreams of marriage; the Shanghai recruits hoped to find eligible bachelors from their native districts at work in the city, while the Japanese girls planned to earn themselves a dowry large enough to impress the young men of the village on their return.[34] For all these reasons both families and daughters expected their stay in the mills to be brief and found the short length of their contracts reassuring.

By contrast, the recruitment of the Bombay millhands was much more consonant with the whole process of urbanisation going on around them. Although their background was no less rural than their Chinese and Japanese counterparts and their circumstances were often equally impoverished, their status tended to be higher within the family and village. Most of the Bombay millhands were men—79 per cent of them in 1922—and those women who did enter the mills were either widows or the wives of millhands and were confined to certain processes. In comparison with the east Asian mills, the Bombay workforce was also old. An official survey carried out in 1930 found that fewer than 11 per cent of the millhands were under 20 years of age, while 28 per cent were over 35. Nearly 40 per cent of them had had more than ten years service in the industry.[35] A majority of the millhands came from middle ranking peasant castes with no tradition of textile work. Whether they were family heads or brothers alternating in an urban job to add to the joint family income, work in the mill was a livelihood of much greater importance to the workers themselves than the supplementary nature of the wages earned by the mill girls of China and Japan.

These differing attitudes to factory work were reflected in the accommodation and amenities that were opened up to the millhands through the recruiting system. Few of the Bombay mills provided company housing; in any case, this form of accommodation was unpopular since the millhand was reluctant to be thrown together with strangers under the eye of hi employer. It was the jobber who acted as a broker between the millhand and the various networks of urban life. If he was not himself a landlord or a moneylender, he could find the worker a congenial tenement, arrange for him to have his meals cooked, fix him up with a loan, introduce him to a grain dealer and ease him into the social and political life of the slums. The jobber's power and patronage lay as much outside the mills as in them. Through his influence the workers became members of an urban community as well as members of an industrial labour force.

In Japan, by contrast, the millhands lived apart from the rest of society. Because the mill girls were so young and because their parents would probably not have agreed to sign contracts otherwise, the mill companies were obliged to build dormitories where the girls were housed and fed and spent most of their lives.[36] With trained labour so much in demand from their competitors, it suited the companies to keep their workers under lock and key. These dormitories became notorious for their poor food, the dirt, disease and despair which they harboured and the harsh discipline which ruled them. Labour turnover seems actually to have increased under the dormitory system, with a large proportion of the girls leaving industry altogether to return to their homes; one mill in Osaka, for example, had a labour turnover of 120 per cent in a year.[37] In response to this some of the mill companies set about improving the dormitories and adding amenities like cultural and educational programmes, company shops and organised recreations.

The impact of these reforms is much debated. The Kanegafuchi Spinning Company, one of the pioneers of reform, succeeded in getting its monthly turnover down from 12 per cent in August 1902 to 4 per cent in January 1906, but even the new rate was high and Kanegafuchi was by no means typical.[38] A surprising amount of malingering was possible within the dormitory system and there were some months when the rate of absenteeism was as high in the Japanese mills as it was under the supposedly more casual arrangements in Bombay.[39] The average length of service in spinning mills was only 1.5 years in 1897; by 1929-30 it was still only just over 2 years and at the outbreak of the Pacific War it had fallen again to 1.75 years.[40] A considerable proportion of mill girls used to brave the company guards and abscond within a matter of months.

This is not to say that progress towards the formation of a working class was steady and uninterrupted. Recruitment through intermediaries, while it eased the early stages of the workers' transition from agriculture to industry, created interests that were essentially local in character and might therefore stand in the way of further collectivism, whether of class or community. I have shown elsewhere how the interests of jobbers and unions came into collision in Bombay and how primordial loyalties survived and were manipulated by jobbers, millowners and politicians in the disastrous strike of 1929.[44] Honig has concluded that Chinese labour history is not simply the history of steady proletarianisation. 'It is', she writes, 'as much a history of workers striking to defend traditional relationships as one of workers demanding improvements in their working and living conditions.'[45] It was recruitment through intermediaries that gave the mill-hands the latitute to bring such relationships into industry. If this went further in Bombay than elsewhere, it also created a workforce that was more open to change and reform than its counterparts in east Asia. Because the jobbers had a formal status on the factory floor as well as informal leadership outside, they were susceptible to a wide range of pressures and persuasion from those around them: government, millowners, local bosses, politicians of various kind and, not least, the millhands themselves. Recruitment through intermediaries was not simply a device for managerial exploitation of the workforce, though it could have this function. It was also a means by which the workforce shaped its own development. In comparison with the history of textile labour in Shanghai and Japan, it can hardly be said that this development in Bombay was 'arrested'.

NOTES

1. M.D. Morris, *The Emergence of an Industrial Labor Force in India: A Study of the Bombay Cotton Mills, 1854-1947* (Berkeley, 1965); R.K. Newman, *Workers and Unions in Bombay 1918-1929: A Study of Organisation in the Cotton Mills* (Canberra, 1981); R. Chandavarkar, 'Workers' Politics and the Mill Districts in Bombay between the Wars', *Modern Asian Studies*, XV (1981), 603-47.
2. E.D. Murphy, *Unions in Conflict: A Comparative Study of Four South Indian Textile Centres, 1918-1939* (New Delhi, 1981); C.P. Simmons, 'Recruiting

and Organising and Industrial Labour Force in Colonial India: The Case of the Coal Mining Industry, c.1880-1939', *Indian Economic and Social History Review*, XIII (1976), 455-85; M. Bellwinkel, 'Rajasthani Contract Labour in Delhi: A Case Study of the Relationship between Company, Middleman and Worker', *Sociological Bulletin*, XXII (1973), 78-97; Royal Commission on Labour in India, *Report* and *Evidence* (London, 1930-1).

3. J. Cheneaux, *The Chinese Labor Movement 1919-1927* (Stanford, 1968); J.W. Bennet and I. Ishino, *Paternalism in the Japanese Economy: Anthropological Studies of Oyabun-Kobun Patterns* (Minneapolis, 1963).
4. C. Lowe, *Facing Labour Issues in China* (London, 1934).
5. For example, S.D. Mehta, *The Indian Cotton Textile Industry: An Economic Analysis* (Bombay, 1953).
6. For evidence on these points see Newman, *Workers and Unions*, chapter II and 'Social Factors in the Recruitment of the Bombay Millhands' in *Economy and Society: Essays in Indian Economic and Social History*, ed. K.N. Chaudhuri and C.J. Dewey (Delhi, 1979), 277-95.
7. Morris, *Emergence of an Industrial Labor Force*; K. Taira, *Economic Development and the Labor Market in Japan* (New York, 1970).
8. Newman, *Workers and Unions*, chapter II.
9. P. Joyce, *Work, Society and Politics: The Culture of the Factory in later Victorian England* (Brighton, 1980), 100-1.
10. Newman, *Workers and Unions*, chapter II.
11. J.W. White, 'Internal Migration in Prewar Japan', *Journal of Japanese Studies*, IV (1978), 81-123.
12. T. Uyeda and T. Minoguchi, *Small Scale Industries of Japan: The Cotton Industry* (Tokyo, 1936), 38; M. Umemura, 'Agriculture and Labour Supply in Japan in the Meiji Era', *The Developing Economies*, III (1965), 284.
13. T. Shindo, *Labor in the Japanese Cotton Industry* (Tokyo, 1961), 36-7.
14. Uyeda and Minoguchi, 33-4; G.R. Saxonhouse, 'The Supply of Quality Workers and the Demand for Quality in Jobs in Japan's Early Industrialization', *Explorations in Economic History*, XV (1978), 46.
15. For a colourful but possibly exaggerated account of conditions see E.P. Tsurumi, 'Female Textile Workers and the Failure of Early Trade Unionism in Japan', *History Workshop*, 18 (1984), 3-27. Tsurumi makes very few distinctions between silk and cotton, large factories and small, and different historical periods. This may be why her account differs so much from that of A.S. Pearse, *The Cotton Industry of Japan and China* (Manchester, 1929). Pearse visited a number of large mills in the 1920s.
16. Saxonhouse, *op. cit.*, 46; Shindo, *op. cit.*, 35.
17. S. Yoshisaka, 'Labour Recruiting in Japan and its Control', *International Labour Review*, XII (1925), 488.
18. Shindo, *op. cit.*, 46-7; Taira, *op. cit.*, 125.
19. Yoshisaka, *op.cit.*; Uyeda and Minoguchi, *op.cit.*, 33.
20. Newman, *Workers and Unions*, *passim*.

rate in all spinning mills was 75 per cent.' Ueda and Minoguchi, op. cit., 5.

37. Hazama, op. cit., 446.

38. Ibid., 416-7.

39. Sumiya, op. cit., [illegible]. See also Pearse, op. cit., 180 and Yamamoto, [illegible]

40. Saxonhouse, [illegible] (1976), 162.

41. [illegible] op. cit., 86.

42. Tsurumi, op. cit., seems to believe that most girls had little choice and were lured into the mills by false promises. This may have been true in the early years of the industry, but by about 1920 some prefectures had been major recruiting grounds for a generation, with particular villages having scores of girls in the mills simultaneously, and it is inconceivable that a reasonably accurate knowledge of working conditions would not have got around. See Ueda and Minoguchi, op. cit., 52-3.

43. Honig, op. cit., and 'The Contract Labor System and Women Workers: Pre-Liberation Cotton Mills of Shanghai', *Modern China*, IX (1983), 421-54; Xia Yan, 'Contract Labour', *Chinese Literature*, 8 (1960), 47-83.

44. *Workers and Unions*, ch. IX. For a comparative analysis of events in Bombay and Shanghai see my 'Vanguard of the Proletariat? Communists and Unions in Shanghai and Bombay, 1927-1929' in *Proletarianisation in the Third World*, ed. B. Munslow and H. Finch (London, 1984), [illegible].

45. Honig, *Women Cotton Mill Workers*, 306.

INDEX